CHINGIZ KHAN
The Life and Legacy of an Empire Builder

CHINGIZ KHAN
The Life and Legacy of an Empire Builder

Syed Anwarul Haque Haqqi

PRIMUS BOOKS

An imprint of Ratna Sagar P. Ltd.

Virat Bhavan

Mukherjee Nagar Commercial Complex

Delhi 110 009

Offices at CHENNAI   KOLKATA   LUCKNOW
AGRA   AHMEDABAD   BANGALORE   COIMBATORE   DEHRADUN   GUWAHATI
HYDERABAD   JAIPUR   KANPUR   KOCHI   MADURAI   MUMBAI   PATNA   RANCHI

First published 2010
Reprinted 2013

ISBN 978-81-908918-9-9 (hardback)
ISBN 978-93-80607-81-8 (paperback)

Published by Primus Books

Laser typeset by Digigrafics
Gulmohar Park, New Delhi 110 049

Printed at Sanat Printers, Kundli, Haryana

To

Kampta Prasad Srivastava
Jai Chandra Sharma
Mohammad Umar (Government High School, Hardoi, U.P.)
C.G. Roy
V.K.N. Menon
N.L. Chatterji (University of Lucknow, U.P.)
Pandit G.S. Sharma
Professor Mohammad Habib
Professor A.B.A. Haleem
My Teachers Now Memory

Contents

List of Maps

Preface

$\mathcal{T}$HE PRESENT STUDY IS THE result of an almost lifelong interest in the subject with unavoidable intermittent interruptions, extending over six decades. For almost three score and ten years, I have made an attempt, not to 'judge' but to 'understand' Chingiz Khan, his work and legacy. The career of Chingiz Khan after his phenomenal rise to power, irrespective of one's views about its nature and consequences, has singular interest. The conquests of Chingiz Khan were as, Rene Grouset said, 'as important a fact for the commerce of the Middle Ages as the discovery of America for the men of the Renaissance'. Poets, politicians, and travellers have been inspired by the achievements of the Great Khan and his descendants. If Chaucer went to him for his unfinished story of Cambuscan Bold, Coleridge was inspired by Qubilai (Kubla) Khan and his palace in Xanadu. Hitler's staff adapted his military strategy and tactics for their formidable Blitzkrieg during the Second World War. And surprisingly, the idealist Jawaharlal Nehru found him 'charming'. Thirteenth-century missionaries such as Carpini and Rubruck had been constrained to admire Mongol society and the discipline and justice therein. Yet the world seemed to have forgotten him and it took a long time for an authentic account of his career and legacy to appear.

As an undergraduate student I was amazed to learn that the founder of the Mughal Empire in India, Zahir-ud-din Babur, was a descendant of the Mongol Chingiz Khan. This orphaned youth, survived a struggle for power and ultimately became a conqueror greater than Alexander! How did that happen? A couple of popular books whetted my curiosity which soon developed into a lifelong interest, if not a passion. I decided to undertake a translation of Ata Malik Juwaini's *Tarikh-i-Jahan Gusha* for my doctoral dissertation. The task had appeared to be simple but soon discovered that I was mistaken as I stumbled over the flowery passages, the puns and allusions and the frequency and fluency with which Juwaini laced his narratives with quotations from the Holy Book, the sayings of the wise, and, above all, lines from well known Persian poets. Drawing consolation (and inspiration) from the life and struggles of the nomad leader, I decided to persevere. Fortunately, Professor M.A. Nami (University of Allahabad) came to my rescue. To benefit from his learning and insights into Persian literature, I spent a summer with him. He led me through the significance of the 'Grand Style', the significance and niceties of Juwaini's style, conveying through puns, turns of phrase, allusions and the sayings of wise men what would not have been advisable to express in plain language.

Although the project had my whole heart it could not, for many reasons, have my undivided attention. The delay turned out to be a blessing in disguise because a Chinese scholar, Wei-Kwei-Wei, came to India to work with my mentor, Professor Mohammad Habib. He loaned me a copy of his draft translation of the *Secret History of the Mongol Dynasty*. I was thrilled, for it showed Chingiz Khan to be a man much different from the one I had till then understood/misunderstood. I was transported to a world neither mysterious, magical nor mythical—and certainly neither devilish nor barbarian—but a real world of men and women engaged in the ordinary, sometimes bloody, chores of life as anywhere else. Chingiz Khan came through as a loyal friend, a loving family man, cruel to his enemies but generous to his own. This was a turning point in my academic pursuits. It prompted me to revert to the subject of my doctoral study.

Having got rid of the shackles of translation and the 'thankless' task of identifying names and locations of places I found myself in muddy waters. Chingiz Khan and his Mongols had not yet been studied by historians of war. Moreover, there was no record of the Khan's career written by any Mongol, as the Mongols had a language but no script and consequently, no written texts. Only the Chinese and Persians could do it, but to his death they had no reason to commemorate his achievements after the unprecedented devastation of their countries and the shattering of their pride by the ferocious Mongol horsemen.

Barring a few scholarly treatises, the literature easily available in English was generally based on secondary 'sources'. The problem with translations is, as I learnt, that they are alternatives but not substitutes for the original texts. Every language has a style of its own, its own idioms, turns of phrase, and social and literary traditions, and Persian is one of the oldest and richest languages. The primary sources are in Persian, Arabic, and Chinese. Those based on secondary sources are useful for providing a second view. This study attempts to present, without prejudice, a comprehensive account of the career and conquests of a great nomad leader, Chingiz Khan, based on the original Persian sources, plus English translations of Chinese sources, and supplemented by the reports of the great thirteenth century travellers and classic studies by modern leading Mongolists. It is an attempt to provide readers with an interesting and readable story of one of the great historical figures of all times, who 'shook, shocked, and moved' his world. Thus I do not focus attention on events and dates but attempt to follow in the footsteps of Ibn Khaldun, father of historiography, Toynbee (who cross references backwards and forwards), Emil Ludwig (for his creative imagination and reconstructions) and Holland Rose (for his interesting and paramagnetic readability).

The Mongols have often been identified with 'bloodshed and devastation', or 'barbarism'. The study, therefore, focuses attention on those aspects of Chingiz Khan that have been overlooked, such as (a) the trials and tribulations of his early life, (b) his conduct and character as a man, a family man, a friend, and a hero, (c) a military general, (d) a law-giver and administrator, and, above all, (e) his achievements in governance.

I consider in the pages that follow the transformation of the unlettered and untutored Mongols into a disciplined people, exemplary rulers of alien peoples with their own civilizations as they became the dominant power in Eurasia for over a century. I draw my net wide to provide a perspective to evaluate this unlettered empire-builder, his policies, and his place in the development of political thinking and administrative policies. Are we justified in lauding ourselves as 'enlightened and civilized', and branding the greatest nomad leader and his peoples as 'barbarians'?

As a student of history, I was in quest of facts, cross-checking them to assure their veracity and the authencity of the narrator, and if possible to fill in the gaps and lacunae in the history of the Great Khan. I have tried to the best of my ability to do what Qazi Minhaj Siraj the thirteenth-century Persian chronicler did, and to piece them together in a readable narrative. I have attempted to provide the reader with the social and political context.

The present work is the revised and enlarged version of my doctoral dissertation approved by the Aligarh Muslim University. The delay gave me the time and opportunity to get my readings up-to-date and discover the latest trend of approaches to the 'Mongol phenomenon'. There has been a trend towards a more careful approach to this enigmatic person, even though the 'tags of barbarism and blood thirstiness' linger. There remain biographical gaps pertaining to the conduct and character of the great conqueror as a man, as a friend, as a legislator and as an administrator, which show his role and place as a history-maker. I have, therefore, attempted to provide a more comprehensive and authentic account of Chingiz Khan in an interesting and readable form.

The basis of a true understanding of the 'Mongol phenomenon' and an authentic account of the life and achievements of the Great Khan (particularly his conquests in Muslim Asia), must lie in the Muslim chronicles of the thirteenth and fourteenth centuries. The reports of the European travellers Carpini, Rubruck, and Marco Polo, the Chinese monk Chang Chuan, and the north African Arab Ibn Batuta, supplemented by Bretschneider's *Medieval Asiatic Researches* and Barthold's studies on Central Asia are invaluable.

One of my main sources has been Ata Malik Juwaini's *Tarikh-i-Jahan Gusha*. A high officer of the Mongol empire, Juwaini and his family as well, occupied key posts in administration. Juwaini's proximity to affairs of the state allowed him first-hand knowledge about the men and events that changed the history of Central Asia.

The *Tarikh-i-Jahan Gusha* is divided into three volumes: the first deals with Chingiz Khan, Ruyuk and Uktae. The work remains the main reference for Chingiz Khan's campaigns in Muslim Asia. Written about AD 1253, *Genghis Qhan: The History of the World-Conquences (Tarikh-i-Jahan Gusha)* details the massacres of Khurasan and the destruction of Merv, Bokhara and Nishapur. He closes his narrative at 1256.

Rashid-ud-din Fazlullah's (1245-1318) *Jamaiut-Tawarikh (Compendium of Chronicles)* is an indispensable source on the history of the Mongols and the life of Chingiz Khan and his descendants. The *Jamaiut-Tawarikh* supplements Juwaini by giving a more detailed account of life and conditions in Mongolia before the rise of Chingiz, the early life of the conqueror, his sayings and military organization, but leave intact Juwaini's account of Mongol campaigns in Muslim Asia.

The *Compendium* is unique because of the variety and sources tapped— Chinese, Mongolian, Turkish, Hebrew, Syriac and Uighur among others. Rashid-ud-din's style is straightforward and ornate.

The *Tabaqat-i-Nasiri* of Minhaj-i-Siraj is one of the earliest works concerning the Mongols, while it also covers the Muslim dynasties of the Indian subcontinent from AD 864 to the Mongol invasion in AD 1260. However, it is only the last chapter (Book XXIII) that deals with the Mongol phenomena, containing information on the conquerors of Hulaka—Chingiz Khan and his descendants, Juji, Uktae, Chaghatae, Batu, Mangu and others. Given his ecclesiastical and somewhat noble pedigree, Qazi Minhaj Siraj got ready acceptance when he emigrated to India (1227) due to the Mongol conquest of Afghanistan.

The work describes the death and destruction due to the Mongol attack in Khusrogun, the mountains of Gharjistan. Interestingly, the facts are corroborated by Juwaini who wrote the *Tarikh* at about the same time, and by the author/compiler of the *Secret History of the Mongols*.

Written in simple prose, though with verbiage, it adequately describes the Mongol invasions among the Indians.

Chief among the Sino-Mongolian sources is the *Secret History of the Mongols* (1228) one of the earliest contemporary extant accounts of Temuchin Chingiz Khan. It is the first and only account of the Mongol leader in the Uighur script. The Mongolian version has no chapters, unlike the seven Chinese versions. The bulk of the book (key chapters) deals with Chingiz. It records the early legends and historical traditions of the Mongols and Chingiz Khan up to his second accession. It details his early struggles for accession and later also served as a handbook for administration and governance for members of the ruling class, in its inclusion of strategies and organizational skills of Chingiz Khan.

I have not been merely concerned with the conduct and conquests of Chingiz Khan but have also tried to find out whether he and his contribution to the art and science of governance and polities have any contemporary relevance.

I should like to remove the misconception that I am soft on the Great Khan or that I aim to give him a good certificate. His devastation of the stretch from Samarqand to the Caspian Sea must needs be acknowledged. Hulaku was to follow later with his notorious sack of Baghdad, which left a deep scar on the Muslim psyche. Were it feasible one would have preferred to seek cover under the pregnant words of Ibn Tiqtiqi: 'There happened what happened of things I like not to mention; therefore imagine what you will, but ask me not of the matter'. One who has experienced the gory 'last days of the British Raj', and the nightmare of the early days of Independence, can understand Ibn Tiqtiqi's anguish.

Having no prejudices and predilections though cognizant of the Khurasan and Baghdad holocausts, and having no illusions about their inherent and integral arrogance, I undertook the ardous task of studying the Mongol phenomenon as 'a voyage of discovery' and as far as possible exploring and reporting objectively and faithfully about the past of a much misunderstood people, the nomadic Mongols. I was astonished to discover what had been generally missed or overlooked by the chroniclers because of the dust, din and haze raised by the clattering of the fierce horse-hooves and war-hoops, by the shrieks of the wounded and dying, by the smoke rising from the masterpieces of architectural beauty and the treasure houses of learning. The historian's vision can be further blurred by the legends, misunderstandings, exaggerated reports, and horrifying caricatures spread by word of mouth in that period.

The study has also focused attention on those aspects of his life and work and, therefore, the significance of the Great Khan as: (a) a man, a family man, a steadfast friend and generous hero, (b) a military genius, administrator, and far-sighted law-giver and, (c) his understanding of governance. The man and his policies have been studied in the context of the contemporary social and political thought, the challenges that he had to contend with, the governing classes of succeeding generations, and the conduct and behaviour of the monarchs of his times.

Chingiz Khan was a man of the people who loved life and, like Babur, enjoyed it. The Mongols have rightfully been proud of him and have loved and revered him. He was not a scourge as generally assumed, but a blessing not only for the Mongols, whom he raised from penury and destitution to plenty and power, but also a blessing in disguise for all those who were prepared and willing to 'hear and obey' him.

It is my most pleasant duty to acknowledge the role of my dear parents, Syed Mahmudul Haque, my father who in spite of his failing health, and mother who in spite of an ever-tightening purse remained steadfast in prompting me to pursue higher studies but could not live to see the fulfilment of a cherished dream. I greatly deplore the loss of my sister, Shamim Zehra Haqqi, my friend and mentor in boyhood, who nurtured and tutored me during school days. She recounted to me stories about great men and women, past and present.

I find it difficult to say how much I owe to my wife, Syedah Zaibun Nissa Haqqi, who was my co-worker and academic guide. She took over the care of the children and relieved me from the worries and responsibilities of household management. Besides, she took keen interest in my research project and the progress of my work. A geographer in her own right, she provided the maps for my doctoral dissertation. It is difficult to say how much I have been missing her since she bid adieu.

It is with great esteem and pleasure that I express my warmest regards, particularly for Kampta Prasad Srivastava, and Jai Chandra Sharma, my schoolteachers, who were for me what a master potter is for his products and in reality, to them I owe the beginning of my academic career. Dr. A.V. Rao whetted my desire for extra-textual studies by loaning me books not otherwise available, C.G. Roy, who sanctioned me free and unrestricted access to his rich personal library as his student at Lucknow, and to boot his gold wristwatch for the Honours Examination, and finally Professor Mohammad Habib, my mentor at Aligarh Muslim University, who in consonance with the true tradition of guru took keen interest in my work and gave me the benefit of his immense knowledge and prodigious memory.

Among those whose valued help and assistance I have to acknowledge I must mention the unfailing courtesy and cooperation of Wei-Kwei-Wei, who allowed me the fullest liberty to utilize his (till then) unpublished draft translation of the *Secret History* in connection with my own thesis on the life and achievements of Chingiz Khan. Without his great gesture of Chinese courtesy and goodwill, the thesis could not have been completed and revised to my satisfaction. I feel deeply beholden to him. Saiyid Zaheer Husain Jafri, Professor and Head Department of History, University of Delhi showed interest in the manuscript of this work. But for him it would not have been published. I am deeply beholden to Professors T.A. Nizami, Mohammad Mahmood, B. Rahmatullah, Absarul Hasnain, and Mohmmad Mustafa for many an out of way act of kindness.

Should I also thank my children Syed Tariq Mahmood, now Professor, Department of Medicine, Immunology, and Rheumatology, State University of South Carolina, Columbia, Former Professor, Department of Medicine, Division of Rheumatic Diseases, Case Western Reserve University, Cleveland, U.S.A., Dr Sohaila Mohsim, Ghazala Javed and Tasneem Aftab who cooperated with their mother to allow me to carry on my academic pursuits and responsibilities.

It would be unfair if I do not make a special mention of Dr (Mrs) Sohaila Mohsim for direct and indirect contribution towards the finalization of the revised text. Following the demise of my wife, she took over the responsibility of looking after me.

It gives me also great pleasure to thankfully acknowledge the contributions of Alimud Din, my stenographer who flawlessly typed from a not very legible manuscript the original version of this study. R.K. Gupta, who displayed exemplary forbearance and expertise in coping with the repeated and innumerable corrections, additions, alterations and deletions in the revised version, and Esha Verma, Research Fellow, Department of History, University of Delhi, who spared some of her valuable time and helped R.K. Gupta decipher and adjust the additions and the 'new field placing'.

I should like to place on record my grateful regards and thanks for what I owe to some of them: Professors of History, Nandlal Chatterji (University of Lucknow), S.C. Saxena (University of Allahabad), and Yusuf Husain Khan

(Osmania University, Hyderabad). I should also like to place on record my deepest regards for my teachers at the Universities of Lucknow and Aligarh, and the London School of Economics. Whatever merits the study may have, the credit belongs to them. I am alone to blame for the content and shortcomings.

I have avoided the use of diacretical marks as I believe they are a nuisance for the general reader, and they are not necessary for scholars familiar with the language. The general reader may find the Index of relevant names and places useful.

Aligarh, Uttar Pradesh   S.A.H. Haqqi

Introduction

HE QARA-KHITAIS, who played a significant role in the history and politics of Central Asia during the twelfth and the early thirteenth century, were originally the neighbours of the Chinese. Living in the southern part of Manchuria, they were quite troublesome to their wealthy and sedate neighbours. They often raided and harassed the Chinese towns and caravans of merchants, but it was only in the tenth century that the Qara-Khitais had the strength and ability to undertake a regular campaign of conquest. In AD 916 they conquered the northern part of China and founded the dynasty known as the House of Liao. The founder of the dynasty, Apaoki, conquered northern Mongolia and in AD 924 he visited Qaraqorum. The house of Liao was, however, expelled from eastern Asia and China in AD 1125 by the Jur-Jun and had thus to move westward (Map 1). This westward movement was not, however, a full-fledged or wholesale migration of the Qara-Khitais; it appears that a considerable section of the Qara-Khitais accepted the rule of the Jur-Jun while others trekked towards the west in two waves. The first trek was disastrous, for the migrants were decisively defeated by Arsalan Khan Ahmad of Kashghar in AD 1128.

Fate was, however, kind to the second group of migrants and crowned their endeavours with the establishment of an independent kingdom in the west. The Qara-Khitais were not unknown to the lands they conquered, for, according to Ibnul Asir, they had already made an unsuccessful foray in AD 1012-13, followed by another in 1017-18. Conquering Balasaqun, they proceeded to occupy Kashghar and Khotan and were strong enough to force A-tisiz (Itsiz Khwarazm Shah) to become their tributary and pay them 30,000 dinars a year. Mahmud Khan of Samarqand was defeated at Khojend in 1131 while Sanjar was defeated in 1141 in the desert of Qatwan. The Qara-Khitais, thus, established a kingdom in the west which was as powerful and extensive as the one they had lost in the east. The Qara-Khitai ruler assumed the title of Gurkhan or 'Khan of Khans'; *gur* may be a derivative of old Turkish *kul* or *kuz,* 'glorious' or 'heroic', and he could style himself as Khan of Khans, for his dominions stretched from the land of the Qir-Qiz in the north to Balkh in the south, from Khwarazm in the west, to Bish-Baligh in the east.

The Gurkhan, allowed his vassal states to have their own native dynasties. In order to have the reins of power and influence in his own hands, however, the Gurkhan granted no fiefs, not even to his relatives, and 'allowed no one command of more than 100 men'. Chinese remained the official language, but no discrimination was made against the Muslims, who continued to occupy posts of honour and influence. It was only when Naiman Kushluk supplanted the Gurkhan that religious persecution raised its ugly head for the first time in Central Asia.

The Qara-Khitais had been greatly influenced by the culture and civilization of China. The Chinese influence was best reflected in their writing, which was based upon the Chinese system: 'small characters, few in number and all arranged in rows'.

We do not have a complete list or accurate chronology of the Gurkhans, but a co-relation of the Muslim and Chinese accounts reveals that there were five Gurkhans. The first Gurkhan died in 1142 and was succeeded by his widow and then by his son in 1150, who ruled for 13 years. In 1163 the Gurkhan's daughter succeeded and reigned till 1178, when she was succeeded by Tirgu or Chi-lu-ku, her brother's son. Tirgu ruled till 1211 when he was supplanted by Kushluk.

The Khwarazm Shahs

The Seljuq Empire did not recover even temporarily from the effects of Sanjar's defeat and captivity at the hands of the Ghuzz, and his death, closely following his escape from captivity, which removed the last hope of retrieving the fortunes of the empire. The first and the foremost provincial governor to profit by the decline and decay of the Seljuqs was the unscrupulous governor of Khwarazm, A-tisiz, the grandson of the Seljuq slave Anushtagin Gharja. Purchased and presented by the Seljuq Amir Bilga-Tagin to the Sultan Malik Shah, 'the clever and courageous Anushtagin rose to become the superintendent of the royal kitchen'. As the revenues of Khwarazm were reserved to meet the kitchen establishments, says Juwaini, Anushtagin was also styled as the

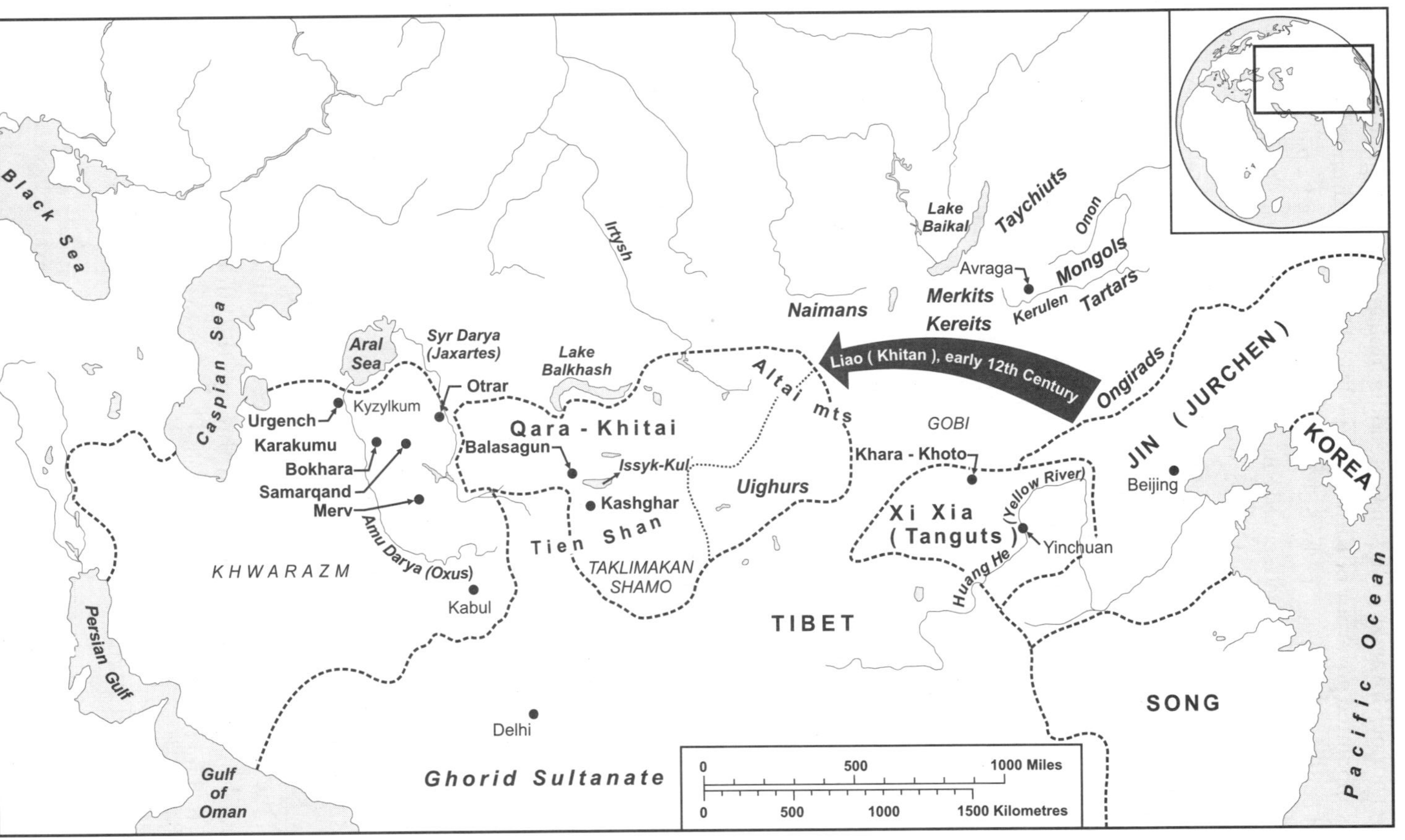

Map 1. The World of Young Chingiz

governor of Khwarazm. His son Qutbuddin Mohammad, brought up in Merv, was appointed governor of Khwarazm by Dad-Habshi bin Altun-taq in 1097, and confirmed in his office by Sultan Sanjar. A just ruler and a patron of arts and literature, Mohammad served Sanjar with complete loyalty and faithfulness till his death sometime in 1127-8 when he was succeeded by his able and ambitious son, A-tisiz, who was destined to found a dynasty and raise Khwarazm to the heights of power. 'With rare perseverance and skill', Barthold remarks, 'he and his successors stopped at no measures to attain their aim, the foundation of a strong and independent kingdom.' An expert in the art of warfare, A-tisiz was held in high esteem by Sultan Sanjar and, according to Ibn Khaldun had been given command of the imperial troops. During the heyday of Sanjar's power and prosperity, A-tisiz remained a faithful vassal, but always with an eye to his own profit.

A-tisiz made repeated bids for the crown when he found Sanjar in trouble or his hold weakening. But he was baulked in his efforts, and without realizing his lifelong ambition, died of paralysis at the age of 59 in 1156. Cultured and learned, A-tisiz was a typical soldier of fortune, daring, insolent, rapacious, and cruel. A-tisiz was succeeded by his eldest son, Abul Fath Alp Il-Arsalan who inaugurated his reign by imprisoning his brother, Sulaiman Shah and executing the Atabeg, Oghul-beg.

With the battle of Qatwan, which reduced the authority and prestige of Sanjar, Transoxiana passed into the hands of the Qara-Khitais and their protégé, Tamghaj Khan Ibrahim, son of Arsalan Khan Mahmud, became the ruler of Samarqand. But Ibrahim's rule was short-lived. The Qarluqs rose in revolt and put him to death. His successor, Chaghri Khan Jalal-ud-din, was determined to teach the unruly nomads a lesson. He executed the Qarluq chief, Payghu Khan, and persecuted the other Qarluq leaders, who sought refuge with Il-Arsalan. Acting on the complaint of the persecuted Qarluq leaders, Il-Arsalan pitted his forces against those of his nominal vassal. In July 1158, Il-Arsalan marched into Transoxiana as the protector and liberator. The Khan of Samarqand was assisted by the roving bands of the Turkmens and the Qara-Khitais. The two armies faced each other on the banks of the Zarafshan but peace was brokered through the efforts of the leading and learned men of Samarqand; the Qarluq leaders were restored to their posts and the Khwarazm Shah returned to his own capital. Il-Arsalan was also ambitious and attempted to expand his domains but could not make much headway.

The death of Il-Arsalan was followed by a civil war between his sons, Sultan Shah and Imaduddin Takash. Takash did not hesitate to turn to the

Gurkhan for help by offering submission and an annual tribute of 30,000 dinars, in return for Qara-Khitai aid against his younger brother Sultan Shah. Unable to match the strength of the force garnered by his brother, Sultan Shah left the capital and Takash was brought back triumphantly to Khwarazm. But friction soon arose between Takash and his allies. When the Gurkhan's envoy arrived to demand from the Shah the price of his enthronement and an increase in the tribute for the continued support of the Qara-Khitais, he met with stubborn refusal. The envoy was reportedly insolent and exasperating and in a fit of wild rage Takash ordered him and his companions to be put to death. Hostilities soon broke out between Takash and the Qara-Khitais and Sultan Shah hastened to take advantage. He entered into an alliance with the Gurkhan, and the Qara-Khitai general Fuma was despatched on a punitive expedition to exact vengeance for the murder of the envoy and to place Sultan Shah on the throne of Khwarazm. However, the expedition did not succeed. The people of Khwarazm, the Khitais discovered to their grief, were indifferent to the pretensions of Sultan Shah. Fuma, however, acceded to Sultan Shah's request for a division, and with the help of the Qara-Khitais Sultan Shah managed to defeat the local Ghuzz chief and wrested Merv, Sarakhs and Tus from the hands of their leader, Malik Dinar. He also ousted Tughan Shah from Nishapur. In 1157, however, Takash occupied Nishapur and an accommodation was arrived at between the two brothers whereby Sultan Shah was allowed to hold Merv, Sarakhs, and a few other towns. But the restless Sultan Shah soon brought about an unnecessary conflict with Ghor. After concluding an alliance with Tughril, an upstart adventurer, who now held Herat, Sultan Shah attacked the territories of Ghor. A struggle between the two Muslim powers was inevitable though on both sides there had been previously an unwillingness to strike.

Takash always considered it his first duty to expand his dominions and consolidate his conquests. No difficulty awaited him in Khurasan, for the Ghorids had made themselves unpopular and were preoccupied with the events in India and elsewhere. Towards the north and east, Takash succeeded in strengthening his hold over Trans-Oxiana by the conquest and occupation of Bokhara, and bringing the Qipchaq tribes under his sway. In the west he subdued Iraq where he was invited by the caliph, locked in a triangular conflict with the Seljuq Sultan and the Atabeg Qutlugh Inanj. In 1194 he took parts of Iraq.

The caliph soon had reason to regret his ill-advised invitation to the powerful Khwarazm Shah, for not only did the Khwarazmians defeat the Seljuq sultan and the Atabeg and subject the people to unspeakable cruelties, the Shah also refused to pay respect to the caliph's wazir and his preposterous demands. He decided to annexe Iraq and demanded the inclusion of his name in the Khutba at Baghdad.

Enemy to every influence and every movement that tended to lessen his temporal power, the Abbasid Caliph Nasir never hesistated to resort to the foulest means to stamp out opposition. Now baulked and crossed in his ambitions over Iraq, he began inciting the Ghorians and the Khitans against the Khwarazm Shah.

In fear for his life as well as for his throne, Ala-ud-din Muhammad Khwarazm Shah sent an envoy to Sultan Ghias-ud-din to effect a reconciliation and a union of their forces for a campaign against the infidel Qara-Khitais. Their ambitions were, however, too identical to permit a harmonious agreement and cordial collaboration, and the Khwarazm Shah was forced to undertake an expedition for the recovery of his patrimony. He took what seemed to be a gambler's chance. 'With the rapidity of lightning' he advanced into Khurasan and by 1203 was able to recover his lost province and drive the Ghorians out of Khurasan. This aroused his ambition to extend his frontiers and take possession of Herat.

Shihab-ud-din the Ghorid Sultan understood and accepted the challenge. Battle was joined in the great plain near Qara-Suza in which the Khwarazm Shah was defeated and Shihab-ud-din besieged Gurganj which was valiantly defended by the people. Hard-pressed, the Khwarazm Shah appealed to the Gurkhan for help, and a huge Qara-Khitai army under the command of Taniko Taraz 'a Turk of great age and wisdom' and hero of forty-five battles, crossed the mountains and marched on Gurganj. Before the Qara-Khitais could surround him, Shihab-ud-din wisely abandoned the siege.

The retreat of the Ghorians was barred near Andkhud by the Khitan general, Taniko Taraz, who instead of marching on to Gurganj, had turned south and was waiting for them. The Ghorians bravely faced the Qara-Khitas who were their equals in courage and strength. Yet, abandoned by most of his men, the sultan showed no signs of cowardice. The issue was long in doubt and it was after a fortnight's battle that the sultan was completely beaten and forced to seek shelter in Andkhud. But Usman, the Sultan of Samarqand, came to his rescue and secured a safe passage for him and his few remaining men to Ghor on the condition that they surrender all arms, ammunition, and belongings.

The decisive battle of Andkhud determined that thereafter, the Khwarazm Shahs and not the Ghorians were to be the masters of Khurasan. Yet Andkhud had made it clear that no Muslim ruler was to thrive in his ambitions of a

Central Asian empire so long as the Qara-Khitais were there. Peace was made between the Ghorid Sultan and the Khwarazm Shah, which promised to prove lasting; for Ala-ud-din wisely demanded no concession injurious to the honour or political interests of Ghor. Herat and Balkh were restored to the Ghorians while the rest of Khurasan was retained by the Shah. Shihab-ud-din and his descendants thus paid a price for his greed, as would, ironically, the Khwarazmians a little later.

Burning with a desire to revenge himself upon the Qara-Khitais, Shihab-ud-din turned a deaf ear to the appeals of the caliph for an expedition against the Khwarazm Shah. For the sake of preserving his prestige as 'Sultan of Islam' and also to revenge himself on the Gurkhan, he flattered the Shah and aided him indirectly at least, to subjugate the Qipchaq. It was not until 1205 that he believed himself strong enough to measure arms with the Qara-Khitais but he was not destined to carry out his ambitious project of a three-year campaign against them, for while returning from India an assassin's dagger claimed him and the dreams of a Ghorian empire in Central Asia did not outlive the great sultan. With Shihab-ud-din departed the glory and grandeur of the Ghorids; for at his death Ala-ud-din annexed the territories of Herat and Balkh and compelled Shihab-ud-din's successor to accept Khwarazmian suzerainty.

In 1208 Ala-ud-din Khwarazm Shah was at the height of his fortunes and appeared to have achieved mastery over Khurasan. Ghias-ud-din Mahmud, the ruler of Ghor, humbled and defeated, was no more than a humble vassal. Now practically supreme in Central Asia, Ala-ud-din felt that it was time to extend his dominions in the north and north-east. But in his prosperity he forgot about the Qara-Khitais, who had aided him against his Muslim rival and put him where he was, he forgot that he and his ancestors had invited the Qara-Khitais into Khurasan as well as Transoxiana and had shown them the fertile valleys and the weakness of the people—knowledge that could have come to them in no other way. Khurasan lay subdued and prostrate at his feet; the rebel governor of Nishapur had been hunted to death; Herat and Bokhara had been finally incorporated in his domains while by a treaty of mutual alliance he had extended his sphere of influence even over the sultan of Samarqand. He now stopped the payment of the annual tribute to the Gurkhan, especially so on account of the insolence and haughtiness of the Qara-Khitai tax keep collectors.

In 1209 the Gurkhan's wazir, Mahmud-Baym, duly arrived to remind the Shah of his dues at a time when the sultan was to launch an expedition against the Qipchaqs. Thinking discretion to be the better part of valour, he did not deem it advisable to give the Gurkhan, as Juwaini says, 'a pretext or an opportunity to molest his dominions during his absence'. He felt it a disgrace even to acknowledge his liability to pay the tribute, and left the affairs or matter in the hands of his mother, Turkan Khatun, as he set out on his expedition. 'Turkan Khatun treated the envoys with due honour and respect, paid over the accumulated arrears of tribute, and sent a number of distinguished courtiers to apologise to the Gurkhan for the delay. But, says Juwaini, Mahmud-Bay—had witnessed the haughty bearing and stubbornness of Sultan Muhammad. He warned assured the Gurkhan that the sultan would never pay him tribute again.'

It is impossible to believe that the Khwarazm Shah did not realize the danger to which he had exposed his newly conquered domains and the noose into which he had put his neck. As sovereign ruler of Muslim lands, on him rested the responsibility of liberating Transoxiana from the yoke of the infidel Qara-Khitais. As early as 1203 he had been in secret communication with the Muslim chiefs and maliks of Transoxiana and had received encouraging response, especially from Bokhara and Samarqand, to unite against the Qara-Khitais. He met a ready response, for the rapacity of the Gurkhan's representatives had become intolerable.

In 1205-6 Sultan Usman of Samarqand also joined the coalition and the Khwarazm Shah rallied his army at Samarqand for the first great campaign against the Qara-Khitais. He could not muster enough Khwarazmians to undertake so formidable a feat as the invasion of the Gurkhan's vast domains, and had to rely upon the contingents of Bokhara and Samarqand, crossing the Jaxartes at Hurkat by a bridge of boats, 'which he afterwards destroyed so that his army might have no hope of retreat', the Khwarazm Shah reached Taraz, where Taniko was waiting for them. Battle was joined in the great plain of Ilash and, after a stubborn battle, Taniko was wounded. He was sent captive to Khwarazm, where he was killed and his body was thrown into the river. 'Every one', says Qazi Minhaj, 'obtained the money he wished to have in his pocket or the slave girl he desired to hold within his arms'. And the Sultan assumed the title of 'a second Alexander', 'Sultan Sanjar' and 'the shadow of God on earth'.

Yet Central Asia was fast proceeding to a catastrophe. The officers of the Khwarazm Shah would engage in such bloody conflicts with the vassal rulers and their subjects, plundering the inhabitants of the country, that the people soon found that they had passed from Scylla to Charybdis. The indignation of the population against the Khwarazm Shah, who had sacrificed them to his officials soon reached breaking point. Even Sultan Usman of

Samarqand, who had only recently married the daughter of the Shah declared for the Gurkhan. Samarqand rose in a popular revolt against the Shah in 1212. The Shah's daughter was forced to barricade herself in the citadel. The Khwarazmians were butchered to the last man and their bodies, says Ibnul Asir, 'cut in halves and pieces of them hung up in the bazars, as butchers hang meat'. As soon as the Shah heard of the uprising, he marched on Samarqand. The town was sacked for 3 days and 10,000 persons lost their lives. Sultan Usman and members of the Qarakhanid dynasty were executed and Samarqand was annexed. Thus Ala-ud-din finally founded an independent kingdom holding Khurasan and Transoxiana.

Had the sultan availed himself of peace and tranquility to diminish the burden on his subjects and to consolidate the defence of his recently conquered and far-flung empire instead of extending its frontiers, he might perhaps, have established his dynasty on a firmer foundation. But as soon as he heard of the disturbance in the Gurkhan's dominions and the rise of Kushluk to prominence, he began a bitter and bloody conflict with the nomads. The hosts of the Khwarazm Shah proved no match for the virile nomads and the guerilla warfare of Kushluk completely foiled and paralysed the efforts of the Khwarazm Shah. In a short time Kushluk brought under his yoke the fertile valleys of eastern Turkestan. Not only did the sultan fail to rescue the Muslims of Kashghar and Khotan from the depredations and the ravages of Kushluk's soldiers, he even proved powerless to guard his Trans-Oxianian frontier and was obliged to follow a scorched earth policy; and 'provinces were devastated so that they should not fall prey to Kushluk'.

'As soon as Muhammad', says Dr Siddiqi, 'had rid himself of his rivals', 'aspired to the restoration in his favour of the universal Sultanate.....' But he failed to understand the man with whom he was going to deal—the Caliph Nasir, as unscrupulous as he was ambitious. Nasir had long been dreaming and scheming to re-establish and restore the power of the Caliphate. It was his dream of the universal Caliphate which was to plunge the lands of Islam into the most bitter of their controversies and to call forth Chingiz Khan from the seclusion of the Mongolian steppes and end with the destruction of Baghdad and the Abbasid Caliphate. Caliph Nasir exhorted the Ghorian sultan to enter into an alliance with the infidel Qara-Khitais against the Khwarazm Shah; he even stooped to enlist the services of the Assassins to remove Oghulmish, the Khwarazmian Viceroy of Iraq and Sharif of Mecca.

So Muhammad's efforts to achieve his aim by diplomatic means were foredoomed to failure. The caliph was adamant and no compromise or solution could be arrived at. Neck or nothing remained his demand and the caliph, with the experience of the Buwayhids, Ghaznavids and the Seljuqs still fresh in memory, declined to put his neck in the noose of Khwarazmian sovereignty on which the sultan, 'Ala-ud-din Khwarazm Shah, was insisting. The sultan did not consider himself in any way inferior to the Buwayhids or Seljuqs and maintained his original position. The 'unscrupulous proceedings' of the caliph furnished a plausible pretext to the Khwarazm Shah to obtain a fatwa for his deposition. Armed with theological sanction, the sultan proceeded to declare the caliph deposed and ordered his name to be omitted from the Khutba and the coinage, and in his place declared Syed Alaul Mulk Tirmizi the rightful and legitimate caliph. He then led an expedition in 1217 to depose Nasir and enthrone the new caliph. But, unfortunately for the Shah, due to the early fall of snow, the troops of the Shah, like the Grand Army of Napoleon, perished miserably in the snowstorms; the Shah himself was lucky to escape. 'A cruel blow', as observes Barhold, 'was dealt to his prestige and position by the failure of this campaign'.

Finding himself in a hopeless position, the Sultan appears to have lost his balance of mind and sense of values. The setting up of a Shia as a caliph was a blunder. The veneration enjoyed by the Caliphate as an institution in the Muslim world is revealed by contemporary writers. The author of *Chahar Maqala*, Nizami Aruzi, had observed much earlier that he was a 'representative of the Prophet'. 'Any one who sought to bring evil upon it (House of Abbasidis)' wrote Ibn Asir, 'was punished for his action or for his evil intentions'. Even as late as the First World War, the name of the Ottoman Sultan was recited in the Friday sermon as Caliph of Islam in regions outside the Ottoman Empire.

It may not be out of place to refer to the insensitivity of the Khwarazm Shahs to the feelings and reactions of their subjects, since the days of Takash on account of their constant alliance with the 'infidel' Qara-Khitais and quarrels with the caliph. Giving expression to the popular anger Maulana Zahir-ud-din Faryabi, according to Qazi Minhaj Siraj, addressed the following apostrophe to Sultan Takash:

O Shah! Since Azam has been assigned to thee by the sword, send an army towards Mustapha's place of rest (*Madina*), then lay desolate the (Holy) Kabah, and bring a fan, and send the dust of the Haram to winds as useless particles. *The crumbling drapery of the Kabah, place in the treasury* and send two or three (dirty) pieces of matting for the Prophet's tomb, when Thou has become a perfect infidel, then send to Khita (the Gurkhan) the head of the Caliph.

Ala-ud-din Khwarazm Shah failed to comprehend the rising tide of public opinion against his family for their 'inveterate hostility to the Caliphate and disgraceful alliance with the Qara-Khitai'. He was unable or unwilling to foresee the consequences of his latest outrage. The order of the sultan was clandestinely disobeyed or repudiated in Khwarazm, Samarqand, and Herat.

Khwarazm Shah was dominated by the haughty and ambitious Turkan Khatun and her mercenary clique. The corporate organization of the Qanqalis and their devotion to Turkan Khatun—who belonged to their clan—had given her the opportunity, and a means to interfere in the administration of the empire 'The influence of this relentless, strong-willed woman and the valour of Turkish warriors', as observes Curtin, 'raised those Chiefs to the highest rank among military leaders, their power was enormous, since commanders of troops governed with very wide latitude.' Amid this aristocracy of fighters the power of the sovereign was uncertain; he was forced to satisfy the ambition of men who saw in all things only their own profit. The troops controlled by those governors ruined every region which they visited.

Turkan Khatun, the head of this military faction, not only equalled her son in authority, but often surpassed him. When two orders of different origin appeared in any part of the Empire, the date decided which had authority. The order on which the date was most recent was carried out and the order of recent date was always that of Turkan Khatun. She employed seven secretaries at all times, men distinguished for ability. The inscription on her decrees was 'Protectress of the world and faith, Turkan, queen of women'. Her device was: 'God alone is my refuge', and 'Lord of the world' was her title.

Under the intolerable pressure of his mother the sultan was driven on his reckless career from madness to madness and crime to crime. His latest acts were to appoint Mohammad bin Sahib as his Wazir, to bestow on him the titles of Nasir-ud-din and Nizam-ul-Mulk, to exile his eldest and ablest son, Jalal-ud-din, to the governorship of the distant and outlying territories of Ghor and Ghaznin, and to nominate the youngest son, Qutb-ud-din Uzlagh Shah (descended from a Qanqali wife), as heir to the throne and to confer on him the provinces of Khwarazm, Khurasan and Masandaran, which were really governed and administered by Turkan Khatun. In the provinces under the government of Turkan Khatun, 'Muhammad's authority was in practice not recognised'. As Turkan Khatun had a great regard for her tribesmen, the Qanqalis, says Juwaini, 'became all powerful. Kindness and mercy were far from their hearts'. They excluded the native population from all posts of importance and power and reduced them to the position of serfs. Their tyranny, says Juwaini, did great damage to the power of the Shah. Thus a violent opposition and hatred was engendered throughout Khurasan and Iraq and not a finger was raised in defence of the Khwarazmian dynasty when it fell on evil days. Barthold remarks:

The bureaucracy, was deprived of all importance; the military caste, at the head of which stood the Sultan's mother, was in open enmity with the bearer of the Supreme power; the priesthood could hardly forgive the Khwarazm Shah for the murder of Majd ad-din and the fatwa extorted against the Caliph; the people liberated by Muhammad from the yoke of the infidel Qara Khitars rose against their liberators, and were put down mercilessly. Muhammad therefore could not depend on a single element of the administrative system, nor on a single class of the population. The issue of the struggle between such a power and the fresh forces of the nomads, united at this time under Chingiz Khan, one of the most talented organisers of all ages, is comprehensible.

The Ancestors of Chingiz Khan

The origin of the Mongols as that of the other Central Asian tribes, is lost in legends. History-tellers and chroniclers later compounded the confusion more by their attempts (fuelled by the compulsions of court patronage), to discover the noble pedigree of their leaders. The *Secret History of the Mongol Dynasty*, for example, would have us believe that the illustrious Mongol tribe came into being from the mating of a heaven-born grey-wolf and a whitish doe, who together crossed a river, called the Tengis, and reached the source of the Onon River, where they settled at the foot of the Mount Burqan (Burkhan). The chronology and careers of the ancestors of Chingiz Khan have been stamped with greatness and glory by obliging chroniclers and court historians who have attempted to trace their ancestry to the Prophet. They are 'Children of Light' and, therefore, worthy rulers of the heavenly born Mongols. The way the widowed Alan Goa (Alan Quwa of Muslim historians), whose chastity was doubted by her sons, has been raised to the dignity and status of 'Mary of the Mongols' by Abu Fazl shows the effort of Timurid historians to give the finest pedigree to the descendants of the great conquerors, Chingiz and Tamerlane.

In the long string of names that adorn the genealogy of Chingiz Khan, Buzanjar, signifying 'Great Sovereign' occupies, next to Alan Goa, pride of place as the law-giver of the Mongols. He is credited with having unified Mongolia by subduing and subjugating the different tribes, including the Tatars. Son of Alan Goa by 'the Man of Light', Buzanjar is said to have been 'enthroned' in Rabi I AH 130 November, AD 747. The next important figure is Qaidu Khan, the sixth ancestor of Chingiz Khan. Greatgrandson of Buzanjar, his claim to greatness rests on a victory over the Jalairs; he avenged the loss and humiliation which had been suffered by the Mongols during the chieftainship of his father. He was not only great as a war leader but constructed a canal which made his territory prosperous and flourishing. It was his grandson, Tumnah Khan, who is credited by the Timurid historians of having made the famous family arrangement, known as the *Altamgha* or 'Award' of Tumnah Khan. According to the Timurid thesis, Tumnah Khan in order to solve the friction between his two sons, Kabul Khan and Qachuli, and in consequence of Qachuli's strange dream, decided that Kabul was to succeed him as Khan and Qachuli was to command the troops and look after the administration.

Kabul Khan duly succeeded his father as the Khan of the Mongols and soon earned the title of *Alanjik* or 'Cherisher of his people'. On account of his reputation as a great administrator, a lover of justice, and a brave soldier, the Kin Emperor (the Altan Khan of Muslim historians) 'invited' him to his court. The Khan of the Mongols, it is said, was received with great honour; the special favours showered upon him only served to arouse the suspicions of Kabul Khan, however. Afraid he would be poisoned, he ran away. He threw up what he had eaten and returned to the feast. The Chinese were amazed and shocked at his hard drinking and at the enormous quantity of food he ate. Later, however the intoxicated Kabul Khan shouted at the Emperor and tweaked his beard. Immediately the enraged courtiers demanded his head. The Kin Emperor was greatly displeased but, nevertheless, accepted Kabul Khan's apology and allowed him to depart; the chroniclers further add that Kabul Khan was given a 'Crown' or headdress and belt.

After Kabul Khan's departure, the emperor was, however, persuaded by his courtiers to recall him—probably to put him to death. Kabul Khan refused to return and continued homeward. His son, Ukin Barqaq, however, fell into the hands of the Tatars, who carried him off to the Chinese Emperor, who put him to death 'by having him mounted upon a wooden ass and nailed to it with iron spikes'.

Kabul Khan was succeeded by Qubila, who was noted for his stature, courage and strength. 'His voice', it is related, 'would pierce the seventh heaven, and his grip was like that of a bear. He could take a strong man, and with both hands bend him like a twig until his back broke. During the cold winter nights he was fond of going to sleep naked before a great fire made of the trunks of trees. He did not care for the sparks of fire which used to fly out and touch him, for, if he chanced to awake, he would fancy the fleas had disturbed him, and he would scratch himself and go off to sleep again'. He is credited with having waged a successful expedition against the Kins and the Tatars and returned laden with immense booty.

Then Bartan succeeded his brother, Qubila Khan, as the leader of the Mongols. He dropped the title of Khan and assumed that of *Bahadur* or Hero. Qachuli died during his reign and, it is said, his son, Irdumji Barlas, was appointed to his hereditary office by Bartan Bahadur. On the death of Bartan, his son Yesukai became the chief of the Mongols. And with Yesukai we reach firmer ground; the twilight of legend and chronicles is replaced by the daylight of history and the fairy tales of mythical and semi-mythical heroes recede and recoil before the stark realities of history, written with blood and fire by Chingiz Khan.

1

The Making of the Man

SINGING JOYFULLY, Yeke Chiraidu of the Merkit tribe was riding home along with his young wife in her cart. Yesukai, of the Borjigin clan, who was hunting and hawking along the river Onon, espied them; and, noting that the woman was very beautiful, he galloped home to call his brothers, Nekun Tai-tsi and Daritai Otchigin to help him to capture her. Pursued by the three brothers, Yeke Chiraidu was frightened and allowed his wife to make the decision. 'These three men look very dangerous', she said, divining their aim and ambition, 'and wish to take your life. I pray you to hurry off. If your life is saved by any means, you can very easily find a woman like me. If you remember me, you can marry another woman and call her by my name.' Taking off her outer garment and offering it to him as a souvenir, she bade him adieu. The three brothers tried to capture Chiraidu and pursued him over seven hills, but when unable to overtake him, they returned to the woman and her cart. With Nekun Tai-tsi as a guide and Daritai escorting it, Yesukai began to pull the cart towards his ordu or tent. The captured woman began to cry, and 'her screams seemed to raise the waves on the Onon River and to shake trees of the forests.' 'Never were my husband's hair blown by the wind,' she wailed, 'nor his stomach suffered from hunger. How hard will it be for him now that he has to leave me.' 'Your husband has by now passed many ridges and crossed many streams,' Daritai Otchigin explained to her, 'your cries cannot make him turn back his head. It is in vain to look for his trail. Be content and stop screaming'.[1]

It was an ordinary case of woman-lifting in twelfth century Mongolia. Tradition dictated how a woman was to behave before and after abduction, and on recovery by the first husband. After the ex-husband had been mourned for, the new husband had to be pleased; and a wise woman, whether lawfully married or summarily abducted, would do her best to establish her supremacy and status in the polygamous household of her new husband. The act of capture was the only marriage ceremony needed; the man's consent was obvious, while a formal wailing on the part of the woman proved that she was at least reconciling herself to the loss of her former lord.

Human history has not recorded a more significant case of wife-lifting: the captured woman, Oyelun, was destined to be the mother of the largest number of connected imperial dynasties the world has seen. Yeke Chiraidu ran away and disappeared from history, while Oyelun remained in her cart to make it.

Oyelun's character was destined to unfold in the years to come. Her life was to see recurrent crises and her intellect and nerves never failed her. Throughout her life she succeeded in persuading, directing, and controlling a son such as no other woman has succeeded in bearing. To get rid of a somewhat humdrum husband and to take the position of the premier wife of a chief, who commanded 40,000 yurts was a change for the better. Oyelun belonged to the Olkunut branch of the desert-dwelling Merkits, but inter-tribal alliances were common in Mongolia and Oyelun's primacy in Yesukai's household was never questioned.[2] It is to be wished that we had a more detailed account of her work in training and moulding the young Chingiz Khan. Intelligent and intrepid, she proved a tower of strength to her son during the days of his difficulties and distress. Strong and resolute, she had a sharp tongue and she was the only person of whom he was afraid, to whose railings, harsh epithets, and invective he did not dare reply. Never except once in his youth do we come across an instance when defied her.

Her new husband, Yesukai, was a tribal chieftain of the steppe famous for his sagacity and bravery which had earned him the title of Bahadur—Khan of the Yakka Mongols, he was lord and leader of 40,000 tents or families. Even his brothers, including those senior to him, acknowledged him as their leader and head of the Borjigin clan. A great warrior, he had succeeded in bringing some of the Taichiut clans under his banner, and helped the celebrated Toghril Wang Khan of the Kereits several times. In recognition and appreciation of Yesukai's valuable services and assistance he had become Wang Khan's *anda* or sworn-friend.[3]

'Say to Kutula, among the seven sons of Kabul Khan and to Kadaan Tai-tsi among my ten sons,' said Anbagai Khan to Barakhachi of the Baisut tribe, 'that I, who am the chief of all you people, have been seized by the Tatars while escorting my daughter to her marriage. Hereafter, you must not forget my unfortunate end. Even if you wear out all your five fingernails or break all your ten fingers, you should avenge us.' For the savage and ferocious tribe of Mongolia, blood called for blood.

Between the Tatars and the Mongols enmity and blood feud were of long standing, and the unfortunate end of Anbagai was only of a series of murders of vengeance and counter-vengeance. Kutula, named by Anbagai and elected Khan by the Mongols, waged a war of annihilation against the Tatars but could not crush them. As chief of the Borjigin clan, a sept of the Mongols, Yesukai had to help his kinsmen against the Tatars. On returning home in 1155 from a successful expedition against the Tatars whose two chiefs, Temuchin Uka and Korbugha, followed him in chains, he found that his favourite wife, Oyelun, had given birth to a son who, as legend would have it, had come into the world with a clot of blood in his hand. In accordance with the old Mongol custom (which required the name of a new born to commemorate some conspicuous incident connected with his birth) the boy was given the name Temuchin—to celebrate Yesukai's triumph over the formidable Temuchin and to commemorate the discomfiture of the Tatars.[4]

To the superstitious Mongols, the birth of Temuchin with a clot of blood in his hand, coinciding with their triumph and victory over their enemies was a great portent. The congealed lump of blood in his fist indicated, the sages and the shamans prophesied, that the new-born babe was destined for a great and bloody career. Long before his birth, it is said,[5] his greatness and glory had been foreshadowed and revealed to one of his greatgrandfathers, Qachuli. Relating his dream to Tumnah Khan Qachuli said:

I saw three stars rise on the left of Kabul Khan, one after another, and these stars having attained the meridian, declined and disappeared, when a fourth star of great magnitude, and very bright, arose from the neck of Kabul Khan, and after sometime many smaller stars separated from it, which shed light over all parts of the horizon; and when the great star had set, they still continued to shine with undiminished splendour. When I awakened from my dream, I found a large portion of the night was still unexpired, and, therefore, again composed myself to sleep; and again I dreamt that seven stars arose from my neck successively, and then an eighth arose, of very large size and great refulgence; several stars also separated from this and shed light over different parts of the earth; and when the great stars had declined and set, the remainder still continued to illumine the heaven.

The interpretation of the astrologers was that three kings of the seed of Kabul Khan would reign successively, but the fourth would be the conqueror of a great part of the inhabited world; he would have many children who would all reign over different parts of the earth; their descendants, for a long period, would succeed them in rank and power. Seven of the immediate descendants of Qachuli would also be rulers in a second degree; but the eighth, whose existence was denoted by the large star, would become the conqueror of the greatest part of the earth; he would have many children, all kings of different countries.[6] There is not a single great ruler or hero in the history of Asia whose advent and great career are not thus foretold by such interesting but apocryphal stories. These stories of dreams and their *post-facto* historically-justified interpretations occur in the literature too frequently. The earliest authorities, including *The Secret History of the Mongol Dynasty*, the *Tabaqat-i-Nasiri* and *Tarikh-i-Jahan Gusha*, are all silent about such dreams and prophecies. It is the later Timurid historians, and court historians who manipulate and reveal in such legends and stories the greatness of Chingiz Khan and his descendants—for obvious reasons.

Of Temuchin's early life and training we hear nothing, but it is reasonable to suppose that as the years rolled by and childhood turned into youth, Temuchin was brought up in the hard and harsh atmosphere of nomadic life, in which the tribal lords and chiefs fought, drank, and duelled, married and slept with their weapons underneath them—a rigorous life in which chief shared the miseries, hungers and privations of their people. For life in the Gobi Desert was anything but calm on plentiful. Carpini comments:

Here are no towns or cities says Carpini, but everywhere sandy barrens, not a hundredth part of the whole being fertile except where it is watered by rivers, which are very rare.

This land is nearly destitute of trees, although well adapted for the pasturage of cattle. Even the Emperor and princes and all others warm themselves and cook their victuals with fires of horse-dung and cow-dung.

The climate is very intemperate, as in the middle of summer, there are terrible storms of thunder and lightening by which many people are killed, and even then there are great falls of snow and such tempests of cold winds blow that sometimes people can hardly sit on horse-back. In one of these, we had to throw ourselves down on the ground and could not see through the prodigious dust. There are often showers of hail, and sudden, intolerable heats followed by extreme cold.[7]

Nomads with their movable houses and immense droves of cattle moved up and down between seasonal camping grounds and fresh pastures; in summer to escape from desert heat and desert storms, from drought and sand, and in winter to avoid the piercing and chilling gale when sand mixed with snow hit their faces, and women and children, huddled in the yurts, would wrap themselves against the cold. Wind and lightning, thunder and ice, tempests, dust and hail, the familiars of nomadic life in the Gobi, must have steeled and strengthened Temuchin and given him that iron physique which withstood the demands of his career. He must have grown up with the boys of his age, fishing in the rivers, taking part in wrestling bouts, learning horsemanship hunting the wild antelope, the hare and the fox, the lizard, the marten and sometimes the bear. It was a rough and rugged life that the Mongols lived, especially in winter when the herds had been consumed to danger point, and no more horses and sheep could be slaughtered to feed the family and they were compelled to live on *kumiz* or fermented milk and boiled millet. Warriors of the tribe would go out on raids to carry off the cattle and horses of other tribes while the hunters went after elusive game. Cattle-lifting and the use of pasture and streams were the major causes of strife between the tribes and, therefore, towards the spring, young men spent sleepless nights to watching the skyline for raiders or to hunt for stray cattle. The 'poor and wretched conditions'[8] in which they lived made the boys learn to go without cooked food for several days. 'The sign of a great Amir', says Juwaini 'was that his stirrups were made of iron. The other paraphernalia of their lives can be estimated from this.' And so Temuchin, sharing his father's tent and learning the soldier's life at first-hand, would have known how to appreciate food, and how to do without it, even how to carry on without sleep.

Nine years rolled by—long stretches on the roads of time, when Yesukai determined that his son was old enough to be betrothed and, according to the tribal law of exogamy, began to look for a bride for Temuchin from among the daughters of the Olkunut tribe. 'Where are you going, Yesukai?' asked Dai Sechen, meeting them on the way. 'I am going to my son's maternal uncle of the Olkuna', Yesukai answered, 'to ask for a girl to be his wife'. 'This son of yours has piercing eyes and a bright face', remarked Dai Sechen. 'Last night I dreamt that a white falcon, which was holding the sun and the moon in its talons, flew to me and perched on my hand. I said to someone that we can only see the sun and moon but now a white falcon has perched on my hand with the sun and the moon in its talons. This must be a good omen. Today your presence with your son here has shown me the significance of my dream. It presages that good fortune will attend your son's courting. We, the Ungira family, have never quarrelled with others for land or subjects. If we have any beautiful girls, we shall be glad that they should sit on the thrones of the royal wives of your imperial family. Generally speaking, in a contract of marriage, the boy is honoured for the position of his family and the girl for her beauty. Yesukai, I have a daughter at home. She is still of a tender age but come and have a look at her.'

Dai Sechen was the head of the prosperous and powerful tribe—the Jungirat, whose fertile pastures lay between the Tatars and the Onguts who dwelt near the Great Wall of China. On account of their geographical position, the Ongut and the Jungirat had closer relations with the Chinese than did the other Mongol tribes, and were, as such, under greater Chinese cultural and political influence. They wore fine and costly garments, their weapons were ornamented, and their *yurts*, or felt-tents were adorned. On account of such differences, the Ongut and the Jungirat were classified by the Chinese as 'White Tartars' or civilized barbarians, in contradistinction to the 'Black Tartars', the appellation by which they referred to the other tribes of the steppes.

On reaching Dai Sechen's *yurt*, Yesukai was impressed by the ten-year old girl, who was exceedingly handsome and well-built. Her name was Bortei. The very next day, Yesukai sought her hand for his son. 'Does a thing appear to be of higher value if it is given only after much begging?' asked Dai Sechen, 'or does it become less important if it is given in reply to a few words of request? There cannot be any reason for allowing a girl to grow old in her parents' house. I give my daughter to your son but let your son stay here as my son-in-law.' Yesukai agreed and as a token of betrothal presented his saddle-horse to Dai Sechen. 'My son is afraid of dogs', said Yesukai before his departure, 'please do not let dogs frighten him.'

The journey to the grazing lands of the Jungirat and his residence with Dai Sechen were an event in the life of the youth who had never before travelled such distances or seen such bare, rocky mountains, accorded hills and wandering dunes which he traversed this time. (The grazing lands of Yesukai's people lay in the fertile valleys between the rivers Onon and Kerulon where game abounded and the hills were covered with forest.)

Life in Dai Sechen's ordu was sweeter and easier. Young Temuchin's eyes must have been transfixed when the Chinese merchants visited his father-in-law's ordu to exchange their fine textiles, painted shields, ivory quivers, and ornaments with the articles which they required, and the Jungirat could supply furs and hides, camels and yaks. From them Temuchin must have heard something of the empire on the other side of the Great Wall—the vast empire where poets were more respected and revered than princes, where soldiers and warriors were paid but looked down upon—a strange country ruled by tradition and culture, philosophy and learning, poetry and music. It would have been a strange and new world that was revealed to the young boy, but the knowledge which he acquired about China would serve him 40 years later, when he would measure swords with people on the other side of the Great Wall.

But Temuchin's stay with Dai Sechen was cut short by the sudden arrival of Munlik, who announced that Yesukai was heart-sick and yearned for his son. To avoid, complications, Munlik did not tell Dai Sechen that Yesukai was lying on his deathbed. He had chanced to cross the camps of the Tatar enemies, and the chief of the clan had recognized him and invited him to partake of their feast. According to the unwritten law of the steppes, hospitality could not be refused. Tired, thirsty and hungry as he was, he enjoyed their lavish hospitality, but failed to read in their dark and sullen faces, their desire to avenge the humiliation they had suffered at his hands thirteen years ago. They poisoned him and he was a lost man when he reached his ordu to see the grief-stricken faces of his followers and the grey eyes of Oyelun.

'Who is near me?' cried Yesukai, unable to endure the torment and separation of his son. It was Munlik. 'My sons are still young. Now my heart fails. Go to see my brothers and sisters-in-law and inform them. But first bring Temuchin back quickly.'

But Dai Sechen had grown fond of the boy and was loth to part with him. 'Since his father is grieved', said Dai Sechen. 'Do take him home. But do not forget to bring him back immediately afterwards.'

It is not certain how long Temuchin stayed with his father-in-law, but it is impossible to believe that Yesukai was poisoned on his return from the bridal mission and Temuchin was immediately recalled. For if the duration of his residence had been so short, Dai Sechen would, in all probability, not have become so enamoured of Temuchin to have kept his daughter waiting for four long years while dangers and difficulties grew thick and fast around Temuchin, and he was hunted by his adversaries, once even made a prisoner with a 'Kang' around his neck! Moreover, all the Persian authorities say that Temuchin was 13 when his father died.[9] I am, therefore, inclined to believe that he remained with Dai Sechen for three years and that it was on some other occasion, not the return journey from the Jungirat, when Yesukai Bahadur was poisoned.

Riding fast, day and night, Temuchin reached his ordu only to find that his father was already dead. Now the question of questions was whether the unruly tribes would accept him as their lord and leader. Amongst the marauding tribes of the Gobi, loyalty lasted only as long as it was an advantage to be faithful to a leader—only as long as he could protect his people and their herds. Struggle for existence and power was the first law of the steppes, and the chief was father to his clan: he had to feed them and guide them; he was to comfort them and protect them against the enemies. Due to his valour and wisdom, Yesukai Bahadur had succeeded in bringing 40,000 families under his banner, but the unruly tribes were not ready to follow the banner of the Yaktails simply because they had done so earlier.

His cousins and relations were the first to forsake the thirteen-year old Temuchin, believing that the death of Yesukai Bahadur was an opportunity for them to try their own luck. The widows of Anbagai Khan, Urbe and Sakatai, set the ball rolling: they refused to share with Oyelun the seasonal offerings and sacrificial meat; Oyelun protested in vain. They encouraged and incited Targutai Kiriltuk and Todoyan Girtei, sons of Anbagai Khan, to desert Oyelun and her sons. Charaga, Munlik's father and an old and loyal attendant of Yesukai, did his best to persuade them to change their mind and remain loyal to their old master's son. 'The deep water is gone', retorted Todyoyan Girtei, 'the bright stone is broken'. But with Yesukai, their leader, dead, who could they turn to? A weak woman and her children, who would lead them only to death and destruction? A youth without experience, of fiery and uncertain character. Never! As a parting kick, one of the deserting Taichiuts wounded the old Charaga in the back. The desertion of the Taichiuts was a signal: it sowed doubts and uncertainties in the minds of others as well, who also resolved to leave the banner of the Yaktails and seek the protection of new and stronger leaders.

Oyelun, the young Khan's mother, was, however, an intrepid woman. Undaunted by the faithlessness of her relations and undeterred by the desertion, she saddled a horse and, holding the banner of the Yaktails[10] in her hand, followed the melting tribesmen. She managed to persuade half of them to return and renew their allegiance to her son, the new Khan of the Yakka Mongols. But soon they too left and joined the Taichiuts.

Sorry and miserable was the plight of Temuchin, and those who stood by him voluntarily chose a life of great hardship. After the three comfortable years at Dai Sechen's ordu, the contrast must have been too bitter, especially when Munlik, who had been entrusted by the dying Yesukai to look after the family, deserted. The youthful Khan had only a handful of men and women, poor, wretched, and frightened. About the same time Sughu Jijan, whose care and counsel would have been of much use and value to the young Khan, also died; his son, Qarachar Noyan, the famous ancestor of Amir Taimur, was still young and inexperienced. Though reduced to drive straits, Temuchin made no appeal to his father's 'anda' as son of his deceased friend or even to his 'father-in-law' for help. He did not appeal to Toghril Khan of the Kereits, the friend and ally of his father, as he did later on, probably because he thought that he should not go to him a supplicant, but as an ally, for the strong aid the strong, and in politics weak and whining friends are greeted with ill-concealed scorn. Nor did Temuchin go to Dai Sechen, for he feared that Dai Sechen might even refuse to keep the engagement of his daughter with him, poor, defenceless and hunted as he was. The girl had been brought up in a richer clan and with all the conveniences and comforts of life. He must first prove himself worthy of being helped. He was not prepared to take any risks, specially with regard to his marriage with Bortei to whom, as his career shows, he was passionately devoted. And it is quite probable that if he had gone to the Jungirats, he might have lost, if not his life, at least the girl whom he deeply loved, like Babur who left Samarqand to save Andijan only to find that he had lost the one without saving the other.

The family of Yesukai Bahadur was now reduced to desperation; they had no pastures worth the name, and no herds to graze them on. They were forced to live on a vegetable diet—unpalatable and distasteful to the nomads. Oyelun had to go out to pick wild onion, garlic and other roots while the boys would go out to fish on the banks of the Onon and to hunt small game like marmot, marten, and rabbits. Living in poor and harsh conditions, and in the midst of hostility and hatred, Yesukai's sons grew up into fine fighters. Tall, bright-eyed and gifted, Temuchin was distinguished from his brother Juji Qasar and half-brother Bektor by his love of power, who excelled him in physique and bodily prowess. Soon they began to quarrel about the game, when Temuchin and Qasar noted that their half-brothers deprived or despoiled them of their share. 'I caught a fish' complained Temuchin to his mother, 'but Bektor and Belgutai robbed me of it.' 'How could you brothers behave like this?' asked Oyelun. 'Apart from our own shadow we have no friends; apart from a horse's tail we have no whip. We suffered injury at the hands of the Taichiuts and were unable to seek revenge. Would you like to follow the example of the five sons of the Lady Alan and remain forever irreconciled? You should not behave like this!'

'Yesterday we shot a sparrow', they grumbled on, 'and it was seized by them; today we caught a golden fish, and they again took it away. How can we get along together in this manner?' Dissatisfied with their mother's sober advice, the two brothers decided to resolve the problem by murdering Bektor and they shot him dead. This fratricide foreshadowed the most terrible trait in his character—to remove all obstacles from his way, never to hesitate for personal or sentimental reasons. Neither mother nor brother nor any one must stand between him and his object. The way he brushed aside his mother's advice shows his singleness of purpose. It was a warning to others and a declaration that he would stop at nothing. He must be his own master.

The murder was appalling—the murder of a defenseless youth without challenge by his own brother. Bewildered by his behaviour, Oyelun was beside herself with grief. 'When you were born', wildly she cried, 'your hand held a piece of black blood. Now you are like a dog that eats the sack that brings her baby, a furious beast who jumps over the cliff. We have no companion except our own shadow and no whip except a horse's tail. We suffered at the hands of the Taichiuts, yet we could not retaliate. How could you have behaved like this?'[11] After this Temuchin resolved to keep the peace and remain on affectionate terms with Belgutai.

The warning about the Taichiuts was not a bit too soon. For the Taichiut chiefs, who had seceded from the banner of the Yaktails, and had deserted the followers of Yesukai, were beginning to get anxious. They had hoped that, abandoned and deserted by all, the family would perish at the hands of robbers or die of poverty and starvation. But the sons of Yesukai were growing up fine and promising. The serpent had been scorched but was not dead.

Marriage and Youth

'We deserted Temuchin's family', said Targutai to his fellow clansmen. 'Now he and his brothers are like little birds with lengthened features, and like the young of wild beasts. In time they may grow too strong for us.' Collecting his followers, he raided the yurt of Oyelun to get hold of Temuchin. The unexpected arrival of the Taichiuts caused confusion and consternation; the children ran hither and thither for shelter, and Kachiun, Temuga, and Temulun were hidden by Belgutai in a cave, trees barricading the path of the pursuing Taichiuts while the mighty bowman and skilled archer, Juji Qasar, shot arrows at the raiders. 'If you hand over Temuchin, your eldest brother', shouted the baffled enemy, 'we will spare the rest of you'. Learning that they were after him, Temuchin mounted his horse and rushed into the depth of the forest. Unable to catch him, the Taichiuts encircled the forest.

Temuchin spent several days in hideouts, waiting for a chance to slip away. He made two attempts to get off, but each time gave up because of portents. First, the saddle of his horse fell to the ground in an inexplicable manner. 'It may be possible', he reflected, 'for the saddle to fall with the girth still fastened; but how can it fall when the breast strap is holding it? Perhaps the Tengri is preventing me.' He spent another three days without food, and when he wanted to leave the forest, found his way blocked by a white rock. 'Tengri wishes that I should stay here longer', thought Temuchin and once again he retired to his hiding place to spend another three days there. Unable to bear the torments of hunger any longer, he resolved to get out. No sooner did he come out than he was seized by the waiting and watchful Taichiuts.[12]

That there was a tinge of superstition in Temuchin, such as usually appears in men of the desert, cannot be denied; but that he was religious by nature as may appear from a superficial study of the previously quoted anecdote, is doubtful. His religion verged on political machinations rather than devotion; even while professing fatalistic belief, he subordinated it to his own designs. Banking[13] on the credulity and superstitions of his people, he constantly alluded to his being the chosen of the Heaven: the Eternal Blue Sky was evoked only to dazzle the vulgar herd.

As it was not customary in those days to put the captives at once to death,[14] Temuchin was taken prisoner and humiliated with a 'kang' or *do-shakka*, a rough and ready portable pellory fastened round his neck. In mocking contempt he was paraded in the Taichiut camp as if he were some beast or bird for show; and, further more, he was made to spend one night in every tent by rotation as if to chasten him of his pride and to break his nerves.

One day the Taichiuts were feasting on the banks of the Onon, a youngster keeping watch on the prisoner. Finding an opportunity, Temuchin struck down the guard and made his escape, taking the stocks with him. Crossing the wooded banks of the Onon he concealed himself up to the nose—in the shallow waters of the Onon with nothing but his head and eyes above water level. Discovering his escape the Taichiuts were at once on his trail. It was spring and the moon was shining bright and clear. It was Surghan Shira who noticed him immersed in the river. 'It is only on account of your cleverness', he remarked to Temuchin, 'that the Taichiut brothers hate you. Be very careful. You may remain lying here, for I will not report you'.

'You lost the man in day time', said Surghan Shira to the Taichiuts, when they were about to make a more determined attempt and a more thorough search. 'How can you find him in the darkness of night? It would be better to return by the same way we have come and search all places on the way more carefully. After that we may disperse for the night. Tomorrow, we shall gather together and resume our search. The man cannot run far off with the Kang on his shoulders.' 'This is the last search', whispered Surghan Shira passing by Temuchin. 'After this we shall go home and return to continue our search tomorrow. After we leave, go home to your mother and brothers but do not tell anyone that I have seen you'. But with the 'Kang' round his neck, Temuchin could not make good his escape. 'I will pass the night in the custody of Surghan Shira', he reflected, 'his two sons Chinbai and Chilaun showed pity on me and loosened my 'Kang'. Now Surghan Shira did not inform the others though he saw me twice and passed away. If I go to him, he is sure to save me.'

Surghan Shira was surprised and staggered to see Temuchin entering his tent, for he was well aware of the consequences, if the Taichiuts discovered their victim hiding there. 'Why have you come here?' asked the baffled Surghan Shira. 'I advised you to go to your mother and sisters.' But his sons, Chinbai and Chilaun, persuaded and prevailed upon their father to save Temuchin. They removed the stock from round his neck, burnt it, and concealed him under wool in a cart.[15]

Believing that someone had hidden Temuchin, the next day the Taichiuts began to search their own camp and probably suspected Surghan Shira or detected some trace of Temuchin's whereabouts there. They made a thorough search of his camp, scouring the rooms, the carts, and even underneath the beds. They were on the point of discovering their fugitive when they began to search the cart and throw off the wool but were put off by Surghan Shira's calm remark: 'It is too hot for any one to be able to survive under all that wool.'

'You had undone me', spoke Surghan Shira with a sigh of relief. 'Had they found you, the fire of my house would have been extinguished for ever. Now go and seek your mother and brothers'. Supplying him with everything required for a journey—a white-nosed sorrel mare, boiled and roasted flesh, a leather-bag of mare's milk—and giving him a bow and arrows but no flint or means of obtaining fire, Surghan Shira and his family bid him adieu.[16]

Little did Surghan Shira guess what part he was playing for the future history of Asia and mankind—and also for the advancement of his own family. Temuchin never forgot Surghan Shira's kindness, and a decade or two later when his word was law throughout the barrens, he rewarded his benefactor handsomely. The descendants of Surghan Shira rose to high ranks in the service of Chingiz Khan and his sons,[17] and the famous Amir Chaupan was descended from him.

Returning home, Temuchin and his family moved on again to their ancestral pastures near the Mount Burqan. It was a small and dejected family assembled around the fire—with no herds of cattle to graze and feed upon, and there was nothing to eat but what they could kill in the steppe and the hills. Temuchin had to go out and hunt marmots and wild mice to support his family. Such were the pursuits and privations of the man who was to redraw the map of Eurasia and to lead the shaggy nomads of the Gobi *from excessive destitution to inordinate affluence, from the desert of poverty to the palace of delight*,[18] and whose descendants were to dress in silks and brocades firing the imagination of poets like Coleridge.[19] (Italics added.)

While the family of Yesukai was thus eking out a miserable existence with nine horses and a few other things they had managed to save, their horses were driven away by Taichiut robbers. The only mount left was the sorrel mare on which Belgutai had been out hunting marmots and wild mice. And so they had to await his return to take up the pursuit. 'I will go for them', said Belgutai as soon as he learnt of the misfortune. 'You should not go', said Juji Qasar. 'It is I who will go.' 'No! neither of you', decided Temuchin. 'I will go myself.'

Riding hard, day and night (or as the *Secret History* puts, 'three days and three nights') after the thieves, Temuchin met a youth tending a big herd of horses and milking a mare. 'Have you seen eight gray horses passing this way?' enquired Temuchin. 'I am Temuchin, son of Yesukai.' 'Before sunrise this morning eight horses such as you describe were driven this way,' replied the young man. 'I can show you their trails.' To Temuchin's astonishment the young man immediately unsaddled Temuchin's mare which was exhausted, and choosing two fresh mounts, said, 'You have come in great difficulty, which befalls all of us, young man. I will accompany you in your pursuit. My father is called Nagu Bayan; I am his only son. My name is Bogurchi.'

The two young men, of their pursuit, on the third day saw Temuchin's horses in an enclosure. Galloping into it, they made off with their horses. The thieves took up the pursuit, brandishing their lances. Temuchin and Bogurchi turning and speeding their horses, rushed with the fleetness of shadows. Arrows flew past them and they heard the angry and hoarse shouts of the pursuers. As their mounts were fresh and those of Temuchin and Bogurchi were already tired, they began to gain on the fleeing youngmen. 'Give me your bow and quiver', said Bogurchi, as he saw the foremost of the pursuers close on their heels and about to hurl his lasso. 'I am afraid that you may be wounded on my account', replied Temuchin, 'I can match him in shooting.' Reining in his horse, Temuchin fit an arrow to his bow and sent it off. The arrow hit the mark and brought the pursuing horseman down. The sun set and it became dark. The thieves lagged behind, and the two friends rode on.

'I could hardly have brought these horses back without your help', said Temuchin to Bogurchi on reaching Nagu Bayan's *yurt*. 'So we shall divide them between us. How many of them you would like to have?' 'I accompanied you and assisted you because I realized your difficulty', answered Bogurchi. 'How can I accept any unforeseen gift from you? I am the only son of my father and shall inherit his properties which are enough for me. I cannot take anything from you. If I did so, what would be the merit of my accompanying and assisting you?'

Nagu Bayan was delighted at the safe return of Bogurchi and pleased with his companion and their achievement. 'Henceforth, you two young men must always help, and never desert each other', said the old man. And they never parted from each other. One of his most loyal and capable generals, Bogurchi became one of Chingiz Khan's trusted Orloks.

The harsh four years in which Temuchin barely survived the hatred of his enemies with all the odds against him, were momentous. They shaped his character and left indelible impressions on his mind. They brought out the qualities of courage, and resolution; they made him steady in adversity. It was in these impressionable years that he developed his fiery energy, his contempt for human life and a determination to use merciless world as it had used him.

No longer an unknown, fortune-tossed outcast, Temuchin had won a friend and secured his first vassal—Bogurchi. The Gobi rang with the tales of his escapades, the daredevil deeds of the youthful descendant of Kabul Khan.

Confident of himself and knowing that while he had nothing tangible, he had a name that excited applause, he decided it was time for him to go to Dai Sechen and claim his betrothed. 'When I heard of the hatred of the Taichiut brothers for you', said Dai Sechen, to Temuchin on his arrival, 'I was grieved and almost lost hope of meeting you again.' Dai Sechen honoured his word even though Temuchin was no longer affluent, nor could he boast of any following worth the name (except his own brothers Qasar and Belgutai, and his comrade Bogurchi). And Bortei was duly married to him. Dai Sechen and his wife, Sotan, accompanied the couple on Temuchin's return journey; Dai Sechen came up to the banks of the Kerulen and then blessing them went back but Sotan accompanied her daughter to her new home and returned after settling her there.

Temuchin now decided to call his comrade and vassal Bogurchi to come and reside with him. On Belgutai's reaching Nagu Bayan's camp and delivering Temuchin's message to Bogurchi, the latter at once mounted a hump backed sorrel horse and, taking only his black cart, left for Temuchin's camp—once again without informing and bidding farewell to his old father. Such was the magnetic influence which Temuchin exercised over those who came into contact with him.

Bortei had brought a sable cloak (with her dowry) to be presented to her mother-in-law. Temuchin determined to make a profitable use of it. Now that his condition had improved a little, he was no longer a hunted and flying fugitive but was master and lord of a yurt of his own, son-in-law of the rich and powerful Dai Sechen, chief of the Jungirats and, above all, a name which was a 'household word' in the barrens. He decided to visit his father's *anda*, Toghril Khan[20] of the Kereits, to remind him of the old ties and renew the family friendship.

Toghril was chief of the pastoral Kereits and lord of the riverain tract along the Great Wall. He was a ruler of great dignity and magnificence, and on good terms with the Chinese. On account of their contacts and communications with the Chinese, the Kereits were culturally superior to most of the Mongol and Turkish tribes. Turks by race, they had walled towns and lived in houses of mud. They were also prosperous and excellent traders. A good many of them had been converted to Christianity, which gave rise to the legend of a mighty King-Prester John ruling over Christians somewhere in the East, whose aid and assistance was desired by the Pope and the sovereigns of Christendom in their struggle against the Muslims.

The self-seeking, Wang Khan was crafty and treacherous. He was the son of the Kereit chief, Kurja Kuz Buyuruk, who had been put to death by the Kin emperor, probably because he had become too strong and powerful to be allowed to consolidate his position. On Buyuruk's death, the throne was siezed by his two sons, Tatimur Taishi and Biku Timur, but Toghril defeated them and put them both to the sword. In this fratricidal war Irge Qara sought the assistance of the Naimans, and Wang Khan was driven out. Homeless and hopeless, Toghril asked for and acquired the assistance of Yesukai and was once again Khan of the Kereits. Probably on account of his harsh character, he could not win the hearts of his people, for next year when his uncle, Gurkhan, rose against him, he was once again a fugitive and a wanderer. Once more he appealed to Yesukai, who marched against Gurkhan. Gurkhan sought safety in Tangut, and Toghril was once again Khan. It was on this occasion that Yesukai and Toghril became *anda* or sworn friends.

Temuchin now decided to go to Toghril and cement the close ties that had existed between his father and the Khan of the Kereits. Taking the sable cloak as a gift, he and his brothers went to the Khan, who received them well. 'In the old days you were in good accord with my father', Temuchin reminded him. 'You are like a father to me now. My wife presented this cloak on the occasion of meeting her mother-in-law, and I have brought it to you, my father.' The greedy Khan was pleased and said, 'I shall collect for you your deserters and gather together your wandering people. Having met you, I will certainly remember all this.'

And so the pleased Temuchin returned to his camp—as poor as before, with no warriors or soldiers following him. It was sufficient that the powerful Khan of the Kereits had consented to treat him as his son and promised to help him recover the following of Yesukai.

Struggle for Survival

Better and more welcome news awaited Temuchin. As soon as he reached his camp the old blacksmith, Jarchiutai, with his bellows on his back, arrived with his son, Jelme. 'When you were born at Delium-Boldak', said Jarchiutai, 'I gave you a swaddling-band lined with sable fur and presented my son, Jelme, to you, but as he was yet of tender age I kept him at home to bring him up. Now I present him to you; let him saddle your horse and wait at your doors.' This addition to his following was an indication of his growing fame and importance among the dwellers of the barrens. He was now the adopted son of the mighty Toghril Khan and the son-in-law of the rich Dai Sechen.

'O Mother! Rise quickly', suddenly shouted the old maid-servant Ghuakchen, just before dawn, 'I hear horses approaching, perhaps the Taichiut brothers are coming. O Mother! Rise quickly.' 'Rouse up the children,' cried Oyelun, 'wake them all quickly.' Bewildered and frightened, all of them got up and saddled the horses. Knowing that this time, if caught, it would not be servitude and slavery but certainly death, Temuchin hurried off towards Mount Burqan, leaving Bortei behind: there was no spare horse and no time to be lost by carrying her on his own mount. Clearly, he loved himself and self-preservation was the keynote of his personality. Incidentally, even after the captivity and concubinage of Bortei amongst the Merkits, he esteemed her above all his wives and concubines, and it was her son, Juji, of Merkit paternity,[21] who inherited his vast dominions. What we know of his other wives and sons—is mere names and shadows. The old maid-servant Ghuakchen, however, made an effort to save Bortei from falling prey to the raiders. Hiding her in a black cart, covered with wool, she drove up the river Tengeli.

'I am coming from Temuchin's house', she replied to the horseman who challenged her. 'I go around shearing sheep for rich families.' 'Is Temuchin in his yurt?' 'His house is not far,' she answered, 'but as I got out from the rear of the house I do not know where he is.'

The horsemen left her unmolested and galloped away but finding the camp empty and nobody except Belgutai's mother, they came back. In the meanwhile the axle of her cart had broken. 'Is there anyone in this cart?' they asked her. 'Only wool inside.' Their suspicious aroused, they decided to search the cart and found Bortei, the young wife of Temuchin. Carrying their prize with them, they followed Temuchin's tracks. Thrice they rode round the mountain but on account of dense forest could not find him. 'By capturing Temuchin's wife', the raiders said to themselves, 'we have answered the old insult offered to us.' These raiders belonged to the three clans of the Merkits— Uduit, Uve and Khaat. For vengeance Bortei was made over to Chilger the Strong, the younger brother of Chiraidu, whose wife had been forcibly seized by Yesukai about two decades ago.

Making sure that the Merkits had actually left for their camps, and had not just a feigned retreat, Temuchin despatched Belgutai, Bogurchi, and Jelme to examine the movements of the Merkits. After three nights they returned to inform him that the raiders had left and so he emerged out of his concealment—once again showing that he valued his life above those of others—wife, brother, or companion. Descending from his hideout in the mountain, he looked towards the sky and striking his breast, said: 'Thanks to Ghuakchen, who possessed the ears of a chunk and the eyes of an ermine, I have had a narrow escape. Mount Burqan has protected my insignificant life; I will make constant sacrifices to it and so will my sons and grandsons.' Then turning towards the sun and taking off his cap and putting his girdle round his neck, he struck his breast, made nine genufluxions and sprinkled fermented mare's milk on the ground. Such was the Mongol method of worship: taking off cap and belt, and hanging the belt a round the neck, signified complete surrender as cap and belt were worn by a free Mongol. Here again we see the hint of superstition.

Temuchin's grief at the loss of Bortei and the little that he owned is not known to us. Dreams of ancestral glory and greatness, revived after his visit to Toghril had probably vanished in a moment; and now, once again, the world was dark. He did not give way to tears as Babur would at the loss of Samarqand and Andijan at about the same age: Temuchin was made of sterner stuff. Luckily, his brave old mother, brothers and the two companions had been saved and they were with him. It was not in him to give way to despair. Keen as he was to live up up to the reputations of his ancestors Aghuz Khan, Kabul Khan and Yesukai Bahadur, and filled as he was with dreams of conquest and dominion, reverses such as this one could not discourage him to sit down and do nothing.

Temuchin resolved to invoke the aid of his adopted father, Toghril Khan. Accompanied by his brothers, Juji Qasar and Belgutai, he went to the Black Forests on the banks of the Tula, where the Khan was camping. 'Last year when you presented me the sable cloak,' spoke Toghril Khan, 'I promised that

I would collect your scattered people. I remember the promise and will annihilate the Merkits and rescue your wife.' 'Go and speak to Jamuka, my *anda,* I will raise a force of twenty thousand men as the right wing here, and ask him to raise the same number on the left wing. Also ask Jamuka to fix a date for the meeting of the two armies.'

Jamuka was a kinsman of Temuchin, for the Jajirat clan, to which he belonged, also claimed descent from the same mythical ancestor, Buzanjar. Jamuka and Temuchin were childhood friends. They had become *andas* or 'sworn friends' with a vow to stand by each other through thick and thin. This was during the lifetime of Yesukai when Temuchin was heir to the Yaktails banner under which 40,000 families were united. But when the hero died and the tribes deserted the youthful Khan, Jamuka forgot his oath. Able, active and ambitious, Jamuka assembled Temuchin's tribesmen under his own banner, from amongst whom a contingent of 10,000 warriors could be raised. He was quite powerful, lording over chieftains of illustrious descent, and had become the *anda* of Toghril, Khan of the Kereits.

As the Merkits were dour fighters and a headache to both Toghril and Jamuka, it did not require much time and trouble for Temuchin to persuade Jamuka to make common cause with him. Pleased at the opportunity to quash the Merkits, Jamuka agreed to declare war on the Merkits, 'to capture all their people'. It was decided that the allies would assemble at Boto-Khan Boghurji on the banks of the Onon, and then cross over into the Merkit territory by means of a pantoon bridge tied with 'pig's-bristle grass' and take the Merkit clans by surprise while they were separate and pasturing in their separate grasslands at Buora-Keyer, Talkhon Arai, and Karaji-Keyer.

The Merkits were caught unprepared. They had not expected Temuchin to fall upon them like this, and with such a great force. They scarcely had time to run to their yurts to seize their weapons and the ordu was filled with confusion and the shrieks of women and children, the screaming of horses, and the clatter of arms and hoofs. Tuqta Bigi and Dair Usun, the chiefs of two Merkit clans, managed to escape in the darkness of night but Tuqta's wife and kin were all captured. With the enemy close on their heels the Merkits retreated and raced down the Selenga. Meanwhile, Temuchin shouted the name of his Bortei, and she rushed forth to seize the reins of his horse. They were re-united in the moonlight. 'I have what I sought', he sent his message to Toghril and Jamuka, and asked them to stop the pursuit of the fleeing enemy. For he may have had reasons of his own, not to seek a blood thirsty revenge for the captivity and humiliation of his bride. He was guided by considerations more portentous than a desire for revenge. It was not in his interest to annihilate the Merkits and thereby leave his allies, Jamuka and Toghril, supreme. He would leave the door open for future conflicts between Merkit and Kereit, and also for a possible of reconciliation of the Merkits to himself at some later date. 'The three hundred Merkits, who had taken part in the raid of Mount Burqan and ridden around it thrice, were massacred without exception; those of their women who were suitable to be made wives, were made wives (by the conquerors); those that were suitable to be made slaves, were made slaves.'

The campaign was extremely successful from Temuchin's point of view. He had made, no doubt, a big impression among the fighting clans. He had also had an opportunity of moving and mixing with the members of the various clans. A year and a half later, when the uneasy alliance between Jamuka and Temuchin came to an end, we find a good many clans flocking to the standard of Yaktails. From the *Secret History* it would also appear that Temuchin took back those of his people who had deserted and joined Jamuka. Moreover, Temuchin utilized the occasion to instil into the minds of the credulous and superstitious Mongols the idea that he was the chosen of the Eternal Blue Sky, who protected and favoured him. 'Wang Khan, my father, and Jamuka, my *andal*', he said in expressing his thanks for their help. 'Through your aid, the Tengri has given me the strength to seek my revenge.'

On return from the Merkit expedition, Jamuka and Temuchin who had renewed their old friendship, camped together at on the Onon. 'The old folk', remarked Temuchin, 'have said that when two persons become *anda,* they seem to have only one life between themselves; they will never desert each other, and they will guard each other's life. Now we must renew our friendship and intensify our affection.' Considering Temuchin's previous experience of Jamuka's adherence to his word, this proposal looks strange. But his position was still insecure. The Taichiuts were still strong; the Merkits might once again attempt to avenge their humiliation. He himself had still to make good his loss. He had to win back from powerful neighbours the flocks and pastures they had appropriated, and the warriors who had joined them. Jamuka would be less dangerous and troublesome as an apparent ally than an avowed enemy. Jamuka for his part, considered it worthwhile to keep terms with Temuchin, who was now under the protection of his own *anda*, the Khan of the Kereits. And so they exchanged gifts to cement their relations, once again became *andas* and, in celebration, arranged a grand feast and slept together under one blanket—the Mongol way of signifying unity of hearts.

Jamuka and Temuchin lived on peaceful terms for a year and a half, watching and studying each other. But real friendship and a union of hearts was not possible. Both were ambitious, aspiring for domination. Each was prepared to remove all the obstacles that lay in his way, as children play with a house of cards. Nothing was sacred in their eyes except their own desire. A breach was inevitable, a clash certain.

The breach occurred in a quite novel and surprising manner. On breaking their summer camp and moving to new pastures, the two sworn friends were riding side by side when Jamuka, talking about their next encampment said: 'Temuchin! If we pitch our camps in front of a mountain, those who graze their horses will have tents to live in, if we encamp by the side of a stream, those who tend the sheep and lambs will get food for their gullets. What is your opinion?' Temuchin could not follow what Jamuka meant and made no reply. Reining in his horse, he remained behind to consult his mother, Oyelun. Now what Jamuka meant by his circumlocutory speech is not quite clear; perhaps it implied that the two friends could not pull on much longer: the sooner they decided to part the better. Buy 'those who tend sheep and lambs' Jamuka meant the common people, while 'those who graze their horses' meant the aristocrats. So this implied that the followers of Temuchin and Jamuka could not pasture their herds together; they should have separate grazing lands or Temuchin should re-think the composition of his following. The majority of Jamuka's followers were common people, herders of sheep. Temuchin, on the other hand, had an aristocratic following, symbolized by 'horses' and 'tents'. But Temuchin had not grasped the implications of Jamuka's words. 'Of Jamuka, your *anda*,' broke out Bortei, 'people say that he loves the new and despises the old. Now that he has had enough of us, do not his words conceal some hostile intentions towards us? We must not stop; we must march on through the night so that we may part from him in good time.'

'Bortei speaks sense', said Temuchin, whose doubts and suspicions were aroused, and he decided to break away from his sworn friend. 'They marched on till dawn', says the *Secret History*, 'when behold, there were men of the Jalair clan…and of the Kiyan clan…and of the Bearin clan; there were Korohi and old Usun…and all the men of the Mene-Bearin clan, all following Temuchin.'

The breach with Jamuka turned the tide in the affairs of Temuchin, for it was followed by desertions and secessions by aristocratic clans and tribes from Jamuka. Prominent and distinguished among those who now joined Temuchin were Daritai Otchigin, his uncle; his first cousin Kuchar; Altan Otchigin, son of Katur Khan, the last great Khan of the Mongols; the eldest branch of the descendants of the famous Kabul Khan; the chief of the Jurki clan; and Subutai, the future conqueror of eastern Europe.

The sentiment of 'divinity' that 'doth hedge a king' had seemingly begun to influence the people. The talents, the exploits, and, above all, the personality of Temuchin attracted them. To cap them all was the seductive simulation of the sky arranging his affairs and ordaining his pre-eminence among the chiefs of the Gobi. 'In a vision I saw', said Qorchi on joining Temuchin, 'a hornless bull draw the lower poles of a big tent along Temuchin's way and shouted, "The Heaven and the Earth after consultation have appointed Temuchin to be the Lord of Dominion. I am carrying this power to him?" When you become the Lord of Dominion, what happiness will you offer me?' 'I will make you a chief of Ten Thousand Families', said Temuchin, who knew the value of such propaganda in the great and ambitious task before him. 'For all the trouble I have taken to reveal to you the great truth,' said Qorchi, 'you will only give me this. What happiness is there in being a chief of Ten Thousand Families? Make me such a chief and permit me to select thirty of the most beautiful girls to be my wives. Besides, you must always grant me what I ask.' Even to this demand Temuchin consented because he understood that every thing and every man had his price, and the price asked was not exorbitant if it could win over the sturdy but superstitious warriors to his side. He could foresee the paralysing psychological influence which such propaganda would have; it would break their will to resist him, whom the Sky seemed to help. It would strengthen the loyalty and devotion of his followers on account of their belief that the 'gods' were on his side.

The rumours and tales thus set afloat, had their effect, for when need of a Khan arose, Temuchin as the only obvious candidate began to be discussed. After considerable wranglings and parleys in which the descendants of Kabul Khan, Altan, Kuchar and Sacha-Beki could agree only on Temuchin, they waited on him and said: 'we have decided to declare you our Khan. When you are our Khan, we will be in the front in every battle against your foes; if we capture any beautiful women and good horses, we will first present them to you; at the hunt we will start first to encircle the game for you to shoot. If we disobey your commands in battle or injure your interests in times of peace, you can deprive us of our families and properties and exile us to a remote country. Swearing allegiance to him, they declared him Khan and gave him the title of Chingiz,[22] which means 'mighty'.

These words clearly define the relations of a Khan with his followers. The Khan was lord and leader but with no power of life and death over his vassals. *For disobedience and treason the punishment he could inflict was confiscation of property and exile.* For his part the leader had to secure them against enemies and lead them to victory, which would mean beautiful captives, good horses, and abundant pastures, all that the heart of a steppe nomad could desire.

The nomads had hitherto been leading an indolent and jealously individual life. The first task to which Temuchin Chingiz set himself, was organization of his ordu, and disciplining the unruly nomads. He realized, that if organized and disciplined, these fierce, ferocious and fearless fighters of the steppe would constitute a formidable power—a menace to towns and tribes. Here was the first step in the ladder to lordship of the Gobi. Having been raided and surprised more than once, he determined to no more oblige his enemies, and to safeguard himself against all eventualities and to meet possible contingencies, he made appointments of trusted and reliable men to various posts, each responsible for his own 'department'. Ogolai, Bogurchi's younger brother, Kachiun Jetai, and Dogulku were appointed to be his archers while Chilgutai, Kubilai, Tokuraun, and Juji Qasar were to be sword bearers; they were to be constantly on guard at his tent. Ungur, Saiketu, and Kadaan Daldur Khan were put in charge of the provisions; Degai was to be master of the shepherds; Kuchigur to superintend the manufacture of carts; Dotai was the manager of the Khan's household. Belgutai and Qaraltai were masters of horse-training while Taichiutti Qutu, Malichi and Mutkalku were to supervise the tending of the horse herds. Argei Qasar, Tahai, Sukegai, and Chaur-Khan were selected to be his messengers, who were 'to be constantly ready so that he may send them off promptly (on near and distant missions) like arrows.'

Temuchin had learnt by experience that people respect a strong man and it was only by use of force and terror, promises of rewards, and generosity that he could capture their imagination and arouse devotion and loyalty to his person. He was generous with rewards to his followers. 'If I am indeed the King,' he could say with Tamerlane, 'all wealth is mine. And if I am not the King, what will it avail me to keep what I already have?' 'I have not forgotten it in my heart', he said to Bogurchi and Jelme, 'that at the time when I was without a following you two, before any others, became my followers: now you shall take precedence over the whole assembly.' 'You that are assembled here', he said turning towards the warriors and aristocracy, 'you parted with Jamuka and decided to join me. If the Sky preserves me and helps me, all of you, my old friends, will ultimately become my happy companions.'

Now Temuchin was once again a Khan, a true descendant and inheritor of Kabul Khan. The danger was over but not the loss. He still had a long way to go to gather and unite all the Mongol clans. But he had shown himself as an able diplomat and a keen judge of men, and a beginning had been made. People changed sides, hesitated, abandoned him, but even when none believed in his star, Temuchin never wavered. The prime cause of his early success without the aid and assistance of others was his iron will and courage which attracted the hardy warriors of the steppe and evoked reverence and enthusiasm. Courage is contagious, and Temuchin had proved himself a worthy and doughty scion of the house of Aghuz Khan. Gifted with an awe-inspiring personality, he had the power to win hearts, which stood him in good stead with his followers, even when his star seemed to be on the decline. His first words and acts on becoming Khan prove his superiority and foreshadow the great genius that would flower within him. Babur and Akbar were only fourteen when called to the throne; Suleiman the Magnificent exercised power and responsibility in his youth; so Temuchin was but one example of precocious development.

Notes

1. Wei-Kwei-Sun, *The Secret History of the Mongol Dynasty,* tr. Igor de Rachewilte, (henceforth referred to as *Secret History*), pp. 9-10. Also see, *The Secret History of the Mongols—A Mongolian Epic Chronicle of the Thirteenth Century,* English Translation (hereafter referred to as *Mongolian Chronicle*), Leiden: E.J. Brill, 2004, pp. 11-12.

2. Rashid-ud-din Fazlullah, *Jamiut Twarikh*, MSS no. 186, Raza Library, Rampur, fol. 95, (hereafter referred as Rashid-ud-din). 'Ala'-ud-din 'Ata-Malik Juwaini, *Tarikh-i-Jahan Gusha,* ed. Mirza Muhammad Qazwini, Gibb Memorial Series (hereafter referred to as Juwaini).

3. Sharfuddin Ali Yazdi, fols. 56-7 MSS no. 186, Raza Library, Rampur, (hereafter referred as Sharfuddin).

4. Rashid-ud-din, fol. 236; Sharfuddin, fols. 56-8; *Rauzat-us-Safa*, vol. V, p. 10.

5. *Rauzat-us-Safa*, vol. V, p. 8; *Shajratul Atrak*, pp. 55-6.

6. *Rauzat-us-Safa*, vol. V, p. 8; *Shajratul Atrak*, p. 57.

7. Rockhill, *Travels*, pp. 170-71.

8. Juwaini, Vol. I, p. 15.

9. Ibid., fol. 240; Sharfuddin, fols. 56-7ff;. *Rauzat-us-Safa*, vol. v, p. 10.

10. H. Howorth, *History of the Mongols,* Part I, p. 50.

11. *Secret History,* pp. 14-15; *Mongolian Chronicle,* pp. 20-1.

12. 'In AH 584 (1187-8),' says Raverty, 'he became a captive in the hands of Turkutas or Turkutae Kariltuk, the Badshah as he is styled, great-grandson of Hammanka of the Tanjuts.' Hammanka is Humeka of the *Shajratul Atrak* or Anbahai of the *Secret History*. But he is the grandson of Qaidu's second son and not, as Raverty relates, the son of Qaidu's second son. The Tanjuts of Raverty are the Taichiuts of the *Secret History* and *Tarikh-i-Jahan Gusha*.

It is difficult to accept the year AH 584 as the date for the capture of Temuchin by the Taichiuts. Having been born in AH 549 according to all Persian authorities, he was 35 years old in that year while Qachiun and Temuga were respectively 31 years and 27 years old. If so, they would have been old enough to fight.

13. Raverty further adds: 'In AH 579 (AD 1183) the Nairuns (i.e. the descendants of Alan Goa by the Light) began to return to their allegiance and Temuchin succeeded in bringing some other tribes under his sway'. This date too cannot be accepted, for Temuchin did not command any tribes until several years after his escape from Taichiut captivity. The kind of life he was leading at the time of his captivity and the showing put up by him against the Taichiuts do not lend credence to Raverty's statement.

Tengri is the Mongol equivalent of God. After their conversion to Islam, the Mongols often referred to God as Tengri Taaila. On the dream and its interpretation appertaining to the conquest of Muslim lands, *Tabaqat-i-Nasiri*, pp. 338-9. Rashid-ud-din, fol. 39.

14. Ibid.

15. Rashid-ud-din, fols. 39-40.

16. Ibid.

17. Ibid., fol. 40.

18. Juwaini, vol. I, p. 16.

19. In Xanadu did Kubla Khan,

A stately pleasure-dome decree:

Where Alph, the sacred river, ran,

Through caverns measureless to man,

Down to a sunless sea.

And there were gardens bright with sinuous rills,

Where blossomed many an incense-bearing tree;

And here were forests, ancient as the hills,

Enfolding sunny spots of greenery.

20. *Anda* means 'companion in battle'. Toghril or Toghrul is described by Raverty as 'a bird used in field sports, one of the falcon tribe, a jerfalcon probably!' Raverty, p. 936, note 5. See also, *Tabaqat-i-Nasiri*, p. 331.

21. Juji means 'unexpected guest'. He was so named on account of the circumstances attending his birth, Rashid-ud-din, fols. 95-6.

22. Rockhill, *Travels,* p. 269, note 1.

2

Struggle for Supremacy

AS KHAN OF THE MONGOLS, Chingiz had an opportunity to prove his ability and to play the role of an ideal nomad chief. The promise which he made to his followers—the promise of a happy life—was clearly a challenge. It must have provoked in different quarters indignation, amazement, contempt, or amusement. People could recall and recount the miseries of his childhood when he had to feed on wild mice and marmots or was a captive of the Taichiuts with a kang round his neck, and still more recently when his bride was the maidservant and concubine of the victorious Merkits. They could repeat these incidents of his life and laugh at the boastful Khan, who promised his followers the best of the pastures and the finest of the women and the horses. The Taichiuts were still formidable and, probably, on the look out for another merry hunt; Jamuka, cunning and cruel, had parted from his *anda* with no goodwill, preparing for a trial of strength. Temuchin could only count on Toghril, the crafty and treacherous Khan of the Kereits, who had no scruples to sacrifice his own brothers and uncles to satisfy his lust for power. So the people could have shrugged their shoulders and made bets whether he would survive three moons or three summers. Yet the depth and variety of his experience were unknown to most people. No one had correctly gauged his intellectual power, his political nerve, or the extraordinary strength of character stored up and disciplined in that titanic frame.[1] The revelations of the next decade would astound the nomads and the world.

The time had come at last to show what the ferocious nomads could do, when disciplined, united under a chief to whom nothing was sacred or unclean, who was determined to concentrate all energy and force towards one end alone, the glory of the Yakka Mongols. Chingiz had studied the men with whom he would have to deal; he was convinced that in nerve and tenacity of will or in mastering any difficult situation, he would not fail.

Temuchin must have realized that if he could inaugurate his rule by friendly alliances with his immediate neighbours, his position would be greatly strengthened. For neither now, nor at any point during his long career, was it his habit to close the doors or drive an adversary into the battlefield unless he was convinced that peaceful negotiations and parleys could not secure his aim. And, therefore, the first step of the new Khan was to send messengers to Toghril and Jamuka inviting their help and cooperation. 'It is very good', said Toghril Khan to Tahai and Sukegai, the messengers of Temuchin, 'that Temuchin has been made Khan. How, indeed, could you Mongols do without a Khan? So take care not to undo what you have done by common consent.' The old Khan of the Kereits was no statesman; he could not fathom or foresee the ambitions of Temuchin. And so he was pleased with the election of his *anda*'s son. But Jamuka was more shrewd and could see much ahead of his nose. 'Tell Altan and Kuchar, who are now with Temuchin', was his laconic reply, 'that as a result of their instigation, Temuchin *anda* and myself were separated from each other. Why did you not declare Temuchin 'Khan' when we were together? What is in your mind that has caused you to declare him Khan now? You all should always remain faithful to Temuchin and let his heart be at rest through your constancy.' Thus, as far as Jamuka was concerned, the attempt at reconciliation failed.

The rivals soon had a pretext to appeal to arms. While Chingiz was engrossed with the affairs of his followers and looked to the discipline and efficiency of his fighting machine, two horsemen of the Ikiras clan, Mulketotakh and Boroltai, appeared at Gulyalgu where he was camping. They had brought news for the Khan which brought him to his feet in a moment. Jamuka had crossed the Alaut Turkhan ridge and was advancing against Chingiz with a force of 30,000 men to avenge his brother's death.

Daichar, a younger brother of Jamuka, had driven off the horses of Juchi Dharmala, a follower of Chingiz. Dharmala was not to be deprived of his horses: he took up the pursuit and, coming up to the raider, brought Daichar down with an arrow shot that broke his backbone. Having recovered his horses, Dharmala returned to his camp. There was nothing new or strange in such an episode. But it fanned the smouldering jealousy of Jamuka into a blaze; to settle matters once and for all, he marched towards Chingiz's camp.

Chingiz did not hesitate; he marched out with 30,000 men to meet the advancing force. The two armies met at Chelaini on the banks of the Onon in which Jamuka had an upper hand. Chingiz had to beat a retreat and seek refuge in the narrow valley by the side of the Onon. Jamuka, however, did not follow up his triumph by a pursuit, as Sultan Jalaluddin was to do later, but contented himself by wreaking havoc on the 'wolves' or chieftains who fell into his hands. Niutai Chakakhaan was beheaded and his body was torn to pieces, tied as it was to the tail of a running horse. The end of some others was yet more terrible.

Jamuka's policy of vengeance failed to achieve its objective which was to strike terror into the hearts of the wavering and to rally his followers more solidly to his flag. It failed on account of its very violence: it served the defeated and discomfited Chingiz as a heaven-sent blessing. A sense of revulsion spread against Jamuka, and people murmured and grumbled at his harsh and cruel behaviour. Chiefs and clans began to desert to Temuchin Chingiz, who knew how to welcome them, and how to hold his men together. Jurchetai of the Urut tribe and Quildar of the Mangut tribe had been the first and the most prominent to leave Jamuka. Now even Munlik, on whom the dying Yesukai had bequeathed the care of his family, returned to renew his allegiance, for, like many others, he now found that love and loyalty to Temuchin no longer clashed with self-interest. Munlik came with his seven sons, one of whom was the famous shaman, Kokchu. Temuchin Chingiz, in need of loyal followers, was pleased with every fresh arrival. He received all without reproach, even Munlik. To celebrate his assumption of Khanship and the arrival and allegiance of fresh tribes Chingiz arranged a grand feast on the banks of river Onon to welcome them. This banquet, however, was marred by feminine petulance and jealousies. 'Why not offer the milk to us before these people', objected Ghulichin and Khuurchin, the two Jurki ladies, displeased by the preference accorded to Oyelun, Qasar, Sacha Baiki, Yebaigi, the little lady or mistress of Sacha Baiki, who were served first. The two women had Sikiur, the master of provisions, beaten for the slight suffered by them. Chingiz, however, remained patient and undisturbed. He asked Buri Boko to deal with the petulant women and bring them to reason, while he directed Belgutai to maintain order outside the camp. But later a further nuisance was created by Buri Boko, who clashed with Belgutai over a stolen bridle. 'Why do you let him treat you like this?' asked Chingiz Khan, who observed all that was going around. 'My wound is not very serious', said the bleeding Belgutai, who also had suffered a broken shoulder. He said, 'Cousins should not quarrel because of me.' But the ire of Chingiz was now roused and he ordered his men to punish the Jurkis and bring them to their senses.

While Chingiz had been struggling for survival and consolidating his gains, the Kin emperor found that the Tatars had become too powerful and were now a menace to his walled and wealthy subjects. Therefore, they had to be punished and their power broken. Since the Tatars were elusive raiders, who refused to offer a pitched battle, but harassed their opponents by their hit-and-run tactics, the Kin Emperor sought an arrangement with the Khan of the Kereits to encircle the Tatars, who could then be crushed between the Kereit anvil and the Chinese hammer. Chingiz learnt about this. It offered him an opportunity to deal a smashing blow to his ancestral enemies. To defeat the Tatars was his dearest wish: it meant revenge for past injuries, and might mean gains in terms of men, money, women and horses. He sent an arrow-messenger to Toghril. 'The Kin have now sent Wang King,' ran the message, 'chasing Meguchin, Saultu and other Tatars up the Ulcha. These people are my great enemies, and have killed my ancestors. Father! Will you help me attack them?' The 'father' agreed, and Chingiz sent his arrow-messengers to the Jurki chiefs, Sacha Baiki and Daichu, to come to his assistance. Six days he waited for them and their warriors, but in vain. They had not forgotten the rough treatment they had received and were in no mood to help Temuchin to further himself. Chingiz and Toghril Khan, thereupon, marched against the Tatars, who were retreating and fleeing from the Chinese; they were hemmed in, their retreat barred and blocked, and were completely crushed at Khusutushi Tuyan.[2] Meghuchin, Saultu, and other leaders were killed and a large number of them were made captives.

This expedition of 1194 was a personal triumph for Temuchin Chingiz. Not only were his deadliest enemies annihilated, the campaign also afforded him an opportunity to test the mettle and efficiency of his warriors. It also strengthened his ordu with the incorporation of Tatar women and children. His position was further improved by the title that Wang King was pleased to confer upon him, Military Commander of the Frontier. Now Toghril became Wang Khan. Above all, he had an opportunity to study Chinese soldiers at first hand—their cunning and dexterity, their gallantry and intelligence but without the recklessness and ferocity of the nomad fighters—knowledge which he was to exploit with deadly effect only a few years later. Successful and satisfied with the results of the campaign, Chingiz and Wang Khan returned to their camp.

Chingiz now acted to tame the Jurkis, to put an end to their insolence and intransigence, and, above all, to show that his orders could not be disobeyed with impunity. Sacha Baiki and Daichu had failed to respond to his summons for the expedition against the Tatars. Old grievances were now raked up, and new charges were levelled against them. It was reported to Chingiz Khan that, during his absence on the expedition, they had killed ten of his subjects, besides stripping naked fifty others at Halil Lake. 'Why do we suffer all this ill-treatment at the hands of the Jurkis?', said the angry Khan. 'On a former occasion we had a feast on the Onon, they beat our master of provisions and broke the shoulder-blade of Belgutai. This time when we asked for their help to avenge our ancestors, they did not come. On the contrary, they want to help our enemy and have now become our enemies.'

The Jurkis were the descendants of the invincible and daring archers of Kabul Khan. Kabul Khan had seven sons and to his eldest son, Ogin Barkat, he allotted his valiant warriors, noted for their strength and archery. It was because of their unbeaten record in battle that they were named Jurki. Chingiz marched against them and defeated them. Sacha Baiki and Daichu were captured and beheaded; the rest of the tribesmen were carried off and incorporated among his followers.

Soon afterwards Buri Boko, another important member of the Jurki clan, was treacherously put to death. Probably Chingiz regarded him a powerful and implacable enemy, for though his principle was to win over and conciliate his opponents, if he found that reconciliation was not possible, he removed a person from his way. Buri Boko was a grandson of Kabul Khan, noted for his strength. Forsaking the sons of Bartan Bahadur, i.e., the family of Yesukai, he had allied with the daring descendants of Barkah. Chingiz Khan had a deep hatred of him and had not forgotten or forgiven him for the skirmish in which he had broken Belgutai's shoulder. He asked Buri Boko to have a wrestling bout with Belgutai. On that occasion Buri Boko feigned defeat, probably to humour Chingiz Khan, and was held down by Belgutai. 'Chingiz bit his lower lip', says the *Secret History*; 'Belgutai, understanding his meaning, pressed his knees on Buri Boko's spine, seized his neck with both hands, and turned it forcefully backward until he had broken Buri Boko's backbone.'

The successful campaign against the Tatars marked a definite improvement in Chingiz's relations with the Khan of the Kereits. He was no longer a fugitive or hunted chieftain to be pitied and patronized by the Wang Khan. The Wang Khan and Chingiz became more attached and intimate with each other. The real reason was that they each needed the other's help. They were, as Chingiz described later on, the two wheels of a cart. The value and importance of this combination was very soon established when, in 1196 the Kereit Khan was faced with the armed resistance and open rebellion of his younger brother, Irka Qara. Irka Qara was assisted by the Naimans and, ultimately drove off the Wang Khan, who sought refuge with Gurkhan of Qara-Khitai. He remained there for about a year and a half but failed to get any help. Hard pressed and in great distress, Wang Khan resolved to appeal to Chingiz. With nothing left but five she-goats on whose milk he lived, a camel, whose blood he drank, and a blind horse, the solitary mount and companion of his wanderings, he marched across the land of the Uighurs and the Kingdom of Si-bsia. Chingiz welcomed him and provided him men and cattle. Restored to his dignity and security, Wang Khan accompanied his ally and benefactor on a punitive expedition against the Merkits—which was a great success and enormous booty fell into the hands of the victors. Probably with an eye to the future and also due to some consideration for the old man, Chingiz offered all the booty—men, women and cattle—to the Wang Khan. Next year, in 1198, Chingiz organized a punitive expedition against the Tatars, while the Wang Khan marched against Tuqta Bigi and gained a decisive victory over the Merkits. Tuqta's eldest son, Togus Bigi was killed while his wife, two other sons and two daughters and a host of others fell into the hands of the Wang Khan. But, unlike Chingiz, the crafty and greedy Khan kept all the spoils for himself.[3]

Chingiz, who noted everything but forgot nothing, remained impassive and maintained the old attitude towards Wang Khan. And, therefore, in 1199, the two friends and allies were again at the head of their joint forces—now against Bue-Ruq, a chieftain of the Naimans. Finding himself unable to cope with the superior numbers of the invading allies, Bue-Ruq left Uluqtaq and crossed the Ulungu river. Chingiz and the Wang Khan followed the fleeing Naiman, and captured Yeditupluq whom Bue Ruq had sent to reconnoitre. Victorious and triumphant, they turned back from the Lake Kizil Bashi but found at Baidarakh Belchir their way blocked and barred by the able Naiman general, Kokseu Saprakh. As it was late in the evening and the sun was about to set, the hostile forces decided to camp for the night—to rest as well as to prepare for the engagement the next day.

'I am like a lark', said Jamuka to the Wang Khan, 'which is attached to the place where it lives, but Temuchin is like a bird of passage whose cries resound in the skies.' 'Why are you attempting to instigate men against your good brother?', remarked Gurin Bahadur. 'Temuchin had formerly sent envoys to the Naimans and this is why he lags behind both day and night', said Jamuka; by insinuation he succeeded in arousing Wang Khan's suspicions about the intentions of Chingiz. Without consulting or informing his ally, the Wang Khan quietly left the field under the cover of night, leaving the camp fires and lights burning to deceive his ally as well as the enemy. Chingiz was surprised at this unexpected and treacherous move of his ally and had to beat a hasty retreat across the Altai and encamped at the river Sali—an inglorious conclusion of a triumphal return march.

Unfortunately for the crafty old Kereit Khan, the Naiman general decided to pursue and attack him instead of Chingiz. The Wang Khan was badly mauled: Koksen Saprakh inflicted a heavy defeat on him, captured the wife of Sengun, the Khan's son, and half of Wang Khan's men and cattle. Making use of the discomfiture of their captor and enemy Wang Khan, the captive sons of Tuqta Bigi, Qutu and Chilaun by name, escaped down the river Selenga and fled to join their father.

Struggle for Power

Badly beaten, Wang Khan once again appealed to Chingiz for assistance. The clever and astute warrior rose to the occasion and, without any words of reproach for the treacherous behaviour of the Kereit chief, he immediately despatched an army under the command of his four distinguished warriors, Bogurchi, Subutai, Muquli, and Boloul. The Mongol soldiers reached Quraan Qut to find that the Kereits had been worsted by the Naimans and that Wang Khan's son, Sengun fleeing on a wounded and lame horse, was about to fall into the hands of the enemies. The timely arrival of Mongol warriors saved the fleeing Kereits, the Naimans were defeated and rolled back, and all the women and people of Wang Khan were recovered and restored to him.

'In the old days', said the remorseful and grateful Wang Khan, the good father of Temuchin saved my people for me; now his son has sent his four great warriors to restore them to me again. Heaven be my witness! I will repay my obligations to him. For whom did the father and son take all these troubles? I am an old man now. Who will rule my people after me? My younger brothers are all unworthy of the trust. Sengun is my only son, but his existence is a matter of indifference to me. Let Temuchin be the elder brother of my son. When I have two sons, there will be little for me to worry about.'

A repentant and chastened Wang Khan met Chingiz in the Black Forest on the banks of the Tula to renew the alliance, to cement the understanding he formally adopting Chingiz as his son. 'We will jointly attack and capture any numerically superior enemy' so ran their agreement. 'When there is a hunt, we will jointly form a semi-circle around the game. If anyone attempts to instigate ill-feeling between us, we will not believe him till we have met and talked over the matter personally.'

The agreement removed the cloud of suspicion that had darkened their relations. It was especially favourable to Chingiz, whose rapidly increasing power and position it tacitly affirmed and recognized, by raising him to the position of heir to the Kereit chief, 'the elder brother of his son'—the provision for the clarification of misunderstandings and settlement of disputes sought to eliminate future possibilities of a rift. No more Jamukas! No more repetition of the sad debacle of Quraan Qut.

The reconciliation effected between Wang Khan and Chingiz in the Black Forest caused alarm and unease among the anxious and routed tribes, the agreement seemed to make clear the aims and intentions of Wang Khan and 'the elder brother of his son' (Chingiz)—subjugation of the tribes of the Gobi and the creation of a grand kingdom of the steppe. It made them realize the gravity of the threat to their independent existence. Jamuka, instigated them to action.

The ceaseless activity of Temuchin's inveterate and inexorable enemy soon bore fruit and, in 1201, eleven tribes—Taichiuts, Saljiuts, Qungpurats, Durmans, Jajarats, Jalairs, Uirat, Merkits, Tatars, Yoorkin, and Qatghin— assembled at Alhui Bulas or the Ulhui River and formed a confederation to fight the Chingiz-Wang Khan axis. They came to an agreement concerning concerted action and swore their strongest oath, by sacrificing a horse, a bullock, a ram and a dog, to be faithful to each other; to them there was no engagement more solemn.[4] 'May that happen to us', they affirmed,[5] 'which has happened to these animals if we break our vow and are false to our sworn alliance.'

Jamuka was elected Gurkhan or head of the coalition and, to take the enemies by surprise and not to give them time to effect a junction, he decided upon an immediate attack on Temuchin Chingiz, who was then on the banks of the Kerulon. But Chingiz was informed of the confederates' plans by Kuritai and he immediately sent the information to the Wang Khan. To meet the impending attack, Chingiz and the Wang Khan assembled their forces and marched up the river Kerulon. The hostile forces met near Chikburkhu and, next day, at Koidin the confederates suffered a crushing defeat and the tribes dispersed to their encampments.[6]

Jamuka retreated along the banks of the river Argun, but was pursued by the Wang Khan, while Chingiz went after Anchu Bahadur, the Taichiut commander of the confederate vanguard. Crossing the Onon, he turned round and awaited the arrival of the pursuing troops. Fierce and ferocious was the battle which awaited Chingiz and the grim encounter lasted all day. During the course of the battle, Chingiz was wounded in the neck by a poisoned arrow and he fainted. 'How is it?' said Chingiz, when, on regaining consciousness, he saw some blood. 'Would it not be better to throw this at a distance?' 'Being in a hurry,' said the loyal Jelme, 'I did not have time to carry it far. Besides, I was afraid of what might happen to you if I left you here alone. I simply swallowed some of the blood straightaway and vomitted the rest on the ground here. By now a lot of it is in my stomach.' 'Well, I was wounded already,' said Chingiz, 'why did you go into the enemy's camp all naked? Had you been caught, you would have had to tell them that I was wounded.' 'No', said Jelme. 'I would have told them that I intended to surrender to them, that when you discovered my intention, you had stripped me of my clothes and that I succeeded in snatching myself out of your hands when about to be executed, and escaped to them. They would have certainly trusted my words, given me clothes, and put me to work. I could then have stolen one of their horses and ridden back.' 'You saved me once when the Merkits made an attempt on my life. This time you sucked the clotted blood out of my wound and, again, when I felt thirsty, you risked your life in order to seek mare's milk to lessen the sourness of my heart. Three times you have rendered me invaluable service, I will never forget it.'

When the day dawned, Chingiz found that the enemy had retired during the night and he immediately rode off to fetch the fugitives.

Next day, Surghan Shira and Jirghuatai, members of the Todogs clan of the Taichiuts, came to him. Chingiz was pleased and asked Surghan Shira the reason for his late arrival, who explained his delay in joining him to the fears and anxieties which he had for his family. 'Had I come earlier my family would have been ruthlessly exterminated by the Taichiuts.'

'Who was the man', enquired Chingiz. 'Who was he who in the battle of Koidin broke the neck of my horse with an arrow?' 'I shot the arrow', replied Surghan Shira's companion. 'If you order me to be executed, my blood will hardly cover more than a palm-breadth of earth but if you spare my life, I will serve you to the best of my ability, I will cross deep torrents for you and crumble rocks to sand.' 'Whenever an enemy has injured me,' said Chingiz, 'he has remained silent about it. But you, who have hidden nothing, are worthy of being my companion.' To commemorate his feat, Chingiz named him 'Jebe'—the arrow—the name by which he is known in history.

The victory over the confederates and the annihilation of the Taichiuts established the position of the new Khan of the Mongols and added lustre to his fame. From all parts of the Gobi, tribesmen began to flock to his banner in increasing numbers, and Jakhaganbu, brother of the Wang Khan, along with the scattered sections of the Kereits, joined the Mongol Khan.

Having finished off the Taichiuts, Chingiz decided to remove the Tatar menace also. In 1202 he led an expedition against the Tatar tribes. Knowing the reckless courage and ferocity of the Tatars, and the possible confusion in the scramble for booty, Chingiz issued a terse but stern order. 'If we are victorious, you shall not seek for booty; when all is over it will be divided into equal shares. If the soldiers are forced to fall back to the initial positions, they shall advance again. He who retreats and does not resume the advance will be beheaded.' The Tatars were decisively beaten in the battle of Dalan Nimurgas, and immense booty fell to the victors. But his distinguished kinsmen, Altan, Kuchar and Daritai, disobeyed the instructions, and no sooner did the Tatar forces give way that they began to plunder the enemy tent. On being informed of their violation of his order, Chingiz asked Jebe and Qubilai to wrest from them all the spoils they had gathered. Chingiz was not the man to connive any disobedience or tolerate any kind of resistance to his authority. His word was law and should be carried out unquestioningly and unflinchingly. This was the first and foremost lesson which Chingiz sought to teach the unruly and haughty nomad of the steppe.

'The Tatars killed my father,' Chingiz said to the members of his family. 'Now that we have captured their men, let us exterminate all Tatar men who are as tall as the axis of the cart and reduce the rest into slavery.' Tatars were his ancestral and deadliest enemies; by no stretch of imagination was there any chance of reconciling and winning them over, and, therefore, their leaders and grown-up men had to be wiped out. But their harmless women could be absorbed and made to increase the strength of his fighting machine while the young boys would be trained and brought up in Mongol families. They agreed, and who could dare disagree with the fiery Khan, who had just a little while ago taught a lesson to his kinsmen?

'What have you decided in the Quriltai?', asked the Tatar Yeke Cheren. 'We have resolved', answered the thoughtless Belgutai, 'to exterminate all male Tatars, who are as tall as the axis of the cart.' Yeke Cheren immediately communicated the news to his fellow-captives and advised them to have their swords ready to meet the executioners. Many fled the camp and entrenched themselves on a mountain nearby. It was only after a sanguinary battle, and sustaining heavy casualties, that the Mongol warriors could storm the Tatar positions. They suffered further losses when the Tatar prisoners fell upon their executioners with swords concealed for the purpose.

The needless loss of his warriors annoyed Chingiz. 'Belgutai', said Chingiz, 'has been guilty of leaking an important resolution passed in the conference of our clan, and this has led to numerous casualties on our side. Hereafter Belgutai is forbidden to take part in any important Quriltai. He will be entrusted only with the outdoor administration of cases of dispute, riot, robbery, theft, and the like. He and Daritai will be permitted to enter the conference after the discussion of its agenda is over, and all its members have drunk their cups.'

Chingiz was now well on his way to sovereign power. In a period of ten years of ceaseless struggle, repeated alarms and dangers, and bloody battles, he had established and extended his authority. His deadliest enemies, the Taichiuts and the Tatars, had been annihilated and were no better than mere names. The united and the most determined effort of the tribes had failed to shake his position. And he was on friendly terms with the formidable Wang Khan, being 'the elder brother of his son'.

But the utmost confidence and esteem which he enjoyed aroused the envy and jealousy of Wang Khan's son and relations, and they plotted together to bring about his downfall. Jamuka, who bore him great enmity, had also joined Wang Khan and, on account of his sagacity and shrewdness, had come to have an influence on Wang Khan's only son, the haughty and thoughtless Sengun who was ill-inclined towards Chingiz.

'Will our daughter enter their door to stand facing the north and their daughter come to our family to sit facing the south?' said Sengun, opposing a marriage alliance with Chingiz. Chingiz had proposed a mutual matrimonial alliance between the two families, offering his own daughter Kuchin for Sengun's son, Tusakha and, in return, the hand of Wang Khan's daughter Chaur Begi, for his son, Juji. Left to himself Wang Khan would have been glad to have such an alliance but the hatred of Sengun for Chingiz stood in the way. Sengun's animosity stemmed from the fact that Wang Khan treated Chingiz with respect and honour, had formally adopted him as his son and was guided by his advice in all matters of importance.[7] This was tantamount to the supersession of Sengun, and whatever chances he had of regaining his father's good opinion, and succeeding to his authority, would be sealed by the matrimonial alliance. And so he had the proposals rejected and, says the *Secret History*, 'this soured the heart of Chingiz'.

There is no need to question the sincerity of Chingiz's desire for a closer understanding in 1202, and an alliance for common ends. There were still many tribes to be subjugated and many a rival to be stifled. But the rejection of his proposals should have set him thinking—regarding the meaning and consequences of Sengun's attitude and ambitions. With Sengun and Jamuka having the ear of the old Wang Khan, and his kinsmen to aid and abet them, would it be possible for him to remain on former terms of intimacy and loyal co-operation with Wang Khan? And if it were not, what would be the consequences of a rupture? Having explored and appreciated the 'political' framework of the Gobi and the new groupings of the tribes, he could not afford to lose the friendship and protection of the Kereit Khan. A breach with him could involve the abandonment of a traditional friendship, estrangement from a valued friend, and, above them all, a perilous groping after a new ally in an uncertain and shifting future. Remaining outwardly calm and on the old terms, he became cautious and remained at an arm's length from his ally.[8]

Now Jamuka had his opportunity to avenge himself upon his rival. He was not the man to fail or falter. He utilized the cooling friendship to drive a wedge between the Kereit chief and the Mongol Khan. Knowing that Wang Khan was attached to Chingiz and would not hear ill of him, he decided to incite the Wang Khan's son. Sengun was young and had no experience of men and affairs; even his father had no good opinion about his abilities. And Jamuka was not wrong in the choice of his tool. 'Temuchin has exchanged messages with the Naiman Tayang through their envoys,' said Jamuka. 'He speaks like a son of your father, but his actions are such that it is foolish for you to trust him. If you do not get rid of him first, it is you who will have to face the humiliation. If you decide to take action against him, I will charge into his camp personally.' Altan, Kuchar and other kinsmen of Chingiz, who had deserted the latter on account of his insistence on discipline—irksome to the independent aristocrats of the steppe—were also there to support Jamuka.[9] 'We are ready', said Altan and Kuchar, 'to kill all the sons of Oyelun for you'. 'I will bind his hands and feet for you', promised Yebugachen Khartayat. 'It would be best to capture his people', suggested Toghril, 'what can he do without his people?' 'Sengun, I will go with you to the top of the tallest tree and down into the depths of deepest river in whatever you plan to do', declared Qachiun Begi.

When Sengun sent Baikhan Todiya to his father to warn him against Chingiz, Wang Khan understood that it was Jamuka, who had incited his son. He refused to believe such treachery from Chingiz, who had so far done him much good service, and no evil. 'Why do you indulge in such speculations?', he asked. 'Both you and Temuchin are my sons. I have placed my confidence in Temuchin and if he conspires against me, God will withdraw his protection from him. Jamuka's fantastic words should not be relied upon.' Sengun was not satisfied, and sent another messenger, but the old man refused to be taken in. Sengun then went himself. 'Father!', he said, 'Even now when you are amongst us, he has no regard for me. One day, when you are no longer with us, it is unlikely that he will permit me to rule over your people whom my grandfather gathered.' 'My son, how can I think of deserting any of my sons? I have placed my confidence in him and God will not protect me if I think ill of him.' Disappointed and disgruntled, Sengun departed in anger.[10]

Now Wang Khan was desperately unhappy. In his sober judgement nothing could be worse than a collision with his adopted son; the pressure of Sengun's appeals and the promptings of jealous counsellors was almost intolerable. The appeal to the memory of his father adjured him to authorize action to save the dynasty; on the other hand, past experience and a sense of honour prompted him to stand firm. Sengun had appealed to him in the name of his grandfather, and continually reminded him that his throne and the future of his children were at stake.[11] What was he to do? Wang Khan shrank at the thought of a rupture with Chingiz, who had rendered him valuable services during the last eight years and had proved himself reliable in an otherwise treacherous world. This would be burning the bridges and blowing up the magazines. He was repelled by the idea; but just as the dropping water wears the rock away, the repeated importuning made him give way. 'May God not withdraw His protection from us', he said. 'My son, why should you desert me? You may do whatever you think fit in order to overcome him. Certainly, you know what you are going to do.'

Chingiz was strong and powerful, and the conspirators professed 'to remove him by means of stratagem'[12] rather than risk an open conflict. 'Some time ago', said Sengun, 'Temuchin asked for the hand of Chaur Begi for his eldest son, Juji; we did not agree at that time. Now we will send her to him saying that we accept his proposal. We will fix a day, invite him to the matrimonial feast, and seize him when he comes here.' The message and the invitation were sent to Chingiz and, accepting it, he set out with ten attendants. On the way he called at the house of his stepfather, Munlik, the husband of Oyelun, and explained to him the purpose of his visit to the Kereit camp. 'When we first asked for their maiden', said the thoughtful and sober Munlik, 'Sengun looked down upon us, and rejected our proposal. What has changed his mind now that he has suddenly invited you to the marriage feast? Temuchin, my son, can't you see through (the trick)? Better not go to them. Why not make a pretext that your horses are thin during the spring and say we are too busy grazing them, and cannot find time to go to the feast.'[13]

Chingiz agreed and returned to his camp, sending Bukhatai and Kiratai as his substitutes for the feast. 'We must act quickly', said Sengun. 'They have discovered our secret. We must now proceed at once and encircle and capture them.'

'We have decided to capture Temuchin tomorrow. I wonder what big reward one will obtain by taking this piece of news to Temuchin's notice,' said Yeke Cheren, the youngest brother of Altan and one of Wang Khan's distinguished leaders, who had been at the discussion and could keep nothing from his wife Alakyit. 'Don't be free with your tongue', she said. 'If any servant should hear us, who knows that he may take it seriously.' By chance at that time, Batai, who had come to deliver mare's milk, overheard the conversation. On returning home, he repeated it to one of his companions, named Kishlik. 'I will go there myself', said the incredulous Kishlik, 'and find out'. 'We should cut off our tongue for speaking what we had just discussed', he heard Yeke Cheren's son, Narin Keyan, say, who was sharpening his arrow. 'Who can shut the mouths of the servants?' 'Bring me my white horse together with the chestnut horse and tie them here', he said, turning towards Kishlik. 'Tomorrow I shall go out riding them early in the morning.'

'I have just learnt that what you said is true', he said to Batai. 'Now we shall both go and report to Temuchin.' Making the necessary preparations for the journey, they galloped off and made the malicious designs known to Chingiz. 'The conspiracy', they requested him to believe, 'is as real as anything can be.'[14]

The situation was desperate: the boys had given him a timely warning. There was no time however to summon his subordinate tribes; the Kereits must have started and may turn up any moment. Chingiz held speedy consultations with his chief companions and they decided to make for the skirt of the mountain Mao-under with their followers and dependants and to leave their tents standing. The women and children were despatched first while the rear was commanded by Jelme, whom Chingiz ordered to scout for the enemy. No sooner had they reached Kharakhaljit Yelait than did Chijitai and other horse-herds bring reports of huge columns of dust raised by the enemy across the Mao-under mountain.[15]

The Kereits raided the Mongol camp in the early hours of the morning but found it silent and deserted. The silence of the graveyard prevailed there, which they had mistaken for the Mongols being in deep sleep.[16] They had come to mow down the warriors and have a merry hunt galloping through the surprised and bewildered camp. They were themselves surprised and confused to find that all life had disappeared—there was no movement, no sign of horses or herds, no running child or woman, except the camp-fires which were still ablaze. The volleys of arrows they poured into the tents to kill sleeping soldiers had been wasted.[17] Chingiz had once again eluded his hunters.

Finding the enemy at his heels and no way to avoid him, Chingiz turned round and made ready to give battle. 'Uncle Jurchidai,' said Chingiz, 'I wish to request you to take charge of the vanguard. What is your opinion?' 'I will lead the vanguard', declared Qaildar. 'When I die, you will take special care of my orphan sons.' 'I will be in front of the Khan', said Jurchidai, not to be outdone, 'with the Uruts and the Manguts as the vanguard of the battle.' And so the two clans took their positions.

Tracking the Mongols, Wang Khan succeeded in coming up. 'Who are the best warriors of Temuchin?' Wang Khan asked Jamuka, when he saw the Mongols deploying for battle. 'The Urut and Mangut tribes are both good fighters', said Jamuka. 'They cannot be dispersed even by close cavalry charges; they are skilful both in the use of short spears and swords, and their standards are either coloured or black; when they appear, we must beware of them.' 'If that be the case', Wang Khan said, 'let the valiant Khadakhji of the Jirgin charge them and be assisted by other commanders.'

Inferior in numbers, Chingiz was not in a position to launch a frontal attack on the Kereits but had to fight a delaying battle. Having arranged his men, he waited for the enemy to open the attack. Elated and believing that they had the enemy in the hollow of their hands, Wang Khan's vanguard, commanded by Khadakhji the valiant, marched straight on, at a quick pace. They seemed to aim at the centre and were immediately charged by the Uruts and the Manguts, who rolled them back. As Wang Khan saw the Jirgins hard-pressed and giving way, he sent out Achikh Skirun of the Tumentubegan tribe to support and reinforce them. The Kereits rallied and fought back with reckless ferocity. In the fierce melee and confusion that ensued, Quildar fell off his horse and the Manguts rallied round their fallen commander and raised a wall of steel round him to protect and prevent him from being made a captive. Finding them locked and in difficulties, Chingiz ordered Jurchidai to charge the enemy with his ferocious Uruts, who delivered a telling blow and scattered the enemy's vanguard. As they wavered and gave way, Wang Khan immediately and repeatedly reinforced them. Oman Dunkhait was sent to rally the broken columns and was backed by the reserves under Shilaiman Tai-tai with 1,000 guards. Grim and stubborn was the fighting; great and tremendous were the stakes; the overlordship of the Gobi was in the balance. Chingiz himself showed 'excessive bravery and even rashness'[18] and, with a general's eye on the field, watched and supported his wings as and when he found them hard-pressed. The disparity of numbers and the courage of the Kereits seemed to make the heroism and bravery of his men ineffective. To surprise and paralyse the enemy, Quildar Noyan suggested to Chingiz that the only chance of success lay in outflanking the enemy and capturing the hill at the rear of the enemy. The *Tulughma* (the famous Mongol sweeping manoeuvre and rapid wheeling movement to charge the enemy's rear) was ordered and carried out.[19] A flanking movement and occupying the enemy's rear always has a restraining effect: it makes the enemy nervous, cautious and holds his advance. The Kereits were surprised and held back. Sengun himself made a last effort to overwhelm and sweep away the enemy. The Mongols met the desperate charge with stubborn determination. Sengun was wounded in the face by an arrow shot by Jurchidai at his father, whom he shielded with his own body. This discouraged the furious Kereits and the lengthening shadows separated the two armies late in the evening.[20]

Discouraged and broken-hearted on account of his heavy losses, Wang Khan retired from the battlefield; the stubborn courage and fighting qualities of Chingiz Khan's warriors had unnerved him.[21]

Chingiz had held his ground in the face of superior and fierce numbers and the Kereit tide had ebbed. But he was not in a position to pursue the retreating enemy—discouraged and disappointed as he was, he thought it advisable to withdraw a little from the field and to re-organize his men. When the morning dawned and he inspected his soldiers, he found his son Uktae, Boloul and Bogurchi missing. 'Uktae, Boloul and Bogurchi, the most trustworthy of all my men,' thought Chingiz, 'lived together and have died together, not wishing to part.' But presently Bogurchi appeared and Chingiz thanked God. 'The enemy had shot down my horse,' he said, 'when I was walking back, I saw the Kereits turn back to guard the fallen Sengun, leaving this horse with an inclining load on its back. I took advantage of the opportunity, cut down the load of the horse, mounted on it and followed the trail back.' 'Soon after, another man was seen approaching on horseback', to quote the graphic and dramatic *Secret History*. 'As he approached nearer, an extra pair of feet were also seen dangling under him. When the horse arrived, it was found that Uktae and Bolul were sitting parallel on its back. Boloul's mouth was soiled with blood because he had sucked out the clotted blood from the arrow-wound on Uktae's neck.' Chingiz was deeply touched and tears flowed down his cheeks!

Boloul informed Chingiz of clouds of dust raised by the enemy trailing towards Burakhat, and Chingiz immediately moved on towards Dalan Nimurgas, and thence along the river Khalkha. He had only 2,600 men, for the tribes had refused to rally to his aid on the ground that he had exceeded his authority and, acting contrary their age-old customs, had picked a needless quarrel with Wang Khan, a struggle they could not cope with.[22]

Dividing his men into two contingents of equal strength, he marched down along both the banks of the river Khalkha. The warriors took to hunting to exercise and to gather food, and it was during one of these hunts that the wound of the gallant Quildar opened, and he died. The brave warrior was buried by the mountain Ornou near the river.

'Remember your matrimonial bond with our princely dynasty,' was the biting message with which Chingiz sent Jurchidai and his Uruts to the Jungirats, who dwelt round the Lake Buyur. 'Submit to us; if not, be ready for battle.' They readily agreed and Chingiz left them unmolested.

Khadaan Daldur Khan, who had lately joined him, informed Chingiz of the bitterness and remorse with which Wang Khan regarded the needless rupture with Chingiz. 'When the wounded Sengun', he said, was brought to Wang Khan, the latter remarked, "you challenged the man whom you should not have provoked. What a pity it is for me (to see) that my son has been pierced by a nail on his cheek, but if life is left within him, he will have another trial". "O Khan! When you had no son", protested Achikh Shiran, "you prayed for one, and now that you have Sengun for your successor, wherefore do you not promote his interests". Wang Khan instructed his people to tend his son with special care and to save him from pirks. From there they marched homeward.'

Pleased with the submission of the Jungirats, Chingiz marched east and encamped on the banks of the river Tungeli. And to profit from the disgust of Wang Khan and to attempt reconciliation, he despatched Arhai Khasar and Shegagai Jeun on his behalf. 'I am now on the eastern bank of the small Tungeli river. The grass here is splendid; the horses are fat. Father, what have I done to incur your wrath which has filled me with fear? If you wished to reprimand me, you could have done it in a peaceful manner as well. Why this policy which attempts to destroy all my possessions? Presumably, some people have come between us. But did we not make an agreement that if either of us was slandered by anyone, we would not believe in it till we had talked over the matter personally? Father, have we had any personal interview this time? Though young, I seem to be old enough; though bad, I seem to be good at the same time. Moreover, you and I are like the two wheels of a cart; when one of these is broken, the cart cannot move. May I not compare myself to a shaft or a wheel ... out of gratitude to my father you said that you would repay his kindness to his sons and grandsons. God knows it ... when you were so hard-pressed that you lived on the milk of five she-goats, drank blood from the veins of a camel and rode a blind horse, as a mark of respect for the old relations between you and my father, I sent my men to welcome you to my camp and levied a tax in kind on my people in order to provide for you. When you captured the Merkits, I left all their cattle and their possessions to you. Later when we pursued Bue-Ruq and met Kokseu Saprakh in battle, you deceptively left lights in your camp and withdrew all your men; but after Kokseu Saprakh had attacked you, seized Sengun's wife and people, and also captured one half of your people in Tiraigatu, you appealed to me again. I sent my four great warriors to restore Sengun's wife and people, together with all your cattle. Thereupon you again expressed your gratitude. Now, whatever may be reason for upbraiding me, please send your men to impart it.'

Wang Khan, already remorseful and sorry for the breach with Chingiz, was greatly touched and deeply moved by the long catalogue of valuable services done to him by Yesukai Bahadur and his son to whom, as a matter of fact, he owed his position and life. He cut open his little finger, drew a little blood, put it in a small birah back vessel and, handing it over to the messengers, said: 'There is good reason for me not to desert Temuchin, my son, but I have deserted him already. If I do him any harm in future, may I be cut up in the same manner.'

Chingiz also sent a stinging and biting message to Jamuka: 'Through your envy and malice for me, you have sown discord between the Khan, my father, and me. In former days, it was a custom that the son who got up first used to drink mare's milk from his father's jade cup. Because I often rose early, you hated me. Now you may drink the whole milk from my father's jade-cup; no one will suffer from your drinking.'

He did not forget to reproach his false kinsfolk, who had violated their oath of allegiance and loyalty, and, going over to Wang Khan, had goaded him into action against Chingiz. 'Why did you two desert me?', ran the message to Altan and Kuchar. 'Kuchar! You are the son of Nekun Tai-tsi. In former days we asked you to be Khan but you refused. Altan! You father was Qutsula Khaqan, who ruled over the Dada people. We asked you to ascend the throne but you also refused .... You all made me your Khan, even against my wishes, and now you have left me and joined Wang Khan. Keep him company to the end. Do not begin a thing without seeing it completed, lest people should blame you and say that you are worthless. Defend well the sources of the three rivers (i.e. the Onon, the Kerulen, and the Tula), and do not let others occupy them as their grazing ground.'

Chingiz admonished Toghril, whom he called 'my slave by descent', for his disloyalty. But it was for Sengun that he reserved the most pointed and cutting language. 'To your father, I am a son born in clothes and you are a son born naked. Our father has promoted our interests equally. Being afraid that I would take precedence over you, you began to suspect me and out of envy and malice you sent me away. Now do not cause any more grief to our father's heart. Go to him by day and by night and dispel his sorrow and loneliness. If you do not get rid of your jealous spirit, you will soon try to be ruler in our father's lifetime and cause him suffering. If you wish to send a message to me, send two persons instead of one.'

Though Wang Khan was willing to come to him, the haughty and immature Sengun was in no mood for a compromise, and certainly not to be cowed. 'Wherefore has he called the Khan his father?' exclaimed the enraged Sengun. 'Just call him an old butcher of men. Why has he styled me his *anda*? Call me old Master Tokhtoa or say that my business is to plait sheep tails.[23] I know the exact meaning of his words. They mean war. And you, Belga Baiki and Todayan, raise the grand standard and graze the horses properly so that they in time be fat and fit for the task. There is no room for doubt now.'

Informed of the heavy preparations for another all out effort against him, Chingiz marched towards the Salt Lake Baljunah, which contained but little water, scarcely sufficient for his men and beasts.[24] Here his affairs began to prosper once again; tribes residing and roaming in that area submitted to him and Muslim merchants called upon him, exchanging their sheep and camels with martens.

While encamped at Lake Baljunah, Chingiz was visited by his younger brother, Juji Qasar, who had made his escape from Kereit captivity. He had only a few followers with him while his wife and three sons Yegu, Yesunga, and Tukhu were still in the hands of the adversary. He had suffered much hardship in his search for Chingiz; he had to content himself with raw hide and sinews of oxen until he could trace his brother. Warm and affectionate was the meeting between the two brothers and they sat down to devise ways and means of overcoming their adversaries. Born and bred in an atmosphere of violence and intrigues they hit upon a ruse.[25] Khaliutar and Chaur Khan were dispatched to solicit an understanding on Qasar's behalf: 'I have not seen the shadow of my eldest brother, I have traversed many routes but I have not seen him anywhere. I have called out to him but he has not heard me. At night I have slept on the earth and looked at the stars in the sky. O Khan, my father, wife and children are with you. If you will send a trustworthy man to me, I will come with him to you.' The envoys were instructed to return and report to the brothers not at the lake but on the river Kerulen, whether Chingiz was immediately to start. For Jurchidai and Arhai were ordered to lead the vanguard immediately and encamp at Arkhalgonji on the Kerulen.

The tired and exhausted companions of Juji Qasar appeared before Wang Khan on their worn out horses and delivered the message. Khan was pleased and this added to the relish and merriment of the feast which he was giving in his golden tent. There was apparently no reason to doubt the sincerity of Juji Qasar's solicitations; his wife and sons were in his hands, while he himself had had no news of Chingiz's whereabouts. 'If this be the case,' replied Wang Khan, 'let Qasar come.' He deputed the reliable Iturkin to accompany the envoys on their way back to Juji Qasar. When they approached the Kerulen encampment, Iturkin's fears and suspicions were aroused by the 'many shadows of figures' that he beheld from the great distance. At once he turned round and galloped off to report the treacherous move. Khaliutar sped after him and, overtaking him, barred his path, but had not the courage or strength to touch him. But Chaur Khan, who had lagged behind, solved the difficulty; for, while the two warriors stood face to face hurling defiance, he brought down Iturkin and his horse by an arrow shot into the hip of Iturkin's horse. The captured Iturkin was brought before Chingiz who sent him to Qasar with orders to put him to death. Informed that Wang Khan was unprepared and unsuspecting, Chingiz decided to take him by surprise. Riding day and night at full speed, he reached the ordu of Wang Khan to find him in the midst of festivities. The Kereits were surrounded and a grim battle ensued in which attempts to break the Mongol ring failed. The battle raged for three days, and was brought to an end by the flight of Kereit Khan, demoralized and frightened because Qarachar Noyan, according to the Timurid historians, struck his horse with an arrow and brought it, head foremost to the ground.[26] Mounting another horse, Wang Khan and Sengun took to flight, leaving their wives and daughters captive in the hand of the victors, and the Kereits saved their lives by surrendering and submitting to Chingiz.[27]

There was no trace of Wang Khan and Sengun. The captives were examined. 'I could not harden my heart to let you take my rightful master and kill him,' answered Khadakh Bahadur. 'I have fought you for three days to give him enough time to escape. Now, if you put me to death, I will embrace death: if you spare my life, I will be at your service.' 'He who did not wish to desert his master', said Chingiz, 'but fought against me to give him an opportunity to escape is really a brave man and deserves to be my companion.' Loyalty was the virtue which Chingiz prized the most, even in his enemies. He spared the life of Khadakh Bahadur and rewarded him for his loyalty and devotion to his old master by making him a commander of a 100 soldiers.

Wang Khan had fled towards the Naimans to seek shelter with their chief, Tayang Khan. At the river Nikun he was captured by a Naiman scout, Ghurisubechi. 'I am Wang Khan', he protested, in vain. The scout could not believe that his miserable captive was the once powerful Toghril Wang Khan, Chief of the Kereits, and put him to death. Sengun managed to escape and succeeded in reaching Chual along with his attendant Kokochu and his wife.

While Sengun went to shoot a wild horse, Kokochu prepared to desert him. 'In the old days', protested the wife, 'he provided you with fine clothes and fed you with good food. How can you now desert your rightful lord?' She refused to accompany him. 'You will not go', retorted Kokochu with savage mockery. 'Do you intend to marry Sengun?' 'It matters not if people say that a woman's face is dog-skinned,' answered the defiant wife. 'Nevertheless, you must give him this gold cup from which he may drink.' Kokochu at last yielded and the wife consented to accompany him. 'How could I accept the services of such a man?', said Chingiz, when he heard their story from them and ordered Kokochu to be killed but rewarded his wife.

The victory over the Kereits was complete and Chingiz was now the most powerful nomad chief in Mongolia. Sengun was no better than a fugitive, fleeing for his life. The Kereits had saved themselves by surrendering to the victors and the victorious Mongol Khan absorbed them among his own people by distributing them among his warriors. Tahai Bahadur of the Saldutai tribe was rewarded with one hundred 'tents' or families of the Jirgin tribe. The two daughters of Wang Khan's younger brother, Jakhaganbu, were selected for marriage: Ibaha for Chingiz and the younger Siyur Qaqtani for Tului. This saved Jakhaganbu's followers from humiliation and slavery.

To celebrate his triumph, Chingiz distributed honours and rewards to his followers; and, at the suggestion of Qarachar Noyan,[28] he had a register made of the names of all those who had accompanied him in his fight, 'high and low, amir and slave, camp followers and servants, Turks and Tajiks.'[29] 'Every one of them', records Juwaini, 'attained high dignity, so much so that even the carpet-layer and camel-drivers lived in wealth and luxury. Some of them (later on) became rulers, while others rose to high offices and became famous throughout the world.' Chingiz was lavish in the distribution of rewards and offices to those who served him with devotion and loyalty. But the highest rewards he reserved for the two boys who gave him timely warning of the treacherous night-attack by the Kereits—he gave them privileges and immunities that had never been bestowed by any ruler. Besides giving them the golden tent of Wang Khan along with its golden vessels and its attendants, he made them *terkhans*, and gave them the Wanghuci—a clan of the Kereits as their bodyguard. *Terkhan*[30] were exempt from the payment of all taxes. He kept for himself all spoils he captured in the battle, and all game he seized in the hunt and was not obliged to share them with others. A *terkhan* had, further, the right of entering the royal presence at any time without previous permission, and was allowed to carry his bows and arrows at the feasts, and to have a flagon of his own. Above all, whatever offence a *terkhan* might commit, he could go unpunished up to nine crimes. These privileges were to be inherited by the descendants of Batai and Kishlik for nine generations. 'These two have saved my life', said Chingiz.[31] 'Now by the grace of the everlasting God, I have subjugated the Kereit people at last and thus secured the exalted throne. Let my descendants constantly remember my obligations to them.' And they did. 'At present', wrote Juwaini, 'there are many descendants of these two persons and all of them are much respected and honoured. They are held dear and prized by the monarchs.'

Chingiz Khan was not content with rewarding his chief followers but decided to humour all his men by assigning to the various tribes different places of honour or *Uruni*. All the tribes were enrolled and grouped into twelve *koors* or divisions, divided into six *koors* of the right wing and six of the left. The *koor* were allotted fixed places and positions both in the court and in the camp, and the same on the battlefield. The two *koors* of the right and left, distinguished by rank and learning, had permission to sit in his presence. The next two tribes of the right and left were stationed at the door of his durbant, and were ordered to stand and superintend the entry and exit of persons to and from the hall of audience. Two tribes of the right and left, composed of the bravest men in the army, were stationed outside the door of the court tent and were allowed to sit. The next two tribes of the right and left were ordered to take their places behind the two preceding *koors* and were permitted to sit. The next two *koors* were also to sit behind the fourth and the last two *koors* were also directed to sit behind them. Men were appointed to superintend the places and movements of the *koors*, both in peace and war.[32]

From the above account it will be clear that Chingiz was not 'abandoned by most of his troops' nor did he 'fly to the desert of Baldjuna' as Howorth[33] believes, and neither was he 'a hopeless fugitive at Baljuna'.

The campaigns against the Tatars and confederate tribes, and the battle of wits and treachery with Wang Khan were neither strange nor of any particular importance in the history of the Gobi, except as illustrating that in inter-tribal conflicts and feuds all means were fair if they achieved the aim; in these there was no sense of honour, which was a normal feature of the unruly nomads' lives; but they were of the greatest service to Chingiz. They put him in touch and closer contact with the tribal chieftains, and enabled him to prove his courage and generalship in the eyes of the best soldiers. The tribal commanders learned to appreciate his true value, and the warriors discovered that the son of Yesukai was a cool and steady leader. When they saw him battle heavy odds and emerge triumphant, they recognized the mettle of the man. In 1194, he was an unknown entity, with no military record to his credit; in 1203 he was an applauded general, a man of courage and power of endurance, a leader whose wisdom, poise and resolution had been tested and acclaimed in arduous campaigns.

Having gained a decisive victory over the Kereits, Chingiz sent envoys to other tribes to demand their submission. Every tribe which submitted, like the Ovirat and the Qinqurat, he incorporated with his own people, and treated it with favour and kindness. But 'those who showed contumacy and refused to submit', says Juwaini, 'he brought under the sword and bled them red by means of the scourges of calamity and the whips of annihilation.' In this manner he succeeded in bringing most of the Mongol tribes under one banner and under his own sway.[34]

This policy of incorporation and integration was a novel experiment which paid good dividends. It impressed Marco Polo, who described it at some length. 'When he conquered a province,' says Marco Polo,[35] 'he did no harm to the people or the property, but merely established some of his own men among them, while he led the remainder to the conquest of other provinces. And when those whom he had conquered became aware how well and safely he protected them against all others, and how they suffered no ill at his hands, and saw what a noble prince he was, then they joined him heart and soul, and became his devoted followers. And when he had thus gathered such a multitude that they seemed to cover the earth, he began to think of conquering a greater part of the world.'

Jamuka and Wang Khan

Facing formidable, almost insurmountable, difficulties Chingiz could have had no cut-and-dried programme. He had a clear conception of the ends he sought to achieve, but the means were determined by the realities of each situation as it arose. Free of scruples, he was always playing for the next stroke. It is not surprising that a marvellous march of events in which each stage seemed to slip into its pre-appointed place, made Chingiz one of the great leaders of the nomadic tribes, at whose beckoning crowns of kings were to roll into the dust.

The rise to power of Chingiz Khan had been looked upon with deep suspicion by the tribes, and attempts were made to stem the tide of his growing strength. His rapid triumph over the Kereits turned the misgivings of his Naiman neighbours into fear. Baibuqa Tayang Khan was alarmed at the news of the discomfiture and death of Wang Khan. He was displeased with the treatment meted out to the venerable and worsted Khan. Tayang Khan's mother Gur Besu, ordered sacrifices to be made to the severed head of Wang Khan. Music was played before it, and the face of the dead Khan seemed to smile, which the assembled people regarded as ominous: the suspicious Tayang Khan crushed the skull with his foot.[36]

'Now even if the dogs bark', protested the veteran Naiman general, Kokseu Saprakh, 'you will read into that an omen. Even your old father once remarked that you have a weak personality and would not be able to safeguard the multitude of his subjects. You are a weakling, and possess no arts or good qualities except hunting and falconry.'

Whatever the truth of this, Tayang Khan was a shrewd judge of men and affairs, and he understood the ambition of Chingiz, who could not be satisfied with the chieftainship of a tribe. 'Is it not that the Mongols aspire to have a supreme Khan? They frightened the old Wang Khan to flee and die outside his country. There can only be one sun in the sky', he had exclaimed, 'How can there be two masters on earth? This is the time to bring them to submission.'

'The Mongols are dull and clumsy and wear dark clothes', said his mother, Gur Besu. 'What useful purpose will it serve to bring them here? Let us keep them at a distance. However, if there be any beautiful women and maids, bring them back. After being taught to bathe, they may serve to milk the cows and goats.' 'Well', said Tayang to his mother, 'that is not difficult. I shall go and deprive them of their bows and arrows.'

'Don't be so proud,' advised the Naiman general, Kokseu Saprakh, who knew the Mongols better. But his advice went unheeded, and Tayang Khan began his preparations for a war against Chingiz. He set about organizing a confederacy, sending an envoy to Alaqush Tigin Quri of the Unqut tribe.[37] Chief of the Unquts,[38] Quri had under him 4,000 tents and guarded the Great Wall against the raids and encroachments of the nomads—Naiman and Mongol. Alaqush was his name, and Tigin Quri his title. Two kings could not exist in one country nor two swords in one scabbard, ran the message; even if he failed to join him, Tayang would cure the malady with the sword himself. The plan was to engage Chingiz in a battle on two fronts.

Alaqush was, however, a sagacious and experienced man, and could discern that Chingiz was the rising sun, Naiman the declining star. Moreover, he was located closer to Mongol Khan, whose battalions might pour any moment into his territory; Baibuqa Tayang Khan was at a remote distance and would not, even if he wished, be able to come to his aid. Besides, he had no stakes in a war between the nomad chieftains to run unnecessary risks; law and order, peace and quiet in the Gobi were not to his advantage: once the hungry nomads had ceased quarrelling among themselves, they would march towards Cathay, ravaging the Ongut territory on their way to and from the Great Wall. If any alliance were desirable with the nomads, self-interest and prudence pointed to Mongol Khan.

'I regret my inability to take charge of your right wing', Alaqush Tigin replied the Naiman Khan; and immediately he despatched one of his chiefs to warn Chingiz about the plans of Tayang Khan.[39]

The envoy met Chingiz at Temiyen-Keyer, where he was out on a hunt. Chingiz held counsel with his chiefs and sons. As it was spring, the horses were lean and thin, and doubts were raised about the wisdom of a campaign at that moment. Yet, if the Naimans were given time to organize a confederacy, the odds would be in their favour. If the Mongols could strike first and give a sudden blow, the conspiracy would be scorched, and they might then deal separately with the hostile tribes. 'Why do you make excuses about your thin horses?' said Daritai Otchigin, who had guessed the impatience of Chingiz, and now wanted to atone for his previous desertion. 'My horses are quite fat. After we have got this information, how can we sit here and wait?' 'What is the use of a man,' said Belgutai, with contempt, 'who lets others deprive him of his bow and arrows? The Naimans have spoken proudly, relying on the expanse of their country and the number of their population. If we surprise them by an attack, we can easily deprive them of their bows and arrows. When we fall suddenly upon them, they will certainly leave behind their horses and abandon their houses to seek shelter in the forests. We should mount and start at once.' Belgutai's plan was, at last, accepted.

Knowing the formidable enemy with whom he was going to deal, Chingiz immediately devoted himself to re-organizing his army. He mustered his troops and, after roll call, reconstituted the men on a decimal basis—into units of thousand, hundreds and tens. In the unit of ten men, the amir commanded the other nine; out of such ten amirs one was appointed amir-i-sadah, commander of the hundred. Similarly, the commander of the thousand was appointed out of the ten commanders of the whole division. This meant that the instructions and orders were to be issued only to the commanders of the thousand to communicate to their immediate subordinates.[40] It gave unity and simplicity to the army organization and secured efficiency with speed. The Mongol troops were no longer a disorderly and disorganized rabble. There was now a chain of command.

With bitter memories of past adventures and experiences, and the recent case of Wang Khan before him, Chingiz took steps against surprise raids and instituted a guard corps, the *keshik*, chosen from 'young men, agile and well-shaped, from the families of Noyans, chiliarchs and centurions, as well as from freemen (*tarkat*).' Eighty warriors were to mount guard at night, seventy soldiers were to serve as attendants. Ogolai 'Cherbi' and Khundus Khalchan were appointed officers of the Khan's personal bodyguard. Arhai Khasar was directed to recruit a thousand fighters 'to stand in the front in battle and serve as bodyguard in peace-time.' The *keshik*, organized on strictly aristocratic basis, were to serve a double purpose: to bind the steppe aristocracy to the person of the Khan and to train and pick out the best for future leadership and imperial service.

Chingiz instructed all the bearers of bows and quivers, the attendant-corps, the body-guards, the masters of provisions, the gate-keepers, etc. to attend to their duties in day time, and to retire at sunset and to hand over the charge of their articles as well as their duties to the night-guards before they left for the night. Those in charge of horses were to keep a constant eye on the animals. The night-guards were to sleep around the tents; the gate-keepers were to stand at the gate. They were to be replaced every three days by turns.[41]

The Naimans and the Merkits

Having made his preparations and reconstituted the army for the great struggle ahead, Chingiz marched against the Naimans. Marching up the river Kerulen, the vanguard under Tebe and Khubilai came into contact with Naiman scouts at Saali-Keyer. The action that ensued showed the Mongols that the enemy was not one that could be trifled with. The Naiman scouts gave the Mongol vanguard a good beating and carried away a prisoner. They could have sent the Mongols flying back to their main army but for the timely arrival of the Mongol army. The Mongol warriors were now wary of an immediate and hasty frontal attack. 'We are inferior to our enemy in number and we have come after a long march', Dodai Cherbi said to Chingiz, 'We should first graze our horses and scatter a sort of dummy force over Saali-Keyer. Let every one of our men lights a fire in five places in the night. Though our enemy is superior in number, it has only an inexperienced weakling as its head. Our device will certainly create doubts among them. When our horses are satiated, we can chase their scouts swiftly, dash straight to their main camp and take them unawares.'

Chingiz consented and the trick was successful. The Naiman scouts were deceived by the innumerable fires which they saw—innumerable as the stars.

They sent a report to Tayang Khan along with the Mongol soldier and his lean horse which they had captured. Tayang Khan[42] concluded that the Mongols were numerically strong but their horses were miserably lean. He sent word to his son Kushluk (Guchluk) advising against precipitate action. 'The horses of the Mongols', he remarked, 'are thin but the starry fixes of their camp indicate that they are numerous. The Mongols are a stubborn and hardy people. They will not close their eye when you touch their eyeballs and will not evade you when you pierce their cheeks. Since their horses are thin, let us break camp and induce them to follow us up to the Altai mountain. Their horses will be thinner while ours will be fat and fit. We shall then turn against them and defeat them.' But like the foolhardy Sengun, Kushluk could not judge the man he was up against. 'How can the Mongols be numerous? Where could they have come from, since the majority are with Jamuka here?'

Kushluk was young, irresponsible, and inexperienced. Yet even experienced men refused to see the merits of the strategy suggested by Tayang Khan. 'Your father, Inancha Belga, had met many a foe like this in old days, but on no occasion did he turn back and expose the backs of his men and the cruppers of his horses to the enemy,' said Ghuli Subechi (Quri Sumajo),[43] who had grown up with him from childhood and was familiar with him. 'Why are you so frightened now? Your father knew your mettle long ago and entrusted the army to your mother, Gur Besu, a woman. Now that Kokseu Saprakh is old, the discipline of our troops has slackened. Your heart is enthralled by your Khatun, and from you the perfume of manhood does not emanate.'

'All of us have the same life that must be taken away by death and the same body that has to bear hardships,' said the enraged Tayang Khan, stung by these taunts. 'Why do you insult me? I have decided now to march into battle against the foes.' And, thus due to lack of that iron discipline and implicit obedience to the chief, which prevailed in the enemy's camp, Tayang Khan was obliged to leave his well-chosen position in the mountains, abandon his sound strategy, and move into the plain to offer battle, where Chingiz was waiting.

Tayang crossed the Orkhon and faced the enemy, who had reformed his lines and was ready for action. Chingiz understood that his enemy was no rabble but an organized confederation of the Durman, Qathgin, Merkit, Ovirat, Jajarat, Tatars, etc., built round the Naiman nucleus. He entrusted the centre to his younger brother, Juji Qassar, the mighty warrior and bowman, while Otchigin took charge of the reserve—an important job in an all-cavalry requirement. When Jamuka saw the disposition and arrangement of Mongol forces, his heart gave way and he concluded that the day was lost. No stickler for lost causes, he gathered his followers and deserted.[44]

Having sounded their horns and kettle-drums, the two armies engaged in battle. In the obstinate struggle that ensued, the Mongol generals, Subutai, Jebe, Qubilai and Jelme distinguished themselves; they charged the enemy like 'wolves chasing the sheep'. The Urut and Mangut clans tore down the resistance of the Naiman troops; even so the troops of the enemy continued the charge and the battle lasted all day. Slowly but steadily the Naimans were pushed back up to the mountain as evening closed in. Tayang Khan was seriously wounded, and his body was so weakened as to be almost without a soul; he retreated to the top of the hill. Though the army was broken and Tayang Khan severely wounded, the Naiman chiefs and amirs still had hopes of recovering the day. Quri Sumajo and others advised Tayang Khan to return to the field for a final charge but he was too ill. Amir Sumajo appealed to him in the name of his wives and their honour. To goad Tayang Khan into action, he flung at him taunts of effeminacy and cowardice, but the old Khan was completely broken. They then decided to fight on their own and carry the struggle to the bitter end rather than see their Khan die before their eyes and be made captives by the enemy. 'Let us show our fidelity to our Khan', they shouted,[45] 'and turn our faces to the enemy.' Like lions they charged at the enemy and fought so valiantly, while life remained in them, as to even gain the praises of their opponents. But they were steadily swept away. Chingiz was impressed by their bravery and courage and wanted them captured alive, but they had sworn to fight to the last, and they inflicted heavy losses on the Mongols as they perished.[46]

Nothing remained for the vanquished but to seek safety in flight; but their retreat was barred by Chingiz, who had ordered his forces to surround the mountain. In the effort they made to get away at night, the Naimans suffered great losses in confusion and chaos—pushing their own men into the abyss and trampling others to death.[47]

The victory was complete. Tayang Khan died of his wounds while his son Kushluk fled to his uncle Bue-Ruq. Their men fled in all directions, leaving multitudes of slain upon the field and roads around. Tribe after tribe, the Durbans, the Qatghins, and the Jadarlan, submitted to the authority of Chingiz. The women of the family of Tayang Khan fell into the hands of the victors. 'You said that the Mongols are dull. How is it then that you have come to me?' asked Chingiz, who enjoyed castigating his enemies when he had the chance. The Naiman females were noted for their beauty, and Chingiz married Gur Besu[48] himself while Kushluk's daughter Liqum Khatun, was given to Tuli in marriage.[49]

With the Kereits annihilated and the Naimans no longer a menace, Chingiz decided to settle old scores with the forest-dwelling Merkits. He marched in autumn of the same year, 1204, against Tuqta Bigi the chief of the Merkits and routed him, but Tuqta and his two sons, Qudu and Chilaun, managed to escape and took asylum with Bue-Ruq. Then Dair Usun presented to Chingiz his beautiful daughter, Qulan; to him as his favourite wife, Chingiz became passionately attached to her and she was to accompany him on his campaign against the Khwarazm Shah. But there was a delay.

'Naya had told us that he was one of the Khan's men,' said Qulan, to explain her three-day stay with Naya and the consequent delay in reaching the Khan's ordu. This enraged the jealous Khan who ordered Naya's execution. 'As there were wandering soldiers, who obstructed our passage, he offered to keep us company. Had we not met him, I do not know what would have happened to us on the way. Torture him not; but with the benevolent permission of my Khan, examine my innocence.' 'With a devoted heart I serve you, my lord,' spoke the doomed Naya. 'It is the humble duty of your servant to bring to you any beautiful maidens and good horses that he comes across. Put me to death if there lurks any intention other than this in my heart.' 'Qulan speaks sense', said Chingiz and was pleased to find her innocent. He was enamoured of her all the more, nor was he less pleased with Naya. 'This man is truthful; he may be trusted with great missions in future.' And on the re-organization of the army at the time of his election as Khaqan, he was appointed commander of the centre.

The wife of Qudu, son of Tuqta, was married to Uktae. Successful and laden with booty, men, women and horses, Chingiz started for his yurt. But drawing nearer home, says Saanang Setzen,[50] he grew timid and reflective. Suddenly he stopped and held a meeting of his generals. 'My first wife Bortei, to whom I was bethrothed in early youth, is the wife and house-mother bestowed upon me by my noble father. In the field, I took to myself Qulan. I now find it hard to present myself to Bortei who awaits me at home. It would be shameful, too, if our meeting in the presence of our newly acquired subjects were to be unfriendly. One of you, then', said the great Conqueror, 'speed in advance to my consort Bortei, and speak to her in my name.'

Surprised were the bold warriors at the trouble which afflicted the Khan, whose word was law, and they were equally embarrassed by the mission assigned to them. Soldiers of fortune, whose eyes did not blink, where swords and spears fell fast and thick, they now seemed to falter. At last Muquli volunteered and relieved the anxiety and distress of his fellow Orloks. He went to Bortei and delivered the Khan's message: 'Beside protecting my own lands, I have also looked around elsewhere. I have not followed the counsel of greater and lesser lords, on the contrary, I have amused myself with the variegated colours of a tent hung with panther skins. I have distant people to rule over and, therefore, have taken Qulan to be my wife', the Khan has sent me to tell you this.[51] The shrewd Bortei understood the meaning of this enigmatic message. For Setzen says: the sensible Bortei thus replied, 'the will of Bortei and of the whole people is that the might of our sovereign may be increased. It is for him to decide with whom he will enter into alliance. Among the weeds are many swans and geese. If it be his wish to shoot arrows at them until his finger be weary, who shall complain? So also there are many girls among our people. It is for him to say who is the choicest. I hope he will take to himself both a new wife and a new house.'

This anecdote is of doubtful authenticity, being mentioned neither by the *Secret History* and Rashid-ud-din nor by Juwaini or any other chronicler. But it throws light on the social life of the Mongols and gives an insight into the softer side of the character of Chingiz, the man of iron will, and his relations with his family.

Thus within eighteen months, Chingiz had struck two decisive blows, which shattered the two most formidable rivals. The year 1203 saw the Kereits completely crushed while in 1204 he had utterly broken the power of the Naimans and the Merkits. Now, all the rivals of Chingiz had been removed but Jamuka Sechen, the arch enemy, sponsor and leading spirit of more than one confederacy against the Mongol. But the defeat of the two coalitions had demoralised the tribes. They were no longer willing to challenge the Mongol. Jamuka was no longer the leader of his tribe: his own people began to desert. Deserted and forsaken by all, the one-time Gur Khan had been reduced to the position of a brigand with five followers. Time and circumstance alienated even these men and, seizing him one day, they brought him to his mortal enemy. 'The black crows have snatched the duck,' Jamuka sent a message to Chingiz, 'the slaves have seized their master.' 'Those who have dared to betray their own master can scarcely be faithful to any one else', said Chingiz, who was always harsh to traitors. 'They should not be left unpunished. Execute them with their sons and grandsons.' And they were to be executed first and in the presence of Jamuka, a befitting nemesis for their treachery.

Jamuka met his end heroically. He was handed over to a nephew of Chingiz with orders to put him to slow death—the Chinese method of torture of cutting off one limb after another and thus destroying the victim. Jamuka bore it unflinchingly and even advised the executioners how to proceed. He observed that if fortune had favoured him and Chingiz had fallen in his power, he would have treated him in the same manner.[52]

But Chingiz was not done with the Merkits yet. They had been beaten but not crushed. The embers of undying hatred for Chingiz still glowed in their hearts and no sooner had he started for his yurt that under Dair Usun they rose in arms and plundered the Mongols who had remained behind. A strong force was despatched to deal with them. The Merkits were once again defeated and scattered. Dair Usun was captured and sent to Chingiz, who was on his march against Tangut or Qashin.[53]

Master of northern Mongolia and no longer worried by formidable enemies in the rear or on his flanks, Chingiz turned towards Tangut: a rich hunting ground for booty, full of cities, fortresses, and fine buildings. Having reached Tangut the Mongols stormed the strong fortress of Liki and levelled it. Lungsi-hien was next to receive the Mongol onslaught. It was a big city, well defended, but fell. Having plundered the greater part of the country, Chingiz returned in triumph to his own yurt laden with immense booty in 1205.[54]

Notes

1. For a pen-portrait by Minhaj-i-Siraj, see *Tabaqat-i-Nasiri*, p. 373.
2. Identified with Chegel Tayin.
3. Khwandmir, *Habib al-Siyar*, (hereafter referred as *Habib al-Siyar*), vol. I, part III, p. 8. Mirkhwand, *Rauzat-us-Safa*, (henceforth referred as *Rauzat-us-Safa*), vol. V, pp. 11-12.
4. Sharfuddin, *Zafarnama*, fol. 58; *Rauzat-us-Safa*, vol. V, p. 11.
5. Ibid., fol. 58; ibid., vol. V, p. 11.
6. *Rauzat-us-Safa*, vol. V, p. 11.
7. Juwaini, vol. I, p. 26.
8. *Rauzat-us-Safa*, vol. V, p. 11.
9. Ibid.
10. Ibid.
11. Ibid., pp. 11-12.
12. Juwaini, vol. I, p. 26.
13. Rashid-ud-din, fol. 38.
14. Juwaini, vol. I, pp. 536-7.
15. Ibid., pp. 57, 37.
16. Ibid., p. 37.

17. *Shajratul Atrak*, pp. 67-8.

18. Ibid., p. 69.

19. Ibid., *Rauzat-us-Safa*, vol. V, p. 12.

20. *Shajratul Atrak*, pp. 68-9; *Rauzat-us-Safa*, vol. V, p. 12.

21. Juwaini, vol. I, p. 37; *Rauzat-us-Safa*, vol. V, p. 12.

22. *Rauzat-us-Safa*, vol. V, p. 12.

23. The work of plaiting sheep's tails and curls was looked down upon by the Mongols.

24. Juwaini, vol. I, p. 37; Sharfuddin, fol. 60; *Rauzat-us-Safa*, vol. V, p. 12.

25. Sharfuddin, fol. 61.

26. Sharfuddin, fol. 61; *Rauzat-us-Safa*, vol. V, p. 12; *Shajratul Atrak*, p. 72. The earlier authorities are silent about Qarachar's great feat on the battlefield.

27. *Rauzat-us-Safa*, p. 13; *Shajratul Atrak*, pp. 71-2.

28. *Shajratul Atrak*, p. 69; Sharfuddin, fol. 60. The earlier authorities again fail to credit the illustrious ancestor of the Timurids with any such role.

29. Juwaini, vol. I, p. 37.

30. Ibid., pp. 37-8; Sharfuddin, fol. 60; *Rauzat-us-Safa*, vol. V, p. 12.

31. Juwaini, vol. I, p. 38.

32. *Shajratul Atrak*, pp. 69-70.

33. Howorth, part I, p. 59.

34. Juwaini, vol. I, p. 38; *Rauzat-us-Safa*, vol. V, pp. 12-13.

35. *Travels*, pp. 118-19.

36. *Rauzat-us-Safa*, vol. V, p. 13.

37. Rashid-ud-din, fol. 20.

38. Rashid-ud-din, fol. 22.

39. Rashid-ud-din, fol. 20.

40. Juwaini, vol. I, pp. 32-3.

41. Ibid.

42. *Rauzat-us-Safa*, vol. V, p. 13.

43. Ibid.

44. Ibid.

45. Ibid., p. 14.

46. Ibid.

47. Ibid., pp. 13-14.

48. Gur Besu is referred to both as Tayang's wife and mother. As, after Tayang's defeat, she was taken by Chingiz as wife, it may safely be inferred that she was young and had the charm and graces for which the Naiman women were famous. The apparent contradiction of her being Tayang's wife and mother may be resolved by a reference to the old tribal custom of a son marrying his stepmother. 'I am old now.' Tayang's father is reported to have said about Gur Besu; 'this woman is still young,' and Tayang should have married his young stepmother when he succeeded to his patrimony. (*Secret History*, p. 68).

49. *Rauzat-us-Safa*, vol. V, p. 14.
50. Quoted by Prawdin, pp. 61-2; Howorth, vol. I, pp. 57-8.
51. Saanang Setzen quoted by Howorth, vol. I, pp. 57-8; Prawdin, pp. 61-2.
52. *Rauzat-us-Safa*, vol. V, p. 14.
53. *Shajratul Atrak*, p. 78. Qashin or Tangut of the Persian historians is the Hsi-Hsia of the Chinese. It was also called Tangut. Hsi-Hsia was re-named Qashin to commemorate Chingiz Khan's successful campaign against Hsi-Hsia. Qashin was also the name of the capital of the country where, according to Raverty, 'the great *caravans* of traders met from the west and south in their trade with *Khita* or China. It was a very rich city, and the abode of learned men (Raverty, p. 950, note). One of the sons of Uktae was named Qashi but whether the boy, as Raverty asserts, gave his name to the place, is not certain. It is also probable that the boy was named after the place.
54. *Rauzat-us-Safa*, vol. V, p. 14.

3

Consolidation

$\mathcal{T}$HE MONGOL TEMUCHIN of the race of the Kiutata has, on the banks river Onon, declared himself Khaqan (Emperor). Thus, in these words, the Chinese Imperial Annals[1] recorded in 1206 one of the most significant events in the life and history of the nomads. 'All is quiet in the distant lands' is the second entry about Chingiz in the Annals, being made twelve years earlier in the year 1194 when he was made Warden of the Marches in appreciation of his services against the Tatars.

Having destroyed his rivals Chingiz became the lord of the tribes in the region between the river Irtish and the Khingan mountains. Now he summoned a qurlitai or great assembly of the tribes in subjection to him. The qurlitai met at Saman Kahrah at the source of the Onon in February 1206 and was attended amongst others by his sons, his noyans and all army generals and captains. There Chingiz set up a white standard consisting of nine tails, and held a great feast.[2]

Chingiz had summoned the qurlitai for a definite purpose—the election of a supreme Khan or Khan of Khans. He could have very well declared himself so, but preferred to humour the chieftains and to observe the tribal traditions, which required an election. There was no question of a real election and the assembly had been called as a formality to endorse the leadership of Chingiz.

'If you wish me to be your ruler', asked Chingiz, 'are you without exception resolved to fulfil all my orders? To come when I summon you, to go wherever I may command you and to slay whoever I may indicate?' The chiefs solemnly promised to obey him under all conditions.[3]

'A person of red colour, seated on a grey horse, appeared unto me (in a dream) and said: "Go thou to the son of Yesukai and say that henceforward he shall not be called Temuchin any more; in future, his title shall be 'Chingiz Khan',[4] said Kokchu,[5] the shaman. Shamans, as communicators with the spirits who knew the secrets of the future, and often went to consult them on a white horse, were held in veneration by the superstitious Mongols. Kokchu was reputed to spend his time in devotion and, wandering in a state of nudity, not affected by heat and cold. It was said that he used to fast and sit naked in the snow until, from the change in the temperature, the snow melted and was converted into steam. He was called *Teb-Tengri* or the Trusted or Chosen of Heaven.[6] He was Munlik's son and probably at his father's behest had stepped forward and announced heavenly blessings and approval for the new *Khaqan*. Munlik, who was now Chingiz's stepfather, did this perhaps to atone for his desertion. Chingiz did not believe in the claims of the Shaman but allowed Kokchu to impress their minds in his favour.[7]

'If Heaven preserves me and helps me, all of you, my old friends, will ultimately become my happy companions', was the promise Chingiz had made to his people on his first election as Khan and he remembered it. Now as Khan of Khans, he decided to reward them for their loyalty. 'Let all those who have helped me, be rewarded for their services and loyalty to me,' he said. 'What extraordinary services have Bogurchi, Muquli and others rendered to you that call for further rewards?' asked Shigi Qutuqu, the scion of a Tatar chief, who had been made a captive in his youth, and wore a golden ring in his nose and a stomach-belt lined with golden tassels and sable. He had been adopted by Oyelun as her sixth son and since then had remained in the family. 'Now what reward are you ready to offer me?' 'You are my sixth brother', said the indulgent Khan. 'You shall have an equal share with all my younger brothers and you will not be punished for the first nine crimes you commit. You will also act as the supreme judge of my people.' 'I am the youngest of your brothers. I dare not take an equal share', said Shigi Qutuqu. 'I shall be satisfied if you give me all the people who live in the mud city.' Shigi Qutuqu went to summon others to receive their rewards.

The first to be rewarded was Munlik, who had married Oyelun and whose son was the shaman Kokchu. 'Without your protection and advice', said Chingiz, 'I would have fallen into the trap that Wang Khan and his sons had set for me. I have always been grateful to you for this and my sons and grandsons will also remember the debt. Henceforth, seated in that corner, you will receive all monthly gifts, and your descendants will also enjoy the same privileges.'

Next he turned to Bogurchi, the friend and companion of his youth who had helped him recover his stolen horses. The only son of a well-to-do father, Bogurchi had left home without informing his father when Chingiz requested him to join his yurt. 'You bore the same hardships as I did', said the Great Khan. 'In the battle against the Tatars at Dalan Nimurgas when it rained at night, you wore a shawl, and stood by me while I slept, to shelter me from the rain so that I could rest till dawn: *you did not change your position except once*. Such have been your most heroic deeds and I need not enumerate the rest. Furthermore, you and Muquli together have advised me on all that should have been done, and prevented me from doing anything reckless. But for this, I would not have attained my throne. Now your seat will be above others in order of precedence, and you may commit nine crimes unpunished. I appoint you Commander of Ten Thousand Families in the country extending westward from here to the Altai mountains.' Thus was Muquli made the ruler of a Khanate, the rulership to be inherited by his descendants. And Naya, who had proved himself worthy of trust and had escorted the Khan's young and beautiful wife, Qulan to his yurt in safety was made the Commander Ten Thousand Families of the centre.

'You spoke the words of revelation when I was young,' Chingiz said to Qorchi. 'You have also accompanied me through all hardships. You said then that if the prophecy was realized, you should be permitted to choose thirty wives. Now, you can select *thirty beauties from among the women and girls of the subject peoples*. All the land along the river Irdish will be your camping ground and the people of the forest near the river will also come under your control. You will defend their country and dispense justice among them. Those who disobey you will be punished.'

Next he turned to Jurchidai, hero of many battles. It was he, who had charged the centre of Wang Khan's army and shot Sengun in the cheek. 'I do not know', said Chingiz,[8] 'what would have happened if that arrow had missed him. When Jakhaganbu who had sought safety for his people by presenting his two daughters revolted after the defeat and dispersion of the Naimans and the Merkits, I owed much to your design in recapturing him and his people. The four thousand men of the Uruts will be under your administration and in recognition of your meritorious services I give you *my own wife*, Lady Ibaha [also spelt Ibaqa]' 'It is not because I dislike your character that I am not keeping you among my other wives,' he had explained to Ibaha, 'My desire is to give you as an extraordinary award to one who has collected my wandering people and brought them back to me. My successors will recognize the reason that calls for such a reward. Your descendants will inherit all your titles. Your father gave me Ashi Timur, the master of provisions, along with two hundred men as your dowry. Now that you are to leave me, let half of them, including Ashi Timur, stay with me as a token of love.'

For vigilance and devotion to his duties Qunan, the personal attendant of the Khan, was appointed leader of the Kenikes tribes and Commander of Ten Thousand Families under Juji. Tolun, the son of Munlik, received the title of Cherbi and was made ruler of the people he had collected and Commander of One Thousand Families under Tuli, the youngest son of Chingiz Khan. Wangur, the master of provisions, was allowed to collect his kin and to also was made a Commander of One Thousand Families. Along with Boloul and Tolun, he was placed in charge of feasts and provisions. 'Steward Wangur (Ouggur) and Boloul' said Chingiz Khan, 'Both of you may ride to the gatherings and distribute the provisions. When there is feast, you two are to sit separately on the left and the right, together with Tolun facing the north, while distributing the provisions.'

'You have tamed many stiff-necked and stubborn persons', he said turning towards Qubilai.[9] 'Along with Jelme, Jebe, and Subutai, you form my four brave warniors. Wherever I order you to go, you will smash the hard stone, break the heavy rock and cross the deep water. In battle I constitute you four as my vanguard; Bogurchi, Muquli, Boloul and Chilaun, my four great warriors, stand beside me; Jurchidai and Quildar stand in front of me. So I have nothing to worry about. Henceforth, Qubilai, you shall be the seniormost man in military affairs. You complained about Beduun being obstinate, so he has not so far been made a Commander of One Thousand Families. Now you and he shall be joint Commanders of One Thousand Families and you shall consult each other before taking action. I shall take note how he fares in future.'

'My mother', said Chingiz to Boloul (Boroqul), 'had adopted you and Shigi Qutuqu, Guchu, and Kokchu, four sons picked up from enemy camps and reared you; she meant that you and her own sons would keep good company. You have accompanied me in all perilous battles; you have never let us pass a night in battle on an empty stomach. Your wife, Altani, saved the life of my son Tuli when the Tatar Khargil Shira had tried to kill him. At Khalkhaljit when I was in battle against Wang Khan, you, Boloul, saved Uktae's life by sucking the clotted blood from the arrow wound on his neck. You have certainly repaid my mother's kindness to you by saving the life of my two sons. You have never slackened in determination to serve me at all difficult times. You are, therefore, exempted nine times from punishment of any crimes you may commit.'

Jelme was exempted punishment for nine crimes while Narin Toghril was rewarded for the services his father had rendered to Chingiz Khan and had died at the hands of Jamuka at the battle of Dalan Baljut.

'What reward do you want?' Chingiz asked Surghan Shira and his sons, who had joined him only lately and whose kindness, when he was a captive of the Taichiuts, he had never forgotten. They expressed a desire for the land of the Merkits along the river Selenga to be their grazing ground, which was readily granted. 'And your descendants', added Chingiz, 'will be given the privilege of wearing their bows and quivers at feasts and they will also be exempt from punishment for nine crimes.' 'Whenever you are in need of anything', he said turning Surghan Shira's sons, Chilun and Chenbe, 'you may come and ask for it yourselves.'

As Jebe and Subutai had no subjects or vassals of their own they were made Commanders of One Thousand Families and were to rule over the people they had collected. Similarly, the Shepherd Degai was commissioned to collect the unattached and unregistered people and also become a Commander of One Thousand Families.

Unparalleled and unique was the scene, rich and sumptuous was the feast, and lavish and generous were the awards, but one thing was apparent; the Khan would have no favourites. Many like Batai and the Tarkhans had, of course, the right of entry to his tent at all times, but they influenced him no more than the others. He would keep the reins of governance in his own hands, and he allowed himself to be advised but not overruled. This singleness of purpose and iron determination accounts for his rise and success and for the strong discipline which distinguished his followers. Terrible as he was, however, he was, not an unattractive nomad chieftain. If he was hard and cruel to rebels and enemies, he judged his men accurately and rewarded them generously. The geniality with which he conversed with his distinguished followers and the amazing frankness with which he recounted their services and his indebtedness to them, draws our admiration. Such admissions reveal his self-confidence too.

After a ceaseless struggle of a decade, the majority of the nomad chieftains had sworn allegiance to Chingiz. He started as a wandering fighter and now the leader of all those who dwelt in felt tents. It looked as if he knew that his hold and command over the unruly nomads chieftains rested on a utilitarian basis. He had their reason, a sense of their interests, their needs and, for the time being, their enthusiasm. For he must have thrilled the heart of the ferocious nomads. Now the prospect of dominion over China would have served to inflame their ambition. He had before his eyes the experience of centuries and the story of nomadic empires, and was determined that his own would not go the way of the Huns, Hiung-un, the Sien-Pi, the Jen-Jena and the Uighurs. And he very well realized that loyalty had no meaning for the horse-riding, flesh-eating and arrow-shooting nomads; they were loyal only to themselves and to their own interests. Once the strong hand was removed, the headstrong and unruly nomads would begin to assert themselves again. The grouping and melting away of the tribes was a common occurrence in the history of the steppes. Chingiz Khan wanted something more durable, an empire which would endure.

Chingiz decided to revive the ancient tribal name of the Mongols and to organize his subjects so as to weld them into one imperial organization. Like the early Abbasids he sought security in an imperial organization that appointed to posts of profit and power, the tried and tested warriors who owed everything to him. But he was wise enough not to disturb the old clan organization by foisting alien chiefs upon them; he appointed their new leaders from amongst those whom they would trust but who were willing to live and die for him. This policy secured the reconciliation of the tribes and the consolidation of his conquests and enabled him to prepare for new struggles and conquests.

Chingiz appreciated the influence which superstition exercised over his hardy and unsophisticated people. 'The Tengri', announced the shaman Kokchu[10] to the superstitious nomads, has spoken to me and said, 'I have bestowed the whole earth upon Temuchin and his descendants. Give him the name of Chingiz Khan.' And they believed what he said. Superstition and terror gripped them, for in his achievements and miraculous exploits they now saw the assistance of the Spirits and the hand of God. 'Heaven has ordered me to govern all people,' he said. 'With the protection and help of the Tengri, I defeated the Kereits and attained the supreme rank.'

Now Khan of Khans, Chingiz decided to harness the influence of the priests: he created the post of *beki* (Begi) or State Shaman. To this post he appointed the old Usun, who belonged to the senior branch of the descendants of Buzanjar. '*Beki* is a high rank', said Chingiz.[11] 'Usun, You are the eldest descendant of Bacrin, you must be the *beki;* as a *beki*, you shall ride a white horse, dress in white clothes, and in every company take the first place; it shall be your duty to find out which year and which moon is auspicious.'

If the pronouncements of heavenly blessings by the Shaman upon the new Khan, and the unity of religion and state which Chingiz achieved by institutionalizing the post of *beki*, grouped and united the nomads into a solid body, Chingiz Khan made it a living organism by infusing into the people his indomitable spirit. The Mongols believed, that they were born to rule the world but so far had been denied their birthright. Had not the gods spoken to them, through the shaman, of their destiny to lord over and 'govern all peoples.' The ethnonym 'Mongol' with its legends and imperial memories, went back to the days of Alan Quwa, Aghuz Khan, and Kabul Khan. Tribes and clans who had nothing to do with the Mongols or even had been on hostile relations with Chingiz, now began to adopt the appellation of Mongol. 'Owing to the greatness of Chingiz Khan and of his clan says Rashid-ud-din,[12] 'the other Turkish tribes, each of which had a distinct name and appellation of its own, have begun to call themselves Mongol.'

Chingiz was, however, not content with conquests; he aspired to an empire that he could bequeath to future generations. No conqueror was ever brought into more difficult and delicate relations with the conquered than the Great Mongol Khan. He had to govern and hold peoples, who prized their independence above life. Had they all combined their forces, it is probable that there would have been no Chingiz Khan and no Mongol Empire. Fortunately for him, they had remained divided and Chingiz played them one against the other, and conquered them one after the other. Moreover, the wise policy of conciliation and consolidation, following upon his triumphs in war, had done much to win the tribes over to his side.

Chingiz knew the treacherous nomads too well: their loyalty was at best doubtful. As Babur was to say,

> Were the Mongols a race of angels, it would still be a vile nation
> Was their name written in gold, it would still be abomination,
> Beware you pluck not a single ear from a Mongol field,
> For whatever is sown with Mongol seed has an odious yield.

The first step for Chingiz was to maintain a sufficient standing army to overawe each separate source of insurrection. He could indeed rely upon the loyal chieftains in his campaigns against the Kins and the Sungs to plunder prosperous Chinese towns. He could trust his subsidiary chiefs and allies along with his own officers in a conflict with the Qara Khitais or Tanguts. But he needed a body of retainers who would look to him for rank and wealth and even the bare means of subsistence.

In 1203 Chingiz Khan had organized his bodyguard of 80 men for night guard and 70 for duty in the day. The guard consisted of archers (*Korchi*), table-deckers (*bawarchi*), doorkeepers (*egudenchi*), and grooms (*akhtachi*). There were also the six *cherbis* who managed the Khan's household while 'one thousand *Bahadurs*' constituted his personal guard; they served as the advance guard in battle and court guards in peace. The Guard had done its work well and he decided to increase its strength and constitute it as the nucleus of his fighting force—like the Guard of Napoleon. But it was to be organized as an aristocratic body; only men of noble blood were to have the privilege of being enrolled in it. 'Now that Heaven has ordered all the nations to be put under my rule, let ten thousand persons from among the people under the Commanders of Ten Thousand, One Thousand, and One Hundred Families, choosing only agile and well-shaped youths from the sons of dignitaries and freemen, be my guard.' The son of a Commander of a Thousand Families was allowed to bring along a younger brother and ten attendants; they were to make their own arrangements as far as horses and equipment were concerned. The son of a Commander of One Hundred Families could bring a younger brother and five attendants while the sons of an officer of ten families and free men (*Tarkat*) were allowed the company of a younger brother and three attendants each. Considering their meagre resources, their attendants were equipped and given horses by the Khan.

To accord with the dignity of the emperor of the steppe 'decreed by Heaven to rule and govern the whole earth', and also in anticipation of the dangerous tasks which lay ahead, the strength of the Guard was raised to a *tuman* or ten thousand. It contained, as before, an 'attendant corps', now increased to one thousand under the command of Ogolai Cherbi, and the archers, now a thousand strong, who were led by Yesun Teye. The six new regiments of a thousand each were captained by tried and tested soldiers— Boghulkhu; Buqa, a cousin of Muquli, Alchidai, Dodai Cherbi; Chanai, a cousin of Jurchidai, and Akhutai. Arhai Qasar was the leader of 'The Thousand Heros', who formed the advance guard in battle and served as court-guard during peace time. 'These guardsmen of mine,' said Chingiz Khan 'will henceforth be called the Great Central Army.'

Dodai Cherbi was in supreme command of the Guard and under his control and directions were the attendants and members of the royal household. On the march, the Korchi and Turgewuls remained on the right side of the Khan's tent while the remaining 7,000 marched on the left side and Arhai's Bahadurs walked in front. Along with them also marched the assistants of the Chief Judge, Shigi Qutuqu, the collectors and distributors of bows, arrows and weapons, the grooms of the official horses, the guardsmen and the Cherbis who were in charge of the distribution of silks. All these special servicemen were to march on the right side while those who were in charge of the tent and carts could march on all three sides.

The night guard consisted of four companies under Buqa, Alchidai, Dodai Cherbi, and Doghulku. The companies were led on duty by their captains in person and remained on duty, by turn, for three nights. 'The archers and the masters of provisions must attend to their duties in the day time,' said Chingiz, 'at sunset they must hand their bows, quivers, utensils, and covers to the night guard before they go to rest for the night. Next morning when hot water is taken in, they must return to their respective duties. If the night guard around my tent catches any one passing by it at night, they must bring the prisoner next morning to me for interrogation. The night guards who come for their turn of duty must show their passes before they enter. The gatekeeper may break the head or shoulder of anyone who attempts to enter my tent at night. Anyone who has to see me on urgent business must first see the night guard and he may enter my tent with them to report to me. No outsider is to be allowed to sit in the two rooms of the night guard.' The night guard, moreover, had to take charge of the rooms, carts, banners, cooked food, covers, utensils, etc., they were held responsible if anything was lost or was unaccounted for. They controlled and supervised the distribution of robes and food. They were to check and challenge all who entered or left the Khan's tent and, to avoid needless delay and vexation, were required to know the overseer of the domestic staff and cattle-herds of his tent. 'The gatekeeper', it was laid down, 'shall stand close to the gate. The two butlers inside the door and the superintendent of the camp will be selected from the guards.' Thus the Guard had to perform multifarious duties. They formed the household of the Khan.

Discipline was stern and rigid. Defaulters and absentees were given thirty strokes for the first offence, seventy for the second, and the third time they were given thirty-seven strokes, expelled, and exiled to a distant place. The officers were required to recite the rules to their men before they came on duty and also to inform them of their turns so as to give them no excuse for errors. Strict secrecy was enjoined about the number of guards on duty and the dates and turns. No one was allowed to make such inquiries, none to give such information. Violation of this rule led to the confiscation of the offender's horses, saddles, and clothes—a severe punishment for a nomad.

The Guard, at the same time, enjoyed great privileges. 'A personal guardsman of mine,' said the Khan, 'is superior to an ordinary Commander of One Thousand, and an attendant of his, superior to an ordinary Commander of Ten or Hundred. If an ordinary Commander of One Thousand attempts to dispute or fight with a guardsman of mine on equal terms, he will be punished.' More than that, the guardsmen were not under the disciplinary control of their own captains and commanders; the Khan had a close watch on them and took personal cognizance of their actions. Breach of discipline or infraction of duty were to be reported to the Khan and decided by him. 'Let any breach of the rule on the part of the men be reported to me. Those who deserve execution, will be executed, and those who deserve thrashing will be thrashed; but if the officer in charge beats his men, he will be beaten in the same manner as a punishment.' The Guard participated in an expedition only if the Khan undertook the campaign in person. And even if only some guardsmen were sent on some campaigns the Khan retained his personal control and supervision over them. 'If any one disobeys you,' said the Iron Khan to Subutai when sending him on a campaign, 'if he is a man I know personally, bring him to be tried by me; if he is not, execute him on the spot.'

The old guardsmen enjoyed a higher rank and esteem than the rest of the army.[13] 'Guardsmen of the night-watch!', said Chingiz Khan. 'You have kept my body and mind at peace. You have guarded my tent on calm and clear nights and on stormy and tumultuous ones as well. You have never caused any delay in urgent business and I greatly owe the attainment of this seat of dignity to your diligence. Henceforth the faithful night guard is to be called the "Old Night Guard", Ogolai Cherbi's seventy attendants the "Old Attendants", Arhai's Bahadurs the "Old Bahadurs"; and Yesun Teye with other archers the "Old Archers". My descendants will remember the service of these guardsmen. Treat them with honour and give them no cause for resentment: and regard them as your good genii.'

The Great Wall and the Golden Khan

In 1207 Chingiz decided to weed out the last remnants of Merkit and Naiman opposition now allied under the leadership of Bue-Ruq. This was the brother of Tayang Khan, and it was to him that Kushluk and Tuqta Begi, the Merkit chief, had fled for shelter. Bue-Ruq had not in the meanwhile been idle; he knew what he was up against and prepared to face the Mongol storm. He was, however, stupefied by the Mongols in the neighbourhood of Ulugh Tagh (Urtu-ola of the Chinese) near the river Suja, where he was hunting. The surprise was complete; Bue-Ruq was captured and killed while his followers dispersed in all directions. Tuqta Bigi and Kushluk, however, managed to escape. They fled towards the region watered by the Irtish but, to avoid hot pursuit, directed their adherents to disperse and rejoin later.[14]

As Chingiz Khan was now near the frontiers of Tangut, he determined to chastise its ruler, Shidarqu, for the non-payment of tribute; the expedition was a complete success. Wuhlahai was captured and so too the capital, Qashin. Shidarqu, thereupon, deemed it prudent to submit to and pacify the Mongol Khan by agreeing to pay tribute. He also submitted to the occupation of his capital by Mongol troops.[15] Next was the turn of the Qir-Qiz Chief, Urus Inal, to receive the summons to submit to the Mongol Khan. Being in no position to offer resistance, he complied.

Meanwhile, Tuqta Bigi and Kushluk had acquired considerable strength, but their activities were not unknown to the Mongol Khan. And as he realized that these chiefs constituted a threat to the security of his frontiers, he decided to set out against them in person. The magnitude of the danger is revealed by the fact that he set out with a vast army in winter when the cold was intense and the water was frozen. On the way, he came across the Ovirats, who readily submitted and guided his troops on to the camp of Kushluk and Tuqta Bigi. The Naimans and the Merkits were overwhelmed by superior numbers, and Tuqta was killed by an arrow shot by a Kunkoor archer.[16] An attempt was made by Qodu, the brother of Tuqta, and the latter's three sons, to carry off his body but, with the Mongols after them, they cut off his head and carried it with them. With Kushluk they fled into the land of the Uighurs, and despatched a messenger to the Idiqut asking for asylum. The Idiqut was, however, a shrewd judge of men and affairs, and decided to have no truck with the fugitives. He slew their agent and marched out to expel them from his territories.[17]

The year 1209 was thus a happy and auspicious year, beginning with the expedition against the Merkits and Kushluk, and concluding with the bloodless extension of Chingiz's rule over the Uighurs. The Uighurs are famous as the most devoted to learning of all Turkish tribes; from them the Mongols received the alphabet and their earliest instruction. 'Idiqut', according to Juwaini,[18] signifies 'The Lord of Power,' and, at this time, Barjuq was the Idiqut. He was a tributary of the Gurkhan of Qara-Khitai, whose Shahna, Shawkam by name, resided in Qara-Khwaja. Shawkam was, however, short-sighted and arrogant, and his extortions enraged the Idiqut, his amirs and even the *raiyyats*. When Mongol victories sent panic throughout Central Asia, Barjuq cast his lot with the all-conquering leader of the Mongols; and Shawkam was killed on his orders. Shawkam, in the words of Juwaini, 'was surrounded in a house that they pulled on top of him.' He renounced his allegiance to the Gurkhan, and sent to Chingiz Khan an embassy. 'When I heard the renowned name of your Majesty,' ran the Idiqut's message, [19] 'I felt as happy as if I had seen the sunlight piercing the clouds or water melting out of ice. If you kindly permit, I will undertake to be your fifth son and serve you to the best of my capacity.' Chingiz was pleased by this offer of voluntary submission and treated the Uighur envoys with favour and distinction. On their return he despatched with them his own envoys, perhaps to fathom the real intentions of the Idiqut and examine his resources. They conveyed the necessary assurances on behalf of the Khan and also his demand that the Idiqut should offer his submission in person.

The Idiqut was satisfied and set out to offer his submission in person. Chingiz Khan, meanwhile had to lead a punitive expedition against Shidarqu, who submitted once again and is said to have sent his daughter to be wed to Chingiz. When Chingiz Khan returned home in triumph, he found Arslan Khan and the Idiqut waiting to render him homage. The Idiqut was rich and had brought costly presents for the Khan. He returned loaded with favours and honours. He rendered assistance in the campaigns against Kushluk, the Khwarazm Shah, and Shidarqu.[20] Arslan Khan was the chief of the Qarluqs and the seat of his authority was Qiyaligh. Rubruck names it Koylak and says it was a great trading centre in his time and had three idol temples, the doors of which were always open to the south. Like the Idiqut of the Uighurs, Arslan also turned to Chingiz Khan for protection. Chingiz honoured him by giving him a daughter in marriage.

All these events secured the position of Chingiz as the overlord of the Gobi. There was now no one to challenge his dominion. Groups of people, or tribes, might rebel here and there, but there was no person to stop him. He now resolved to settle scores with his Chinese neighbours. The nomads of the Gobi had always cast covetous eyes on the wealth and women of China. Their relations with China were old and can be summarized as raid and trade. For the shaggy nomads of the steppes, China was the land of splendour, the cradle of luxury, the entrepot for necessities. With consummate skill and great dexterity, the Chinese rulers had thwarted all their attempts to unite and unify. The Great Wall was built to guard the flourishing towns and cities which excited the curiosity and cupidity of the 'barbarians'. It was in pursuance of the same policy of divide and control that Kabul Khan had been poisoned, and Hamanka and Ukin Barqaq nailed on the cross.

Chingiz knew, because of the trade that China was formidable; he was well aware of the state of affairs there, and gained knowledge of the roads across the Great Wall, the location of fortresses, and the disposition of troops. To strengthen morale Chingiz sought to make his Chinese expedition a campaign of vengeance for past injuries. He recounted to his officers and counsellors the cruelty of the Chinese to his ancestors and harangued them about the wrongs the nomads had suffered at the hands of the Chinese. The Tengri had now chosen him and assured him of victory against his enemies.[21]

Before setting out on his great enterprise, Chingiz sent an envoy to the 'Son of Heaven' to demand peace on his own terms. The task of the envoy was unenviable, for he was to intimate to the Chinese monarch the unpalatable news of the unification of the nomadic tribes under the suzerainty of Chingiz Khan. Nothing could be more galling to the Chinese monarch than to be so addressed by the chief of the shaggy nomads, whom they had heretofore looked upon with scorn and contempt; and nothing could risk the life of an envoy more than the communication of such a message. Moreover, the envoy had also to obtain first-hand knowledge of China. The mission was perilous, the task delicate. With his unfailing judgement of men, Chingiz picked an old attendant, Khwaja Jafar[22] by name. He was shrewd, cultured, and noted for his eloquence.

'It has come to thy knowledge that we, by Heaven's favour, have been chosen from among all the Mongols to hold the reins of Empire and guidance', ran the message of Chingiz Khan to the Kin Emperor.[23] 'The fame of our conquering host, which is resounding in all cities and countries, must have reached your ears. During the course of our conquering career, those who were fortunate submitted to us without delay and became our allies, and received our grace and favours. But those who attempted to rise and resist us, their houses, goods, property, and dependants were wiped out. Praise and honour to High Heaven, our dominion is so well ordered that we can visit Cathay. We are now starting for Cathay with an army which is like a roaring ocean and we can meet enmity or friendship with the same tranquil feeling. If the Golden Khan in his wisdom selects the way of friendship and concord, and fully welcomes us, we will confirm him in the government of Cathay. If he cannot come himself, let him send presents and his honoured sons to us. But Heaven forbid, should be resist, he would go the way of the others.'

The message offered no basis for any settlement compatible with the dignity and legendary claims of the Golden Khan. The Golden Khan was furious and sent the Khwaja back with an equally insulting answer. Khwaja Jafar had, however, carried out the necessary investigations about roads, routes, and the military preparedness of Cathay.[24]

Meanwhile, Chingiz Khan had not remained idle. He arrived at an understanding with the Khitan chief, Yehieu Liuko. The alliance was solemnized by the breaking of an arrow and the sacrifice of a white horse and a black ox, which signified the determination of the contracting parties to stand together. The Khitan chief undertook to assist the Mongols in their campaign against the Kin while the Mongol Khan promised to restore him to the sovereignty of Liauting.

Spring had set in, and it was now time for the Mongol Khan to start on his great expedition. Chingiz decided to whip up the morale and intensify

the self-confidence of his warriors by invoking the blessings and assistance of
the Tengri.[25] The Mongol families were directed to assemble at the base of
the mountain and it was enjoined that men be separated from women, children
from their mothers; and, says Qazi Minhaj,[26] 'for three whole days and nights,
all of them remained bare-headed; and for three days no one tasted food and
no animal was allowed to give milk to its young. Chingiz then entered the
tent for three nights and day; and, during this period, all the people assembled
there were crying out, Tengri! Tengri!' At dawn, on the fourth day, Chingiz
Khan came out of his tent and announced to the eager and credulous populace
that Tengri had been gracious to grant him victory against their ancient
oppressors. For three days, the Mongols feasted and, on the fourth day, the
avalanche moved on towards the land of culture and song. Yamah Noyan and
Guiguik led the vanguard while a contingent of 10,000 soldiers, under
Toghachar was left behind to guard the Khan's hearth and home and keep the
conquered tribes quiet.[27]

On receiving news of the advance of the Mongol hosts, the Kin Emperor
set out with a huge army with a strong force to guard the entrance into his
territory and to harass the enemy—but to no avail. For Chingiz had entered
the Kin territory through a different route, investigated and negotiated by
Khwaja Jafar.[28]

Having crossed the Great Wall, Chingiz Khan despatched his troops in
various directions to carry fire and sword and strike terror into the hearts of
the population—'disaster, plunder, devastation, and slaughter' as Qazi Minhaj
would put it.[29] Soon the Chinese advance guard received information that
the Mongols had captured a rich town and, unaware of the near approach of
the Chinese troops, were busy dividing the booty and enjoying their triumph.
No better opportunity, thought the commanders, could be had to take them
by surprise. By a rapid march in the dead of night, the Chinese troops contrived
to reach the Mongol camp the next morning. The Mongols, who were busy
cooking rice for their morning meal, immediately mounted their horses and
flung themselves upon the Chinese. The Chinese had to face the furious charge
of the Mongols, and suffered heavy losses. The main Chinese army under the
Emperor fared no better, the Emperor having to seek safety behind the walls
of his capital.[30]

Having seen the fighting qualities of the Mongols, the Kin Emperor, like
the Sultan Ala-ud-din Khwarazm Shah, was unnerved and he consulted Wang
Khan about the feasibility of buying off the Mongols. 'Have the Heaven and
Earth', said the equally frightened Minister,[31] 'turned the wheel of fortune
and is a change of dynasty imminent? The *Dada* (Mongols) have become so
strong that they have finally defeated our mighty army and captured our

impregnable Tsu-Yung-Khun. If we persist in carrying on the war to its ultimate end, we will have to face the possibility of a defeat which may mean the complete disintegration of our army. But if for the time being we surrender to the *Dada* Khan and beseech him to withdraw his forces, we will have time to decide about the measures we should take. Besides, I learn that the *Dada* men and horses are suffering from the inclemencies of the weather and an epidemic. Let us send girls, gold, silver, and silks as presents to the *Dada* Khan and see if he will agree to a peaceful settlement.' 'Wang Khan speaks with wisdom,' said the Kin Emperor and asked him to negotiate a settlement. Chingiz was pleased and accepted the terms: peace, presents and the hand of the princess.[32] 'Using the silks for packing the gold, silver, and other valuables,' says the *Secret History*, 'Chingiz's men loaded their horses and cattle to their fullest capacity and moved away.'

The irrepressible ruler of Tangut had, meanwhile, roused the ire of the Mongol Khan by his unsatisfactory behaviour and Chingiz, therefore, marched against him. Shidarqu, however, thought prudence to be the better part of valour and decided to submit. 'When I heard the name of your Majesty, I was overcome by fear,' submitted Shidarqu. 'Now will you let me be your right wing and serve you? My people are of sedantry habits and cannot come to the muster at an urgent order. With your kind permission we will present Your Majesty the products of our country such as the camel-hair, silks, falcons and hawks.' Chingiz once again agreed to forgive the Tangut ruler.

On returning to his camping grounds Chingiz received the news that the Kin Emperor had evacuated his capital. The Golden Khan, it seemed, had no faith in the accommodation arrived at with the Mongols and had decided to shift his capital out of Yen-King (Khan Baligh of *Rauzat-us-Safa* and the city of Tamghaj of *Tabaqat-i-Nasiri*). The site of Pyen-lyang appealed to him; forty leagues in circumference and surrounded by a triple wall, Pyen-lyang was situated on, and on one side protected by, the river. 'The breadth of the river is so great,' says Khwandmir,[33] 'that, between early morning and evening, a boat passes from one side to the other, and returns with considerable exertion.' The environs of the city were also celebrated for the fruit they produced.[34] The Golden Khan was nervous and, on his way to his new capital, grew suspicious of his Qara-Khitai soldiers and ordered them to be disarmed. The Qara-Khitais refused to be disarmed, which they could very well have construed as the prelude to their slaughter. The Golden Khan was enraged and ordered their commander to be executed. The defiant soldiers, thereupon, deserted him and drove away with the cattle belonging to his son. Profiting from the confusion and chaos prevailing in the Khan's dominions, one of their adventurous chiefs rose in revolt, brought several localities under his authority and, to consolidate his position, went over to the Mongols.[35]

The transfer of the capital was a confession of weakness on the part of the Kin Emperor, a declaration that the 'Son of Heaven' was no longer confident of holding his own against the shaggy nomads. The transfer of the capital was a tacit recognition of the formidable power that the Mongols had become under the leadership of Chingiz Khan. The disaffected and the disloyal were not slow to exploit the new phase in the old struggle between city-dwellers and tent-dwellers.

Chingiz Khan was also one of those who watched with interest the moves and turns on the chessboard of Chinese politics. The significance of the transfer of the capital could not have been lost upon him, especially as it amounted to a repudiation of the recent concord with the Mongol. Disloyalty, sedition and confusion now plagued the Kin dominions and no better opportunity could be had to finally settle old scores. When the Kins stopped his envoys from proceeding through their territory on 'a goodwill mission to the Sung' Chingiz marched against the Kin Emperor in 1214. A strong contingent was despatched towards Khurja (Corea of the European travellers) to prevent the Chinese from receiving reinforcements from there while the main army marched on Pyen-Iyang. The old capital was strongly garrisoned and all the endeavours of the Mongols to take the city by assault were repulsed. The Mongols, thereupon, decided to reduce the city by siege. The city was encircled and the blockade was merciless with the inevitable result that want and famine raised their ugly heads. To relieve the distress of the heroic defenders, the Chinese emperor arranged for a convoy of provisions which was intercepted by the Mongols. The Kin emperor was devastated and he poisoned himself. Although the defenders continued to hold the town and put up defiance, the inadequate provisions ultimately forced them to surrender.[36]

Chingiz despatched Wangur and two other men to take possession of the treasures of the Kin Emperor, prepare a record of the same, and bring them to him.[37] When they reached Yen-King to take charge of the treasure, the Kin treasurer, Kada, offered gold, silks, and other valuables to Wangur and his fellow officers as personal gifts. Wangur, Arhai and Khasar accepted them, but Shigi Qutuqu refused the gifts, 'Hitherto the gold and silk in Chungdu (central capital) belonged to the Emperor of the Kin,' said Qutuqu; 'now they belong to Chingiz. How dare I take anything for myself?' When they returned, Chingiz enquired if his officers had accepted gifts. 'Shigi Qutuqu reported the truth to him.' Explaining his refusal of the gifts, Shigi Qutuqu added that since the city had been taken by force of arms, all the booty belonged to the Khan; it would have been otherwise if the city had not been besieged and taken by force.[38] Chingiz was pleased and rewarded him, but admonished Wangur and the others.[39]

The Teb-Tengri

Meanwhile Juji had been entrusted with the task of subjugating the Uriankhai people on the left and right banks of Lake Baikal; the dense forests provided them abundant game and their main occupation was hunting. Juji returned laden with immense booty. Among the presents he brought for his father were falcons, horses, and sables. Chingiz was pleased and awarded the conquered people to him.

Next was the turn of the Ghuli Tumat tribe,[40] one of the offshoots of the Uriankhai people. Safe in the mountains and shielded by dense forest, they had refused to bow to the rising Mongol Khan. On an earlier occasion they had successfully defied the Mongols and two Mongol officers, Qorchi and Khudukha Baiki, were eking out a miserable existence among them. Determined to put an end to this menance, Chingiz Khan designated the distinguished Boloul as the commander of the expedition against the Tumat tribe. By this time the ruler of the Daidutul was dead, and his wife had succeeded to the chieftainship of the tribe. She was intrepid and active. For, though Boloul took ample precautions against any surprise and despatched scouts for reconnaissance, the Mongol troops were ambushed one night and suffered heavy casualties; Boloul was killed.

The news of the disaster which had befallen his men roused the fury of Chingiz; the death of Boloul was a great loss. To avenge the humiliation, he decided to march against the enemy in person but Bogurchi and Muquli managed to persuade him to send a tried and tested warrior. So Dorbedokhsen was commissioned to lead the avenging host. He proved himself a sound general and a great tactician. 'Dorbedokhsen,' says the *Secret History*, 'kept his army under strict discipline. He feigned an attack at the spot which the enemy had formerly selected for its ambush, and then secretly marched through Khulaanbuka, a pathless tract. To enable his men to march through it, he sent in advance a number of men, each of whom carried ten straps on his back to beat those who stopped with them; he also had axes, saws, chisels, and other tools for cutting down the trees that stood in their way. The army at last came to the top of the mountain from which they could look down at the Tumat people as if (into a room) through a ceiling-window. The large army marched straight, and all of a sudden fell upon the enemy, who was caught at the feasting table.'

The triumph was complete, the humiliation was avenged, and the conquered people were distributed by Chingiz Khan among his mother, younger brothers, and sons. He was, however, still displeased with his uncle, Daritai Otchigin, whom he now wanted to disown for having once deserted to Wang Khan. 'This uncle of yours is the only living monument of your father, left to you,' pleaded Bogurchi Noyan. 'How can you disown him?' The appeal to the memory of his father touched the heart of Chingiz, and he consented to forget and forgive the failing of his uncle.

The reconciliation between Chingiz and Daritai was opportune; for immediately he was face to face with the overweaning pride and presumptions of the Teb-Tengri, the shaman Kokchu, the fourth son of Munlik. Munlik had seven sons, all ambitious and power-hungry. They were not satisfied with the position that Chingiz had conferred on the family. Shaman Kokchu was a great asset to his scheming and ambitious brothers. The nomads held him in great reverence and 'whatever he commanded,' says Juwaini,[41] 'they carried out.' Consequently, they gained adherents and were puffed up with their own importance. One day they had a quarrel with Qasar, the younger brother of Chingiz, and had no hesitation in beating him up. 'You used to boast that no one can challenge you,' Chingiz rebuked his crestfallen brother. 'How, then, have you been beaten by them?' Qasar left the tent and did not face his brother for three days. This encouraged the sons of Munlik to drive deeper the wedge between the two brothers. They came the Teb-Tengri to communicate to Chingiz the will of the gods. 'The Everlasting Sky', he said, 'has sent a Spirit to reveal his command to me. First, Temuchin will rule over the nations, and then Qasar's turn will come. If you do not eliminate Qasar, your power will be uncertain.' Chingiz was shaken. Oyelun was immediately informed of the departure and destination of her masterful son; and she was no less quick in going after him that night in a cart pulled by a white camel. She reached Qasar's camp at sunrise and found him bound, deprived of his hat and belt; Chingiz, who was interrogating him, was 'surprised and alarmed' at the sudden appearance of his mother. 'Oyelun', says the *Secret History*, 'stepped down from the cart, unbound Qasar, returned his hat and belt to him and squatted down in fury. Then uncovering her breasts, she declared: 'Do you see? These are the breasts both of you have sucked. What crime has Qasar committed that you wish to destroy your own bone and flesh? When you were an infant, you could suck out this breast while Kachiun and Otchigin together could not suck out the other but Qasar alone could release me of all my milk. Therefore, you, Temuchin, had wisdom in your heart while Qasar had strength in his arms. Whenever the people rebelled, Qasar quelled them with his bow and arrows. Now that all the enemies have been subdued, you wish to get rid of Qasar? When his mother's anger had spent itself, Chingiz said to her, 'Mother, you have made me afraid and ashamed.'

The Khan was not, however, reconciled to his younger brother; the words of the shaman still rankled in his mind, and a little later, Oyelun was shocked to learn that Chingiz had deprived Qasar off most of his people. It broke her heart and she died soon after.

Meanwhile, adherents had been gathering round the Teb-Tengri, who had not only the halo of direct communication with the Tengri, but also the prestige of being the stepson of Oyelun. Daily he grew in strength and soon his adherents became comparable in number to those of Chingiz himself. Even the men of Otchigin deserted their standard and went over to the Teb-Tengri; and Shagur, whom Otchigin asked to take them back, was beaten up. Next day, Otchigin fared no better when he was surrounded by the scowling brothers, who appeared bent on manhandling him. 'How dare you send your man to take away our people,' they shouted and Otchigin was frightened. 'I should not have sent the man,' he submitted. But they were not satisfied and compelled him to kneel down inside their tent and atone for the affront.

'Early next morning,' runs the graphic account in the *Secret History*, 'before Chingiz had risen from his bed, Otchigin came, knelt before him, recited his grievance and wept. Before Chingiz could speak, his wife, Bortei, stretched herself and covering her breasts with the quilt, exclaimed in tears, 'who are they? The Khoughutan have thrashed Qasar before this and now they have compelled Otchigin to kneel. What kind of order is this? If they have the daring to challenge your brothers, who are strong as cedar trees, while you are alive, will your people, like flocks of birds or like grass bowing to the wind, submit to your weak and simple sons when you are no more with them? She wept bitterly.'

The shaman and his brothers had over-reached themselves, and Bortei's intervention proved effective. It forced the Khan to have done with Kokchu and his pretensions. 'When the Teb-Tengri comes to me today,' Chingiz said to Otchigin, 'you may do with him what you like.' 'A little later,' says the *Secret History*[42] 'Munlik came with his seven sons. As soon as the Teb-Tengri sat down on the western side ready to join the feast, Otchigin stepped up to him, siezed him by the collar and said, "Yesterday, you forced me to kneel. Now we shall have a fight." Otchigin began pulling the Teb-Tengri out of the tent. Chingiz told the two not to measure their necks in his presence. So they pulled each other out of the gate. Then the three picked warriors (of Otchigin), waiting outside, came forward. They seized the Teb-Tengri, broke his spine and threw his body down. Otchigin came back to the tent and said, "Yesterday, the Teb-Tengri made me confess myself guilty; today, when we had just begun the wrestling competition, he lies there and refuses to get up. So he is but an ordinary competitor." Munlik, the father of the priest, understood the situation and exclaimed in tears, "Khan! I have been a faithful companion of yours from the time when you had not ascended the throne." At this moment Munlik's six other sons rushed through the gateway and stood round the fire-basin, rolling up their sleeves. Chengiz was alarmed; he stood up and ordered them to make way for him. Surrounded by his archer-guards he came out of his tent and saw that the Teb-Tengri was dead. He ordered a tent to be put up to shelter the body, and then, breaking camp, started for another place.'

Precautions were taken to keep and protect the corpse of the Teb-Tengri inside the tent. The door and aperture at the top of the tent were closed and a guard was left behind to watch the tent. On the third day, it was reported that the corpse was missing and had apparently disappeared through the opening at the top. 'The Teb-Tengri,' observed Chingiz, 'had beaten my brothers and slandered them unfairly; so the sky did not love him any more and took away his life along with his body.' 'You failed to restrain your son from the attempt to rival me, which cost him his life,' he rebuked Munlik. 'Had I known that you were such a man I would have undone you along with Jamuka, Altan, Kuchar, and the rest. But, if one speaks a word in the morning and changes it in the evening, or says something in the evening and withdraws it next morning, what shame he brings upon himself in the estimate of the public! As I have previously promised you exemption from the death penalty, let the matter be closed.'

This episode reveals Chingiz Khan's capacity for cool calculation. He was a methodical person who left nothing to chance or to be decided in a casual manner. He was patient and tolerant of the presumptions and pretensions of the seven sons of Munlik as long as they did not affect his position and power. The moment, however, he realized that the shaman was aspiring for dominion,[43] he decided to eliminate him. No one was to thwart his will.

Kushluk and Tuq Tughan[43]

When Chingiz Khan had defeated Baibuqa Tayang Khan, his son Kushluk had fled towards Bish Baligh, and from there to the frontiers of the territory of Kuja. In utter poverty he wandered in the mountains while his followers dispersed. In desperation he decided to go to the Gurkhan's court and bide his time. There he was received with due courtesy and treated with honour. When the Khwarazm Shah began hostilities against the Gurkhan, some of the Khan's own amirs in the eastern part of his territory, rebelled. They intrigued and negotiated with Chingiz Khan and with his assistance, freed themselves from the Gurkhan's yoke. Finding the time opportune, Kushluk decided to fish in the troubled waters of Qara-Khitai. 'If you permit me,' he said to the Gurkhan,[44] 'I will go and collect all my wandering followers, who are now scattered like sheep without a shepherd in and around Imil, Qiyaligh, and Bish Baligh. Everyone is molesting them. They want a leader. To bring them to your assistance the time is opportune, as Chingiz Khan is preoccupied with Cathay. I am always at your service and ever ready to carry out your wishes.' The Gurkhan was pleased with Kushluk's fair-seeming offer and gave him the title of 'Kushluk Khan'. As soon as he realized his mistake the Gurkhan issued orders to have him brought back, but it was too late. For Kushluk had 'started off like an arrow shot from a strong bow'[45] and was out of reach. On reaching Imil and Qiyaligh, he was joined by Tuq Tughans, who was also an amir of the Merkits, and had fled on hearing of the rising power of Chingiz Khan. The scattered Naimans soon gathered round Kushluk. Even those in the Gurkhan's forces, who were in some way related to him, joined him and soon he found himself at the head of a considerable army. He began to plunder and ravage territories; he would attack one place and then another till his followers increased and his army became strong. He then turned towards the Gurkhan, attacking and ravaging his territories.

When Kushluk heard of the rising power of the Khwarazm Shah, he sent repeated embassies to negotiate an alliance and, ultimately, they entered into an agreement that the Khwarazm Shah would attack the Gurkhan from the west while Kushluk marched from the east; if the sultan were the first to attack and defeat the Gurkhan, he would have as his share all the territory up to Almaligh and Kashghar; if Kushluk were the first to attack him and conquer Qara-Khitai, he would have the country up to the Jaxartes. The Gurkhan was accordingly attacked from both the sides, and Kushluk took the lead. The troops of the Gurkhan were stationed at great distances and could not cope with the invading hosts and retreated. Meeting little or no opposition, Kushluk reached Uzkand, plundered the treasury and went on towards Balasaqun, where the Gurkhan was stationed. Battle was joined on the banks of the river near Balasaqun; Kushluk was decisively defeated; but most of his followers were captured. Later, when he heard that the Gurkhan had returned triumphant after his battle with the Khwarazm Shah, and had begun to behave capriciously towards his subjects, and that his levies had also gone back to their homes, he decided to make another attempt. During the Gurkhan's absence in the east he had raised and equipped a fresh army and, now with the rapidity of lightning, he rode out against the Gurkhan, attacked him unawares, made him prisoner, and became master of his kingdom. He forced the Gurkhan to give him his daughter in marriage. Having strengthened his position in Qara-Khitai, he once more marched against Awzar Khan of Almaligh and killed him. Meanwhile, the inhabitants of Kashghar and Khotan had raised the standard of revolt. The Gurkhan had kept in prison the son of the Khan of Kashghar; to sow dissension and cause disunion in the ranks of the rebels, Kushluk now released him and allowed, rather asked, him to proceed to Kashghar. The rebel amirs were, however, too alert and wary to accept the 'Trojan horse'; even before the Khan's son could step into the city, they seized him and killed him at the city gates. Finding the rebels determined, Kushluk decided to starve them into surrender. He sent an army against them at the time of gathering the harvest. Unable to collect their harvest for three or four years, and faced with scarcity and paralyzed by famine, the people of Kashghar submitted. Kushluk went there with his army; he billeted a soldier in every house so that the city came under collective control. 'Violence, wickednesss and sedition reigned supreme', says Juwaini.[46] 'The idol worshippers did whatever they wanted and there was no one to prohibit them.'

Having obtained possession of Kashghar, Kushluk moved towards Khotan, one of the most inaccessible regions of Central Asia. It was easily subdued and became a victim to Kushluk's violence and intolerance. For an unknown reason, he had developed an intense hatred against Islam, and now strove to compel the Muslims to abjure their faith. He allowed them to choose between Christianity or idol worship, or the wearing of Chinese dress. The Muslims opted for Chinese dress and prayed for deliverance from the intolerant yoke. The muezzin's call to prayer was stopped, mosques and schools were closed. One day, Kushluk drove the celebrated theologians and doctors of law into the open plain and began discussing religion with them. 'Who is there in those rows?' said Kushluk to the three thousand leading imams assembled there, 'who can dispute with me about matters of religion and state, without keeping back anything and without fear of punishment?' In his ignorance, comments Juwaini,[47] he believed that there would be none among them, who would have the courage to refute and reject his words; and that, in truth, if any one dared to start the discussion, he would, because of Kushluk's majesty and awe, try to save himself and his life; instead of inviting on himself the thunder bolt of calamity, would prefer to confirm Kushluk's lies and falsehoods.' But he was mistaken and Imam Ala-ud-din came forward and sat before Kushluk, prepared to speak the truth. A discussion began about religion and the imperturbable imam began to question and answer Kushluk with surprising confidence. 'Truth', says Juwaini,[48] 'overcame falsehood and the scholar the ignorant.' Defeated in discussion and silenced by argument, Kushluk resorted to obscene and senseless words about the Holy Prophet. This provoked the imam, who cried out: 'Dust in your mouth, O Kushluk, you accursed enemy of the Faith.' The imam was instantly arrested and Kushluk asked him to abandon Islam and adopt idol worship. For several days the imam was tied up, naked, hungry and thirsty. Food was denied him but, like the prophets of old, the imam bore the torture with fortitude. He was then nailed to the gate of his college. The imam, however, till his dying breath, kept advising the people that religion should not be cast away owing to the persecution and tortures of the tyrant. So he ultimately gave up his soul to the Lord and 'passed from the poison-house of this world to the garden of eternity.'[49] Buddhist supremacy was once again established, while cruelty and endless trouble overtook the people.

But at last 'the arrow of prayer hit the mark of acceptance.'[50] Having decided to conquer the territories of the Khwarazm Shah, Chingiz Khan despatched troops to suppress the mischief of Kushluk and Tuq Tughan and, thereby, secure his flanks. Kushluk was at that time in Kashghar and abandoned the town without offering battle. The Mongol forces were welcomed as the Mongol troops asked for nothing but the whereabouts of Kushluk and allowed everyone to follow his religion unmolested. Once more the Muslim call to prayer sounded five times a day and public worship was permitted. The inhabitants killed each of Kushluk's soldiers quartered in their houses. Mongol troops were sent in all directions in pursuit of Kushluk. Wherever he went the Mongols arrived in pursuit. They chased him[51] to the borders of Badakhshan; entering the formidable defiles by the Wararni Pass and reaching the banks of the river Surkh-juyan, Kushluk took the wrong road and entered a blind pass and was seen by a party of hunters. When the Mongols arrived they arranged with the hunters for the capture of the fugitives, the hunters retaining all that the captives had on their person. The Mongols cut off Kushluk's head and took it away with them, the Badakhshani hunters got much booty consisting of cash and jewels. The provinces of Kashghar and Khotan up to the frontiers of the sultan's dominions were now added to the empire of Chingiz Khan.

As Tuq Tughan, who had allied himself with Kushluk during the period of his ascendancy, had retired to Qum Kibchik after the defeat of Kushluk,

Chingiz sent his eldest son, Juji to crush him. Advancing by rapid marches, Juji overtook the fleeing Merkit chief at Taraz and, in the sanguinary conflict that ensued, he annihilated the Merkits. Tuq Tughan was slain and Juji was returning laden with spoils when he was challenged by an unexpected adversary—Sultan Ala-ud-din Khwarazm Shah.

Having disposed off the affairs of Iraq (1218) and leaving his 15-year-old son Rukn-ud-din in charge of the government of the province, the Shah had set out for Transoxiana and then Nishapur. He gave himself up to wine and women. Having thus enjoyed himself for more than a month, he moved on to Bokhara, where again the old warrior succumbed to the irresistible call of the table and the harem. Having assembled his troops and levies, he then decided to march against Kushluk, who had been, as already pointed out, carrying forward an ambitious and expansionist policy. On reaching Samarqand, the Shah once again surrendered to the pleasures of wine, women, and song. Here he received news about the movements of Tuq Tughan, the chief of the Merkits, who was fleeing from the Mongol army led by Juji. To guard his territories from their incursion and ravages, the sultan marched towards Jand. On receiving intelligence that Tuq Tughan's were not mere predatory movements but that he was being pursued by a strong army of the Mongols, the sultan retraced his steps to Samarqand. Gathering his men, he once again started for Jand 'to bring down two birds with one stone.'

In the meanwhile, Kushluk had been defeated and slain. Continuing his advance, the sultan reached Taraz, lying between the two small rivers Qamij and Qali—a tract where 'twilight did not disappear at all from the sight.'[52] The Shah found the plain red with blood and strewn with the mutilated bodies of the dead and dying. A search was conducted, and one among those who had fallen was discovered to be alive. From him the Shah learnt that the Mongols had there overtaken the fleeing Merkits, that Tuq Tughan and his followers were defeated and that Juji was now on his way to rejoin his father. Finding both birds to have slipped from his hands, the Shah set out in pursuit of the Mongols. He overtook them and prepared to engage them. The Mongols had no instructions to fight all and sundry. They had been sent on a specific mission and, having accomplished their task, were returning to their Khan's ordu. Juji explained the situation to the Shah and cautioned him against needlessly provoking hostilities but to no avail. Forced to fight, the Mongols turned round to face the hosts of the Shah. And the sky rang out with the clatter of clashing weapons and the sound of the whizzing spears. Sanguinary was the battle and the Mongols fought hard to avoid being overwhelmed by the superior number of the Shah's forces. The right wings of both armies broke their opponents; and, putting every ounce of energy and fury in their bid to rout the enemy, the Mongols launched a heavy attack against the Shah's centre, and ultimately forced it back. The symptoms of wavering in the ranks and the imminent peril of captivity to which his father was exposed, called out the best in Sultan Jalal-ud-din. None excelled him in dauntless valour on the day, and, in the thick of battle, he called to the band fighting under him and charged at the Mongols. The counter-charge was successful, the attackers were repulsed, and the Khwarazm Shah extricated out of a perilous position. The battle continued to rage with unabated fury till the night prayer when each army retired to its camp. The Mongols had now witnessed the bravery of the Sultan's troops. This knowledge was to be of immense use two years later when Chingiz Khan led his forces against the Shah. Lighting numerous fires in their camp, the Mongols quietly retreated during the night and joined Chingiz Khan.

The sultan was unnerved by 'the vigour and tenacity of the Mongol troops,' says Mirkhwand,[53] 'and he became filled with apprehension and misgivings.' Without doing or daring anything more, he returned to Samarqand, a changed and dispirited man, irresolute and bewildered.[54] 'Fear and dread of the Mongols took possession of his heart and mind', says Qazi Minhaj; he never again came up against them.[55]

Notes

1. Quoted by Prawdin, pp. 82-3. Besides giving the title of *Khaqan* (Qaan) to Chingiz Khan, they bestowed the title of *gut ony* (Prince of State) on Muquli.
2. *Rauzat-us-Safa*, vol. V, pp. 14-15; Sharfuddin, fols. 62-3.
3. *Tabaqat-i-Nasiri*, pp. 332-3.
4. Juwaini, vol. I, p. 28; vol. V, p. 15.
5. Ibid.
6. Ibid.
7. *Rauzat-us-Safa*, vol. V, p. 15.
8. He was also to be in charge of 4,000 uruts.
9. He was also given joint charge with Beduun who had not been rewarded with a unit of 1,000 as he was 'stubborn'. The Khan also added that he would examine his future 'conduct'.
10. Juwaini, vol. I, p. 28.
11. Ibid.
12. Rashid-ud-din, fol. 245.
13. Ibid., pp. 95-6; Ibid., pp. 158-9.
14. *Rauzat-us-Safa*, vol. V, pp. 14-15; Sharfuddin, fol. 66.
15. *Rauzat-us-Safa*, vol. V, p. 14; Howorth, p. 65.

16. *Shajratul Atrak*, p. 81.

17. *Rauzat-us-Safa*, vol. V, pp. 14-15; Sharfuddin , fol. 65.

18. Juwaini, vol. I, p. 32.

19. Ibid.

20. Ibid., vol. I, p. 33.

21. *Rauzat-us-Safa*, vol. V, p. 16.

22. *Tabaqat-i-Nasiri*, p. 333.

23. *Rauzat-us-Safa*, vol. V, p. 16; *Habib al-siyar*, vol. I, part III, p. 9.

24. Ibid.

25. Ibid. According to Qazi Minhaj, however, Khwaja Jafar was sent 'under semblance of traffic; and Altan Khan commanded that he should be imprisoned.' He remained in prison for a good while but contrived to escape and reach Mongolia, and conveyed the necessary information to Chingiz Khan.' *Tabaqat-i-Nasiri*, p. 333.

26. Ibid., pp. 333-4; *Rauzat-us-Safa*, vol. V, p. 16.

27. *Tabaqat-i-Nasiri*, p. 333.

28. *Habib al-siyar*, vol. I, part III, p. 9.

29. *Tabaqat-i-Nasiri*, p. 334; *Rauzat-us-Safa*, vol. V, p. 17.

30. *Tabaqat-i-Nasiri*, p. 334.

31. *Rauzat-us-Safa*, vol. V, pp. 16-17; *Habib al-siyar*, vol. I, part III, p. 9.

32. The gist of the conversation is the same in *Rauzat-us-Safa,* vol. I, p. 17, *Habib al-siyar*, vol. I, part III, p. 9.

33. *Rauzat-us-Safa*, vol. V, p. 17; *Habib al-siyar*, vol. I, part III, p. 9; *Shajratul Atrak*, p. 83.

34. *Rauzat-us-Safa*, vol. V, p. 17.

35. *Shajratul Atrak*, p. 84.

36. *Rauzat-us-Safa*, vol. V, p. 17.

37. Ibid.

38. *Shajratul Atrak*, p. 85; *Rauzat-us-Safa*, vol. V, pp. 17-18.

39. *Rauzat-us-Safa*, vol. V, p. 18; *Shajratul Atrak*, p. 85.

40. *Shajratul Atrak*, p. 85.

41. Ibid., pp. 97-8; Ibid., I.R. 165-6.

42. Juwaini, vol. I, pp. 28-9. For details of the quarrel between Shaman and Qasar and then between Shaman and Otchigin, younger brother of Chingiz, see *Mongolian Chronicle*, pp. 170-2.

43. Juwaini, vol. I, p. 29.

44. Ibid., pp. 46-55; *Rauzat-us-Safa*, vol. V, pp. 1521-3; Sharfuddin, fols. 74, 81-3, 89-90.

45. Juwaini, vol. I, pp. 46-7.

46. Ibid., p. 47.

47. Ibid., p. 49.

48. Ibid., p. 53.

49. Ibid.

50. Ibid., p. 55.

51. Ibid., p. 49.

52. Ibid., p. 50.

53. Raverty, *Tabaqat-i-Nasiri*, pp. 267-8.

54. *Rauzat-us-Safa*, vol. IV, p. 141.

55. Juwaini, vol. I, pp. 120, 133; Sharfuddin, fols. 90-1; *Rautzat-us-Safa*, vol. IV, pp. 141-2.

56. Raverty, *Tabaqat-i-Nasiri*, p. 270.

4

The Great Campaign

AFTER HIS VICTORY OVER the Gurkhan, Sultan Ala-ud-din Khwarazm Shah had not been able to curb his desire for the fabulous wealth of China. But at this time he received the news of the rise and conquests of Chingiz Khan. For first-hand information about the nomad conqueror, particularly to obtain as Qazi Minhaj informs us, 'information reflecting the condition and strength of the Mongol forces and their weapons, war equipment and provisions, to achieve this objective, the Khwarazm Shah dispatched an embassy under Baha-ud-din Razi to the nomad court'. Baha-ud-din Razi was 'of noble nature, and of lineage, a descendant of the Prophet' and so the Qazi, based his account of the mission on Razi's authority.

The embassy was received with respect and Chingiz Khan expressed a desire for peace and friendship with the 'ruler of the West' and unfettered trade relations between the two empires.[1] In accordance with the prevalent custom, Chingiz Khan sent 'a great number of rarities and gifts for the Sultan'. To establish closer relations he also sent a return embassy, headed by Mahmud Yalvaj, Ali Khwaja of Bokhara, and Yusuf Kanka of Utrar.[2] Seated on a magnificent divan and surrounded by the officers of his court, the Shah received the embassy in state. 'The high dignity and the resplendent glory of our royal house and the wide extent of our realms,' so ran the personal message of the Khan,[3] 'are a matter of common knowledge. As our dominions are coterminus, I deem it important to cultivate peace and strengthen the ties of friendship with you. None of my sons do I hold dearer than you. As you know God has bestowed on me the sovereignty of all lands of the east and of all the territories which lie on the borders of your own. All the chieftains of Cathay, Mongolia, Turkistan and all Mongol tribes are now obedient to my commands, while those who refused to submit, I ground into dust. My territories abound in silver mines while bold and daring warriors flock under my colours. So innumerable are the cities, towns, and territories administered by my men that I have neither the need nor the desire to seek fresh conquests. If you are also inclined to peace and friendship, let traders and caravans on both sides come and go, and let the precious products and ordinary commodities be conveyed from one territory to the other. This will be of advantage to both of us and cement our ties of friendship, amity and peace.'

As the message, with its presumption of superiority, was delivered, a bitter smile is said to have curled the lips of the fierce monarch. The envoys were courteously dismissed but Mahmud Yalvaj, the leader of the delegation, was summoned to the Shah for a midnight interview.[4]

'You are a Muslim born here in Gurganj,' said the Shah,[5] handing over a precious jewel to Mahmud Yalvaj. 'You should, therefore, answer my questions honestly. Be truthful and conceal nothing from me. Now tell me if Chingiz Khan has really conquered Cathay.' 'I swear by God,' replied Mahmud Yalvaj. 'My chief has spoken the truth, and soon the Sultan will come to know of it.' 'But do you know the wide extent of my dominions?', asked the Shah, warming up. 'You have no idea of my armies. How dare your Khan address me as his son? Tell me, now, how strong is his army?' Mahmud Yalvaj trembled at the fury behind the Shah's words; shrewd courtier and diplomat that he was, he resorted to equivocation.

'As compared to the Sultan's boundless forces,' he said, 'the troops of Chingiz Khan are like a shining candle flickering before the sun.' The Shah was pleased and his wrath subsided. A treaty of peace and friendship, allowing free commerce, was concluded and the envoys set out to submit their report to the Great Khan.[6]

Nassavi alone among all the 'contemporaries' gives an account of the 'midnight' interview, but he does not record the source of his information. Nor does he say whether anyone else was present. Mahmud is said to have agreed to be the Shah's 'eyes and ears' at the Khan's court. Was this out of fear?[7]

During their brief sojourn, the embassy would have scanned the forces of the Shah with the eyes of practised warriors and realized that he was prepared for hostilities. The walls and towers of his great cities were in complete repair, and mounted with catapults and ballistics. His magazines were stocked with all the munitions of war; he had a mighty host of 400,000 soldiers; his squadrons of cavalry were ready to scour the country and carry on either defensive or predatory warfare. As they walked through the paved streets and crowded bazaars of the different cities and towns of Transoxiana, they would have observed stately palaces and sumptuous mosques; bazaars crowded with silks and cloth of silver and gold with jewels and precious stones, and other rich merchandise, perhaps they longed for the time when all this wealth should be their spoil.

'The country about the two great rivers and their tributary streams,' says Lane-Poole, 'was one of the most fertile in Asia. Farghana itself was prodigal of fruit and laden with heavy harvests. Abundantly watered by the Sir, and sheltered on all sides from the outer world by fostering hills—save where a gap to the south-west opened out towards Samarqand—the little province smaller than Ireland, was a garden, an orchard, a vineyard. Grapes and melons ripened to perfection at Andijan, innumerable mills splashed in the watercourses and ground the grain yielded by the generous earth. The beautiful gardens of Ush, a day's march to the south were gay with violets, tulips, and roses in their seasons, and between the brooks the cattle browsed on the rich clover meadows. At Marghinan, a little to the west, the third city of Farghana grew such apricots and pomegranates that a man would journey from afar to take them: many years after he was banished from his land, Babar recalled with a sigh the flavour of the dried apricots stuffed with almonds which were so good at Marghinan. The luscious pomegranates of Khojend were not to be despised, but the melons of Akhai—who could resist the melons of Akhai, which had not their equal in the world, not even in the spreading melon fields of Bukhara? If he thought of the apricots of Marghinan in the days of his exile, Babar suffered the dreams of a Tantalus when he remembered the lost joys of the melons of Akhai. But there was more sustaining food than melon-pulp among the hills and woods of his native land. The pastures nourished herds of cattle, sheep and goats cut their devious tracks on the mountain sides, pheasants, white deer, hares, wild goats, gave sport to the hunter and his hawk. Farghana indeed was a land of milk and honey, an axis of plenty between the deserts of Khiva and Takla Makan. The snow-capped hills that clipped it tempered its climate, and during the heats of summer welcomed its inhabitants to their cool retreats.'[8]

Chingiz Khan seemed to be gratified at the evident peaceful intentions of the Shah. He issued strict orders for the implementation of the agreement. Even an embassy[9] from Caliph Nasir failed to goad him into a needless conflict with the Khwarazm Shah. Chingiz was not one to crack the hard nuts of others; probably he shrank from a conflict whose outcome was uncertain.

The treaty of commerce and friendship was beneficial for the subjects of the two mighty monarchs. Since the Mongols had no cities as their permanent abode, and merchants and businessmen did not visit them frequently, wearing apparel and carpets were scarce among them, and the profits in transaction with them were notorious. The treaty now opened new vistas of commerce and trade for the subjects of the Khwarazm Shah. 'Towards the end of Sultan 'Ala-ud-din Khwarazm Shah's reign,' says Juwaini, 'peace and quiet, safety and tranquility had reached a high level; the greatest prosperity prevailed; the roads were safe and disturbances were quelled. Consequently, if there was any hope of trading and profit in the East or in the West, the merchants went there.'[10] Three merchants, Ahmad Khujandi, Ibn Amir Husain, and Ahmad Balhich were among the first to avail of the benefits of the treaty. They collected enormous qualities of gold cloth, brocade, zindichi cloth, and other articles of merchandise they deemed profitable, and set out on their journey. Chingiz Khan had, by now, crushed all rivals and rebels, and exemplary law and order prevailed in his dominions. To guard the routes and protect travellers, he had posted sentries and guards (qaraqchis) on the roads, and had ordered them to let pass merchants safely. Whatever articles were worthy of the Khan were to be sent on to him with their owner. When this caravan reached the frontiers of the Mongol Empire, the qaraqchis selected the merchandise of Balhich and sent him to the Khan. His stock was displayed before the Khan. He asked the *ballishes* of gold for every fabric, which had cost him from ten to twenty dinars only. Chingiz Khan was enraged by his impudent statement. 'This man', he said, 'behaves as if no cloth has come to me.' He ordered the cloth which had accumulated in the treasury of the ancient Khans to be shown to the merchant. The stock of Ahmad Balhich was written down and then given to plunder and he was dismissed.

His companions were then summoned and all their stock was brought before Chingiz. But having become wiser, and in spite of great insistence, they refused to name a price for their goods, and stated that they had brought them as a gift for the mighty Khan. Chingiz ordered the merchants to be paid at the rate of one gold *balish* for each piece of gold embroidered stuff, and one silver *balish* for every two pieces of cotton and zindichi. Balhich was lucky to receive the same generous price for his confiscated goods. The merchants were treated with courtesy and, as a mark of respect, were put up in tents of white felt.[11]

At the time of their return, Chingiz Khan ordered a trading caravan to be equipped and subscribed by his Noyans and chieftains, which would go to Muslim lands to do business. The order was carried out and a caravan of 450 men, all Muslims, set out for Samarqand and Bokhara along with enormous qualities of gold cloth, brocade, zindichi cloth and other articles of merchandise as presents for the Shah befitting the courtesy of one great chieftain to another. 'Merchants of your territories came to us,' ran the message he sent to the

Khwarazm Shah. 'We are sending them back having dealt with them in the manner they would relate to you. We are also sending a trading caravan to purchase and bring the wares of that side. After some time, the confusing materials of our mind will terminate with our concord and agreement while the measures of perverseness and enmity will come to an end.'[12] Along with them, the names of four prominent Muslim merchants are mentioned: Omar Khwarja Atrazi Hammal Maraghi, Fakhrud-Din Dizaki Qukahri, and Amirud-Din Haravi, which indicates that travel and trade relations were already well-established between Muslim traders and the Mongols, and that the mission from Chingiz Khan was, most probably, intended to further extend and strengthen, on an official level, existing trade.

Laden with gold, silver, silks, *targhu*, and other precious commodities the caravan reached Utrar, where it excited the greed of the Shah's governor, Ghayir Khan. Qazi Minhaj mentions the incident at two places. The caravan comprised 500 camels. The goods were forwarded by the Governor to the sultan, and he is corroborated by Ibnul Asir. The goods were sold to the merchants of Bokhara and Samarqand, and the money was appropriated by the sultan. The details about the rarities carried by the caravan are fascinating and only persons of a high calibre and character could have withstood the temptation to cast covetous eyes on the merchandise loaded on camel-backs. Among them, 'The trustworthy' Baha-ud-din singled out for official mention 'a maggot of gold as big as camel's neck so that it was necessary to carry it on a cart ... camels laden with gold, silver, *khaza-i-khitae* (a special kind of coarse woven silk), *targhse* (silk fabric red in colour), *kanduz* (bearer?), *sameer* (sable), raw silk, and elegant and ingenious things from Chin and Tamghaj.' The governor's anger, it is stated, was further aroused by the impertinence of one of the merchants. Cupidity, jealousy or stupidity, whatever may have been the real cause, prompted him to detain the caravan and send a report to the Shah that the movements and conduct of the merchants was highly suspicious. Such situations were not uncommon in those days: merchants did gather information. Without considering the consequences of his action, the sultan issued orders for the immediate execution of the whole caravan and confiscation of the merchandise. The terrible news of the Utrar catastrophe was conveyed to the Mongol Khan by a solitary camel-driver,[13] who had managed to escape.[14]

On receiving the news of the Utrar catastrophe, Chingiz Khan behaved with his usual caution and self-control, and tried to bring the sultan to reason. He dispatched as his envoy a Turk, Ibn Kafraj Bughra, with two Tartar attendants, to demand satisfaction and the surrender of the perfidious governor. Whether the Shah felt that war could not be avoided, or feared the indignation of Turkan Khatun and her Qanqali mercenaries, or was overwhelmed by a sense of prestige, he ordered the Mongol envoy to be killed and his attendants expelled and their beards shaved off. The Mongol invasion of the Muslim world was thus assured, and, with it the greatest tragedy in the cultural history of Asia.[15]

Why the sultan took such a tactless step in dealing with the nomad conqueror is understandable though not excusable. It is impossible to believe that he underrated the power of the Mongol Khan. One can only suppose that his advisers urged upon him the improbability of a 'Tartar' invasion of his dominions; for, even after the terrible lesson of 1218 when he had two years' respite, he took no steps to placate Chingiz Khan, or prepare adequately against an invasion. What is inexplicable is the Shah's failure to handle the situation diplomatically instead of providing the Khan an excuse for an invasion. He displayed none of the consummate diplomatic and military skill that had made the first years of his reign among the most brilliant in Khwarazmian history: 'Thus causing countries to be laid waste, the world to be disheveled, the people rendered homeless, without a domicile and without a chief. For every drop of blood then shed,' as Juwaini laments, 'a river of blood was made to flow. Each victim's head was paid for by a thousand heads, and for each dinar a thousand were taken.'[16]

The Shah's success had gone to his head and he had become an unconscious addict of wine, women and song like the rest of the Muslim aristocracy. The Shah chose to become a fugitive, vainly seeking justification for his follies, frolic, and faults in the malignancy of the stars. He awaited favourable change of stars, which would turn the tide in his favour, while his people were slaughtered, his glorious heritage of architectural splendour was torched, and starving men and women, old and young, innocent children were heroically defended their homes.

Flattery has been said to be the last infirmity of a noble mind. It may be debatable whether Ala-ud-din was gifted with 'a noble mind' but he was, without doubt, conceited and short-sighted. He was ambitious and motivated by a wish to become the second Sanjur the Seljuq, if not the second Alexander the Great. Unfortunately for the Shah himself and his dynasty, and also for his subjects, Ala-ud-din Khwarazm Shah was surrounded by self-serving, servile, and short-sighted courtiers, incapable of or unwilling to him regarding his thoughtless actions and preposterous designs. The Shah was not a good judge of men and was unable and unwilling to choose and include in his entourage men of character and sagacity, who could tender honest but unpleasant advice. Lacking composure, self-control and honest and talented advice, he sailed like a rudderless ship in a stormy sea. He had to contend with many problems. The first and the most pressing was, perhaps, the unconcealed ill-will of his step-mother, who was a law unto herself; her Qanqali Turkish officials, who constituted a constant and dangerous threat to his position and to the stability of his power. The insolence and avariciousness of the Qanqali bureaucrats, the unwillingness and inability of the Shah to control them and his failure to sort out a working arrangement with his stepmother, were all driving a wedge between the oppressed but sullen people and their lawful but hard-shackled sovereign. The situation was heading toward anarchy. Further, contrary to the advice of his seasoned father, the successful founder of the Khwarazmian empire, that he should strive to stick to his policy of friendship with the Gurkhan, Ala-ud-din Khwarazm Shah extended his borders by annexing the smaller monarchies that had till then been working as buffer states between the Khwarazmians and the nomads of Central Asia and China. Unlike the great empire builders, Ala-ud-din paid little or no attention to the urgent necessity of consolidation. Hankering after the shadow rather than the substance of power, he picked a running quarrel with the caliph, and thereby further antagonized his subjects.

Referring to Humayun's chequered life and sudden accidental death, Stanley Lane-Poole remarked in his inimitable style that Humayun tumbled through life as he tumbled out of it. He added if there was an opportunity to tumble, he was not the man to miss it. It can be similarly said of Ala-ud-din Khwarazam Shah that he lived in and by conflict, and that if there was an opportunity to pick up a conflict, Ala-ud-din was not one to let it go. He seems to have relished conflicts and that alone seems to explain his uncalled for 'rush and brush' against Juji and the rash order to massacre the Mongol trades on the charge of espionage. By his unbecoming and irrational execution of the Mongol envoy and shaving off the beards of his two attendants, made retribution inevitable. Ala-ud-din Khwarazm Shah was a Turk. Bravery has been said to be the heritage of Turks, and the Turks have amply demonstrated through history that the adage is no hollow saying. Two shining examples of dogged determination and indomitable courage heightened the background of Ala-ud-din Khwarazm Shah, one right in front of his nose. Shihab-ud-din Ghori one of the illustrious stars of God, but also one of his troublesome contemporaries and the other long after him, Zahir-ud-din Babur, the founder of the Mughal empire in India. Shihab-ud-din suffered two shattering defeats, first by the Qara-Khitais at Audkhad, and the second at Tarain at the hands of Prithvi Raj Chauhan. But he did not lose heart and plodded on to gain a historic victory to found the first Turkish empire in India. Zahir-ud-din Babur was badly worsted and mauled by Shaibani Khan in his struggle to regain his patrimony but did not throw up his hands in despair; instead, he won an empire for himself and founded a dynasty in India.

The outcome of the actions and misdeeds of Ala-ud-din were grim: hundreds and thousands dead, prosperous towns and cities torched, mounds of smoking granaries, and innumerable orchards and fertile fields trampled by ruthless Mongol horsemen marked the trail of one the greatest holocausts of history. Chingiz Khan, however, even after the Shah's unpardonable behaviour displayed astonishing diplomatic finesse in his conduct. He conveyed to Qazi Baha-ud-din Razi, the Khwarazmian envoy, his reaction to the Shah's deplorable misconduct and his conception of kingship and immunity of envoys.

The outrageous conduct of the Khwarazm Shah came as a rude shock to the Mongol Khan who had desired peaceful trade relations between the two kingdoms. The leader of a people who lived by war and plunder, this man had tried to effect an honourable settlement. Though a 'barbarian', he had believed in the inviolability of the envoys and the sacredness of treaties. But this had been misunderstood and misinterpreted. His rage now knew no bounds, and he prepared to take revenge. Climbing to the top of a hill, he uncovered his head, loosened his girdle, put it round his neck, and for three days and nights prayed for victory and vengeance.[17]

Chingiz Khan decided to first quell all the disturbances and disorders in his own dominions. His inveterate enemies, Kushluk and Tuq Tughan, had been exercising power and could continue to do so during his long absence for the war in the west. They were extending protection to deserters of his army and encouraging all those who were opposed to him. He therefore as we have seen, despatched Juji, Yamah Noyan and others to put a final end to mischief. He had despatched envoys to the sultan to protest against his unreasonable behaviour and hostile actions, to inform him about his advance towards his territories and ask him to prepare for war.[18]

The Khwarazm Shah had meanwhile been, rather belatedly, making preparations for the conduct of the war, but no great soldier seems to have participated in his councils; his arrangements were ill-conceived, inadequate, and self-defeating. Gigantic as was the power of the Shah, he divided his forces and despatched them to various towns and fortresses. This move shows his ignorance of what was going on in the Mongol camp and of the strength of the enemy. The Shah failed to appreciate the sound advice of Jalal-ud-din to take the enemy by the forelock, challenge him at the natural frontier provided by the Jaartes, and bar his passage there instead of allowing him to ravage places at his will and gain access to provisions for his men, fodder for the cattle, and artisans and skilled workers to act as slaves. He wasted precious days in councils of war—that sure sign of the chief who does not know what to do. He did not even send a man to the banks of the Jaxartes to observe the enemy. He probably had a fixed idea that the Mongols would never cross the river and the line of his fortresses; that the Mongols, after a short but swift plundering campaign as customary with nomads, would return to their native steppe. Utrar held the key of the regions along the Oxus, and commanded the routes. Had the Shah remained in that position he could have placed Chingiz Khan in dire straits. But, though his army was large, he resolved not to take a stand. His advisers, suffering from the misconception that the barbarian Mongols would not be able to reduce their fortified towns, urged the Shah to retreat beyond the mountains of Ghor and Ghaznin and there raise a new and strong army. The Sultan's eldest son, Jalal-ud-din, alone raised his voice against the counsels of retreat, and entreated his father to fight the enemy, and defend his kingdom and country as befitted the family of the Khwarazm Shahs. The young Jalal-ud-din could have saved the Muslim world from the hoofs and whips of the Mongol horsemen. He had the ability to fight when to others it was futile even to try. He foresaw the futility of the Shah's trust in the strength and impregnability of his fortresses. Realizing, perhaps, the truth of the adage that the strength of the walls is never greater than the courage of their defenders, he cautioned against the demoralising policy of shutting up the warriors inside the towns. Reckless and more daring than the Shah, the young and energetic Jalal-ud-din urged active resistance, out into the open battlefield. Scoffing the idea of raising a new army to smash the barbarian invaders while veterans were scattered all over the land, he pleaded for holding the line of the Jaxartes, where the enemy would be exhausted. In case the Shah decided to follow the policy of masterly inactivity, of leaving things to the stars, he pleaded for permission to defend the frontier. 'If fortune favours me,' he said,[19] 'I will carry off the ball of desire with the "Chaugan" of Divine aid; but if fortune favours me not, at least the people will not curse and say: "They have collected taxes and tribute from us for so long, and at a time like this, they renounced our affairs, and abandoned us to be captive to infidels." It was to no avail. The sultan's panic was so great that the sage advice of his son was considered the mere lisping of an infant.'[20]

The Shah was unnerved by the forebodings of the astrologers, who pronounced the conjunction of the stars unfavourable. The counsels of his mutually jealous courtiers harped on the theme that the Mongols would not be able to hold the lands for long. Perhaps also due to his own irresolution and cowardice, the sultan decided not to defend the line of the Jaxartes but to divide his forces and despatch twenty or thirty thousand men apiece to all the important towns and cities.[21] 'Each one of the Maliks, in accordance with the commands of Sultan Muhammad, was in some part or other,' says Qazi Minhaj, 'and they put fortresses in repair, surrounded the cities with ditches and made preparations for war and the defence of their fortresses as far as it lay in their power.'[22]

The Persian chroniclers (and perhaps Raverty) are all not unjustifiably critical of Ala-ud-din Khwarazm Shah's refusal to heed the advice of Jalal-ud-din as in their opinion he was capable to face the impending onslaught with courage and determination but was instead held off.

He was, according to Yajai and other trustworthy writers, the greatest, the most noble minded, the most warlike, the most devoted of the sons of his father, and the most worthy of the diadem of sovereignty. His valour rivalled that of Rustam and Isfandiyar, and he was able, skilful, and sagacious. If there was any man in those days capable of coping with Chingiz successfully, it was he; from his subsequent heroic actions there can be little doubt that his efforts could have been crowned with success, if only his advice had been acted upon, or he had had the direction of affairs, and had been seconded by his brothers, nobles, and subjects, with that unity of purpose so essential in the hour of danger. His brothers, however, were selfish beyond measure, and cared for nought but their own interests inconspicuous pleasure, excess whilst Jalal-ud-Din[23] was kept in constant attendance upon his father, contrary to his own inclinations.[24]

We may picture the grim delight of the nomad chief when he learnt that his enemy had decided to quit his position and allow him unhindered passage of the Jaxartes. Chingiz Khan was about to set off on his great enterprise. He had received pledges of friendship from the tribes along the route; Kushluk and Tuq Tughan had been eliminated, and his troops had been well received by the Muslim inhabitants of Kashghar and Khotan; both were among the most renowned cities of Turkestan. His army numbered some 600,000, all fine cavalry. He set off in the spring of 1220 at the head of his troops; he knew that he would have to leave some men behind en route; he was obliged to detach and leave behind a part of his force for the defence of the home. He knew the difficulties of the route; he was perfectly aware that he would expose his army to peril and loss while scaling the Roof of the World, and crossing the dangerous defiles of Badakshan. But there was no other route and the army was to ride through stark steppes and climb steep hills whatever the obstacles, dangers and risks. He would cross the Pamir and the Lob

Nor[25] (where the Russians would lose a division six hundred years later). He may also have been aware of the fact that the Shah had been frightened by his first encounter with the Mongols and was unnerved. He knew that the people of Samarqand resented the policies of the Shah and one could fan the smouldering flames of discontent. The nobles were jealous and hostile to the Shah; the theologians hated him for his quarrel with the Caliph, and the general population heartily disliked the barbarous Qanqalis. He prepared with the greatest care but with extreme secrecy, the extraordinary plan of his invasion. He seems to have planned his strokes with masterly calculation to take the Shah by surprise.

The army with which Chingiz Khan set out was the best equipped and the most organized army the nomads had ever had. It had been trained with skill and care. It possessed nearly all the services of a modern army, a commissariat, hospital, and transport administration; an intelligence department; an excellent body of sappers, miners and pioneers; beasts of burden and spare horses; and explosives and burning naptha. According to Qazi Minhaj, the warriors were each given a patty provision for the long journey and a skin of water (with instructions to supplement it with *humiz* and milk of their mares) for every unit of ten horsemen. They also had a vast number of horses to supplement their mounts and, probably, for food in case of emergency, 'so numerous that their numbers cannot be computed'. 'They turned their faces towards the land of Islam', one may presume, with confidence and high hopes of a successful campaign. The superiority of this army consisted in the greatest elements of military strength—its discipline. It had been accustomed to victory for years, and had confidence in its leaders. And Chingiz Khan had lieutenants worthy of himself—Subutai, an admirable cavalry chief and a brilliant soldier, Yamah Noyan, and other distinguished names.

Welcomed by allied chiefs and passing through friendly and subject territories, the Mongol army made its way with comparative ease. On his way Chingiz Khan was joined by feudatory chiefs and vassals such as Arsalan Khan of Qiyaligh, the Idiqut of the Uighur, and Suquagtagin of Almaligh.[26]

Utrar, Jand and Khojend

The Mongols struck their first blow at Utrar (Maps 2 and 3),[27] the chief city of Turkestan and the scene of the ghastly massacre of the Mongol merchants. Situated on the east bank of the Jaxartes, immediately below its confluence with the Chimkant, it was the key to the fertile valley of Farghana. Strongly fortified and populous—it had 70,000 inhabitants within its four walls—Utrar was famous for its bazaars.

The sultan had placed 50,000 men of the 'external army' under Ghayir Khan to guard Utrar. As the clouds of war gathered thick and fast, he reinforced the army with a contingent of 10,000 troops under Hajib Qaraja. Ghayir Khan had exercised the greatest energy and industry in preparing for the onslaught. The citadel and the city fortifications were carefully examined and strengthened, sentries and troops were posted at the gates and over the battlements. Weapons and provisions were stored to face a prolonged siege.

When the neighing of Mongol horses, the clatter of their armour and the war whoops of the Mongols announced the arrival of the invading host, Ghayir Khan went over the ramparts to survey the field. His heart sank at the sight of six hundred banners fluttering in the open field, with one thousand horsemen under each banner[28] investing the town from all sides. The city rose to the challenge and gave battle. Finding himself unexpectedly delayed at Utrar, Chingiz noted that the sultan had dispersed his forces to defend many important cities spread over his territory, so that there was no possibility of him barring his march on the plains of Transoxiana and Khurasan. Accordingly, he arranged his troops in four great divisions. The first commanded by Uktai and Chaghatai was to act against Utrar; the second contingent was directed against the cities from Jand to Lake Aral and was placed under the command of Juji; the third division under Saktu Buqa and Alaq Noyan was sent up the rivers Fanakat and Khojend. While these three divisions were to take the cities on the Syr Darya, he himself with Tuli set out for Bokhara to prevent the Shah from reinforcing any of his garrisons between the two rivers. By means of converging drives on the Amu Darya from the north to the south-east against Bokhara, and south of Utrar, to the north-west, also against Bokhara, he planned to rout the Shah's troops on the flanks of his Samarqand group. It was a complicated operation, requiring mobility. But he had confidence in his men—and they fully justified it.

The Mongol avalanche had come to a dead halt against the walls of Utrar. Uktai and Chaghatai pushed on the siege with vigour but the city stood like a rock. Mongol forces beat against it, the flame-throwers and the miners sapped it, the Mongol soldiers perished on its threshold in ever-increasing numbers, but the city held out and went on fighting. At last after five months' heroic resistance the besieged were reduced to dire straits and Qaraja sounded Ghayir Khan about capitulation. 'If I play false to my sovereign,' said Ghayir Khan, 'what excuse will I have? How shall I escape the rebuke and reproaches of fellow Muslims?'[29] Scorning the very idea of surrender, he held out. Qaraja

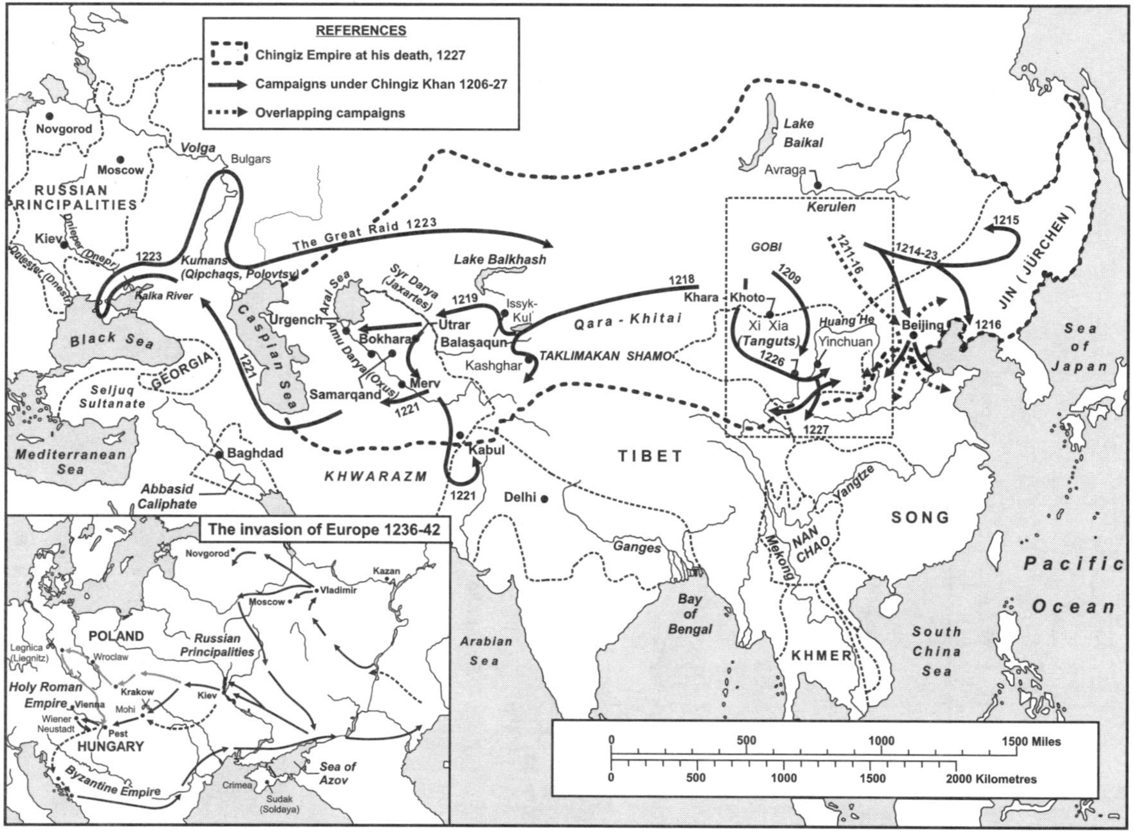

Map 2. The Campaigns, 1206-27

REFERENCES

Chingiz Empire at his death, 1227
Campaigns under Chingiz Khan 1206-27
Overlapping campaigns

Pacific Ocean

Sea of Japan

JIN (JURCHEN)

SONG

KHMER

South China Sea

Lake Baikal

Avraga

Kerulen

GOBI

Khoto

Xi Xia (Tanguts)

Yinchuan

Huang He

Beijing

Yangtze

NAN CHAO

Mekong

TIBET

Ganges

Bay of Bengal

Khara-Khoto

Qara - Khitai

TAKLIMAKAN SHAMO

Issyk-Kul'

Kashghar

Kabul

Delhi

Arabian Sea

Lake Balkhash

Utrar

Balasaqun

Syr Darya (Jaxartes)

Bokhara

Merv

Samarqand

Urgench

Amu Darya (Oxus)

Aral Sea

KHWARAZM

Baghdad

Abbasid Caliphate

The Great Raid 1223

Kumans (Qipchaqs, Polovtsy)

Caspian Sea

GEORGIA

Seljuq Sultanate

Black Sea

Mediterranean Sea

Kalka River

Dniestr (Dnestr)

Dnieper (Dnepr)

Kiev

Moscow

Novgorod

RUSSIAN PRINCIPALITIES

Volga Bulgars

1215
1216
1214-23
1211-16
1209
1226
1227
1218
1219
1221
1223

1500 Miles
2000 Kilometres
1000
1500
500
1000
500

The invasion of Europe 1236-42

Novgorod

Kazan

Vladimir

Moscow

Russian Principalities

Kiev

Sea of Azov

Crimea

Sudak (Soldaya)

POLAND

Wrocław

Krakow

Legnica (Liegnitz)

Holy Roman Empire

Wiener Neustadt

Vienna

Mohi

Pest

HUNGARY

Byzantine Empire

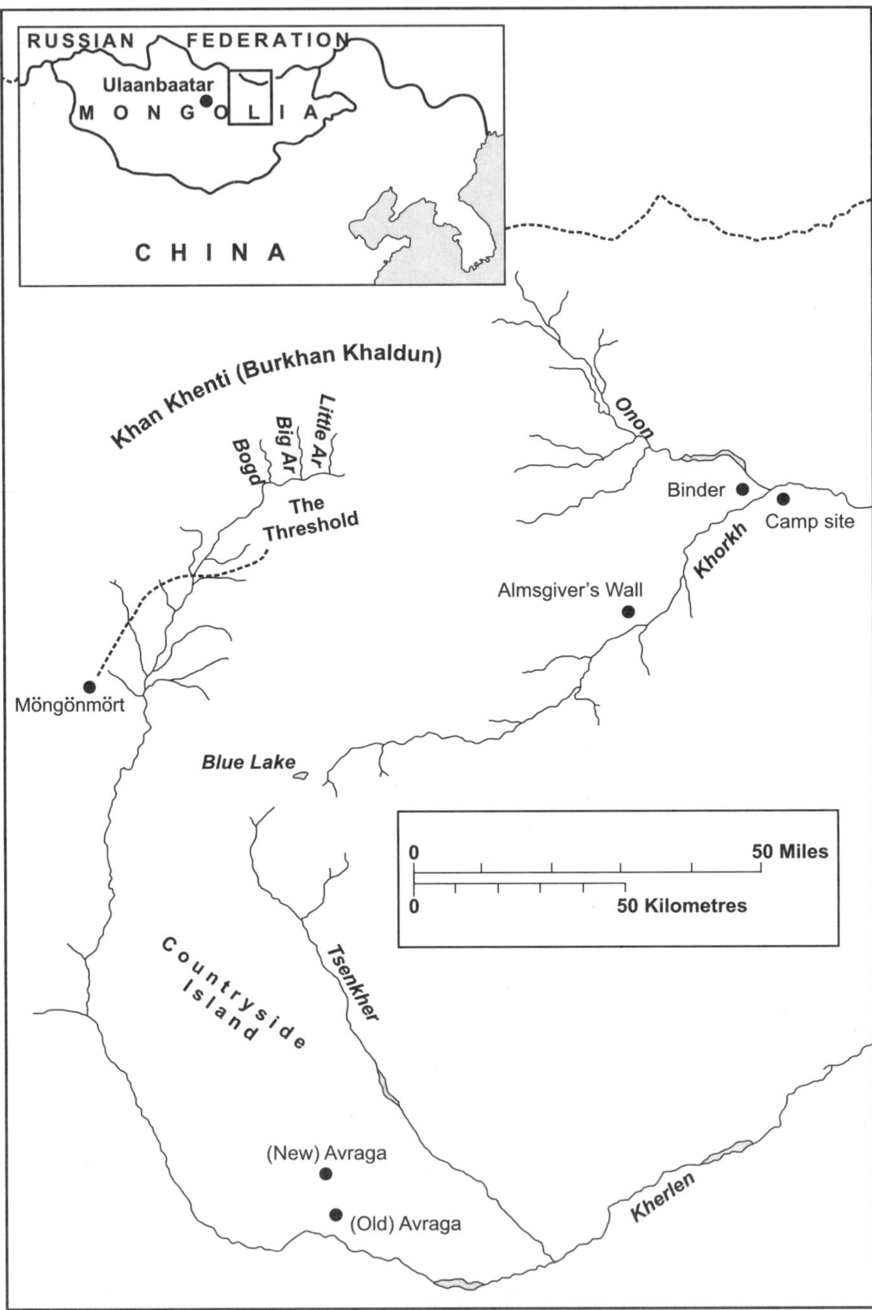

Map 3. The Mongol Heartland

acquiesced and did not pursue the matter. But his nerves had failed, and self-preservation was now his only thought. Hoping to receive favourable treatment, he left the town by the Sufi Khana Gate in the cover of night, with his troops, and submitted to the enemy, who without delay rushed in by the same gate. Qaraja was disappointed in his hopes. The Mongols imprisoned him and his followers; they reproached and reviled him for his ingratitude and disloyalty to his sovereign. 'How can we,' they said, 'expect faithful service from one who has not been true to his old benefactor?'[30] Qaraja and his followers were executed. The inhabitants of Utrar were then driven out of the town and the city given to plunder and pillage.

Resolved to fight to the last, Ghayir Khan threw himself into the citadel with his 20,000 valiant men. The fortress proved too strong for the Mongols to be carried by storm and so they resolved to starve out the defiant garrison. Their provisions were running short and there was no visible sign or hope of any relief. They made several sallies and inflicted heavy casualties on the Mongols, and held out for another month. At last Ghayir Khan was left but with two of his followers. Even then he carried on the unequal and now fruitless struggle. He refused to submit, for he was afraid—not of death which he had faced too often—but the sufferings and sorrows of servitude. The Mongol troops entered the citadel and surrounded the tower where he had taken refuge. As they had been directed to capture him alive, the Mongol soldiers made no attempt to kill him. When his two faithful companions also fell and he ran short of fighting material, he resorted to hurling bricks at his enemies, which were handed to him by a slave-girl. It was only when the bricks were exhausted that the Mongols rushed on him from all sides. Even then he carried on his stubborn resistance and, by various devices and assaults, threw many of them down before falling into the hands of his enemies. He was bound hand and foot and carried to Chingiz Khan who had molten silver poured into his eyes, ears, and throat.

The city had been plundered and was desolate. Now they razed the walls of the citadel to the ground. Of the few people left in that place, and the master artificers who had escaped the general massacre,[31] some were imprisoned and some were driven along with the army, to exercise their trades in the Mongol camp.

While Uktai and Chaghatai were hammering at the gates and walls of Utrar, Juji was laying waste the prosperous and pleasant region of Farghane stretching about a hundred miles along the upper Jaxartes. This was the land for which Babur, ensconced in Hindustan, did not cease to pine. Juji[32] had been commissioned to act against the cities from Jand to Lake Aral. Saqnaq, capital of Qipchaqs on the banks of the Oxus near Jand, was the first town he came across on his route. To avoid a siege and the consequent delay, Juji sent Hasan Haji to negotiate a surrender. Hasan was a Muslim merchant and, after many years of service with the Mongols, had risen to prominence. On account of his past affiliations and relations with the inhabitants of Saqnaq, Hasan Haji could be trusted to have a favourable audience. But when he reached Saqnaq, he found that the inhabitants were not prepared to hear him. For they looked upon him as a traitor to his country and a renegade to his faith. The people raised a tumult and put him to death. Juji then set upon Saqnaq. No respite was given to its defenders. From morning to sunset, storming parties carried on a relentless assault in successive relays. The siege lasted only seven days and, when the city was finally taken no mercy was shown to the vanquished. The place was razed and the inhabitants massacred to atone for the murder of the envoy, Hasan Haji. Hasan's son was appointed governor of the district.

Continuing on his way, Juji captured the towns of Barjaligh-Kent and Ozgand, and as their inhabitants had refrained from offering active resistance, they escaped general massacre. But Ashnas, the next town offered stubborn resistance; its garrison of vagabonds and rascals as the pro-Mongol historians call them fought to the last man.

When news of this spread Qutlugh Khan who had been posted at Jand by the sultan evacuated the town and sought safety in flight. Crossing the Oxus, he made for Khwarazm. When news of this reached the Mongol camp, Jintimur was despatched to treat with the inhabitants and advise them to surrender. But at Jand, there was no chief or leader. Everyone talked and behaved as he thought fit and prudent, and Jintimur had to face popular fury and hostility to all proposals of submission to the infidels. Jintimur got wind of the conspiracy to take his life like Hasan's and, with consummate politeness and wisdom, he foiled and paralysed them. Reminding the people of the fate which had overtaken Saqnaq on account of Hasan Haji's murder, he humoured them with the promise that their lives and properties would remain safe if they submitted without resistance. This satisfied the people and they allowed him to return untouched. On his return to the camp, he reported to Juji all that he had observed and experienced there: the conspiracy to kill him and his escape by means of skilful persuasion and flattery, their weakness and deficiency in 'war material', and above all, differences of opinion among them. Juji had not intended to make an immediate move on Jand but, on learning of the confused state of affairs there, decided to profit by the enemy's weakness and unpreparedness. Reaching the environs of Jand on 4 Safar AH 616 (22

April 1219), he opened a sudden assault on the city. Its inhabitants had never seen a battle or experienced a siege, and so they imagined that the Mongols would never be able to scale the high walls of their citadel. They only shut the gates and climbed on the city walls and towers to watch the besiegers, but made no arrangements for defence or to organize resistance—while the Mongols threw bridges over the ditch and prepared to storm the place. The invaders did not have to exert themselves, for they mounted the walls from all sides and opened the gates without encountering the slightest resistance. Not a single soldier was wounded or injured on either side. As the inhabitants had abstained from active opposition and violence, Juji treated them with consideration. Their lives were spared, only the ringleaders who had spoken fiercely to Jintimur were put to death. The citizens were driven out of their homes and dwellings into the open country, where they remained for nine days while the town was plundered. The defences of Jand were levelled to the dust. Ali Khwaja of Bokhara, a trusted and experienced man, was appointed governor of the town and was given wide powers to administer the locality. From Jand, Juji despatched a contingent of ten thousand under a Mongol general to Shahr Kent. The town was easily and speedily occupied and a Mongol Shahna was left there. Juji thereupon set out to join the main army under Chingiz Khan.

Meanwhile, the third Mongol army under Saktu Buqa and Alaq Noyan, was successfully operating against the towns up the river Fanakat. Proceeding from Utrar, the Mongol commanders reached Fanakat[33]—afterwards known as Shah-Rukhia, in honour of Timur's son—standing immediately below the confluence of the Angran and the Jaxartes and commanding the great Khurasan road from Samarqand to Shah. It was a place of considerable importance and was noted for the turbulence of its inhabitants. Probably that was the reason why it did not have fortified walls. On the arrival of the Mongols, the garrison commander Iyal-Ku Malik, finding himself unable to defend the town shut himself up with his Turkish troops in the citadel. For three days he offered stubborn resistance and defended the citadel vigorously. But then he lost heart, opened the gates, and came out to ask for quarter. Grim was the fate of the garrison; the soldiers were sorted out and separated from the civilians; some of them were put to the sword, while others were killed by arrows. The victors divided the people into groups of ten and hundred, selected the artisans and the young for siege works, and marched on Khojend.

Situated on the southern bank of the Jaxartes, Khojend[34] was celebrated for its vineyards and gardens,[35] for its trade, and for the bravery of its citizens. The city had a citadel and when the Mongol columns arrived, the people retired behind its walls. At this time the city had an intrepid governor, Timur Malik by name. Timur Malik had constructed a lofty fortress at the point just below the city where the Jaxartes is joined by its tributary, and determined to hold out as long as possible, he entrenched himself in it with a thousand loyal and brave warriors. The Mongols surrounded the city and the fortress but could not lay their hands on Timur Malik. They reduced the city, and then as their missiles and arrows were making no effect upon the fortress, decided to construct a causeway across the rivers. The young men of the city were, accordingly, collected in crowds and assistance was also requisitioned from the nearby towns and villages, which had been subdued, until 50,000 men were assembled together to help the force of 20,000 Mongols. They grouped the prisoners into gangs of ten and hundreds and over every ten placed a Mongol to force the unhappy prisoners to bring stones to the river bed from the hills three *farsangs* away. The Mongols then dropped these stones into the river so as to form a dam.

Undaunted by the heavy odds against him the resourceful Timur Malik prepared for the impending battle. He had twelve boats constructed, which were covered with felts plastered over with a mixture of fresh clay and vinegar so as to render them fireproof. The boats had windows or portholes through which arrows and other missiles could be discharged. Every day, at daylight, six of them rowed over to each shore to shoot at the Mongols and prevent the construction of the causeway while at night the besieged garrison made desperate attacks and sallies to destroy the dam. Thus, the besieged made desperate efforts to prevent the completion of the causeway. The hail of arrows and stones continued day in and day out; the daily battle of the boats against the artillery went on. Finding his efforts of no avail and his provisions running out, the Iron Commander decided to leave. He had already arranged for seventy boats and he loaded them with his effects, placed his family therein, and one night, embarking with his warriors, he launched into the river. Once aware of his flight, the Mongol forces set out in his pursuit along both the banks of the river. At every place where they could offer opposition, Timur Malik would draw near with his own vessel, and shoot his arrows which, says Juwaini 'never missed their mark'. He drove off the Mongols and again pushed on with his vessel. Fighting and fleeing, fleeing and fighting, he reached Fanakat, where he found a chain stretched across the river. Timur Malik was not, however, to be checked and stopped by such devices, and 'with one blow of an axe he cut the chain into two',[36] and pushed on. But the Mongols were equally relentless. They followed him down the river and passed an intermittent shower of arrows from both banks till he reached the environs of Jand and

Barjaligh-Kent. Meanwhile the news of Timur Malik's flight had reached Juji and, to bar his progress, he posted forces on both banks of the river and built a pontoon bridge on which were mounted catapults. Becoming aware of the formidable preparations made down the river, he landed near Barjaligh-Kent, and, with the speed of fire, fanned by a strong wind, he made for Khwarazm. The tenacious Mongols still pursued him, but Timur Malik was not one whose courage or resolution could be broken. Whenever the Mongols drew near, he would turn around and fight a rearguard action until his family had made some progress forward. The pursuit and the unequal combat lasted for several days during the course of which most of Timur Malik's men were wounded and killed, while the number of the pursuing Mongols kept increasing. They seized all his baggage, but he would not yield and, with the few men remaining, continued his flight. At last his few remaining followers were killed and Timur Malik was left alone, 'all alone, on a wide sea.' He now had no means of defence but three arrows, one of which was broken with its head gone. Three Mongols were still after him and gaining ground. Drawing the broken and headless arrow from his quiver, Timur Malik, the unerring archer that he was, shot it through the eye of one of them, and blinded him. 'Two arrows still remain in my quiver according to your number,' he called to the two surviving pursuers, 'and they will not miss the mark.' The Mongols fell back and he reached Khwarazm safe. No sooner did he arrive at Khwarazm than he began gathering men for the struggle against the Mongols. He surprised the town of Kint, killed its Mongol Shahna, but, then thinking it inadvisable to stay in Khwarazm, set out to join Sultan Mohammad—who was now a fugitive and fleeing from one place to another to escape the Mongols.

A few more words about the later career of Timur Malik would not be out of place. Tired of the wandering life that attendance upon the Khwarazm Shah entailed, he renounced the world and became a recluse or *darwesh*. Disguised as a *darwesh* and wandering from place to place in Iraq-i-Ajam, he finally settled in Syria. But when the troubles subsided and the country return to normal, the love of his country impelled him to leave his hiding place. On reaching Khojend he found that by the orders of Batu Khan, his son had inherited his property. 'Will you recognize your father if you were to see him?,' he asked his son. 'I was only a sucking babe when I was separated from my father,' he replied. 'I have, however, an old slave who knows him.' And the slave did recognize his old master. But there were many persons who owed him money and they refused to acknowledge the veracity of his claim. At the time Uktai Khan was the supreme ruler of all the Mongols and was celebrated for his munificence and magnanimity, and Timur Malik set out to lay his case before the Mongol Khaqan. On his way to the imperial court, Timur Malik called at the court of Qadqan Ughlan, a prince of the royal family, who, displeased by his haughty bearing, put Timur Malik in chains. Soon after, he was recognized by the Mongol into whose eye he had shot his unerring arrow. Timur Malik was interrogated about his struggle against the Mongols, and he answered in the same insolent tones in which the questions were put. Offended, the savage Mongol shot an arrow at his old adversary which, as he exclaimed, answered for all the arrows he had discharged against the Mongols. Timur Malik died.

Severe and uncompromising, Timur Malik stands out in striking contrast to the degenerate nobles and the imperial dignitaries who looked on as the empire went to pieces. They made no attempt to fight but withdrew to their country estates where luxury and degenerate enjoyment beautified their last days. Had there been a few more devoted soldiers like Ghayir Khan and Timur Malik, they might have brought the titanic Mongol onslaught to a halt.

Bokhara and Samarqand

Having despatched the Mongol contingents under his elder sons and the Noyans to subjugate the various cities and towns of Transoxiana, Chingiz Khan, accompanied by Tuli, set out for Bokhara.[37] When he reached Zarnuq, he sent his envoy Danishmand Hajib to inform the inhabitants of his arrival and to advise them to surrender. Though the people had been terrified by the sudden arrival of a huge host, they did not give up hope and decided to fight. To clinch the issue they wished to murder the Mongol emissary. Getting wind of their intensions, Danishmand Hajib loudly declared, 'I, a Muslim and the son of a Muslim, have come to you in accordance with the will of God and in obedience to the order of Chingiz Khan, I have come to you as a messenger to warn you of the ill-consequences of resistance and to pull you out of the whirlpool of annihilation and blood. The great Khan is himself here with several thousand warriors. If you attempt to resist him, these walls of yours will be razed to the ground and the extensive plain round your city will become a river of blood in no time. If you listen to me and decide to submit according to my advice, your lives and properties will be saved.' The confident tones in which Danishmand spoke and the ring of sincerity in his speech convinced the citizens of the futility of resistance. The town submitted and was spared a general massacre. The inhabitants were, however, driven out of the town to give the Mongols a free hand to plunder. The city fortifications were destroyed and the young men were recruited for siege works at Bokhara. Having given his horses rest and fodder, Chingiz Khan made ready for Bokhara. As Zarnuq[38] had escaped general massacre and destruction, it was named Qutlugh Baligh or the Fortunate City.

The advance guard under Tair-Bahadur was sent to summon Nur. Some Turkoman guides with knowledge of the routes and the roads led the troops to Nur by a hitherto unknown road, which from that date has been called the 'Khan's Road'. The inhabitants of Nur were taken by surprise and had time only to shut the gates. Tair-Bahadur sent them an emissary, advising them to follow the sensible example of Zarnuq. After protracted negotiations, as the inhabitants were not sure of the arrival of Chingiz Khan in person, and also at the same time wanted to be wary of the sultan, they agreed to send an envoy with gifts to him to beg for his protection. Tair-Bahadur was satisfied, accepted a few presents for himself and set out towards Bokhara. When the envoy from Nur presented himself before the Mongol Khan, he was directed to surrender the town to Subutai. When Subutai reached Nur, the town was duly surrendered. He asked the inhabitants to evacuate the town, taking with them only provisions, agricultural implements, and cattle, and to leave their houses as they were—to be plundered by the troops. Having recruited sixty men for siege works at Dabusiya, Subutai marched off. The miseries and privations of the people were not yet over. Soon after Chingiz Khan reached Nur and the citizens had to arrange for a proper reception and welcomed him by offering him provisions, scarlet silks and other costly things. Chingiz Khan demanded a year's taxes in advance, which amounted to 1500 dinars. Setting out from Nur, he reached Bokhara (February 1220)[39] and camped before the gate of the fortress opening on the *registan*, the great sandy plan.

Samarqand and Bokhara were the two chief cities of Transoxiana. If Samarqand was the political centre, Bokhara was the religious metropolis. Ever since its foundation it had been the focus of religion and learning. 'In the East', says Juwaini in true Oriental style, 'it is the dome of Islam, nay more—it is the Medina of these regions—its villas and suburbs embellished with the whiteness of the learning of the Muslim divines and jurists, its quarters adorned with the pavilions of persons of illustrious lineage.'[40]

Situated at a short distance south of the river Sughd, the main town was dotted with beautiful villas and gardens, mosques and markets, public baths and open squares, and measured a league along every direction. The suburbs and towns lying all round the city extended a further nine leagues. The entire town was enclosed by a wall measuring over a hundred miles in circuit with seven iron gates.

Bokhara was at this time garrisoned by 20,000 troops under Kok Khan, a Mongol deserter, and had been reinforced by 12,000 horsemen under Kashli Khan, the Amir Akhur of the Khwarazm Shah. The amirs and generals, Hamid Bur, Sunj Khan, Kashli Khan, and Kok Khan planned to surprise the Mongols during the night and cut their way through to join the sultan. Under cover of night, the sortie was made through an apparently unguarded gate. The Mongols had, however, became aware of their plan and the nightguard had prepared to give them a fierce reception and pursuit. No sooner did the flying garrison reach the Oxus than they were attacked by the Mongols, who after a relentless pursuit put nearly all of them to death. Bokhara had no alternative but to surrender to the enemy. There was no 'several days' siege.'[41] The leading divines and distinguished men of Bokhara issued forth from the city at dawn and surrendered on 21 February 1220.[42] Accompanied by them, Chingiz Khan entered the city to view the town and its fortifications. Entering the Great Mosque, impressed by its beauty and majesty, he stopped near the pulpit and enquired if it were the palace of the Shah. On being told that it was the principal mosque, the House of Allah, he dismounted, ascended two or three steps of the pulpit, and, addressing the people present, said 'In the countryside there is neither fodder nor meat. It is bare of hay and grain. Give fodder to my houses, open the doors of your storehouses and give us provisions.'

To further demoralize the inhabitants and to celebrate his triumph, and, probably, to create fear and awe all around, he allowed his horsemen to revel and feast in the Great Mosque.

The most precious containers of the Koran were brought into the courtyard of the mosque, the sacred leaves of the Korans were trodden under foot, and the chests in which the Korans were kept were converted into troughs for their horses. The wine-cup followed in succession and the singing women of the town were brought into the sacred building to sing and dance. The Mongols thus feasted and held high revel while the imams, the nobles of the city and other high dignitaries were handed the head-stalls of the horses to hold. The sacred leaves of the Korans were flung everywhere on the ground and trampled under the hoofs of the ponies.[43]

It was a strange scene for the terror-stricken Muslims. 'Maulana, what is the meaning of all this?', said Imam Jalal-ud-din, one of the most respected divines of Transoxiana. 'O Lord! Am I awake or a sleep ... is this a bad dream?' 'Remain silent,' replied Imam Rukn-ud-din, the wrath of God is on us. It is not the time to protest or cry.'

After two hours in the Great Mosque, Chingiz Khan rode out into the open square, where Id prayers were offered. He asked the inhabitants of the town to name the wealthiest and the most distinguished among them. Two hundred and eighty persons, one hundred and ninety belonging to the city and the rest foreigners but domiciled in Bokhara, were thus brought before him. To them he enumerated the defects and failings of the Muslims and denounced the treacherous conduct of the Khwarazm Shah. He spoke in Mongol dialect and was interpreted in Persian by Danishmand Hajib. 'O people!', he called aloud, 'you should know that you have committed great sins and your chiefs and leaders are great offenders in this respect. You may ask me what proof I have for this assertion of mine. Here it is, I am the scourge of God sent on your heads. If you had not committed great sins, God would not have delivered you into my hands to punish you for your misdeeds. What is still left in your houses you need not bother about, whatever you have hidden or buried, you must bring to me.'

Chingiz Khan had ordered the inhabitants to drive out the soldiers of the Shah and give them no shelter; but, as Juwaini observes, 'to drive out of the city and citadel the garrison of the sultan was a task impossible for them.' The poor people did whatever they could but in vain. It was also brought to Chingiz Khan's notice that the citizens had given refuge to the soldiers of the Shah and he ordered the town to be given to flames. As the buildings in the city were mostly made of wood, the greater portion of the city was quickly reduced to ashes, only the Great Mosque and a few other brick buildings remained.

The Mongols now turned their attention towards the citadel where Kok Khan had shut himself and his garrison of 20,000 Qanqalis. They forced the inhabitants of Bokhara to participate in the battle for the citadel. Kok Khan defended the citadel with grim determination. The besieged made repeated sorties and, time and again, inflicted heavy losses on the Mongols but all the vigours of the blockade began to tell on the defenders. They were determined to fight to the last, to die but not to give in. At last the Mongols filled the ditch with dead bodies of men and beasts, stones, rubbish and the like, and scaled the walls of the fortress. Kok Khan, the governor and all those found inside the citadel—the number is given at 30,000—'including grandees and great men, the servants of the sultan, who were treated in the most contemptuous manner, and their females and children were carried away into slavery. The city walls and the citadel were razed to the ground. All the inhabitants of the city, with their women and children, were then asked to go outside the city on to the plain, leaving behind all their possessions in their houses. They were allowed to take nothing with them beyond the clothes they wore. Skilled workmen and young men of sound physique were then picked out to do the siege work at Dabusia and Samarqand. Fortunately for the inhabitants there was no general massacre and they were allowed to return. But, as Prawdin observes,[44] 'by the time the Mongols withdrew, Bokhara had ceased to exist as a military position from which the Shah might have been able to threaten Chingiz Khan.' When an inhabitant of the devastated town was questioned about the fate of Bokhara and her new masters, he said, 'They came, they dug, they burnt, they murdered, they robbed and they went away.'

'A more succinct and graphic account of the Mongol conquerors', says Juwaini,[45] 'could not be given.' Nothing remained of the beautiful Bokhara, the city of academics and orchards, but the Great Mosque and a few buildings, built of brick. It took more than a century to recover from the harrowing Mongol devastation, for Ibn Batuta found its mosques, markets, and colleges in a state of ruin.

Situated on high ground at a short distance from the river Soghd, Samarqand with its innumerable canals, stone-paved streets, lead pipes, and smiling gardens, orchards and stately palaces, was, as Si Yu Ki put it,[46] 'a delicious place'. There were gardens and groves, extending for more than a hundred *li*. 'Even Chinese gardens', according to Si Yu Ki,[47] 'could not be compared (with those of Samarqand), the gardens in that country are very quiet; not even the singing of birds is heard there.'

At the time when Chingiz Khan reached near Utrar, Samarqand was reputed for the strength of its defences and the bravery of its garrison, and all felt that years would be required to reduce the city, not to speak of the citadel.[48] Chingiz Khan decided to first conquer the adjoining districts and thereby clear his rear of enemies before he advanced on Samarqand. To have all his troops at his disposal for the great effort against the strongly defended city, he directed his sons and the Noyans to reduce northern Transoxiana, and then converge on Samarqand while he finished Bokhara and the neighbouring districts.

Having recruited a large number of prisoners at Bokhara to do sapper's work at the siege, he set out for Samarqand by way of the beautiful valley of Soghd (or Zarafshan). On his way he did not molest the towns which surrendered, and even where opposition was offered, as at Sar-i-Pul and Dabusia, he did not stop.

Arriving at Samarqand, Chingiz Khan encamped at 'Kok Serai', Muharram 617/ March 1220.[49] Here he was joined by the three army corps, who had completed their work of subduing northern Transoxiana. These divisions brought with them firm and stalwart captives, men who might be of use in siege work.

Of all the towns and cities, Samarqand was the most strongly fortified. It had an army of 110,000 of whom 60,000 were Turks and the rest Tajiks, 'each of whom was the Rustem of the age.'[50] Besides, there were twenty fighting elephants of formidable appearance. There were a number of generals like Shaikh Khan, Bala Khan, and others but no great soldier like Timur Malik or Ghayir Khan to organize resistance or inspire the defenders with their indomitable resolution never to yield. Under a bold and experienced commander, Samarqand could have given an honourable account of itself.

Chingiz Khan spent two days in riding round the city and reconnoitring its high walls and iron gates, its battlements, the deep ditch and other defences. On learning that the Shah was not in the town, he despatched Subutai, Yamah, and his son-in-law Toghachar Gurgan, with 60,000 troops[51] to pursue the Shah giving him neither time nor opportunity to organize resistance.

To demoralize the besieged garrison and civilians, Chingiz Khan ordered his captives also to be assembled and drawn up before the city in army formation. It was a clever device to dismay the defenders, for when they looked at the enemy from their walls and towers, they found the Mongols 'more numerous than the sand-particles of the desert and the rains drops.'[52]

The besieged garrison made a sortie from the city gates and attacked the Mongols. The battle was fiercely contested for hours, and the Turkish soldiers of the sultan excelled that day in skill and bravery. They inflicted heavy casualties on the Mongols, took a large number of prisoners, and carried them off into the city but they themselves lost a thousand men. Chingiz Khan was incensed and, the following day, himself mounted a horse and assumed the control of the troops. Having posted men all around the city, he ordered the kettle-drums to be sounded for a general assault. The besieged poured out of the city gates and offered furious resistance until the evening prayers. Finding the Mongols stubborn and the investment complete, the besieged sought to break their iron blockade by the use of their fighting elephants. The elephants made some impression on the enemy's line, smashing through the ranks of the infantry. Yet, maddened by cuts and wounds given by Mongol darts and lances, they broke loose, running on the field like ships without rudders, trampling down friend and foe.

The heavy losses suffered by them in their sorties and the failure of the elephants against the Mongol cavalry disheartened the besieged and differences concerning the prosecution of the struggle arose amongst them. The Shaikhul Islam and the qazi favoured submission and surrender to the enemy. They waited on Chingiz Khan to ask for terms. He promised them 'protection against his anger'[53] and permitted them to return to the town. As arranged between them, they opened the Namazgah Gate at the time of morning prayers and the Mongols rushed into the town. They did not molest the town folk who ran pell-mell for safety, but busied themselves levelling the walls and defences. The demolition was carried on with marvellous rapidity and singleness of purpose. For a whole day and night, the Mongols paid no attention to the inhabitants; at night the work was carried on in torchlight. When all the walls had been razed to the ground, the Mongol troops entered the town.[54]

Men and women were, as was now customary with the Mongols, driven out in batches of hundreds into the open plain. An exception was made in the case of the qazi and the Shaikhul Islam and their followers. They were exempted from the outrages inflicted on the rest. The number of people is said to have amounted to more than 50,000. It sounds incredible but Samarqand had an area of 750 acres, was densely populated and, according to Si Yu Ki,[55] had 'a population of more than a hundred thousand families, but after the occupation only the fourth part remained behind.' The Mongols plundered and pillaged the open houses. The inhabitants had only themselves to blame for their sorrows and sufferings. Secure within their mighty walls, they might have held the Mongols at bay. It was on account of their internal disputes that one of the strongest places admitted the enemy after so tame a defence. It was lucky for Chingiz Khan that there was someone in the impregnable town to open the gates.

With the city completely in the hands of the Mongols, the garrison was in a desperate position. The citadel had more than 30,000 troops under Alp-Khan, Sersigh-Khan, Ulagh-Khan and others but they were now completely hemmed in—with no prospects of relief and with no hopes of surviving the siege. Alp-Khan decided to make an attempt to escape. With one thousand chosen and daring warriors, he came out of the citadel, charged through the Mongol force, cut his way out, and succeeded in joining the sultan—and conveyed the dismal news of Samarqand's inglorious end.

Infuriated by that successful sortie the Mongols tightened the blockade and closely surrounded the citadel. The besieged garrison still held out and defended itself obstinately. The Mongols, thereupon, destroyed the dam of the Jakardiza canal, whose waters flooded the land surrounding the fortress and undermined the walls. The Mongols then launched a vigorous assault and succeeded in penetrating the citadel. The garrison, now numbering only a thousand, but all brave and unyielding, continued to fight. Overwhelmed by superior numbers, they retired to the Great Mosque only to continue the heroic struggle. Revolving arrows and burning naptha were freely used by the combatants until 'the Great Mosque and all those within were consumed by the fire of this world but baptised by the water of eternity.'[56] Everyone found within the citadel was slaughtered.

Grim was the fate of the survivors and of the 30,000 Qanqali and Turkish troops, who had surrendered and deserted. They were grouped into tens and hundreds and their foreheads were shaved in the fashion of the Mongols as a sign of their incorporation in the main army. Lulled into security, they were, one and all, massacred in the night. The Mongols appreciated courage and devotion but never trusted deserters. Their logic was simple and ruthless: one who was not true to his own master could not trusted to be loyal and faithful to them. Skilled craftsmen and artists, numbering 30,000, were selected and bestowed by Chingiz Khan upon his sons and relations. Another 30,000 or more young warriors were picked for military service and siege works. It was only then that the remaining inhabitants were allowed to return to their dwellings on payment of a ransom of 20,000 dinars and a Mongol Shahna was appointed over the city. Several times afterwards levies were made and people were recruited for Mongol forces. The city was, consequently, desolated and ruined. When Ibn Batuta visited the town in the fourteenth century, he could still see the effects of Mongol devastation. The city was without walls and gates and only a few houses remained in the midst of a maze of ruins.

Should one wonder or lament at the stupidity and inability of the Qanqali Turkish troops to learn from the terrible fate of all the traitors at the hands of the Mongols, or condemn them for their depravity and dishonourable conduct. Trying to save their lives at the cost of their honour, they could do neither, and betrayed both their monarch and their country.

Notes

1. *Tabaqat-i-Nasiri*, pp. 335-6.
2. Rashid-ud-din, fol. 187; *Rauzat-us-Safa*, vol. V, p. 23.
3. *Rauzat-us-Safa*, vol. V, p. 23; Also Rashid-ud-din, fol. 188 and *Tabaqat-i-Nasiri*, p. 336.
4. *Rauzat-us-Safa*, vol. V, p. 23.
5. Ibid.
6. Ibid.
7. This episode reminds us of a similar predicament faced by Raja Birbal, one of the 'nine gems' of Emperor Akbar's court, on a similar mission to the court of the Persian Shah. The Raja was asked about the relative power of the Shah of Iran and that of his sovereign. The astute Raja politely submitted that his master

was like the new moon while the Shah was comparable to the full moon. Deservedly famous for his cool and calm temperament no less than his wit and humour, the Raja later on elucidated that 'new moon' indicated 'rising power' while full moon implied 'declining power'.

8. Babar, pp. 26-8.

9. *Rauzat-us-Safa*, vol. V, pp. 23-4.

10. Juwaini, I, p. 58.

11. Ibid., p. 60.

12. Ibid., pp. 60-1; *Rauzat-us-Safa*, vol. V, p. 24. According to the *Mongolian Chronicle*, p. 182, Kuqhna was head of the envoys, hundred in number.

13. *Tabaqat-i-Nasiri*, p. 337. The camel driver, according to the venerable qazi, had gone to one of the public baths, and could, therefore, make his escape by the fire place.

14. Ibid.; Juwaini, vol. I, pp. 60-1.

15. Juwaini, vol. I, p. 62.

16. Ibid., p. 61.

17. Ibid., pp. 61-2.

18. Ibid.

19. Juwaini, vol. II.

20. Raverty, p. 275.

21. Juwaini, vol. I, pp. 64, 68, 91.

22. *Tabaqat-i-Nasiri*, p. 342, also Raverty, pp. 276-7.

23. Raverty, p. 285.

24. *Tabaqat-i-Nasiri*, p. 338; Raverty, p. 273. But he knew that his was an army which was disciplined, devoted and dependable, like the Light Brigade immortalized by Tennyson, as it was capable of braving and overcoming all obstacles and opposition, irrespective of the nature, dimension, strength of the obstacles.

25. Juwaini, vol. I, pp. 62-3; Rashid-ud-din, fol. 195.

26. Juwaini, vol. I, pp. 63-6; Rashid-ud-din, fol. 196; Sharfuddin, fols. 97-8.

27. *Tabaqat-i-Nasiri*, p. 338.

28. Juwaini , vol. I, p. 65.

29. Ibid.

30. 'The lives of the inhabitants were spared', says Howorth (Part I, p. 76) and that too, in the face of all the Persian authorities. *Tabaqat-i-Nasiri*, p. 338; Juwaini, vol. I, p. 66; Rashid-ud-din, fol. 166; Sharfuddin, fol. 97.

31. Juwaini, vol. I, pp. 66-70; Rashid-ud-din, fols. 196-8; Sharfuddin, fol. 98.

32. Juwaini, vol. I, p. 70, Rashid-ud-din, fol. 198.

33. Juwaini, vol. I, pp. 71-4; Rashid-ud-din, fols. 198-200; Sharfuddin, fol. 99.

34. Ye-lu-Chutsai, like Babur three centuries after him, was deeply impressed by its excellent fruits, especially pomegranates. Khojend, he said, 'abounds in pomegranates. They are as large as two fists and of a sour-sweet taste. People take from three to five of this fruit and press out the juice into a vessel. That

makes a delicious beverage for slaking thirst.' Bretschneider, *Medieval Researches,* vol. 1, pp. 19-20.

35. *Rauzat-us-Safa,* vol. V, p. 28.

36. Juwaini, vol. I, pp. 64, 75-85; Rashid-ud-din, fols. 201-3; Sharfuddin, fols. 95-7; Ibnul Asir, vol. XII, pp. 166-9; and Nassavi, p. 44, gives only a brief account.

37. Not Tashqand as Howorth asserts, Part I, p. 78.

38. Ibnul Asir, *Tarikh al-Kumil,* vol. XII, p. 168; *Tabaqat-i-Nasiri,* p. 339.

39. According to Juwaini (vol. I, p. 79) and the later compilers, Chingiz reached Bokhara on Muharram, AH 617 March 1220.

40. Cf. Howorth, Part I, p. 78.

41. *Tabaqat-i-Nasiri,* p. 339.

42. Juwaini, vol. I, pp. 80-1.

43. Prawdin, *The Mongol Empire,* p. 170.

44. Juwaini, vol. I, p. 83. The Russian experience, a few years later, was no different. 'And the Tartars turned back from the river Quneifer, and we know not whence they came, not where they rid themselves again. God knows whence fetched them against us for our sins.' *The Chronicle of Novogorod,* Eng. tr. Campden Society, 1946, p. 46.

45. *Med. Res.,* vol. I, p. 21.

46. Ibid., p. 81.

47. Juwaini, vol. I, p. 91.

48. *Tabaqat-i-Nasiri,* p. 340; Ibnul Asir, vol. XII, p. 169.

49. Juwaini, vol. I, p. 91.

50. *Tabaqat-i-Nasiri,* p. 341; Timurid historians put the figure at 30,000, which I find hard to accept for reasons given in the chapter: 'The Mongol Avalanche'.

51. Juwaini, vol. I, p. 92.

52. *Habib al-siyar,* vol. I, part III, p. 12.

53. According to *Tabaqat-i-Nasiri,* p. 340, it was taken on 10th Muharram.

54. *Med. Res.,* vol. I, p. 78.

55. Juwaini, vol. I, p. 95.

5

The Mongol Avalanche

IN KEEPING WITH HIS POLICY of hunting down the Shah and allowing the provinces no time to rally round their monarch, or organize resistance to the Mongols, Chingiz Khan decided to reduce Khurasan, one of the most flourishing provinces of the Shah's empire. With Khurasan wrested from his hands, the position of the Shah, both materially and strategically, would become desperate; the empire would be cut into two unwieldy portions unable to help each other; and the Shah would be deprived of the immense resources of Khurasan. For this important and also formidable task, Chingiz Khan's choice fell on his youngest son, Tuli, styled the Ulugh Noyan or the Great Captain. Trained and tested by his father, Tuli was admirably fit to carry out the manoeuvre.

Having crossed the Oxus with Balkh with Bamian reduced to ashes, Chingiz Khan ordered Tuli to proceed to Khurasan with 80,000 horsemen— warning him against of the honey-tongued Khurasanians, to spare those who submitted, and to annihilate those towns and cities that dared to defy him. Toghachar Gurgan, the younger brother of Qarachar Noyan and Chingiz Khan's son-in-law, was commissioned to go with him. In Rabi I 617/May 1220, Tuli set out from Taliqan and proceeded towards Khurasan.

Imagining the triumphal march of Subutai and Yamah Noyan across Iran and Iraq, Tuli had conceived an early conclusion of his task. He directed Toghachar to proceed to Nishapur and accept its formal surrender.[1] For the elders of the city had promised Subutai and Yamah to give up the town when summoned to do so. But much water had flown down the Murghab since then. A short while after the departure of the two Mongol generals, rumours spread that the sultan had defeated and overpowered them in Iraq, and people were confirmed in their beliefs by complete absence of all news about the movements and whereabouts of the Mongol columns; the spirits of the people rose high, and they thought the time opportune to throw off the hated Mongol yoke. The contagion of revolt and resistance affected the inhabitants of Tus and, at the instigation of their commander, Siraj-ud-din, the troops killed the Shahna of Tus, and sent his head as a trophy to Nishapur. This was reported to the Mongol commandant Qishtimur at Ustawa by Syed Butarab, appointed by the Mongols as the head of the chiefs of Tus. Surreptitiously, he slipped out of the town and informed Qishtimur of the brewing storm in Tus and Nishapur. But Qishtimur had only a force of three hundred horsemen to look after the herds and cattle, and sent an agent to inform the Ulugh Noyan, now marching down upon Khurasan. Without waiting for reinforcements or a reply, Qishtimur marched upon Tus, and overpowered and captured Siraj-ud-din, who had only a thousand men to fight under him. Qishtimur put most of them to death and as a precautionary measure, demolished the ramparts and the city walls. Consequently, when Toghachar Gurgan arrived with ten thousand men and the leading amirs as the vanguard of Tuli, and appeared at the gates of Nishapur in the middle of Ramzan, AH 617 November 1220, he found the people determined to resist. The inhabitants behaved with great courage and bravery; they made daring and repeated sallies upon the Mongols and inflicted heavy casualties. On the third day, they launched a furious attack from the side of the Qaraqunh tower, and vigorous was the shower of darts and revolving-arrows from the towers and the ramparts. In the unremitting hail of stones and arrows Toghachar Gurgan was killed by a chance arrow.

Finding the city strongly garrisoned and amply provisioned, Toghachar's deputy, Nurka Noyan, decided to raise the siege, and divided his force into two bodies to march by two different routes. He himself took the direction of Sabzwar, four days' march due west of Nishapur. Very strongly built, it had markets covered by a wooden roof on arches and specialized in the production of grapes and other fruits. The inhabitants put up a brave and spirited defence but, after assailing it for three days and nights, the Mongols stormed the town and massacred the entire population, said to be seventy thousand. The other half of the Mongol force set out for Tus to help Qishtimur to reduce the remaining fortified portion of the town. The inhabitants of Nuqan and Qar offered stubborn resistance, and fought many battles; the Mongols, however, ultimately captured the two places and put all the inhabitants to the sword.

Emboldened and encouraged by their success, the inhabitants of Nishapur rose in open revolt and lost no opportunity to harass the Mongols. Whenever they got news of any Mongol detachment, they set out to surprise and waylay it. But during the winter provisions became scarce, the prices of commodities shot up and the inhabitants became distressed. To keep up the morale, the rebel leaders refused to allow the people to go out; with the Mongols swarming in Khurasan, it was also imperative for security reasons not to people out and risk valuable information reaching the enemy.

Najeeb-ud-din Bahaul Mulk, 'the storyteller', had been appointed by Sultan Muhammad to replace Mujirul Mulk as the Governor of Merv.[2] No sooner did he take charge of his important post than he received news of the sultan's flight across Tirmiz, the confusion and distraction in Khurasan, the coming of terrible enemies from beyond the Pamirs, and the letter of the sultan, 'adorned with the imperial signature and illustrated by the marginal notes of cowardice and pusillanimity.' 'Soldiers, warriors and officers', ran the royal prescript,[3] 'should take refuge in and defend the fortress of Muragha. Those persons who do not possess sufficient means for migration should remain where they are, and submit to the Mongol hordes on their arrival and thereby save their lives and property. They must accept their Shahna and show respect to their orders.' Bahaul Mulk inspected the citadel of Muragha and, finding it unsuited to the rigours of a Mongol attack, he marched off to Taq Yazar and fortified its strong citadel. He left behind as his deputy at Merv a lowly person, who was a Naqeeb and had Mongol leanings. Shaikhul Islam Shams-ud-din Harsi concurred with him in his intentions to submit and surrender the town to the Mongols, but the Qazi and the notables were strongly opposed to all such proposals. It was at this critical juncture, when the people were divided and demoralized, that the troops of Yamah Noyan and Subutai approached Merv. As they had no time to spare, the troops were content with verbal protestations of loyalty and costly offerings and passed on without molesting Merv.

With the Mongol thunder clouds clearing, one of the sultan's guides, Buqa, a Turkoman, came out into the open, collected a body of daring Turkoman adventurers like himself, and, with the help of the anti-Mongol party inside the city, wrested Merv from the feeble hands of the *Naqeeb*. He busied himself with strengthening the defences of the city and welcomed the broken remnants of the sultan's forces into the town. Meanwhile, the sultan had sought refuge in the islands of the Caspian Sea, and Mujirul Mulk, who had been his stirrup-bearer and in constant attendance since his removal from the governorship of Merv, set out for the city of his hopes and ambitions. Having had a taste of pomp and power, Buqa was not willing to give up his newly-acquired position and refused to allow the ex-governor to enter the city. Mujirul Mulk took up a position in the garden of Mahiabad facing the

Sarmajan Gate and waited for the reaction of the people. He was soon obliged to find a number of Maraghzi Sarhangs flocking around him and the inhabitants also came out to support him. Assured of the citizens' support, one day at noon he boldly entered the city—and did not meet any opposition. Rather he found that the Maraghzi troops had deserted Buqa and were ready to serve him. Buqa had now no alternative but to wait upon Mujirul Mulk and offer his loyal services to the former governor of the town.

Having now gathered a large number of followers and warriors, and once again back on the seat of power, Mujirul Mulk lost his mental equipoise and he considered himself to be deserving of more than a mere governorship. He began to entertain dreams of a royal throne for himself on account of his presumption that he had blue blood: his mother had been pregnant by the sultan when she was conferred in marriage upon his father. This made the Shaikhul Islam jealous and indignant. The Shaikhul Islam correctly estimated the hollow and unstable foundations of Mujirul Mulk's power and so maintained secret communications with the Qazi of Sarakhs, a relation of his, who had accepted a Mongol Shahna. Mujirul Mulk was not unaware of the treacherous conduct of the Shaikhul Islam but, on account of his learning and influence, did not dare, to lay his hands on the traitor without convincing evidence. Soon, the Shaikhul Islam's letter to the Qazi of Sarakhs was intercepted. Armed with an open and conclusive testimony, he summoned the Shaikhul Islam, and questioned him about his relations and correspondence with the Mongols. The Shaikhul Islam stoutly denied having any dealings with them or having sent them any information of any kind, until he was confronted by the intercepted letter. The traitor turned white and was utterly confounded, and the indignant Mujirul Mulk contemptuously asked him to depart. But the Sarhangs would not allow him to go scot-free. They hanged him, head downwards, and dragged the corpse by the leg to all the four corners of the town. The corpse was then cut into pieces, and the mutilated body was thrown to the dogs. Mujirul Mulk now began to adopt daring steps against the Mongols. He despatched troops to harry and harass the inhabitants of Sarakhs for having submitted to the yoke of the Mongols and for allowing a Mongol Shahna to lord over them.

Learning of the state of affairs at Merv and the power and prominence attained by Mujirul Mulk, the ambitions and aspirations of Bahaul Mulk were kindled and he appealed to the Mongol amirs of Mazandran. In return for their assistance, he promised to send them as annual tribute one silk garment for each and every house. His proposals met with ready acceptance and he was given 7,000 Mongol troops to get hold of Merv. But he was sadly ignorant of the conditions in Merv, the hold of Mujirul Mulk over the town, and the determination of the citizens to remain free. On reaching the Shahristan, he became a wiser and sadder man and decided to achieve by diplomacy what he would not get by force. 'If formerly some ill-feeling and distrust existed between us,' he wrote, to Mujirul Mulk, 'that has now vanished; as the power of the Mongols is such that wisdom and foresight alike demand that no other road save submission and obedience be traversed. At this time 7,000 Mongols with 10,000 levies are on the way to this part along with me. Regret and sorrow will follow if you do not submit to them. Nasa and Baward, they reduced in a moment. Now out of mercy and to gain your friendship, I am sending you messengers to inform you of these events so that you may withdraw from the struggle and may refrain from throwing yourself into the whirlpool of calamity and bloodshed.'

The letter made a deep impression on the advisers of Mujirul Mulk, who began evacuating the city at once. Soon, however, they got over their nervousness and realized the foolishness of believing a traitor. The agents of Bahaul Mulk were summoned and cross-examined individually about the strength of the Mongol troops accompanying him. They confirmed the statement of Bahaul Mulk, and Mujirul Mulk ordered them all to be put to death—an open declaration of his determination to hold on to the last. He despatched from Merv the remaining 1500 Turkish troops of the sultan to drive out the enemies. When Bahaul Mulk and his allies received the news of the murder of the messengers and the despatch of the troops against them, they beat a hasty retreat from the vicinity of Sarakhs while the Sarhangs of Bahaul Mulk deserted him and dispersed. The Mongols, however, imprisoned the unlucky Bahaul Mulk, carried him off to Tus, and struck off his head.

The troops of Mujirul Mulk pushed on as far as Sarakhs and captured Qazi Shams-ud-din, for he had welcomed Yamah Noyan, provided him with essential supplies, and, on his behalf, assumed authority over Sarakhs. He was made over to the son of Pahlwan Abu Bakr Diwana, whom the qazi was said to have unjustly put to death; and to avenge the murder, the dutiful son slew the qazi. As there had been no news of the Mongols for a considerable time, people began to indulge in wishful thinking about the defeat of Mongol forces. Mujirul Mulk and the notables of Merv were also relieved at the sudden absence of all news about the Mongol armies; they gave in revelry. Soon, to disturb them in their pleasure came Iftikhar-ud-din, the amir of Amuiah, with the unpleasant news of the Mongols having reached Amuiah and the investment of the forts of Kalat and Nau—and that they were on his trail. Mujirul Mulk paid no heed to this warning. Incensed, Iftikhar-ud-din took up his quarters with the Turkomans. Soon thereafter a contingent of 800 Mongols came in search of the fleeing Hakim of Amuiah and attacked the Turkomans. Fortunately for Iftikhar-ud-din, Ughul Hajib and Shaikh Khan arrived with 200 men from Khwarazm. They charged the Mongols from behind and brought down the majority of them. However, some of the Mongols, whose horses possessed greater stamina and speed, managed to flee the field, and were pursued by the Turks and Turkomans. The victors succeeded in taking sixty captives, who were then paraded in the streets of Merv and put to cruel death.

Shaikh Khan and Ughul Hajib did not stay but marched on to Dasht-i-Jard, upon which the Turkomans chose Iftikhar-ud-din as their chief and left the service of Mujirul Mulk. They also planned to capture the town but the vigilant Mujirul Mulk received information of this in time. Foiled in their attempt, they retired and camped on the banks of the river flowing by Merv. From there they began to plunder the villages around, and the suburbs of the city, up to its very walls, and appropriated everything they could lay their hands on. While Merv was being thus harassed by the predatory Turkomans, Tuli was marching down with his 80,000 horsemen and an equally strong contingent of levies drawn from the towns that had submitted or that fell on his way.

On his arrival in the vicinity of Merv, Tuli sent forward his advance guard, 4000 strong,[4] to reconnoitre the country and they arrived at the camps of the Turkomans at night. The latter numbered 12,000 and were more than a match for them. They prepared to ambush the Turkomans as soon as they set out of their camps, in parties, to ravage and plunder the countryside. Juwaini describes the encounter:

Early at dawn they marched towards the gates to attack the town, and the Mongols, who had formed an ambuscade for them, sat motionless. The Turkomans did not suspect the presence of such foes, and each detachment of the Turkomans, as they came up, was attacked unawares and slaughtered. Having broken their strength, the Mongols made for their encampments. The Turkomans, whose numbers (including old men, women and children) exceeded 70,000 were defeated by a handful of men, a great number of them threw themselves into the river (hoping to escape) and perished while the rest were scattered and dispersed.

The Mongols acquired vast and valuable booty, which included no less than 60,000 quadrupeds—oxen, camels and sheep. Next day, on Muharrum, I 618/25 February, 1221, Tuli arrived before the gates of Merv.

Prosperous and pleasant as Merv was, it was famous for its libraries. 'Verily but for the Mongols', wrote the anguished Yaqut, 'I would have lived and died there, I could hardly tear myself away.' Among its more celebrated libraries were the two of the Friday Mosque with more than 12,000 books, and that of the Khanqah, which contained 200 volumes, each according to Yaqut worth 200 gold dinars.

With 500 horsemen, Tuli came before the Ferozi Gate and began an inspection of the walls and the fortifications. He rode round the city and spent six days inspecting its defences and, on observing the mighty fortifications, the huge bastions, the deep trenches and sturdy towers, he commented that the town was impregnable. The bastions were too massive and strong to be stormed and the innumerable soldiers within the town could successfully sustain the siege. Tuli decided to let a long slow siege of Merv cause famine. He planned a strict blockade so that no provisions would reach the besieged. The city was completely encircled by his troops and 10,000 soldiers were posted to watch each gate while he pitched his camp opposite the Shahristan Gate near the Great Mosque. Probably he expected the theologians and the divines, as at Samarqand and Bokhara, to make a deal with him.

On account of the preparations he had made, Mujirul Mulk faced the Mongol hosts with courage and confidence. To incite his men to greater efforts and more daring deeds, he gave out handsome rewards. On the first day, the besieged, numbering 200, came out and launched a fierce attack on the Mongols and in no time slaughtered a thousand Mongols. Tuli Khan was enraged and himself decided to lead the counter-attack with 20,000 men, in which he pushed them back into the city. The Mongols tightened the blockade and took steps against surprise attacks by the besieged. The struggle went on for 22 days, the besieged making desperate sorties but to no avail. As the siege progressed, the inhabitants began to feel the effects of the blockade. Without expectation of relief and reduced to dire straits, their spirits began to waver. Moreover, the refugees from Balkh, Samarqand, and Bokhara who had gathered here narrated their heroic struggles against the Mongols, which further reduced their morale, and induced them to come to terms with the besiegers before it was too late. Mujirul Mulk finally consented and Imam Jalal-ud-din, one of the most venerable divines of Merv, went to the Mongol camp as his envoy to ask for terms. The Imam offered 20,000 dinars, 30,000 camel loads (*kherwars*) of grain, 100 ambling horses and 100 Hindu and Turkish slaves as a ransom. Merv was also to have a Mongol Shahna, and pay annual taxes. The terms were attractive and were accepted. Tuli conferred upon the imam and his associates robes of honour and treated them with courtesy.

Pleased, Mujirul Mulk now set out with ten of his principal officers for a personal audience with the Ulugh Noyan. He was stopped before the audience tent or pavilion of Tuli Khan, and was asked to give an assignment of 300,000 dinars as a gift to the prince, and another hundred thousand dinars for the officers and soldiers of the Mongol army as ransom for the lives of the inhabitants. He complied and wrote down the names of two hundred wealthy persons, who were brought back into the Mongol camp. Though they had sworn their strongest oaths not to harm or molest the citizens, the Mongols racked and tortured the people to extract their hidden gold and silver, so much so that 10,000 people died of torture. Orders were then issued for the mutilation of Mujirul Mulk, the massacre of his attendants, and the destruction of the city. Mongol troops poured into the town and the inhabitants were driven into the open countryside. The captives were distributed among the troopers, and three to four hundred victims fell to the share of each and every soldier. 'People were killed in such large numbers', says Juwaini, 'that the bones of the slain formed mountains and the desert ran red with the blood of the dear ones.' The walls and fortifications of the city were then destroyed, the citadel was levelled to the ground and the pulpit of the Mosque was burnt.

Before setting out for Nishapur, Tuli appointed Amir Zia-ud-din Ali as Governor of Merv and left with him a Mongol Shahna, Barmas by name. Amir Zia-ud-din had been spared on account of his having retired from public life and leading the life of a recluse. He was reckoned among the notables of Merv and was now to rule over such inhabitants as might have escaped from the Mongol sword by concealing themselves in holes and corners. When the Mongols had departed, about 5000 fugitives assembled once more to lead a miserable life in the desolate town. But there was still more misfortune in store for them. Twice the Mongol columns passed by Merv, and each time they slaked their desire. When Syed Iz Zuddin Nassaba, a man renowned for his virtue and piety and held in high esteem, sought to count the number of those slain, he was assisted by many people and even then the party remained occupied for thirteen days and nights. The number of dead, excluding those slain in holes and corners, villages and plain, amounted to over 13,00,000 souls. The figure, though staggering, is nonetheless not improbable.

Under the wise and paternal administration of Amir Zia-ud-din, Merv was soon on the road to recovery and prosperity. He repaired the city walls and the citadel, made liberal grants of money to the inhabitants and the people began to flock to Merv. He took all possible steps to mitigate the suffering of the people, until one of the Sultan's army leaders, Kushtagin Phalwan appeared before Merv and invested the town. The people's hostility to Mongols bubbled over and Amir Zia-ud-din found the ground slipping beneath his feet.

He realized that without the affection and loyal support of the people, he could not successfully carry on the struggle and the formidable task of rehabilitation, and retired to the fortress of Muragha along with his few followers and Mongol contingent. Kushtagin entered the town and took immediate steps to complete the work of rehabilitation. He undertook measures for the repairs of the city dams, the restoration of agriculture, and the repair of public buildings. But, as Juwaini puts it, 'the water of fate had damaged the dam of his life and damned the water of his life in the wells of calamities.'[5] The news of Qarachar Noyan's arrival at Sarakhs unnerved him and he abandoned Merv at night with 1000 distinguished horsemen. He was pursued, overtaken, and defeated near the village of Sangbast; most of his followers were killed. After his flight the administration of Merv was taken over by his agents. Learning of all this the Mongol generals Turbay and Qabar set out from Nakhshab and, within a fortnight of Khushtagin's flight, Turbay appeared at the gates of Merv with 5,000 horsemen. The town was immediately taken; the inhabitants, numbering more than 100,000, were slaughtered. The city walls, palaces, and mosques were destroyed. The Mongol Amirs then drew off leaving Humayun Sipahsalar, styled Aq Malik, to exterminate the people who had escaped the general massacre. He carried out his task with the fiendish cruelty. Under his orders the muezzin, a Muslim from Nakhshab, began to cry the summons to prayer; hearing this the people came out of their hiding places in the belief that the terrible butchers had left. They were captured and shut up in the Shihabi Madrasah and were later thrown down from the roof. Not more than four persons remained alive in the town.

As there were no troops stationed in Merv or its neighbourood, the people who had sought shelter in the neighbouring villages or the steppe, flocked to the town and soon it began to throb with life under the leadership of Amir Arslan. But Merv was not fated to enjoy a peaceful existence. A daring Turkoman from Nasa came to Merv and lorded over the inhabitants for six months. He undertook pillaging expeditions to the Mongol baggage lying in Marwarrud, Panjdih, and Taliqan, and carried off their cattle. But he was soon killed in an attempt to capture Nasa. Meanwhile, a punitive expedition against Merv was well under way, and Qaraja Noyan appeared in the town quite unexpectedly with 1000 men from Taliqan. He plundered the town, massacred every one he caught and appropriated their grain. He was followed by Qutuqu Noyan with an avenging army of 100,000 men, who plundered the town. The inhabitants were treated with unheard of cruelty: some were roasted on fire while others were racked and tortured to death. He remained in Merv for forty days and did not leave alive even 100 souls in the town and its surrounding villages. There were, besides, no victuals left to suffice for them. Merv was thoroughly desolated and depopulated and there remained no more than ten or twelve Hindus, who had been living there for the last ten years and had no other place to live or go to!

Leaving Amir Zia-ud-din behind to look after Merv, Tuli had set out for Nishapur[6] 'to avenge the death of Taghachar Gurgan'.

'Nishapur is the largest and richest town in Khurasan. It occupies an area of one *farsang* and has many inhabitants. It is a resort of merchants and the seat of the army commanders. It has a citadel, a suburb, and a Shahristan. Most of its water is from the springs and has been conducted under the earth. It produces various textiles, silk and cotton. To it belongs a special province with thirteen districts and four territories.'[7]

'No town in all Khurasan,' said Ibn Hauqal, 'was healthier or more popular than Naysabur, (Nishapur) being famous for its rich merchants and the store of merchandise coming in daily by caravan,' on the eve of the Mongol invasion. Yaqut said that he had seen no finer city in all Khurasan and that its gardens were famous for their white currants and other fruits.

Although Nishapur is situated in a stony tract of country, the Mongols brought along with them, from a distance of several marches, so many loads of stone that they lay in great heaps all round the place and not a tithe was used. The grim mood in which Tuli Khan advanced upon Nishapur was revealed by the massacre of all the inhabitants of Tus and its villages. The inhabitants had also been preparing for the awful encounter. The walls and fortifications of the town had been strengthened and, among other things, they had disposed on the towers and the ramparts 3000 *tir-charkhs* or machines shaped like rockets, to discharge iron projectiles filled with inflammable materials three hundred catapults, and other instruments.

In spite of these preparations the people were discouraged by the tremendous odds pitted against them, and so thought it advisable to negotiate and seek an accommodation with the Mongols. The chief qazi, Rukn-ud-din Ali, was accordingly sent to tender submission and ask for grace and mercy. Tuli was inexorable, refused the offer of tribute and offerings, and detained the qazi. On 7 April 1221, early in the morning, the attack commenced but was resisted by the besieged. Next day the Mongols renewed the assault with energy and vigour but the garrison kept up the battle all day garrison. By the afternoon of the third day the Mongol dead had filled the moats in several places. The attack was then renewed on all sides, especially with greater vigour than ever before on the side of the Qaraqush tower and the Gate of the Camel Drivers; battering rams were used with effect, and several breaches were made. Then came another furious attempt to storm, fiercely resisted. The Mongols launched a simultaneous attack on every side, by the ramparts and by the gates. The defenders fought with the courage of desperation and caused havoc among the besiegers. But they were inferior in number and bodily strength and in the end the storming party gained the walls, established itself within the city, and forced the defenders back. The defence continued but was hopeless. On Saturday, Tuli arrived at Jankark, three *farsangs* from Nishapur, and the Mongol troops rushed into the town. The inhabitants fought on. With the shrieks of their wives and children ringing in their ears, they fought in the streets, on their thresholds, and in their houses; they continued fighting until they fell. The superior numbers and discipline of the Mongols at last brought the struggle to an end and the town was at their mercy (10 April 1221).

The Mongols made a search for Fakhrul Mulk and at last dragged him from a cellar underground; to make them put him to death quickly he reviled and abused them, and the Mongols killed him. The inhabitants, men and women, were driven out into the open country and massacred for Tuli had issued strict orders that no one was to be spared, man, woman, or child. They were cruelly slaughtered, an expiatory sacrifice to the spirit of the dead Toghachar. The walls and houses were razed to the ground, and Nishapur was effaced from the map. The daughter of Chingiz Khan, who was the Khatun of Toghachar,[8] then entered the city at the head of her own followers, and caused all that could be found to be slaughtered with the result that no living creature, not even a dog or cat, was left alive. Only 40 mechanics and artisans escaped. They were carried off to Turkistan. Separate heaps were made of men's, women's and children's heads.[9]

Next came Herat,[10] celebrated for its climate and flourishing gardens. The city had in Amir Shams-ud-din Muhammad Juzjani an able and energetic governor, who foreseeing the movements of Tuli Khan, had made careful preparations and collected ample provisions to withstand a Mongol siege. Even the approaches to the city had been strongly guarded. On approaching the green and luscious pastures of Shabartu in the vicinity of Herat, Tuli sent Zanbur to call on the governor, the qazi and the elders of the city to surrender. In case of contravention and resistance, they were threatened with dire consequences. But Amir Shams-ud-din was not cowed by threats. 'Let not that day come for me to be subject to Mongol infidels while breath remains in my body,' he declared and had the Mongol envoys immediately put to death. He had taken charge of the city not to surrender but to defend it.

When Tuli learnt of the murder of his envoys he issued immediate orders for the siege of the defiant city and to kill every Tajik they could lay their hands upon.

On the first day of the siege of Herat there were 30,000 casualties.[11] In Amir Shams-ud-din, Tuli seemed 'to have caught a Tartar', fighting with grim determination. He had the Mongols at bay for seven days. The Mongols suffered heavy casualties, including the loss of several important amirs and 1700 of lesser note. Incensed, Tuli decided to lead the assault in person on the eighth day. The defenders came out in parties of hundreds and two hundreds, and Malik Shams-ud-din also sallied forth to quash the storming party. Bitter and obstinate was the encounter, which ensued. Fighting with reckless courage, Malik Shams-ud-din performed feats of valour and his followers inflicted heavy blows on the Mongols, who were on the point of yielding, when the issue was capriciously decided by a chance arrow which hit and killed Shams-ud-din.

The death of Shams-ud-din left the people without a leader, and was the signal for division and demoralization among the people. The civilians and the ecclesiastics now raised their voice for seeking an accommodation with the besiegers. The soldiers and citizens who were devoted to Sultan Jalal-ud-din were for holding out till the last drop of blood.

Tuli had expected an early conclusion of the siege. He was vexed at the delay and alarmed at the heavy losses suffered by his forces. Meanwhile, the verdant plains and the smiling suburbs of Herat had tickled his fancy, and he desired to spare the city the horrors of a siege. And so, learning of the differences among the besieged, he decided to achieve by mildness what he had failed to get by force. Attended by 200 horsemen, he approached the Firuzabad gateway and removing his headdress, called out: 'O! Men of Herat! Know that I am Tuli, the son of Chingiz Khan. If you desire to save your lives and those of your women and children, cease all further resistance and submit; pay into my coffers the same amount of taxes you have been paying to the sultan.'[12] He promised them on oath that, if they submitted and opened the gates, no harm or injury would be done to them. And the citizens agreed to submit.

Amir Iz-zuddin Harawi, head of the guild of weavers and manufacturers,[13] was the first to go out for an audience with the Ulugh Noyan. Accompanied by 100 persons of his craft, each carrying nine pieces of silks of various kinds and of great price (for which Herat was celebrated), he went to the audience tent and was received well. He was followed by the chief officials and elders of the town. Tuli accorded them gracious treatment but the twelve thousand soldiers and dependants of Jalal-ud-din were put to death. Tuli appointed Amir Bakr Maraghani the Governor of Herat and its dependencies, and his own favourite attendant Mangatae was made Shahna.

Having performed the task assigned to him, the conquest of Khurasan, within the incredibly short period of three months, Tuli set out to join his father who was then encamped near Taliqan of Khurasan.

In three months, the world-siezing Tuli
Captured these[14] all to the gate of Sistan.
He razed and he slew, he swept and he clutched;
Not a person remained, neither great nor small.

Pursuit of the Shah[15]

While the Mongols were overrunning northern Transoxiana, Sultan Muhammad held aloof from every action. The encounter with the Mongols under Juji had unnerved him. The diversity of opinion among his commanders and ministers increased his hesitation. The best warriors declared that Transoxiana was lost, but Khurasan and Iraq must be guarded; troops must be concentrated, a general levy enforced, and the Amu Darya defended at all cost. Others advised him to fall back upon Ghaznin, and there meet the Mongols; if beaten, the Shah might retire beyond the Indus! This being the safest course, Sultan Muhammad favoured and decided to adopt it.

Jalal-ud-din, the only brave man in the Shah's family, was opposed to both projects; he would not hear of retreat, he would stop the invasion at the Oxus. He was opposed to the policy of abandoning flourishing districts and towns to the mercies of the invaders, and the subjects to cruel torments and bitter humiliations at the hands of the uncouth barbarians. He realized that the Mongols did not merely want the upper hand, they wanted complete victory, not merely the legendary riches of Transoxiana, the sacking of Samarqand and Bokhara, but the conquest and occupation of the fertile lands and valleys—the destruction of the Khwarazmian empire. He urged resistance, to smash the advancing hosts. 'If you need to retire to Iraq,' he said, 'give me the permission to fight and the command of the forces—I will drive back the Mongols, and liberate the empire.' But the Shah would not agree. To make matters worse, the superstitious and bewildered Sultan was also overwhelmed by the forebodings of his astrologers, who declared that the stars were not favourable and it was useless to attempt any effective opposition to the enemy.

Jalal-ud-din's appeals fell flat. Every discussion was fruitless. The Shah treated all his son's reasons as folly and the effusions of youthful exuberance.[16]

Having decided to retreat, the sultan left Samarqand by way of Nakhshab. At the same time he sent swift couriers to Khwarazm to inform his mother of his plans and asked her to proceed towards Mazandaran with all his family and effects. The callous Turkan Khatun drowned all state prisoners in the Oxus before she left the capital—never to see it again.

When the sultan reached Balkh, he was joined by 'Imadul Mulk, the Prime Minister of his son, Rukn-ud-din, who held Persian Iraq as an appanage. He had great influence on the Shah and plans was changed at the instance of 'Imadul Mulk. Imadul Mulk was drawn towards his birthplace, the home of his family, and he persuaded the irresolute and dispirited Shah to go to Persian Iraq. No sooner did he leave Balkh, than he received the shocking news of the fall of Bokhara, followed by the disgraceful betrayal of Samarqand by the qazi and the Shaikhul Islam. He now lost all hope of retrieving his fortunes, more so because of the mutinuous and treacherous conduct of his men. He was then accompanied by troops, who were disaffected and demoralized, the majority of them belonging to the tribe of his mother and her kinsmen. They had no love or loyalty for the shah; and now finding his fortune on the decline, they conspired to get rid of their unlucky sovereign. Even previous to this the Sultan's Diwan, Badr-ud-din Amid had deserted him and gone over to the enemy. To create discontent and disaffection in the sultan's demoralized camp, he contrived forged letters[17] to fall into the hands of the sultan. These letters purported to be written by his amirs, offering their services to the Mongol Khan and his acceptance of their services. This caused deep estrangement and suspicion between the sultan and his disgruntled amirs, some of whom now conspired to kill him. Forewarned, the sultan changed his pavilion in the night and in the morning found it 'like a sieve pierced through and through by arrows'[18] (discharged by rebellious soldiers). Finding the sultan unharmed and their plan foiled, his rebels deserted the camp and crossed the Oxus to join the conquering Mongol troops. The sultan now became disconcertingly suspicious and nervous, and set out in haste for Nishapur. His nerves having failed him, his vision clouded by deceit and treachery, he created confusion and consternation among the people by advising them to shift for themselves, to avoid opposition, and come to some arrangement with the advancing Mongols.

When Chingiz Khan reached Samarqand, he received news of the sultan's flight to Khurasan and the dispersal of his forces to the various cities and towns of the empire. Judging that his enemy was cowed and beaten, he decided to send his officers to pursue him across his realm—to prevent him from rallying his provincial nobles or the hardy mountaineers of Afghanistan. He had, it appears, numerous spies in the enemy's camp, and was probably informed by the treacherous elements, of the divided counsels prevailing in the Shah's council and the disaffection in his camp. It is one of the gifts of a great captain to understand the character of his adversary, and Chingiz Khan evidently took an accurate measure of the sultan and his nervous advisers. Holding counsel with his amirs and noyans he observed that the Shah was terrified and torn between conflicting opinions. He had crossed the river Tirniz with very few troops and even those who were not the most devoted and loyal. Chingiz planned not to give the Shah any time or opportunity to rally and to reduce him to such terror that he would think of nothing but his own safety. By this time, he had the whole of northern Transoxiana under his control and it was in the interest of the Khan to fight, if needed a decisive battle with the Sultan. So he decided to send Yamah Noyan, Subutai Bahadur, and Toghachar in pursuit of the Shah and allotted them 60,000 troops for the task.[19]

'Pursue him throughout his Empire and do not rest until you have captured him', commanded Chingiz Khan. 'If you come up against him and find yourselves not strong enough to cope with him, do not turn aside but inform me and the Ulugh Noyan, Tuli, will reinforce you. Spare the towns and people who submit and leave Shahnas with them but destroy ruthlessly anyone who gets in your way. You are to turn the sultan's empire upside down and rejoin me by way of Derbend, the city of the Iron Gates.'

No doubt this force was small and its task formidable—to hunt the ruler of the mighty Khwarazmian empire to death and in his own kingdom. But it was a trained and veteran army, directed by masters of war, one of whom Subutai, at least, was next to the Khan himself, the greatest captain of the age and the future victor of the great Battle of Kalka, and opposed to them were disaffected troops under a general suffering from fear complex.

On his way to Nishapur, when the sultan reached Kalat, near Tus, he was persuaded to stay there and make a stand. For Kalat was reputed for its strength and was favourably situated—a valley enclosed within lofty hills said to be of seven leagues' circumference. Fortified and energetically defended it could, like the Pass of Thermopylae, baffle the Mongol hosts. But the sultan soon changed his mind and after a brief riotous stay, abandoned the place, and reached Nishapur on Safar 12, 617/18 April 1220. Feeling safe behind the strong and fortified walls of Nishapur and probably sick of his wretched life, he sought to forget his formidable enemies by giving himself up to pleasure and revelries.[20]

Eat, drink and be merry
For tomorrow we die.[21]

Trusting that the Mongols would never be able to cross the Oxus and reach Nishapur, he plunged into feasting and merrymaking such that he neglected all affairs of state. People complained of the overindulgence and neglect of kingly duties in vain. Suddenly, however, he was disturbed in the peaceful enjoyment of his pleasures by the unexpected news of the crossing of Tirmiz by three Mongol leaders.

The three Mongols were of course Yamah Noyan, Subutai Bahadur, and Toghachar Noyan who had been commissioned to hunt down the Shah. Starting from Samarqand 'with the speed of a river descending from the mountain into the valley',[22] they crossed the Oxus at the Panjdeh ford and pushed on till they reached Balkh. The elders of Balkh sent a deputation to wait on them and offered them provisions, scarlet silks, and other costly presents. They accepted submission and gifts, left with them a Shahna and allowed them to lead their placid and tranquil life. Recruiting road guides, they sent Tarsi with the advance guard and set out for Herat. Yamimul Mulk, the governor of Herat, was taken by surprise and, unable to offer opposition, placated and pleased the Mongol commanders by providing them supplies. He offered verbal submission and obedience, but did not admit the Mongols into the city or accept a Shahna. Subutai Bahadur and Yamah Noyan were more concerned with following and tracking their prey, the sultan, than with the conquest and occupation of towns and cities. Satisfied with verbal assurances and the supply of provisions, they marched off towards Zawah. Following upon their heels was Toghachar, who refused to be satisfied with Yaminul Mulk's protestations of loyalty and attempted to storm the town. Compelled to fight, the governor gave a creditable account of himself. He inflicted heavy casualties on the Mongols, and at the same time despatched emissaries to the two Noyans to complain of Toghachar's conduct. By the time instructions from them arrived, Toghachar was killed and his defeated troops proceeded to join the two Noyans.

When Subutai Bahadur and Yamah Noyan reached Zawah—a fine town with a strong castle built of bricks—they asked the inhabitants for supplies. Zawah was a richly irrigated town with 50 dependent villages, and produced corn, cotton, grapes and much other fruit. It was also a silk manufacturing centre. The inhabitants paid no attention to their demands and shut their gates. Even threats and solicitations failed to have effect and they refused to give the Mongol troops anything. Since they were in a hurry, the Mongols proceeded onwards. When the inhabitants saw from their walls the Mongol banners moving on, they sounded their trumpets in glee and railed at the passing Mongols. But this raised the ire of the Mongols and they returned to storm the town. They attacked it furiously from three sides. After three days' hectic fighting, they stormed the place and massacred all the surviving inhabitants—men, women, and children. They destroyed heavy articles which were difficult to transport and, without delay, pushed on to Nishapur 'like the autumn blast or clouds of spring, slaughtering all who they came across and destroying all they possibly could.'

Meanwhile, the Sultan had been feasting and merrymaking in Nishapur. He had lost all hope and courage, and urged the people to disperse and seek safety in flight, but how or where, say—he did not perhaps himself did not know. He despaired that large armies had not been successful in their attempt to check and defeat the Mongols, and, wherever they went, famous cities and centres of government, they showed no mercy and spared neither man, woman nor child. Strong citadels and fortresses had failed to save the people from defeat, disgrace and dishonour. 'If, however, you disperse now,' he told his people, 'it is possible that most of you and certain that some of you, will be saved. Arms and fortifications are of no avail against the Mongols.' But he failed to realize that the strength of the walls is never greater than the courage of its defenders and that the impregnability of cities and citadels is measured by the heroism of their defenders. Ghayir Khan and the valiant Timur Malik had shown that the Mongol onslaught could be checked by resolution and resourcefulness. But the Shah was terrified and bewildered. 'Old age and misfortunes have shown their faces while youth, prosperity, and health have departed,' he said when he observed the changes wrought on his face in a glass. 'What is the remedy for this affliction, which is like the dregs in the cup of time and how is this knot to be loosened which has been tied by the revolving sky?'

The people were, however, more optimistic and not prepared to suffer voluntary exile and servitude. The sultan at last gave his unwilling consent to carrying out the necessary repairs and fortification of the ramparts. As there was no news of the Mongols, the sultan's fears were set at rest and he despatched his son, Sultan Jalal-ud-din for the defence of Balkh. But when the news arrived that the Mongols had crossed the Oxus and were nearby, Jalal-ud-din fell back. The Shah left the city under the pretext of a hunting excursion and 'thenceforward', as Prawdin observes, 'he was nothing but a hunted beast in fear of death, lacking strength for resistance and the courage for a fight. His only chance seemed to be to run away and so, attended only by the few who remained faithful to him, and a sovereign in not more than name, he hastened on across what had been his realm, westward, ever westward, through deserts, over mountains, across the whole of Persian Irak [*sic*] ....'[23]

The sultan left behind Fakhrul Mulk, Ziaul Mulk and Mujirul Mulk to administer the affairs of Nishapur. When he retired, one of his most devoted and loyal servants, Sharfuddin, who was a minister and president of the sultan's council, set out from Khwarazm to take charge of the city and organize its defence. Unfortunately, he died three stages from the city and his thousand troops refused to stay in Nishapur but marched off to join the Shah. The next day, 18th of Rabi AH 617/23 May 1220 the advance guard of Yamah Noyan and Subutai Bahadur under Tarsi appeared before the gates of Nishapur. The Mongols tortured and administered oaths to everyone they met in order to extort information about the sultan's movements. They called on Fakhrul Mulk and his colleagues to surrender the town and submit to the authority of Chingiz Khan. 'I govern the city on behalf of the Sultan,' replied the astute Mujirul Mulk. 'I am an old man of the class of the people of the pen and only know how to use the pen. Speed on after the Sultan. If you overcome him in battle, the country shall be naturally yours and I too will be your man.' At the same time he supplied them provisions and fodder for their horses. Day after day, Mongol troops arrived, took rations and marched off. On Rabi 1, AH 617 / 5 June 1220 Yamah Noyan and Subutai Bahadur arrived and summoned the ministers and the leading divines. The shrewd and cautious ministers sent out, with presents and offerings, three persons from among the middle-class people bearing their names and offered to hold themselves as the Khan's slaves. Yamah Noyan advised them to refrain from opposition and resistance. 'Set not your trust in the strength of your walls nor in the number of your troops', warned Yamah Noyan. 'Whenever any Mongol horseman or envoy reaches you, welcome him and do your utmost to help him and do whatever you are told. Thus only can you preserve your houses and property.' As a sign of their having surrendered and entitled to Mongol protection, the inhabitants were given a *yarligh* of Chingiz Khan in Uighur script, stamped with the red seal of the Khaqan: 'Amirs, Elders and all persons shall know that God had delivered to me the empire of the earth from east to west. Whoever submits shall be spared but those who do not surrender shall be destroyed along with their wives, children and dependants.'[24]

As the sultan was their object and they were afraid of losing his trail, Yamah and Subutai separated and pushed on by different routes to meet at Ray. Subutai Bahadur made for Tus by the Jam route. Wherever the people surrendered, he spared them but whoever dared resist was annihilated. Towns lying east of Tus, Nuqan and its dependent villages surrendered and escaped Mongol ravages. But Tus refused to open its gates. Well built and thickly populated Tus was famous for its waters and trees, and still more celebrated for the number of religious teachers, writers and poets it produced. Seat of the celebrated Abbasid propaganda, it played an important role in the political and cultural history of Islam—being the birthplace of some of the greatest figures of Islamic history such as Firdausi, Omar Khayyam, Nizamul Mulk and the great mystics Abu Yazid Bistami, Husain bin Mansur Hallaj, and Imam Ghazali. Tus was easily stormed and suffered the usual fate—complete destruction of the town and a general massacre of the inhabitants. Setting out for Damghan, when Subutai reached Radkan, the beautiful wooded district and its verdant meadows pleased Subutai and he contended himself with the appointment of a Mongol Shahna. No demands were made upon the inhabitants nor were they molested in any way. Proceeding by way of Khabushan, where he killed a good number of the inhabitants 'on account of their haughtiness', Subutai reached Isfarain, thickly populated and noted for its fine grapes and good markets. As the city refused his summons, Subutai ordered a general massacre. Meanwhile, Yamah Noyan was on his way to Mazandaran by the Juwain route and dotting the line of his march with blood, arson and loot.

The sultan was all the while eluding their attacks by a circuitous and headlong flight. Setting out from Nishapur, he reached Ray only to learn and lament that Mongols had made their appearance in Khurasan too. Changing his plans, he made for Qazwin, where his son Sultan Rukn-ud-din was encamped with his 30,000 Iraqi soldiers. He despatched his own mother Turkan Khatun and some members of his family to the strong fortress of I-lal in Mazandaran and his son Ghias-ud-din along with his mother and others of the royal family to the fortress of Qarun-duz commanded by Taj-ud-din Thughan. From there he sent messengers to summon the veteran warrior Nusrat-ud-din from Lur. One of the greatest of the ancient Maliks, he was the Atabek of Lur and the father-in-law of the sultan's son Ghias-ud-din. Styled Hazar-saf probably on account of his bravery and valour on the battlefield, the sultan could rely on the sanity of his counsel as much as on the strength of his arms. Pending his arrival, the sultan held counsel with the amirs of Iraq, who advised him 'to take shelter in the fortress of Shiran-Koh, make it the seat and centre of his operations and from there concert measures to oppose the enemy.'[25] The sultan went to inspect Shiran-Koh and its defences. 'It is not safe for my refuge,' he said. 'It cannot be defended against the Mongols.' This discouraged his followers all the more. Soon afterwards, the sultan was joined by Malik Nusrat-ud-din Hazar-Saf. 'We should start this very hour,' he advised. 'Between Lur and Fars there is a range of mountains, called Tang-Teku. Crossing it we enter a rich country and there we should take shelter. There we shall collect 100,000 warriors, guard the mountain passes and meet the Mongols with courage and determination. We are sure to triumph and our victory will put new hope and courage in the hearts of our armies which are now overwhelmed with fear and dejection.' The sultan's suspicions were, however, roused and he suspected that Nusrat-ud-din had ulterior designs and wanted the sultan in his power. So he decided to remain in Iraq and rally his scattered forces. Soon, however, the sultan was shocked by the news that Ray had fallen and the Mongols were near by. At the coming of the Mongols, his followers began to desert him. Malik Nusrat-ud-din also left, and with hardly any attendants, the sultan with his sons made for Qarun-Duz.

The Mongols were now close upon his heels. Leaving a garrison at Amol[26] to besiege the fortress in which the sultan's harem and children were hiding, Yamah Noyan pushed on towards Ray. Meanwhile, Subutai reached Damghan, which refused to submit. As the inhabitants had sought shelter in the famous fortress of Gird-koh, west of the city, and as he had no time to spare, Subutai proceeded, killing people on the way. Next he reached Simnan, where again he put a large number of people to the sword. The two commanders met at Ray. The inhabitants of Ray were torn by bitter sectarian feuds and divided into hostile sections—the followers of Imam Abu Hanifa, and those of Imam Shafai. As the Hanifites had once burnt the mosque belonging to the rival group, the latter decided to aid the Mongols. The leading members of their sect welcomed the Mongols into the city, and incited Yamah Noyan to a merciless massacre of their opponents. The Mongol general obliged, but, a supporter of Chingiz Khan, he could not appreciate treachery, he could not trust those who had not been loyal to their own fellow citizens, and he put them also to the sword. The total number massacred is placed at about 100,000. Famous for its pottery,[27] Damghan was a prosperous town and did not recover from the ravages of the Mongols. Jackson remarks:

Some Iranian Jeremiah might well find cause to lament over that vast heap of ruins, six miles south-east of Teheran, which once formed the city of Ragha, or Rages, the metropolis of ancient Media, and one of the oldest centres of civilization in Iran. Sanctified as the cradle of Zoroastrianism, hallowed for a day by the presence of the angel Raphael, exalted by princes and cast down by conquerors, this city that was great among the nations is now but a mass of crumbling walls, mounds, hollows, and ruined water-courses, with but few signs of life amid the dust of ages—treasure hunters dig for coins and pottery amid its deserted tumuli, and brick-hunters demolish its walls for building materials to be used in Teheran.[28]

Learning that the sultan had fled to Hamdan, the two Noyans again branched off in his pursuit, Yamah setting out for Hamdan and Subutai making for Qazwin and the neighbouring districts. On Yamah Noyan's arrival the governor of Hamdan, Majd-ud-din Alaud-Dawlah thought it best to submit. He accepted a Mongol Shahna and supplied the victor horses, clothes, victuals, and drinks. Having lost trail of the sultan, Yamah Noyan turned to plunder and devastate Kizrud, Khurramabad and Nihawand. But Subutai Bahadur was hot on the heels of the fleeing monarch.

Subutai's troopers overtook the sultan's party and directed a few arrows at the flying horsemen but did not recognize the sultan. The latter was seriously wounded by their chance arrows but, fortunately for him, his horse was unhurt and he reached Qarun-duz in safety.[29] He remained there only for a day, took a few horses from the amirs there, and set out for Baghdad. On learning how narrowly they had missed the sultan and his party, the Mongols returned to besiege the fortress of Qarun-duz. They attacked the town with energy. Furious was the fighting, with the Mongols wishing to get hold of the castle and the Shah and his loyal garrison holding them back to give the fleeing sultan time to distance himself. As soon as the Mongols received information that their prey had once again escaped, they abandoned the siege and marched off in pursuit. On the way they captured the sultan's guides who revealed the plans of the latter about going to Baghdad. But the sultan had in the meanwhile changed his mind and also his route. He made a detour to the fortress of Sarjahan, stayed there for a week, and then set out for Gilan. The Mongols once again lost his track and, believing that the road guides had deceived and misled them, killed them and fell back. Having had a week's rest, the sultan resumed his flight and reached Astarabad, where he had lost his treasure. The Mongols were, however, again on his heels and he retired to Amol. Baffled by the vigour and tenacity of the Mongol who were relentless in his pursuit and turning up in every place and at unexpected hours wherever he reached, the sultan consulted his trusted amirs. They advised him for the time being to retire to one of the islands of the Caspian Sea, where, at least, the Mongol horsemen would not be able to disturb and molest him.

Very soon, however, the news of his latest hiding place leaked out and Yamah Noyan despatched a column after him. Once again the sultan was, however, fortunate to elude the hunters. He had, by way of precaution, moved to another island and when the Mongols reached the first island, they had to return disappointed. The Mongols now fell back to invest the fortresses of Qarun-duz and I-lal where the sultan's family had sought refuge.[30] Qarun-duz was speedily stormed and razed to the ground. They next turned to I-lal, where Turkan Khatun and the others were hiding. It was a strong fortress and the Mongols decided to reduce it by starvation. The fortress was well provided with water; for it had cisterns, which once filled, stored enough water to suffice and last for years. 'No one could recollect the time when the inhabitants of I-lal ever faced a water shortage,' says Khwandmir, 'But during the period of the Mongol investment, the cisterns dried up and no rain fell. For want of water Turkan Khatun, the Wazir Nasir-ud-din and others came down (and surrendered). Almost at the moment of their reaching the foot of the fortress, heavy rain began to fall and the downpour was such that water flowed out under the portals of the fortress'.[31]

The fortress was plundered and immense booty fell into the hands of the Mongols. Besides precious stones and gems, they got 10,00,000 red dinars and 1000 kharwars (ass-loads) of silk fabric. The captives and booty were forwarded to Chingiz Khan, who was at the time in Taliqan[32] and ordered all the males, however young, to be killed but spared the females for servitude. When Sultan Muhammad, who was eking out a miserable existence on the Caspian Sea island, heard of the fall of the fortress and the consequent outrage to his family, he died of a broken heart and was buried in the clothes he was wearing at the time of his death.[33] To such straits had been reduced the once all-powerful Muslim ruler of Central Asia that his heir and successor, Jalal-ud-din could not procure a winding-sheet for his father's grave.[34]

The Khwarazm Shah died a victim not to his destiny but to his vices and lack of a constructive policy. He never attempted to organize his far-flung dominions and conquests into an efficiently administered empire. He was an ambitious adventurer but not a statesman or empire-builder. There had been no need for a massacre at Utrar. Chingiz Khan had, perhaps, had no inclination to invade the regions beyond the Tianshan mountains but was goaded into it. Even if a conflict with the Mongols was inevitable, the sultan could have weathered the storm had he been the man he was in AD 1200. His mental and physical faculties seem to have been impaired by a life of debauchery. The Khwarazm Shah despaired of his success even before a serious trial of strength. The battle against Juji's forces had come to him as a shock; it engendered in his mind an excessive fear of the Mongols and a complete distrust of his own ability to cope with them.

The enormous numbers of the enemy and the graphic report of his spies dismayed him, while rumours of treachery were rife in his camp. The lack of courage and the spirit of distrust is strikingly evinced by the discussion which the Shah had with his chiefs. The Shah demanded courage which he himself did not possess. Gloom and hopelessness had settled over his camp. The struggle was lost even before the enemy had struck a blow.

Having lost the trail of the sultan, Yamah Noyan fell back to Hamdan where he came to learn that a large number of the sultan's forces had assembled at Sajas under the leadership of Kooch-Buqa Khan and Buktagin Salahdar. To leave them no time to plan and prepare for action, Yamah Noyan immediately set out against them. He defeated and dispersed them. The two Mongol commanders overran the whole of Iraq, carrying death and destruction to most of the towns and cities. Qazwin alone put up a heroic resistance. The inhabitants were brave and warlike and had a big fortified wall dating from the days of Caliph Harun-al-rashid. It enjoyed great strategic importance as it guarded the passes from Tabaristan to the shores of the Caspian Sea. The Iraqis here fought stubbornly and it was after desperate street fighting that the Mongols captured the city. Subutai then ordered a general massacre. The number of those slain totalled no less than 50,000. Having ravaged the greater portion of Iraq, Subutai and Yamah retired to spend the winter in the meadows of Ray. With their men and horses rested and refreshed, they set out for Azerbaijan in the spring. Zanjan was the first town to be tackled. It was thickly populated but was carried by storm and all the inhabitants were massacred without compunction. Ardbil was the next city to be reduced. Next day Governor Jahan Pahlwan of Tabrez was defeated and his son Atabek Aurang bought off the Mongols by offers of submission and cattle. Having reduced and ruined most of the towns and cities of Iraq and Azerbaijan, the Mongols wintered at Mughan—a fertile district with verdant gardens all round. While encamped there they were attacked by ten thousand Georgians who were defeated and repulsed after sustaining heavy losses. They then appealed to the inhabitants of Tebrez, Diar-i-Bakr and Diar-i-Rabi to help and join them against their common but unknown enemies. They decided to assemble for the campaign in the spring. The Mongols had in the meantime to invade Georgia. Luckily for them they received unexpected help and reinforcements from Aghush, the Turkish slave of the Atabek Wzbek. He had assembled a considerable following of Turkoman, Kurdish, and Khalji mercenaries. Reinforced and also refreshed by their stay at Mughan, the Mongols invaded Georgia, plundering and ravaging the country until they reached Tiflis. The valiant Georgians were prepared to give a brutal reception to the marauding hosts. The advance guard under Aghush received a severe drubbing and, like Wellington at Waterloo, was on the point of yielding when the timely arrival of Mongol columns saved the day. The Georgians, unable to cope fled.

In Safar, 619 (March 1222) the roving Mongol columns turned towards Muragha. Seventy miles south of Tabrez, it was 'a large town, flourishing and pleasant, with running waters and flourishing gardens.'[35] It was especially reputed for its fragrant melons, honey-like in taste, green within and red outside. The inhabitants refused to submit and resisted the Mongols for a week. The city was taken by storm, the inhabitants butchered, and the place given to flames. Subutai and Yamah then set out for Ardbil but fell back on learning the strength and valour of its ruler, Muzaffar-ud-din Kokbari—to find Iraq up in arms.

Due to excessive snowfall in the winter of 1222 the roads were blocked and the communications were cut off. There was no news of Subutai and his Mongols and people imagined all sorts of things about the departed barbarians. Jamal-ud-din Aibah, one of the notables of the late sultan who had held the governorship of Iraq, rallied the scattered followers—'rogues and vagabonds' as they are styled by the court historians—and decided to make a bid for the cause. His example was emulated by the citizens of Hamdan, who raised the standard of revolt and killed the Mongol Shahna. They imprisoned Ala-ud-dawlah in the fortress of Kurbat on account of his having previously submitted to the Mongols. As the spring came, Yamah Noyan re-entered Iraq to avenge the murder of the Mongol Shahna and re-establish Mongol authority. Jamal-ud-din Aibah now panicked and offered to submit, but Yamah Noyan was inexorable. He was out to teach the fickle Iraqis that it was not wise to play with the Mongols. Jamal-ud-din and his followers were all put to the sword. He then turned towards Hamdan. The notables and dignitaries wished to negotiate with the Mongols, but the chief *faqih* or theologian persuaded them to resist the infidel barbarians. It was only after a three-day struggle that the resistance weakened. On the third day, the *faqih* was killed and his death made the people leaderless. The Mongols entered the town by a secret underground passage. The inhabitants were massacred and the town reduced to ashes.

> Gone the great sun-temple where
> Golden stair rose over stair;
> Gone the gilded galleries,
> Porticoes and palaces;
> And the plaintive night winds plead

> For the memory of the Mede,
> Sob for alien ears to heed,
> Pilgrim train and caravan,
> Round the walls of Hamadan.[36]

Next was the turn of Tabrez, whose Atabek, Yuz Bek, had sought safety in flight. The venerable Shams-ud-din Usman, reputed for his learning and sagacity, however, displayed consummate tact in dealing with the Mongols and succeeded in buying them off by timely submission and valuable presents. A mercury ointment which proved 'to be very valuable and useful to the Mongols in freeing their persons from certain troublesome parasites'[37] especially pleased them. They accepted his offer of submission and sent a Shahna to Tabrez.

Subutai Bahadur and Yamah Noyan now turned towards Khuwi and Salmas, carrying death and destruction to the territories they passed until they reached Nakhchawan, where all the inhabitants were massacred. Bailqan was the next city to be attacked. The inhabitants were prepared to submit but in the general confusion and tumult, the Mongol emissary was killed and hence the city was stormed. The Mongols exacted terrible vengeance. The women were violated and the entire population massacred. They then marched off to Ganjah, which obeyed the summons, submitted and appeased them by costly and lavish offerings.

At Ganjah the Mongol generals received information that Georgians were preparing to avenge last year's humiliation and were ready to attack them. Subutai and Yamah Noyan set out to meet them. Subutai Bahadur marched forward to engage the enemy while Yamah Noyan lay in ambush with 5,000 men. The Mongols were driven back but, fortunately for them, the Georgians failed to drive home their advantage. Instead of routing the retreating Mongols, they took to plundering their baggage, thereby giving Subutai time to rally his men and return to charge the disorganized enemy; besides, they were surprised by Yamah Noyan. Suffering heavy losses, 30,000 killed, the Georgians retired and rejoined their chief, Malik Daud, at Tiflis. Impressed by the vigour and valour of the Georgians, the wary Mongol generals decided to risk no more engagements with them and marched off to Shirwan, where they laid siege to its capital, Shamakhi. They pushed on the siege with energy and vigour, filled the ditch with the dead bodies of animals, horses, asses, bullocks, cows and even sheep, and stormed the town. As at Bailqan they again violated the women, massacred the inhabitants, and destroyed the city.

Having conquered all Iran and Iraq, the generals desired to carry out the instructions of Chingiz Khan and return to their yurt by way of Derbend, the City of Iron Gates. Strangers to an entirely unknown region, they did not know the roads or routes by which to proceed. The only practicable road across the Caucasus lay through Derbend. 'It is a town', as described by the stout William Rubruck, 'whose eastern end is on the sea shore and there is a small-sized plain between the sea and the mountains across which this town stretches to the top of the mountain adjoining it on the west; so there is no road higher up, on account of the steepness of the mountain, nor any lower down by the sea, but only straight through the town where stands the iron gate from which the town takes its name.[38] On the top of the mountain is a strong fort; its width, however, is but a stone's throw. It has very strong walls without moats, and tall towers.'

Baffled and perplexed, the Mongol generals resorted to a stratagem. 'We do not intend to molest your territory any more,' ran their message to the Shirwan Shah.[39] 'Send unto us some persons so that we may settle terms with them, and then we will depart.' The innocent Shirwan Shah was pleased and hastened to comply. He sent ten of his nobles to buy off the Mongols, but no sooner did they reach the Mongol camp than the crafty commanders had one of them beheaded. 'If you conduct us safely through the Derbend and beyond it,' they said to the terror-stricken nine, 'you will be set free; otherwise, we shall send you to join your departed comrade.' The frightened nobles guided the Mongol troops through and beyond the mountain barrier. The crossing of the Derbend by the Mongols was, says Khwandmir,[40] a feat which no army had accomplished save the Macedonian Alexander.

Beyond the Barrier, the Mongols crossed over into the territory of the Alans. Living on the northern skirts of the Caucasus, the Alans were famous warriors and armourers. 'They form at this day the greatest and noblest nation in the world, the fairest and bravest of men,' noted Marignolli.[41] 'They are Christians according to the Greek rite', observed Rubruck,[42] 'and use the Greek writing and have Greek priests.' To give the Mongols a hard time, the Alans had combined forces with the savage, pugnacious and semi-nomad tribes of Qipchaq. The confederates mustered to bar the passage of the Mongols. Already tired and exhausted, the Mongols were 'alarmed and frightened' by the fighting qualities of the hosts opposed to them. Subutai and Yamah Noyan decided to extricate themselves by resorting to diplomacy.[43] 'We are men of the same stock as you, while the Alans are aliens and foreigners,' ran their secret message to the Qipchaqs.[44] 'You have united with alien races against your brothers. Let us enter into a covenant of peace and friendship.

Whatever you may desire to have in the shape of money or goods, we will furnish you, provided you give no aid to the Alans and leave us to deal with them.' The offer was accepted and the Mongol commanders sent gold, valuables, and costly presents. The Qipchaqs withdrew and the Mongols then attacked the Alans savagely. Not content with the immense booty which they obtained, the Mongols went after the Qipchaqs to wrest from them what Subutai and Yamah had given them. The Qipchaqs had not anticipated this and were caught unprepared. Suffering heavy losses, they fled across the Danube in 1224 and sought the protection of the Russians against the 'devilish' horsemen 'from unknown lands, speaking an unknown lauguage, but determined to enslave all the peoples'.

The leader of the fugitive tribes was *Kotyan*, father-in-law of Prince Mstislav of Halicz. 'They have siezed our country,' was his warning. 'Tomorrow they will sieze yours.' On the instigation of Mstislav the Gallant the Russian princes decided to combine and unite their forces and crush a possible future enemy.[45] Subutai, however, was reluctant to fight the Russians; he wanted to return to Mongolia and rejoin his master. 'The Mongols have nothing against the Russians,' said the Mongol envoys. 'It is the pagans whom we wish to destroy. We are as the Russians in that we worship one God. Profit by our offer, and avenge yourselves upon the enemy, who has warred against you in the past.' The Russians, however, seized the Mongol envoys, put them to death and continued their march. 'You have murdered our envoys, attacked our outposts and want war,' said the Mongol envoys sent to make an official declaration of war. 'So be it. We had planned no evil against you. We both worship one God, is impartial and will judge between us.' But the problem was not so simple: Subutai had to encounter a host of 80,000 warriors. A frontal attack or pitched battle was out of the question and the wily general took to flight. The Russians were encouraged by the apparent fright of the fleeing Mongols. They took up the pursuit, which lasted for twelve days during which the pursuer became disorganized; the Mongols then turned round and charged at Mstislav of Halicz, who had taken the lead, 'unwilling to run the risk of having to share the honour of victory with anyone else.' The Mongols gained a decisive victory.[46] The Russian contingents and the Qipchaqs as they came up fared no better. 'The defeat,' as Curtin says, 'was overwhelming; hardly a tenth of the men under those rash leaders escaped, six princes and seventy distinguished voevodas were killed.'[47] For once the victorious Mongols did not follow in pursuit, for they had no assignment or instructions for the lands beyond the Danube; Chingiz Khan was now on his way back to Mongolia and in 1224 they set out to rejoin him.

Khwarazm[48] and Tirmiz

With the conquest of Samarqand, Transoxiana lay prostrate at the feet of the shabby Mongol conquerors. As the three Mongol corps under his sons and noyans had done their job thoroughly, and, higher up the Oxus, Jand and Barjalighkent had been secured, Transoxiana and its subject territories passed out of the hands of the Khwarazm Shah. To give him no time to rally resistance, Chingiz had despatched Subutai, Yamah, and Toghachar. Now he decided to subdue Khurasan and clear it of his enemies. At the same time, he directed his three elder sons Juji, Changhatae and Uktae to proceed at the head of a great army, 100,000 strong, and reduce the territory of Khwarazm.

Situated to the west of the Oxus, Urganj, called al-Jurjania by the Arabs, was a centre of trade and the meeting place of caravans for the Ghuzz territory. Visiting the town in 1219, Yaqut was impressed by its prosperity. 'I have', he wrote, 'never seen a mightier city, or one more wealthy or more beautiful.' 'Khwarazm was, at this time, in a hopeless condition. With the neighbouring territories groaning under Mongol heels, it was like a tent whose ropes had been cut off. Moreover, the proud imperial city had no member of the royal household to assume direction of affairs and to whom the people could turn. Army officers and nobles like Khumar Tegin, Mughul Hajib, Er-Buqa Pahlwan, and Ali Darughini formed the ruling junta. To tide over the difficult period of stress and strain, Khumar Tegin was elevated to the throne. The choice was dictated by his relationship with the hated but all-powerful Queen Mother, Turkan Khatun.

The Mongol princes set out for Khwarazm by the Bokhara route and, for the purposes of scouting and reconnoitering, directed an advance guard to proceed ahead.'[49] The commander of the advance guard made a remarkable move, an instance of astonishing stratagem. He sent a small party of horsemen to reconnoitre and collect the enemy's cattle foraging outside the city walls. When they appeared before the gates of the town with the livestock, the townspeople mistook them for thieves and roving cattle-lifters. By the time the Mongol scouts were on their way back to report, the Khwarasmians sallied through the 'Gate of the World' and fell on their rear. The Mongol troopers turned round and faced them. The Mongol advance guard rushed out of their ambushes and blocked their way in the rear. The surprise was fatal and the discomfiture of the Khwarazmians complete. The number of casualties is given as 100,000 certainly an exaggeration, as such a large number of warriors would not have gone after 'loafers and vagabonds' just to retrieve the 'stolen' cattle. In the confusion the Mongols managed to enter the town by the Aqabilan

Gate. They penetrated deep into the town, as far as the Tanaurah quarter. They did not, however, feel safe inside the town, for the water courses made it difficult for the action of troops. But they launched another attack the next morning. This time, however, the intrepid Faridun Ghori, with 500 warriors, was at the gates and foiled their attempts to once again get into the city.

When Juji, Chaghatae and Uktae arrived at Khwarazm with the main army, leisurely they went round the city, inspecting its defences and fortifications. They also sent envoys to exhort the inhabitants to submit, but were rebuffed. The city was then closely surrounded. As there were no stones in the neighbourhood to feed their catapults, the Mongols recoursed to a substitute. They made manjaniq-balls out of the trunks of mulberry trees. While they were busy preparing for the siege, they kept the besieged on tenterhooks by occasional assaults on the city and alternating them with emissaries to persuade them to give up resistance. Reinforcements had also been summoned from the conquered districts. Finally, when their armaments and 'materiel' had been prepared and assistance in the shape of men, tools and materials had arrived, they directed an all-out attack on the city. The besieged had been equally active and were determined in their resistance. Hard was the fate of the Muslim prisoners and levies, who were used against their own countrymen, and were assigned the perilous duties of filling up the ditch and undermining the city walls. The havoc caused by the Mongols and their superiority in numbers and equipment disheartened Khumar Tegin. Convinced of the futility of resistance, he sought to save himself by submission. He stepped out of the gate and surrendered. Profiting by the confusion and depression that now prevailed, the Mongols scaled the walls and planted their banners on the ramparts. Their war-whoops shook the entire city but the citizens stood firm and fought with great tenacity. 'They resisted the Mongols in every street and quarter of the city, renewed the struggle in every alley and barricaded every entrance.'[50] Using burning naptha the Mongols set fire to the city but in the end they were beaten back. Though the battering rams were used with effect and a breach was made, the besiegers failed to establish themselves within the city. Though most of the city was destroyed, the besieged obstinately carried on their defence. Disappointed in their hopes of a speedy victory and immense booty, the Mongols decided to divert the waters of the Oxus upon which the city's water supply depended. They despatched three thousand men to capture the bridge from where they could command the city. The besieged charged at them, surrounded them, and put them to the sword. This success gave fresh courage to the defenders and the defence continued with even greater energy.

Meanwhile, jealousy and quarrels broke out between Juji and Chaghatae. The siege was now commanded and conducted with little vigour and as little success. Five months rolled on without any visible achievement. Chingiz Khan was much vexed and alarmed at the delay and the ill success of his arms against Khwarazm. For Tuli had reduced the great cities of Khurasan—Merv, Nishapur, Herat, etc.—in only 3 months. Uktae distinguished by tact and judgement, was thereupon appointed supreme commander, and by his discreet and tactful handling, he smoothed matters and reconciled the two brothers.[51] The siege was then again carried on with vigour, and after two months' hard and desperate fighting, in 1220 the Mongols planted their banners on the city walls and established themselves within the city. The defence continued but it was manifestly hopeless. The next thing to be done was an attack on the city itself. Four streets led up to it from the walls, each of which was barricaded and tenaciously defended. House by house, and quarter by quarter, Khwarazm was stormed, the defenders gradually forced back by the superior Mongol strength. The scene of destruction, which followed, was terrible. Most of the city was reduced to ashes.

The fortifications were then razed to the ground, and its inhabitants driven into the plains. Strict orders were issued to separate the women from the men, but not out of mercy. The women, who were fair and pleasing to the barbaric conquerors, were distributed among them. The remaining unfortunate ones were arranged in two rows, facing each other and stripped naked. 'The women of your city are good pugilists, therefore, the order is that both sides should set on each other with their fists.'[52] With the terrible Mongols standing round them with their swords drawn, the woman had 'to deal blows upon one another until at length the Mongols fell upon them with their swords.' As for the men, their fate was no less terrible. Over a hundred thousand artisans and craftsmen were picked out to serve the Mongols. The rest were massacred. The number of the slain is staggering and beggars belief. 'The number of those slain in Khwarazm,' wrote Juwaini, 'is incredible and I will, therefore, not put it down.'[53] But others, like Khwandmir and Sharfuddin have done so. According to them every warrior slew 24 men and the forces numbered more than a hundred thousand. This refers only to the captives who were butchered after the capture of the city and does not include those who fell fighting for the defence of their city.[54]

It is related[55] that Shaikh Najmud-din Kubra, or the Elder, was at this time living in Khwarazm. One of the greatest Muslim mystics of the day, Chingiz Khan had received reports of Kubra's great piety, learning and sainthood and, true to his practice of revering religious men, he directed his sons to spare Kubra and give safe conduct to him, his family and dependents. When the investment of the city was complete, they, accordingly, sent a message advising him to leave the town. 'We have decided to wipe out the people of Khwarazm and annihilate all resistance. The Shaikh should, therefore, come out and leave the city so that no harm should come to him.' 'How can I desert my relations, friends and followers, all of whom are in the city?' The Mongol princes offered safe conduct to him and ten of his relations. 'But they are more than ten.' The Shaikh replied. 'You are allowed to take 100 men with you.' The number was ultimately increased to a thousand. 'How can I desert the people who were with me in days of peace and comfort, in times of calamity and distress?' His attendants counselled him to accept the Mongol offer and save his precious life but, the worthy son of a heroic city, he decided to die where he had lived. 'I have dwelt in Khwarazm in its prosperity and shall not leave it in the days of its misfortune,' said the venerable Shaikh. 'I will take my chance with the others, await my fate, whatever it may be, and not fly from the Almighty's decree.' He died fighting. One wonders what would have been, the course of history, if there had been a few more cities like Khwarazm, a few more daring commanders like Jalal-ud-din and a few more saints and Sufis like the great Shaikh, preferring death and destruction to dishonour!

When Samarqand and the cities of Transoxiana had been conquered and he had despatched Chaghatae and Uktae to Khwarazm, and several contingents into various parts of Khurasan, Chingiz Khan passed the winter of 1220 in the neighbourhood of Samarqand. From there he moved on to the meadows of Nakhshab. The town was surrounded by fertile fields and orchards and was famous for its markets and grapes. When the summer came to an end and his troops had been refreshed, he rode by way of Timur Qalah, whence he sent Tuli to reduce some towns and cities of Khurasan. On drawing near Tirmiz[56] he sent envoys to invite the inhabitants to submit. Tirmiz was a flourishing city and was defended by a strong fortress. 'It was', says Miles, 'a virgin city, having never been taken. Alexander the Great besieged it six years (or months?) without effect, and was at last obliged to make pact with the inhabitants and retire.'[57] The inhabitants had taken refuge behind the walls of their fortress which was partly surrounded by the waters of the Oxus;[58] it was garrisoned by troops from Sistan under the energetic Amir Zangi Abihafs.[59] The citizens were proud of their warriors, both with regards to their strength and their equipment. No wonder they refused the summons and prepared for a vigorous defence. Chingiz Khan was furious at their defiance and obstinacy, and ordered a continuous assault on the city. It was a bitter struggle, and the Mongols kept on an incessant attack on the fortress for days and nights on end. The Mongol catapults at last effected several breaches and, on the eleventh day, the place was taken by storm. The inhabitants were driven out into the open plain outside the city and, were, according to the usual Mongol practice distributed among the soldiers. Men, women and children all were massacred; none was spared. When they were about to finish their bloody work, they came across a woman who said that if they spared her, she would give them a magnificent pearl. When they demanded it, she told them that she had swallowed it. 'One of great value, like in an oyster-shell, and like a pearl oyster-shell they treated her: they opened her bowels and found it; and after that, it was usual with them to treat their prisoners in this way in hopes of finding jewels.'[60]

Having done with slaughter and massacre, Chingiz Khan advanced on the districts of Lingrat and the neighbourhood of Saman, and spent the winter there. These districts felt the full impact of Mongol hoofs; rape, plunder and death stalked the countryside. As the winter of 1221 came, he crossed the Oxus.[61]

Notes

1. Juwaini, vol. I, pp. 136-8, *Rauzat-us-Safa*, vol. V, p. 36.
2. Juwaini, vol. I, pp. 119-33; *Rauzat-us-Safa*, vol. V, pp. 34-6.
3. Juwaini, vol. I, 2nd copy.
4. It is impossible to accept the strength of the advance guard, i.e. 400, as given by the pro-Mongol historians.
5. Juwaini, vol. I, p. 130.
6. Ibid., pp. 134-40.
7. *Hududul 'Alam*, p. 102 (tr. By V. Minorsky).
8. She was not, as Howorth makes out, 'leading the avenging force at the head of 10,000 men.'
9. 'Having had a pair of oxen yoked to a plough', says Qazi Minhaj, 'Tuli had driven them over (the area on which) the city (stood) so that not a vestige of buildings thereof remained.' *Tabaqat-i-Nasiri*, p. 351.
10. *Tarikh-Nama-i-Harat*, pp. 67-72, *Rauzat-us-Safa*, vol. V, pp. 37-8. Qazi Minhaj gives a brief account of the siege and struggle at Herat but says that the city sustained the siege for 8 months, *Tabaqat-i-Nasiri*, p. 351.
11. *Tarikh-Nama-i-Harat*, p. 68.
12. *Rauzat-us-Safa*, vol. V, p. 37.
13. *Tarikh-Nama-i-Harat*, p. 71.
14. The cities of Merv, Nishapur, Herat, Tus, and other places in Khurasan which were reduced by his troops.

15. Juwaini, vol. I, pp. 112-16; Rashid-ud-din, fols. 205-9; Sharfuddin, fols. 102-7.

16. *Rauzat-us-Safa*, vol. IV, pp. 141-2.

17. *Nassavi*, pp. 37-8.

18. Rashid-ud-din, fol. 206.

19. I have preferred *Tabaqat-i-Nasiri's* account to the versions of the pro-Mongol historians.

    Juwaini, Rashiduddin, Sharfuddin, Mir Khwand and Khwandmir wrote under the patronage of the Great Conqueror's descendants, and, being court historians, were inclined to praise the Mongols. On most occasions they appear to lessen the number of Mongol forces but at the same time magnify the strength of their adversaries.

    It is incredible that Chingiz Khan, prudent, and solicitous of the safety of his men, should assign only 30,000 men to Subutai and Yamah Noyan in their famous expedition to hunt down the Khwarazm Shah in his own kingdom and, then traversing half of Asia, negotiating tortuous defiles and difficult passes, rejoin him in Mongolia.

    It is most probable that the two commanders had 60,000 Mongol soldiers under them as would be commensurate with their hard task; for, Shigi Qutuqu Noyan was given 30,000 horsemen to guard the routes to Kabul, Ghor, Ghaznin and Gharjistan. Making allowance for those killed, disabled, or carried off by disease, a force of 30,000 was too small. Considering the resolute fighting at Herat and other places, the desperate hand-to-hand and street fighting at Qazvin, and then the terrible encounters with the formidable Alans, Qipchaqs, etc., it is impossible to believe that a force of 30,000 horses could achieve such exploits. Even the 60,000 horses given by Qazi Minhaj seems to be an understatement.

20. Rashid-ud-din, fol. 206.

21. Ibid.

22. Juwaini, vol. I, p. 113.

23. *The Mongol Empire*, p. 176.

24. Juwaini, vol. I, p. 114; Rashid-ud-din, fol. 207.

25. Rashid-ud-din, fol. 207.

26. Cf. 'The Mongols passed it by, unaware that Turkhan Khatun, the sultan's mother, and her young children were then hiding there.' Howorth, vol. I, p. 82. Yamah was better informed.

27. Curzon, vol. I, p. 349.

28. *Persia, Past and Present*, p. 428.

29. Rashid-ud-din, fol. 208.

30. Nassavi, p. 48.

31. *Rauzat-us-Safa*, vol. IV, p. 143.

32. Ibid.

33. Nassavi, p. 48.

34. Rashid-ud-din, fol. 208.

35. *Hududul 'Alam*, p. 142.

36. Quoted by Jackson, p. 59.

37. *Rauzat-us-Safa*, vol. V, pp. 30-1.

38. *Travel*, p. 262.

39. *Rauzat-us-Safa*, vol. V, p. 31.

40. Ibid.

41. *Cathay and the Way Thither*, vol. III, p. 248.

42. *Travels*, p. 88.

43. Rashid-ud-din, fol. 222.

44. *Rauzat-us-Safa*, vol. V, p. 31.

45. *The Mongol Empire*, pp. 215-18; *The Mongols in Russia*, pp. 221-4; Howorth, part I, pp. 94-6.

46. *Rauzat-us-Safa*, vol. V, p. 31.

47. *The Mongols in Russia*, p. 222.

48. Juwaini, vol. I, pp. 96-101; Rashid-ud-din, fols. 209-12; Nassavi, pp. 92-4; Sharfuddin, fols. 107-9.

49. Juwaini, vol. I, p. 97.

50. Ibid.

51. Rashid-ud-din, fol. 211.

52. *Tabaqat-i-Nasiri*, pp. 378-9.

53. Juwaini, vol. I, p. 101.

54. *Rauzat-us-Safa*, vol. V, p. 32; Sharfuddin, fols. 108-109. According to Rashid-ud-din, the number of the slain was 12,00,000, fol. 211. According to Ibnul Asir (vol. XII, p. 182) the people sued for peace but this was refused; after the general massacre, the dam on the Oxus was destroyed, and the town was flooded.

55. Rashid-ud-din, fol. 212, *Rauzat-us-Safa*, vol. V, pp. 32-3; Sharfuddin, fol. 109, *Shajratul Atrak*, pp. 153-4. Maulana Jalal-ud-Din Rumi in his celebrated *Nafuhatul-uns* (pp. 486-7) has recorded that the martyred Maulana had many disciples who had a status and renown of their own. Such were Shaikh Majdud-Din of Baghdad, Shaikh Su'adudin of Hamad, Baba Kamil of Jand, Shaikh Raziud-Din Ali Lala, Shaikh Saifud-Din Bukhari, Shaikh Najamud-Din of Ray, and Shaikh Jamalud-Din of Gilan.

56. Rashid-ud-din, fols. 212-13.

57. *Shajratul Atrak*, p. 149, Footnote.

58. *Tabaqat-i-Nasiri*, p. 342.

59. Ibid.

60. Ibid., p. 342; Juwaini, vol. I, p. 102.

61. Juwaini, vol. I, p. 102.

6

The Last Phase

$\mathcal{H}$AVING BURIED HIS FATHER, Jalal-ud-din left the islands of the Caspian Sea to take charge of his 'patrimony'. He set out for Khwarazm, which was then garrisoned by 90,000 Qanqalis. His younger brothers, Arzlaq Sultan and Aq Sultan, held sway over Khwarazm and were attended upon by the valiant Timur Malik, Ughul Hajib, Kujaek Tegin, and Nuh Pahlwan. Highly talented and valourous, Sultan Jalal-ud-din Mangbirni was the hero of the soldiers and an idol to the people.

It may not be out of place to say a few words about the controversy surrounding the sobriquet Mangbirni attached to the name of Sultan Jalal-ud-din. It has been variously interpreted and, therefore, differently pronounced, for instance, as Mengou Virdi or Birti (eternal or God-given), as 'Meng bureuni' (having a mole on the nose) and so on. The explanation given by Hodivala, as against those offered by, Raverty and Ranking, Houdas and Houston, etc., is the best, befitting to the valour and bravery that sent the Persian chroniclers into raptures concerning Jalal-ud-din. Hodivala points out that Sultan Iltutmish honoured Khan-i-Azam Izz-ud-din Kabir with the Turkish title or sobiquet of Mangbirni (or Mangira Manbirini) in recognition of his exploits as a warrior. Khan-i-Azam already enjoyed the sobriquet Ayar-i-Mazda, meaning a warrior who was a match for a thousand (warriors). Sultan Jalal-ud-din deserved the eulogies sung in his honour, as Browne has observed: 'Across the dark days of Chingiz Khan's invasion, when the Persian sky was obscured by the smoke of burning towns, and the Persian soil was soaked with the blood of her children, the personality of Jalal-ud-din Khwarazm Shah flashed like some brilliant but ineffective meteor'.[1]

Handsome, generous and of iron physique, Jalal-ud-din enjoyed universal respect and popularity.[2] He alone had raised a voice for a face-off with the terrible Mongol hosts. His arrival in Khwarazm inspired enthusiasm among the well-wishers of his dynasty and the hope that he alone could deal with the Mongols. But even in the hour of supreme danger his younger brothers remained selfish beyond measure. In spite of the most solemn agreements between the brothers not to molest each other, the selfish and petulant amirs egged Arzlaq Sultan on to do away with Sultan Jalal-ud-din.[3]

If ever any prince inherited a bed of thorns, it was Jalal-ud-din. He ascended the throne or rather succeeded to the nominal suzerainty of a kingdom in chaos, paralysed by the selfish and short-sighted intrigues of its nobles and the petulance of the royal household. The country was bleeding under the heels of the most destructive human avalanche till then known to history. The miseries of the people beggar belief, but that made no impression on the factious, self-seeking, and short-sighted amirs, who were averse to a strong man holding the reins of government. To further their own aims and ambitions, they desired that one of Jalal-ud-din's younger brothers, weak and inexperienced, who would do their bidding, should ascend the throne.

Finding that his brothers would not accept him as their leader and that the amirs were conspiring against his life,[4] Jalal-ud-din decided to forsake the city. Accompanied by a small but devoted band of followers, he left Khwarazm and proceeded, by way of Nasa, to Shadyakh (of Nishapur). But the Mongols had reached Khwarazm territory and at Istawa[5] he came face to face with a Mongol contingent, which blocked his path. Fighting with desperate fury, the sultan and his horsemen broke through the Mongol lines and reached Nishapur in safety. Staying there for a couple of days, he rested his horses and recruited as many men as he could gather. He left for Ghaznin by way of Zuzen just in time to escape his Mongol pursuers, who then set out in his pursuit until they reached a place where the road branched, and where the sultan had posted Malik Iylderk with a small force to fight a rearguard action to give himself time, and then to take the wrong road. The loyal contingent carried out the instructions and the Mongols lost the sultan's track.

When Jalal-ud-din reached Zuzen, he found its gates shut. He wanted to rest there a while, but the citizens, said to be aggrieved, refused to open the gates on the specious excuse that they were too afraid of the Mongols and the dire consequences that any attempt at apparent opposition might entail. The weary sultan pushed on to Mabarnabad, where he stayed for a while and left at midnight. The Mongols were, however, once again on his track and reached the place next morning. It was only when Sultan Jalal-ud-din reached Yazdawiah, 75 miles south-west of Herat, that the Mongols gave up the pursuit, and the sultan reached Ghaznin on 17 Zil Hijjah, AH 617/12 February, 1221. The governor of the city, Yaminul Mulk, who had 50,000 men under him, received the sultan outside the town. The arrival of the sultan gave the people new confidence and courage and they flocked around his standard. Among the notables to join him were the amirs of Ghor, Aminul Mulk of Herat, and Amir Saif-ud-din Ighraq with his 40,000 warriors. The tide seemed to have at last turned and the sultan was now a real ruler of devoted men, not a hunted fugitive fleeing for his life.[6]

Determined not to give his adversary time and opportunity to organize and rally his troops and people for a united and determined resistance, Chingiz Khan despatched Shigi Qutuqu towards Ghaznin to hunt down the young sultan. Jalal-ud-din was becoming formidable and a headache to the Mongols. On reaching Ghaznin the sultan married the daughter of Amin Malik and set about establishing and restoring his authority. He set out of Ghaznin and proceeded to Parwan (also written as Barwan), where he received the news of Walian[7] being besieged by the Mongol generals Takjak and Malghur. As the condition of the besieged was serious and they were on the point of being forced to yield, the sultan left his baggage at Parwan and hastened to relieve the besieged fortress. The fighting was bitter and the Mongols lost up to a thousand men. They fled across the river, destroying the bridges behind them. Immense booty fell into the hands of the sultan, who distributed it among his soldiers, and then returned to Parwan. The defeated remnants of the Mongol contingent rejoined Chingiz Khan and informed him of their debacle. He immediately ordered Shigi Qutuqu Noyan[8] to ride out with his 30,000 horsemen against the daring sultan. As soon as Jalal-ud-din received news of the Mongols approaching Parwan he set out to meet them; he set his troops in battle array, posted Aminul Mulk and Saif-ud-din on the two wings, and took personal command of the centre. In his grim determination to do or die, he ordered his troops to dismount and bind the reins of their horses round their waists, probably to form a solid phalanx against the enemy charge, and to prevent them from impetuously launching, without orders, a cavalry charge. As the right wing, under Aminul Mulk, was the strongest division of the sultan's army, the Mongols made it the chief target of their onslaught, and their heavy and repeated charges at length forced it back; but the vigilant and agile sultan promptly and effectively reinforced these columns and enabled Aminul Mulk to hold his own and ultimately regain lost ground. It was a terrific encounter in which not a single man turned his back; great feats of heroism were performed on both sides and only the enveloping shadows of the night separated the two armies.

Next morning when the two armies were busy preparing for battle the sultan's troops were loathe to fight as they saw the ranks of another division drawn up in the rear of the Mongols. The sultan was approached and advised to make an orderly retreat to the hills and from that vantage ground fight them but, like Babar at Fatehpur Sikri against Rana Sanga; he would not hear of such a proposal. He inspired his men to face the enemy and fight courageously. Shigi Qutuqu Noyan had tried a ruse to overcome the enemy. He had dummies made out of felt and put them on the pack-horses—to give the false impression of fresh arrivals.[9] The Mongols now changed their tactics; they transferred their best men to the right wing and directed their chief efforts against the sultan's left wing under Saif-ud-din. The left wing was, however, composed of the choicest troops and their valour and spirit and unerring archery forced the Mongols back. Seeing the Mongol lines retreat the sultan ordered the drums to be sounded for a general cavalry charge and, mounting their horses, the Muslims rushed upon the enemy. The fleeing Mongols rallied, made a stand against the sultan's advance-guard, and inflicted heavy casualties; but the sultan routed the Mongols with terrible losses. The Mongol leaders escaped and, with the shattered remnants of their troops, joined Chingiz Khan at Taliqan.

Having gained a hard-earned and decisive victory, the sultan's troops took to plunder and, most unfortunately for him, a quarrel arose between his followers over the division of spoils. In the heat of the dispute about a horse, Aminul Mulk struck his whip over the head of Saif-ud-din's horse. As the sultan was powerless to decide the dispute or effect a compromise between these powerful men, Saif-ud-din Ighraq[10] left the sultan's camp with all his troops at night. This weakened the sultan's power and completely shattered whatever chances there were of saving the territories of Ghor and Ghaznin from the Mongols. Deprived of half his forces, the dejected sultan retired to Ghaznin.[11]

The crushing defeat sustained by Shigi Qutuqu came as a rude shock to the Mongol Khan and, having learnt of the desertion of Saif-ud-din and his troops, he decided to hasten for revenge. By then, Jalal-ud-din had given ample proof of his daring horsemanship and skill on the battlefield. His request to his father, 'Give me the command of the armies and I will drive them across the Jaxartes' had not been mere bravado; he had proved himself more terrible in action. Even with his depleted forces he encountered the Mongols three times after the Battle of Parwan, and 'on all three occasions success and victory rewarded him.'[12] Leaving his heavy baggage at Buqlan, Chingiz Khan set out against Bamian, where he was detained unexpectedly for a month. The resistance was stiff and Chaghatae's son, Mutukan, was killed in action. The death of his grandson enraged the fiery Khan and he issued strict orders for the complete destruction of the town. The city was stormed. Bamian was then renamed Mao-baligh or 'the City of Woe'; it was no longer a city but heaps of smouldering ashes. Chingiz Khan pushed on towards Ghaznin with all possible haste and advanced by double marches 'turning day into night and converting night into day in such a way that even food could not be cooked.'[13]

Jalal-ud-din was by then in no position to offer battle; he decided to retire beyond the Indus. Leaving behind a garrison to defend Ghaznin, he started his odyssey. At Kajlah he left behind Uz Khan to fight a rear-guard action, but this plan was foiled, and Uz Khan failed to hold the Mongols. On reaching Ghaznin, Chingiz Khan learnt that the sultan had left the town fifteen days ago and set out after him, leaving Mahmud Yalvaj as governor of the town. The Sultan flew towards the Indus with all possible speed. Time in this case was of essence and the Mongols urged forward their horses. The great task was to stop the sultan from crossing the Indus with his followers and his harem. Proceeding by forced marches, the Mongol overtook the sultan on the banks of the Indus, but he was, as ever, ready to fight and or ranged his men for battle. The Mongol troops hemmed him in from three sides; they were disposed in semi-circles round him, their wings resting on the river. Chaghatae and Uktae had also arrived from Khwarazm to reinforce their father. Chingiz Khan issued orders to his men to capture Jalal-ud-din alive.

The gallant sultan bravely faced the battle;[14] but his lines were compelled to fight back-to-back, in order to face the Mongols from three sides; his horsemen had no space to manoeuvre. In this unfavourable position, the volleys of Mongol arrows had terrible effect; and when they closed in on their enemy in a converging attack, the battle was decided. The sultan showed great intrepidity and his men fought with heroic courage. During the early hours of the battle it looked as if they, by sheer superiority of their fighting spirit, would roll up the armies of the Mongol Khan. Khan Malik repulsed the left wing of the Mongols while the sultan himself charged the enemy's centre and broke it. The Mongols suffered heavy casualties but destroyed the flanks of the sultan, commanded by Khan Malik and Amin Malik. In the centre, the sultan led his men and, as usual, nothing could withstand him; they pressed forward bearing Chingiz Khan and his flag back with the light of victory in their eyes. They made their way into the heart of the enemy lines; but the wise measures of the Mongol chief now had their effect. With the sultan's wings broken, the Mongol flanks closed in and converged. A murderous conflict ensued, perhaps for hours; no quarter was given, no prisoners were made. The broken ranks of still fiercely fighting men were hemmed in like sheep for slaughter, the battle once lost became general butchery. Amin Malik who commanded the right wing, fled from the field and made for safety to Peshawar, but was intercepted by the Mongols. The sultan alone, though hard-pressed, held his ground and with only seven hundred men, fought till noon. Charging the Mongols left and right, over and over again, he threw the enemies back. But all was of no avail; the superior numbers of the enemy at last prevailed and they kept on steadily contracting the area a round him. Juwaini describes the scene thus,

When he [the sultan] perceived that his situation had become desperate and had gone beyond name and fame, he surveyed the scene with tearful eyes and fevered lip. At this crisis, Ujash Malik, the son of his maternal uncle, seized the reins of his horse and dragged him away. With his heart filled with a thousand pangs and with weeping eyes, he bade adieu to his wives and children, and relations and dependents, called for his horse to be saddled and brought forth, and, having mounted, once more like the crocodile plunged into the sea of conflict. Having forced back the enemy (for a short distance), he wheeled round, divested himself of his armour, seized his canopy and whipped his horse to plunge into the (fast flowing) Indus, although the water was at a distance of ten yards or more below the bank. Like lightning he descended on the river and with the swiftness of wind he crossed it.

This crossing is unique in the history of the River Indus. The great river has been crossed by two other stalwarts, four years earlier by Sultan Iltutmish in his pursuit of Qubacha, the 'Sultan of Sind', and by Ranjit Singh, on the back of an elephant! And in both those cases, the ford was rocky and shingle, slow-moving, and hardly knee-deep.

'When Chingiz Khan saw the sultan in the act of crossing the river; he galloped to the bank; some of the Mongols wished to throw themselves after him into the river, but Chingiz Khan forbade them, and they took to their bows. A group who witnessed the scene relates that, as far as their arrows could reach, the water was red with blood (for several of the sultan's followers had followed his example). The sultan had only a sword, a lance and a shield. The heavens above looked down upon him with wonder and amazement as though they said—

> Never hath the world beheld a man like this,
> Nor heard of one among the heroes of ancient times.

On reaching the opposite side safely, the sultan rode upwards along the bank until he reached a spot facing his own camp, and beheld the plunder of his family, treasures and followers while Chingiz Khan was astride his horse on the opposite bank. The sultan now dismounted from his horse, loosened the girths, took off the felt saddle-cloth, together with his cloak and arrows, and laid them in the sun to dry, and spread his canopy on the head of his spear and sat underneath all alone to shade himself from the sun.'[15]

Amazed by such courage and resolution Chingiz Khan placed his hand to his mouth and said to his sons: 'It seems incredible that such a father should have begotten such a son. Every father would want a son like him. Since he has escaped the vortex of fire and water, and reached the shore of safety, countless deeds will be achieved by him, and vast trouble caused. It would be fallacious for any prudent man to be heedless of his actions.'

This was not the first occasion when the Khan had commended the bravery of a notable adversary. During the campaign against the Chin Emperor, (July 1251) an army officer, Chang Jo was brought prisoner and asked to kneel before the officer commanding the troops. 'If you are a general so am I; a man of spirit can die, but he will not humiliate himself.' Impressed by his courage and sense of honour, he was offered service under the Mongols but refused. However, when he was told that his parents were Mongol prisoners, filial ties and affection and the desire to save them sapped the general's determination he agreed to fight for the Mongols.[16]

All who fell into the hands of the victors were slaughtered, including the sultan's young children, while the women of his harem were spared for captivity and concubinage. The riches of the sultan, consisted mostly of gold and coins, and on the day of battle, he had ordered them to be thrown into the river. Chingiz Khan, therefore, deputed pearl divers to fetch whatever was possible out of the river. For mopping up operations he himself moved north and sent Uktae down to subdue refractory chieftains.

Refused asylum by Iltutmish (who was himself not sure of his own position and the foundations of his power), disheartened by the jealousy and unconcealed dislike, even opposition of his brothers, deprived of the support of Amin Malik, his father-in-law, who had been killed by the Mongols, Jalal-ud-din was in a desperate position. Even so he decided to once again try to regain his tattered patrimony.[17] Fortune seemed to have smiled on him and for a while some leaderless but brave men flocked under his banner. Jalal-ud-din had already earned fame for his feats of valour and the news of the Battle of Parwan had inspired some sullen Khwarazmians to rally around him. Town after town rose in revolt under the mistaken idea that the tide had turned and the hated barbarians on the way out. For this, people were to pay dearly later on. The revival of drooping spirits and the general exuberant mood helped Jalal-ud-din recruit a sizable fighting force but it was too late to expel the invaders. The task was in any case sabotaged by his petulant brothers and the selfish amirs. The luckless sultan had neither time nor the necessary manpower and material for a decisive confrontation against the Mongols. He spent the last years of his life practically on horseback, fighting both against those who should have joined him in a common cause against a common enemy, and the Mongols, who were tracking him; he even defeated Noyan Charmoghan but all to no avail. Weakened by age, incessant struggle, and heartbreak, he disappeared like a luminous star from the political horizon, to survive as a legend. Although there were a number of credible and incredible accounts of disappearance (demise), the celebrated historian, Ibnul Asir, was uncertain of his end.

It is idle to speculate the outcome of the Battle of Indus if there had been no quarrel over a horse between two valiant warriors, and no desertion by Saif-ud-din. Not only did the victors and the vanquished at the Battle of Indus, make history, two horses also found a niche in history, one for making a twenty-foot jump into the deep and fast flowing Indus and carrying the sultan to safety the other for causing an irreparable rift between the commanders of the two wings of the sultan's army.

With news of the unrest and sedition in Tangut and Cathay, Chingiz held a meeting with his sons and chiefs about the future course of action. Should they return to Mongolia immediately, or stay on till they had finished with Sultan Jalal-ud-din? It was thought inadvisable to leave behind such a dangerous adversary as the dashing sultan, who laughed 'only at the tips of his lips'.[18] So it was decided to send a force to Kutch, Makran and India to discover the whereabouts and intentions of Jalal-ud-din and another towards Ghaznin, the centre of the sultan's hope, and when spring arrived, to set out for their homeland. Chaghatae with a large force was sent after the sultan and Uktae on his mission to Ghaznin.

Marching up the river Indus, Uktae advanced on Ghaznin, carrying fire and sword through the districts he passed. On his arrival at the capital of Sultan Mahmud, the inhabitants surrendered without the least show of resistance, but to no avail. On account of the activities of the sultan, Ghaznin was razed to the ground; the inhabitants were turned into the open country and, with the exception of artisans and mechanics, all were slain. Leaving Qutuqu Noyan behind to look after the prisoners and the artisans, Uktae marched off to Khurasan by way of the Garm-Sir of Herat. In the meanwhile

Chaghatae reduced Makran and the surrounding territory and spent the winter at Kalinjar on the banks of the Indus. Its governor was Salar Ahmad. He submitted and did his utmost to supply the requirements of the Mongols. The climate was, however, unwholesome and many Mongols fell sick. The Mongols had such a large number of prisoners with them that in every tent there were at least ten to twenty captives. Being natives of the soil, the captives were unaffected by the malady that was sapping the strength of the main army. They performed all sorts of duties and cooked for the soldiers. Perhaps the ill health of the warriors or the shortage of rations made Chaghatae apprehensive of a revolt by the captives, and he decided to have all of them killed. Each captive was commanded to clean a specific amount of rice and the captives, ignorant of their impending fate, completed their task with speed in a week. Tired and exhausted, they were slain while they were asleep.

Chingiz Khan despatched two of his commanders, Turbai Taqshi and Bala Noyan, with two tumans or 20,000 horses, to hunt down Sultan Jalal-ul-din, who was now in India. The Mongol army crossed the Indus and besieged the fortress of Biyah. Formerly, it was governed by Qamr-ud-din Kirmani but he had been lately overpowered and driven out by one of the sultan's amirs. The fortress of Biyah was reckoned among the strongest citadels but it was carried by storm and the inhabitants given to the sword. Next they advanced on Multan. As in the vicinity of Multan there were no stones, the Mongol scouts fetched them from great distances. Crossing the river on a hastily constructed wooden bridge, the two commanders appeared before the gates of Multan and immediately launched their catapults into action. The inhabitants offered stubborn resistance and the siege dragged on. At last the walls were breached at several points and the fortress was about to fall, when the severity of the summer compelled the Mongols to raise the siege. Foiled in their attempt to reduce the town, the Mongols set out to rejoin Chingiz Khan, ravaging the provinces of Multan and Lahore and dotting their route to Ghaznin with arson and loot, ruined fields and desolated towns.[19]

This was, however, not the end of Mongol forays into Indian soil. Having seen the wealth of India, they continued to raid the north-western region, including Lahore, Multan, and even Sind. Lahore became a dependency and the Mongols as reported by Qazi Minhaj, were a constant threat 'as far as the frontiers of Delhi'. Not just the north-western mountains of India, even the Indus had ceased to be a geographical boundary. The Turkish sultans of Delhi, Iltutmish (1210-36) and Balban (1266-87), though distant, appear to have been knowledgeable about the formidability of Mongol power: Iltutmish refused asylum to Jalal-ud-din after the Indus battle. When turning down the advice of a courtier to conquer south India, Balban had said, 'it will not be an act of wisdom to leave Delhi to go on distant campaigns in these days of turmoil and insecurity, when the Mongols have occupied all lands of Islam, devastated Lahore, and made it a point to invade our country once every year. Maintaining peace and consolidation in our own kingdom is far better than invading foreign territories....'

Ghor, Ghaznin and Gharjistan

The victories of Sultan Jalal-ud-din over the Mongols had spread joy throughout Khurasan. At last the Mongols, thought the people, had met in the dashing and reckless sultan a man who would drive the barbarians back into their barren and forbidding steppes.[20] To the highly cultured and sophisticated people of Iran, the rough yoke of the rude Mongols was extremely galling and, therefore, to profit by the turn in the tide (which seemed to be heralded by the successive Mongol defeats between Bamian and Ghaznin) all Khurasan rose in popular revolt against the hated and uncouth invaders. In all towns and cities of Khurasan Mongol Shahnahs and their proteges were killed. But the people were soon disillusioned, Jalal-ud-din was overthrown on the banks of the Indus and the infuriated Mongol avalanche moved on towards Khurasan.

'From whence have these people whom I have killed come to life again?' said Chingiz Khan.[21] 'Henceforth the heads of the people shall be separated from their bodies so that they may not come to life again.' Uktae was specially chosen to carry out the instructions. With a huge army he set out for the reconquest and exemplary punishment of the hot-heads in Ghor and Khurasan. On reaching the Blacksmith's Boundary (Pul-i-Ahangaran), between Ghor and Ghaznin, Uktae camped near Firuz-koh and directed Sadi Cherbi and Mankadhu Cherbi along with several Noyans to march against Sistan while Abkah Noyan was sent with a strong contingent of 10,000 catapult workers to reduce the strong fortress of Gharjistan. Ilchikdae Noyan was deputed to subdue the hill tracts of Ghor and Herat.

Ghor, Ghaznin and Gharjistan were no longer the power centres they once had been. But, as Muhammad Habib once put it, 'every stone of the land was imbued with associations of bygone greatness.' Sultan Mahmud and his son Masud had made Ghaznin a great and beautiful city, a centre of life, knowledge and learning. It was under the patronage of Sultan Mahmud that the great Persian poet, Firdausi, composed the famous epic—*Shahnama*—the voice of Persian nationalism. Ghaznin also occupies a place in the history of Persian mystic thought. It was in the reign of Bahram Shah that the first, and one of three great Persian mystic poets, Abul-Mujd Majdud Sinai, flourished. Of *Hadiqa* and *Diwan* fame, his poetry is distinguished by originality and grace. The other two great poets are Shaykh Farid-ud-din Attar and Maulana Jalal-ud-din Rumi, probably the greatest of them all.

The decline and fall of the Ghaznavids was followed by the rise of Ghori rule under the vassalage of Sultan Sanjar. Of the 'Seven Stars of Ghor' two deserve special mention, Ala-ud-din and Ghiyas-ud-din. Ala-ud-din was an educated person but had, in a war of revenge, defeated Bahram Shah, and torched the majestic Ghaznin, gloating over the feat. This earned him the nickname *Jahansoz* (World Burner). The second 'star', Ghiyas-ud-din, on the other hand, earned everlasting renown as the founder of the first Turkish Empire in India (in 1206) who paved the way for the rule of successive Turkish dynasties.

Sistan defended itself bravely and the Mongols had to fight hard before they could enter the town. The inhabitants were obstinate in their resistance and, even when the struggle was manifestly hopeless, they held their ground and fought hand to hand; women also fought in the streets and in every building without asking for quarter.[22]

Having reduced the mountaineers of Ghor, Ilchikdae Noyan advanced on Herat. Impressed by the verdant meadows and groves and gardens of Herat, Tuli had earlier come to terms with its brave defenders and the town had been lucky to escape the usual Mongol fire and sword. But the contagion of revolt which had spread all over Khurasan at last infected its inhabitants too. The victories of Sultan Jalal-ud-din encouraged them to throw off the hated Mongol yoke. Following the example of the other rebellious towns, Herat also declared independence by murdering the Mongol protégé Malik Abu Bakr and the Shahna Mangatae. 'This comes through your withholding the sword from the Heratis !,' duly commented Chingiz Khan. Chingiz Khan asked Ilchikdae Noyan to proceed to Herat with 80,000 men from the main army and also to levy, on his way, men and materials from all the places which had submitted: Balkh, Shipurghan, and others. With immense arms, ammunition, and levies, Ilchikdae Noyan appeared at the gates of Herat, and, with his huge army of 1,30,000 and closely invested the place.[23]

The inhabitants, too, had made elaborate and thorough preparations for the inevitable and bitter siege. They had been fortunate to get the services of Malik Mubariz-ud-din Sabzwari, the valiant defender of Firozkoh. Under his leadership the people had sworn an oath not to yield or ask for quarter but to fight on till the last.

Ilchikdae Noyan placed 30,000 men on each side of the town and issued strict orders against indiscipline or misdemeanour. To bring out the best in his men, he also held out promises of rewards for distinguished performances. The blockade was tight but the town was, defended with equal skill for a period of more than six months. Malik Mubariz-ud-din and Khivaja Fakhr-ud-din kept up the morale of their men by personally supervising the defence and by an equally lavish distribution of gold and silver. They made spirited sallies and inflicted heavy casualties on the besiegers.[24] Exasperated by the long delay and the steadily mounting losses sustained by his troops, Ilchikdae Noyan decided on an all-out effort and ordered the moats to be filled for a continuous assault on the town. On account of the heavy and prolonged battering by the Mongol catapults and ballistics, the city walls had become 'honey-combed', and then a breach of about 50 yards was made at a place. The people, however, offered stubborn resistance and successfully warded off all Mongol attempts to enter into the city. But the rigours of the siege at last began to distress the desperate and sore-pressed defenders. The ever-increasing reinforcements and the effectiveness of the Mongol artillery, however, made the people despondent and voices were now heard, seeking an accommodation with the enemy. While the inhabitants were paralysed by dissent the Mongols launched a heavy assault on Friday, Jamadi II, A.H. 619 July, 1222[25] and forced their way into the town through the breach. The inhabitants fought valiantly and no quarter was given nor prisoners made. The people were all massacred—men, women and children; the town was sacked and the buildings demolished. The numbers of those slain stagger belief; 16,00,000 people are said to have been killed in Herat, but considering that Herat was one of the most prosperous and thickly populated cities of Khurasan and behind its walls the inhabitants of many towns and villages had come to seek refuge, the figure is credible.

Having reduced Herat to ruins, Ilchikdae Noyan advanced on Kaliun while Sadi Cherbi and other great Noyans set out for Sistan.

Built by Sultan Baha-ud-din Sam, Kaliun was a strongly fortified town, reputed to be the strongest fortress in those parts, 'the like of which,' wrote Qazi Minhaj, 'is nowhere to be found, neither in loftiness and sublimity or in stability and solidity.'[26] 'Situated on a rock, a thousand cubits high, it could be approached only by a narrow and steep mountain path too rugged and too difficult for any living thing to mount it with the exception of reptiles. The fortress had seven wells of perennial water so that the inhabitants were never in want of water. There was also productive land inside. Kaliun was, therefore, self-sufficient in its requirements both of food and water; it had, consequently, defied the Khwarzam Shah for no less than ten years. At this time the fortress had in the two sons of Abu Bakr commanders worth their weight in gold, 'two heroes of renown and in themselves, two huge elepants of war, exceptionally tall in stature, so tall,' relates Qazi Minhaj 'that when they used to accompany Sultan Muhammad Khwarazm Shah (on horseback) in procession with their hands placed on his stirrup, their heads were higher than that of the sultan.' Ikhtiarul Mulk Daulat Yar Tughra was the amir or Governor and he soon showed that he was fit for the post. In this place, though the Mongols had all the neighbourhood, he maintained himself for about two years. He kept his enemies engaged by perpetual surprises and stratagems. He won no victory over them, but kept them at bay and the siege made no progress. (The place was amply provisioned and strongly garrisoned.) The Mongols were soon beset by these vigorous sorties, which created confusion in the camp; burning, ravaging and destroying everything they could lay their hands upon, the daring defenders could be traced, like a hurricane, by the devastation they had made. To guard the camp against the sudden and oft-repeated sallies of the daring skirmishers, the Mongols raised a strong wall around the fortress—the besiegers thereby making manifest their determination not to raise the siege, rather than their bravery in maintaining the struggle.

The intrepidity of the garrison, reached such a pitch that it was impossible for the Mongol forces to obtain sleep at night out of dread of them, and so these infidels completely enclosed the entire fortress with a circular wall, in which they placed two gates, facing the fortress, with walls before them, and men were told off to keep watch at night. A trustworthy person related that a fox had remained at the foot of the rock on which the fortress of Kalium stands, within the circumvallation of the Mongols, and, for a period of seven months that fox had no way by which he might get out, so strictly did the Mongol troops guard this wall.[27]

The brave defenders were, however, not daunted by the huge wall, which sealed them off from all help and assistance. The blockade was now tightened and a vigorous siege was maintained. Months rolled on without any visible effect on the Mongols who were confident in the ultimate success of the twin concomitants of blockade and famine scarcity, to wreck havoc and demoralize the besieged.

Finding the area inaccessible, the Mongols had given up all hopes of taking the place by storm and resolved to thrust to a blockade until a year elapsed and Sadi Cherbi arrived from Sistan. The arrival of fresh troops encouraged the Mongols to attempt more active operations against the citadel. The rigours of the siege, at last began to distress the desperate and sore-pressed mountain-dwellers, now beset by disease and food shortage. Reduced to subsist on dried flesh, pistachios, and clarified butter, the besieged began to suffer from swollen heads and feet, which assumed the proportions of an epidemic and died in large numbers. But even then the possibility of surrender or capitulation did not cross their mind and it was only after sixteen months of heroic resistance during which the garrison had been thinned to only 50 men, twenty of them suffering from swollen feet, that one of them went over to the enemy and informed him of the miserable plight of the defenders. The Mongols immediately prepared to storm the citadel. Throwing all their valuables and costly belongings into the wells and setting fire to their dwellings, the last remnants of the garrison opened the gate, charged the storming Mongols, and perished fighting.

The reduction of Kaliun paved the way for Mongol operations against the still more formidable and impregnable fortress of Fiwar, ten leagues away, on a high rock too difficult to approach by land. It could be defended by a very small force. The inhabitants were unceasing in their efforts, repairing the breaches and eagerly looking for an opportunity to sally forth and set fire to Mongol tents. Finding the citadel formidable and inaccessible, the Mongols abandoned attempts to take it by force and resolved to reduce it by blockade. Tulan Cherbi and Arsalan Khan of Qiyaligh settled at the fortress and the siege dragged on for more than ten months, turning into a severe blockade. No more food could be introduced nor could reinforcements, if any, reach them. Scarcity and famine slowly sapped the strength of the garrison and reduced their numbers until 'the whole of the garrison', says Qazi Minhaj, 'were dead, and, throughout the whole fortress, there were not more than seven men alive, and out of them four or five were sick'. It was only when the remnants of the proud garrison had been reduced to such a wretched and miserable condition that one of them deserted his comrades and went over to the enemy. He informed the Mongols of the miserable conditions inside the citadel. In 1223 the citadel was stormed, and the miserable defenders butchered.

The fall of the strong fortresses of Kaliun and Fiwar synchronized with the Mongol conquest of Firozkoh, which had earlier defied all their attempts. In AH 617/1220-1, Uqlan Cherbi had appeared before the gates of the town, but the inhabitants offered stubborn resistance. Having closely invested the place, the Mongols pushed the siege but the brave defenders held out with determination. Uqlan Cherbi raised the siege after twenty-one days, and retired. Soon, however, dissensions arose and the inhabitants turned against the commandant of the fortress, Malik Mubariz-ud-din, who had to shut himself up in the citadel north-east of the city. The citizens now accepted the overlordship of Malik Qutub-ud-din of Ghor, who appointed his own cousin, Imad-ud-din Zengi, to administer the city. Weakened by internal dissensions, the town was unable to defend itself against the Mongols when in AH 619/1222-3, Uktae sent a force to reduce it. Malik Mubariz-ud-din refused to bend knee to the victors but, as his position was now untenable, he left the place and made for Herat.

The Mongol tide of conquests and victories, however, was met with a check and came to a dead halt against the impregnable fortresses of Tulak and Saifrud of Ghor. Built on solid rock and unconnected with any other mountain, Tulak was said to be constructed by Manuchihr, a semi-legendary figure of Iran. It had a perennial supply of water and the stony well, which supplied all the water the inhabitants needed and had a diameter of 20 yards. The fortress was of exceptional strength and was commanded by the famous Amir Habashi, who, on account of his great skill and proficiency in the use of the lance, was styled 'Nezoh-war'. 'In Khorasan and Khwarazm,' observes Qazi Minhaj, 'there never has been one so skilled in the use of a lance as he. "If I were to lie down on my back upon the ground and take a staff in my hand," he used to proudly assert, "I would defend myself against four men with spears." In short, he was an excellent man and his good works were many, and his charities countless.'

In AH 617/1220-1 the Mongols made repeated attempts to storm the place but failed. It was only a year later, when Qutuqu Noyan arrived with 40,000 troops, that the amir agreed to submit and pay tribute to the Mongols. The inhabitants, who had no objection to accept and even acclaim the overlordship of the barbarians, were bitter about the payment of ransom. They mocked and satirized the amir. Feelings running high, the troops too joined in the popular agitation. They captured the amir and delivered him and the fortress to Malik Qutub-ud-din of Ghor. Malik Qutub-ud-din took measures to strengthen and guard the fortress against the Mongols; and to give the inhabitants a sense of security, he placed his own son Malik Taj-ud-din Mohammad to supervise the administration. A year later, when the Mongols turned against Tulak, they found the entire population up in arms against them. For four years the inhabitants defended themselves with courage and determination and 'in the end,' says Qazi Minhaj, 'it continued safe from the hands of the infidels.'

Saifrud was another fortress that held out against the Mongols. Built by Sultan Baha-ud-din Sam, it was reputed to be the strongest citadel of Ghor. Malik Qutub-ud-din Husain had been entrusted by the Khwarazm Shah with the task of repairing and strengthening the defences of the citadel. The Malik had, however, only completed the construction of a reservoir capable of holding enough water for the inhabitants to last 40 days, when the Mongol hoofs were be heard in the mountain of Ghor. Finding the people shut up in the strong citadels or safe in the inaccessible defiles of Ghor, the Mongols began to collect animals and cattle and the Ghorians suffered heavy losses in their attempts to recover their quadrupeds. Saifrud was invested by a strong Mongol force under Mangutah Noyan, Qarachah Noyan, and Ite-Siz Noyan. Learning that the besieged had only a limited supply of water, they surrounded the fortress and pushed the siege with vigour. Finding the Mongols determined to reduce the town by blockade, the Malik ordered water and provisions to be rationed and controlled. Each individual received about half a gallon of water and four seers of grain. Qazi Minhaj describes the scene thus,

There was an immense number of quadrupeds in the fortress and as many as they were able to cure by drying, they slaughtered and the remainder, amounting to the number of 2,44,000 odd, perished for want of water. The carcasses were thrown from the ramparts of the fort on to the glacis on the side of the hill (on which it stood), and the whole face thereof, for a depth of some 40 yards, was completely strewn with the carcases of the dead animals, so that not a yard of space of the whole hill could be seen but for them—there was no horse in the fortress but one, the private horse of Malik Qutub-ud-din Husain, for the use of which 'the water expended in the Malik's ablutions used to be set aside and was collected in an open vessel so that the animal might drink it'.

The siege was thus maintained for fifty days as the besieged ran short of water. Weaker than the rest, one of the besieged went down the fort and informed the Mongols of the straitened affairs inside the fortress. Malik Qutub-ud-din held a meeting at the time of afternoon prayers and it was resolved that 'the next morning, at the break of the day, they should put all the females and children to death with their own hands, throw open the gateway of the fortress, and that every man, armed with a naked sword, should conceal himself in some place within the fortress, and, when the infidel Mongols should enter it, they, with one accord, should fall upon them with their swords, and should continue to fight them until they should attain the felicity of martyrdom.' The valiant defenders began to embrace each other and bid adieu to their near and dear ones when to their great astonishment and unbounded joy 'at the time of evening prayer, Almighty God, the Most High and Holy, opened the doors of His mercy upon them, and, out of His boundless beneficence, sent clouds so that, on the summits of the mountains around and parts adjacent, until midnight, the rain of mercy descended, and the snow of compassion fell, in such a way, that, from the army of infidels, and the champions of the faith within the fortification, a hundred thousand exclamations and cries arose in wonder at the succour of the Most High God.' At this strange and unexpected succour to the besieged, which provided them with water for another month or two, the Mongols raised the siege and, as Qazi Minhaj would have it, 'went to hell until the following year.'

More trouble was, however, in store for the inhabitants of Saifrud. No sooner was Sultan Jalal-ud-din overthrown on the banks of the Indus than did the Mongols turn to Ghor. In view of the brave garrison's past showing, the Mongols this time made elaborate preparations and the fortress was invested by strong force, fully equipped and provisioned for a long siege. It consisted of both cavalry and infantry and included several amirs of importance. Malik Qutub-ud-din had, however, not been idle; anticipating a second and more vigorous attempt by the Mongols, he had been storing provisions and constructing water reservoirs, and so, when the Mongol force appeared he was not terrified by their numbers. Mongol attempts to storm the fortress were resisted. 'The greater the efforts and endeavours the infidels made', says Qazi Minhaj, 'the stronger became the affairs of the fortress, and the more intrepid grew the warriors of the faith.'

Finding the fortress too strong to be stormed and the Malik too wary and energetic to be easily outwitted, the Mongols decided to get hold of the place by means of a trick. They proposed a truce and stipulated that for three days the inhabitants of the fortress should go to trade their commodities for gold and silver in the Mongol camp and purchase there the garments and cattle they required. After three days' barter, they promised, they would raise the siege and retire. Suspecting an ulterior design or trick the Malik refused to be taken in but not so the inhabitants. Exhausted and tired by two months of constant and heavy fighting, they were anxious to accept the terms. Against the better judgement and advice of Malik Qutub-ud-din, the people forced his hand and the truce was agreed. For two days there was brisk and eager shopping in the Mongol camp and no incident occurred. The people moved about freely and traded as if in their own marketplaces. But on the third day when they went out to the Mongol camp, they were startled by the sudden sounding of kettle-drums and shouts. They did not have to ponder long over the strange phenomenon, for immediately armed bands of Mongols rushed out from the gullies and ravines, from behind rocks, pack-saddles of animals, and bales of cloth. The unsuspecting merchants were paralysed by the sudden massacre and those who attempted to resist were intercepted and cut down by the merciless Mongols. Among the captives thus taken were 280 persons of distinction and 'every family', says Qazi Minhaj, 'had to mourn for the loss of a member or two.' While the fortress was prostrate with grief and mourning, the Mongol Noyans asked Malik Qutub-ud-din to ransom the captives. Fearing another ruse, he refused. The relatives of the captives, now wiser, did not press him to deal with the unscrupulous enemy.

The Mongols now decided to storm the fortress. The wary Malik was, however, alert.

He gave directions so that all the great blocks of stones lying about on the face of the hill near the fortress were speedily placed in such a manner that the touch of a child would move them from their places and send them rolling down. More than a hundred great stones as big as mill-stones, and handmill-stones, fastened to beams of wood, at the extremity of each beam a millstone, they had drawn out; and those beams were fastened to the battlements of the fortress by ropes. All the men of the fortress were divided into two bodies: one-half were concealed on the top of the ramparts, behind the battlements, and the other half outside the fortress, at the foot of the ramparts, behind the great blocks of stone. Malik Qutub-ud-din Husain enjoined that, until the sound of the kettle-drums of the fortress arose, not a person should show himself.

Next morning, the Mongols launched their expected assault (AH 620). Under cover of their shields more than 10,000 Mongol warriors advanced upwards and, meeting no opposition, were lulled into the belief that the inhabitants and garrison of Saifrud were unprepared. When they had ascended the hill and were about 100 yards from the fortress, the appointed signal was given; 'all raised a shout, cut away the millstones, beams and ropes,' says Qazi Minhaj, 'and sent the great stones rolling down. Almighty God so willed it, that not a single individual among the infidel could escape being killed, wounded, or disabled; and, from the summit to the base of the hill, Mongols and renegades lay prostrate together, and a great number of their grandees, Noyans and Bahadurs went to hell'.

The Mongols were overwhelmed by the complete destruction of the storming party and were now convinced that the fortress was in the hands of an energetic and skilful commander. They raised the siege and, to make amends for their failure against Saifrud, attempted to storm the fortress of Tulak. They laid a carefully planned ambush for the besieged garrison but it was unsuccessful. Suffering heavy losses they abandoned the idea of reducing Tulak and withdrew.

The defeat of Jalal-ud-din, on the banks of the Indus, put paid to all hopes of driving away the barbarians and reviving the lost splendour and glory of the Khwarazm shahs. Malik Qutub-ud-din now decided to abandon Saifrud, which was like a tiny island in the midst of a raging ocean, and retired to India where he hoped to start a fresh career.

He was joined by other Maliks of Ghor, Seraj-ud-din, Saif-ud-din and others, and they set out for India with their families and dependants. They were, however, overtaken at the river Arghand by a Mongol force under Qazil Manjuk. He had been directed to reduce those territories of Khurasan which were still flying their own flag. Proceeding by way of Herat, Isfizat, and Tulak, he reached Saifrud, which he found in a defenceless state. It was easily captured. From the prisoners, Qazil Manjuk learnt about the departure of the Maliks for Hindustan. In haste he pursued them and overtook them while they were throwing a pontoon bridge over the river Arghand. The fugitives were in no position to offer battle to the Mongols. Malik Saif-ud-din and his followers, made for the hills and reached Ghor in safety. Malik Seraj-ud-din, however, refused to fly, gave battle, and died fighting. Fighting with great skill and emulating the daring feat of Sultan Jalal-ud-din, Malik Qutub-ud-din whipped his horse into the raging river and crossed over to the opposite shore. Only a few of his followers could join him. The rest, men and women, including his daughters and sisters, warriors and chieftains of Ghor, fell into Mongol hands and were butchered.

> The boast of heraldry, the pomp of power,
> And all that beauty, all that wealth ever gave.
> Awaits alike this inevitable hour,
> The paths of glory lead but to the grave.

Chingiz Khan was camping at Taliqan beside the Pushtah-i-Numan when he received the news. To counteract the effects Jalal-ud-din's resounding victory might have had on his recently subjugated Muslim territories, seething with discontent and wounded pride, Chingiz Khan set out in person to crush the young sultan. As the roads were impracticable for his wheeled carriages, and the route lay through narrow ravines and steep passes of Gharjistan, he had to leave his treasures and heavy luggage behind. Trusting to the terror inspired by his arms, he left only a small force to guard it at Buqlan.

But the wary Mongol chief was mistaken in his appreciation of the hardy mountaineers of Gharjistan. Protected by a ring of strong fortresses, excavated in the rocks at Rang, Pindar, Balarwan, Laghri, Sabekji, Suja Khanah and above all, Ashiyar, and blessed with perennial springs, the wary mountaineers looked with contempt upon the neighbouring amirs and their armies encumbered with all sorts of equipment and baggage. The strong fortress of Ashiyar was, at this time, commanded by Amir Muhammad Maraghini, who had earned a name for his vigour and energy. Undeterred by consequences and Mongol reprisals, he set out for a marauding expedition against the Mongol camp at Buqlan. The Mongols were taken unawares and the surprise was complete. Overpowering the Mongol contingent, he set free their prisoners and returned with immense booty, including horses and wheeled carriages. Encouraged by this success and with a growing appetite for booty, he looted the Mongol camp on one or two more occasions. Retribution was, however, near at hand.

Having overthrown Sultan Jalal-ud-din on the banks of the Indus, Chingiz Khan directed Uktae to ravage the mountain territories of Ghor and Ghaznin that were still independent and defiant. Abaqah Noyan, with a tuman of *manjaniqchis* or catapult-workers, was sent to reduce the strong citadel of Ashiyar. Amir Muhammad soon showed that he was not only proficient in looting the Mongol heavy baggage and cattle-lifting, but equally alert and active in holding his own against heavy odds. The Mongol battering-rams failed to make any effect upon the rock-carved citadel and it was decided to blockade the fortress. Amir Muhammad had collected provisions for sustaining the Mongol blockade. The siege dragged on for 15 months but at last the much dreaded famine and scarcity of provisions reared their awful head. The besieged had to subsist on leaves and carcasses, yet held out until, thinned down by scarcity and epidemic, they were reduced to subsist on human flesh. Qazi Minhaj describes the terrible scene:

As long as there were provisions and flesh, 'they used to consume them, and when food of that kind failed, affairs reached such a pitch that they were want to eat the flesh of whoever was killed, or who died to that degree, that every person used to keep his killed and dead for curing and eating. Some have related and they are responsible for the veracity or otherwise of their statement, that there was a woman of the minstrel class in the fortress of Ashiyar. She had a mother and a female slave. Her mother died, and she dried her body; and her female slave likewise died, and she dried her body also. She sold the flesh of both of them, so that, from the two corpses, she acquired 250 dinars of pure gold. At last she also died'.

The entire population thus perished and there remained 30 men. Amir Muhammad, still refused to surrender. The conditions were now unbearable and the remnant population killed the amir and threw his head towards the besiegers in the hope of grace and mercy. But to no avail! The Mongols stormed the citadel and slaughtered them all.

Thus the 'last hurdle' was overcome, the 'Final Frontier' conquered, and the great campaign stamped Chingiz Khan as the greatest conqueror of the age.

The campaign against the most powerful Muslim ruler had been expected to be tiring but, except for some sporadic, even memorably striking instances, it appeared to fizzle out. The mountaineers of Ghor, Ghaznin, and Gharjistan, however, showed that the war between the 'ruler of the Sunrise' and the 'ruler of the sunset' could have been of epic proportions had the Khwarazmians been blessed with a skilful, determined and courageous leadership. Whereas at Thermopylae, man after man fell, to be replaced by another brave heart, the mountaineers had no narrow pass to defend but a whole region and the scattered towns. Town after town was grimly defended and led by gallant leaders, the people heroically stood up for the defence of their town and their honour—men and women, old and young, braving all odds, scarcity of water and perils, loss of near and dear ones, hunger and disease, even subsisting on carrion—but still carrying on the hopeless struggle till the last breath, reciting that dishonour is worse than death. They deserved an elegy, an epitaph worthy of the sacrifice. But no eye was left to shed even a tear.

The Campaign Against Tangut

On account of the prolonged and protracted absence of Chingiz Khan from Mongolia, the rulers of Cathay and Tangut had begun to waver in their allegiance to him. They began preparations for throwing off the hated Mongol yoke.[28] As decided earlier, Uktae and Chaghatae had done their jobs well, and Chingiz Khan could now afford to return to his native land. From Peshawar, he marched by Bamian and arrived at Buqlan where he had previously left part of his baggage; he spent the summer there in the pleasant meadows of the locality. When autumn came, he decided to resume his homeward march. Daroghas were appointed for the administration of the various towns and cities, but it is doubtful if they were assigned any troops. Crossing the Oxus, he reached Bokhara, where he asked the Sadr-i-Jahan to bring to him someone well-versed in Muslim law and theology. Qazi Ashraf, along with an equally leading preacher was presented to the Khan. Chingiz Khan enquired from them about the creed and customs of the Muslims.[29] 'We believe the Creator of the universe to be All-powerful. High above all things,' they said. 'There is nothing like unto Him.' 'I have nothing to say against it', declared the Khan. They told him about Revelation, Prophethood, Prayers, and Fasting, to all of which he nodded general approval. Chingiz expressed himself against the pilgrimage to Mecca, however: 'The whole world is the house of God,' he said. 'Prayers will reach him wheresoever they are offered.'

Barthold rejects the historicity of the 'Bukhara interview' for two reasons; Ibnul Asir does not mention it, and the objection to 'pilgrimage to Mecca', was too sophisticated to come from a nomad chieftain. But silence on the failure by Ibnul Asir to mention the 'interview' is no argument; we should make due allowance for the distances involved in reaching the account/tales of what happened in far-off lands, and also the importance attached by the 'trustworthy' narrator to the events that he had come to know.

The discussion over, Chingiz Khan proceeded towards Samarqand in AH 618-19/122-3 where he spent the winter. To summon his eldest son Juji, who was ill-inclined since his supercession at the siege of Khwarazm and had retired to his appanage in the Qipchaq steppes, Chingiz sent a messenger directing him to move from the steppes of Qipchaq and to drive before him game, consisting mostly of wild asses, for the customary grand hunt.

Chaghatae and Uktae took up quarters at Qarakul near Bokhara and during the winter were absorbed in fowling and bird-hunting; weekly, it is said, they sent fifty *kharwars* or camel-loads of game to their father until there remained no more of it and the winter drew to an end. As soon as the spring set in, Chingiz Khan resumed his return journey. On the way back he displayed unusual cruelty. As if to emulate and improve upon the triumphal procession of the Roman generals, he ordered the unfortunate and aged Turkan Khatun and the other captive ladies of the fallen dynasty to march in front of his troops, bare-headed and bare-footed, to lament the loss of their pomp and glory, the downfall of their empire and the death of their near and dear ones. This miserable procession is said to have been asked to raise lamentations all through the journey to Mongolia; the story seems to be apocryphal and doubtful as the *Secret History* and Juwaini both mention that it was at the time of leaving for Mongolia that they were commanded 'to sing a dirge on the Sultan and his empire'. Moreover, it is against common sense and also physically too much and too exacting for the 'delicate' ladies to perform it and still survive the vigours of the arduous journey. Turkan Khatun lived on to bemoan the disgrace for which she was partly responsible till 1230 when death relieved her from her sorrows and miserable state.[30]

On the banks of the river Fanakat, Chingiz was joined by Chaghatae and Uktae and, advancing by regular marches, they reached Qalan Yazi, where they were joined by Juji, who, as directed, was driving the game on from the opposite side. The troops were now ordered to encircle the game, and the two steadily moving pincers met at Uqa. Chingiz Khan mounted his horse and entered the ring to enjoy the favourite Mongol hunt. The wild-asses, which Juji had driven on from the steppes, were dapple-grey like the sheep:

on account of the rough journey they had had, their hoofs were worn out, and they were provided with horseshoes. When the Khan, his sons and Noyans had done with the sport and were tired, the remainder of the animals were his and allowed to escape. On his knees, then, Juji presented himself before his father. Among the costly offerings which he had brought were 1,00,000 horses, every 20,000 of which were of different colours.

Chingiz Khan spent the whole summer on the steppe of Qalan Tashi, where he was joined by his two great noyans, Subutai Bahadur and Yamah Noyan, and a great Quriltai was held. Honours and rewards were distributed; some Uighur amirs were also brought there to be executed. Juji was given permission to proceed towards the steppes of Qipchaq and administer his appanage. Resuming his march in autumn, Chingiz Khan reached his ordu in the spring of 1225 after an absence of seven fateful years in which the course of history was vitally changed.

On reaching his ordu Chingiz Khan was met by his two grandsons, Qubilai Khan and Hulaku Khan, both to be famous later in history. Hulaku was nine and Qubilai Khan a year older. On the way to meet their grandfather, Hulaku captured a small deer and Qubilai a hare. 'As it was a custom among the Mongols, on the first occasion of boys capturing game to anoint the middle finger with flesh and fat of the game, which anointing is termed *aghameshi*,' says Rashid-ud-din,[31] 'Chingiz Khan himself anointed the fingers of his grandsons and held grand feasts and banquets to celebrate the event.'

This event is described thus by Howorth: 'on the banks of the Imil he was met by two of his grandsons, afterwards very celebrated, namely Kubilai and Khulagu, one eleven and the other nine years old. They had killed their first game, and, according to Mongol custom, Jengis pricked their middle fingers to mix some blood with their food and drink, a kind of baptism of the chase.'[32]

To celebrate his triumphant return to his own yurt, Chingiz Khan held a feast. Howorth remarks:

What a wonderful gathering that must have been. 'We are much impressed in reading the history of the middle ages, with the effect of the Crusades, which brought the parochial-minded chivalry of Western Europe into contact with the land of so much gorgeous romance as the East, and gave an impetus to thought and action, and an enlargement of view that had more than aught else to do perhaps with the social and mental revolution of the revival of learning. But what were the Crusades as an experience to the journey of Jingis (Chingiz) and his troops? Born and accustomed only to the dreary steppe-lands of the Gobi desert, and its girdle of pine-covered mountains, their triumphant march led them through the very garden of Asia, among its most refined and cultured inhabitants, and through its most prosperous cities. Every step must have been a new chapter of romance, such as boys in England find in the Arabian Nights, and the vast caravans of treasure that they carried back with them must have been objects of intense wonder to the wives and daughters of the returning warriors, and the tales they told of their adventures must have seemed like the romance of ballad makers rather than the truthful experiences of ingenuous soldiers. Nor were the crowds of captives, chiefly artisans, a less important, if a somewhat picturesque, element in the cavalcade. With them there went to the furthest East all the knowledge and craft possessed by the Muhammadans, and if we find the period of Mongol supremacy in China to be a period of revival in art and manufacture, a period of great literary energy, we must not forget what a number of names in the administration of that period are Persian and Turkish; and how the rubbing together of two widely different civilizations, which have crystallised apart, such as those of China and Persia, necessarily leads to a vigorous outburst of fresh ideas and discoveries.'[33]

The feast must have been grand and the gathering unique in the history of the nomads. But during all this time the mind of Chingiz Khan was at work, busy planning a campaign against the haughty ruler of Tangut, who had had the audacity to refuse the summons to accompany the Khan of Khans on his expedition to the land of the setting sun. 'If your strength is not adequate, you need not be Emperor,' was the scornful comment of Shidarqu's courtier, Ashaganbu, and the Tangut ruler endorsed the same by his silence and refusal to be 'the right hand' of Chingiz Khan in his campaign against the Khwarazm Shah. 'How dare Ashaganbu say such a thing? What difficulty is there if I turn my forces against him,' exclaimed Chingiz.[34] 'But this was not my original intention. If God protects us, we shall attack him after returning from (the campaign against) the huci-huci.' It was the disturbing news of the wavering loyalty of the rulers of Cathay and Tangut, and their preparations to throw off the Mongol yoke, which had hastened the return of the Mongol Khan.[35] An expedition was all the more imperative as a coalition between the Kin and the Tangut was imminent; the death of Muquli had re-awakened the fighting spirit of the Kin and they had ventured to attack and recapture some of the towns which had been occupied by Muquli.

Having passed the winter in pleasure and jollity, Chingiz Khan reorganized his men and set out for Qashin, the capital of Tangut. Uktae and Chaghatae accompanied him, but Tuli was allowed to follow later as his wife, Siur-Quti-Bigi was stricken with small pox. About this time, Chingiz received the news of the death of his eldest son Juji.[36]

Carrying fire and sword, the Mongols wrought great havoc; the number of the slain was staggering and the land was littered with corpses. When the

Mongols reached Ling Chau, near Ning Hia, the capital of Tangut, Ilu Burqan went out with a large army to relieve the distressed town; the Tangut army numbers is put at 5,00,000 which is difficult to accept; probably it was 50,000 strong. The battle that ensued was sanguinary. It is said that the number of the slain reached the colossal and staggering figure of 3,00,000.[37] 'Three corpses were found, after the battle, standing on their heads,' reports Rashid-ud-din. 'Among the Mongols it has become firmly established that for every ten Tomans or 1,00,000 persons slain on the battlefield, one of the killed was made to stand on its head.'[38]

Unable to make any further resistance, Ilu Burqan fled to the fortified and massive walls of his capital. Chingiz, thereupon, determined to ravage and reduce the Kin dominions while he could trust to the twin concomitants of the siege to bring Ilu Burqan down to his knees. The heat and dust of Multan had saved India from the ravages of the Mongol horsemen, and, now an awful dream of Chingiz came to the rescue of the Kins; a temporary respite, however, as events turned out later. The awful dream[39] warned the great conqueror that his end was near; and Chingiz was greatly disturbed. 'Are my sons, Chaghatae, Uktae and Tuli distant or near?' enquired Chingiz as he got up from his dream. 'They might not be more than two or three *farsangs* distant,' answered Baisuqa Aqa, the son of Juji Qasar. The Khan directed them to be summoned and, the next day, they presented themselves before their father. 'I have some counsel to hold with my sons and a confidential matter which I wish to communicate to them,' Chingiz said to his amirs and noyans, 'I desire to be private with them for a while.'

'My beloved ones,' said Chingiz,[40] 'the time approaches for me to take my last journey and the period of my dissolution is at hand! By the power of the Almighty, and the aid of providence, I have acquired and consolidated for you an empire, so extensive that from one side of it to the other is one year's journey.' To impress upon them the need of unity and cooperation, Chingiz Khan narrated to them the parable of the many-headed serpent. 'Be sure,' he advised them,[41] 'that if you all hold together and support one another, your enemies, however strong and powerful, will not triumph against you. But if you do not have one leader, whose laws and commands are obeyed and carried out by all the others—brothers, sons, relations and dependents—your fate will be the fate of the many-headed serpent. One night the cold was extremely severe and a many-headed serpent wanted to seek a secure hole to escape from the frost. But when it put one of its heads in any hole, the other heads quarrelled until exposed to the cold all the heads perished. But the serpent that had only one head and many tails, went into the hole, sheltered its body and all its tails and escaped the frost.' He then asked them whom they would wish to succeed him. 'Our father is sovereign,' said Uktae, Chaghatae and Tuli with one voice.[42] 'We are his servants and will obey what he commands.' Chingiz Khan thereupon designated Uktae as his successor and advised them to be united and sincere in their obedience to Uktae as Khan. Not satisfied by their verbal assurances, Chingiz Khan required them to give their agreement in writing and a solemn covenant that they would not deviate from his commands and allow no consideration to upset the arrangement about succession to the Khanship. The Quriltai was, in other words, held only to confirm Uktae's succession. 'The Great Khan,' says Rashid-ud-din, 'further advised that, when his death should happen, no lamentations whatever were to be made, and that it should be kept a profound secret.'[43] His death was to be kept secret, not simply because, as Raverty has observed, 'the ruling passion of treachery was strong even in death'; his aim and objective could also have been to prevent any attempt on the part of the subjugated nations and races to overthrow the Mongol yoke. He might have wanted the princes and Noyans, with their troops, to reach their headquarters before his death was announced. With his characteristic thoroughness Chingiz further advised that the moment Ilu Burqan came to the Mongol camp, he should be put to death,[44] for he seems to have become convinced that no value was to be attached to the offer of fealty and submission by the Tangut ruler.

The sons took leave of their father and made for their respective camps while Chingiz Khan led his troops against Tingnash and Khurjah (Korea). The fame of his arms had already travelled ahead of him and, on reaching Liwaq Shan, he found that the rulers of Tingnash and Khurjah were ready to submit and acknowledge his suzerainty. Among the presents for him was a bowl of the finest pearls and Chingiz ordered them to be distributed among those whose ears were pierced; 'those whose ears were not already bored,' adds Rashid-ud-din, 'had them bored quickly and received pearls.' Even then a good number of pearls remained undistributed. 'It is a day of largesse,' said the Khan, 'let the pearls be scattered so that the people may pick them up.' And for a long time after, it is said, pearls used to be found there.[45]

Ilu Burqan had meanwhile been convinced of the futility of his endeavours against the Mongol Khan, and deemed it prudent to seek reconciliation. Accordingly he sent envoys, with presents and his offer of submission: 'If the Great Khan will grant me pardon and guarantee my safety and security, within a month I will pay him homage in person.' The Khan agreed to forgive the past and pledged his word for the safety and security of the ruler of Tangut.[46]

The 'pledge' contrary to Chingiz Khan's general principle, may have been prompted by some pressing reason or consideration at the back of his mind. During the campaign against Tangut, the Khan had had a near fatal fall when his reddish-gray' mount, named Josutoboro had been brushed by the fleeing white asses. Badly hurt, the Khan had had a restless night. And he was requested by the Orloks and commanders to call off the campaign for the sake of his health. The Khan had refused, though the 'fall' had been considered by some trusted associates as a bad omen. Perhaps, the Khan might have recollected the stratagem or 'peaceful gesture' he employed against the unforgettable Kin city of Volhoi when he asked for 1000 carts and 10,000 swallows to raise the siege. Tying tufts of cotton wool to the tails of the swallows and setting them alight he set them 'free'. With their tails on fire the terrified creatures made for their haunts, and causing confusion and stampede set the city on fire and paved the way for the Mongol triumph. Perhaps Chingiz had learnt something from his commanders, who achieved by 'solemn pledges' given and broken, their objectives in Khurasan and Derbend.

The pledge which Chingiz now gave to Ilu Burqan was contrary to the strategy he had earlier advised his sons and amirs to follow. It appears that Chingiz Khan, who always attached the greatest importance to the pledged word, made an exception in the case of the Tangut ruler. Ilu Burqan, according to Qazi Minhaj, had been a thorn in the side of the Mongol Khan, and was quite formidable and, therefore, might have proved a sore headache to Chingiz's successor. Ilu Burqan, thought Chingiz, should be eliminated at all costs, and provoking of his own sense of honour, not for the first time, should have been silenced by the reasoning that his word was binding on him alone, not upon the regent or his successor, who should have a 'doctor's mandate' to do what was best in the interests of the empire. By the time the repenting Tangut ruler arrived to offer his homage and submission, he would be dead and Tuli, as regent, would be free to exercise his 'individual judgement'—and put him to the sword.

Chingiz Khan died on fourth of Ramzan, AH 624 / 16 August 1227[47] at the age of 73 (Map 4).[48] His death was kept a profound secret. Unaware of the death of his adversary and equally unsuspicious of the fate awaiting him, Ilu Burqan set out from his capital to offer his homage to Chingiz. When he arrived near the Mongol camp, he was duly received and welcomed by Mongol amirs and noyans; but when he approached the ordu of Chingiz Khan, Ilu Burqan and his attendants were all killed by the Mongols.[49]

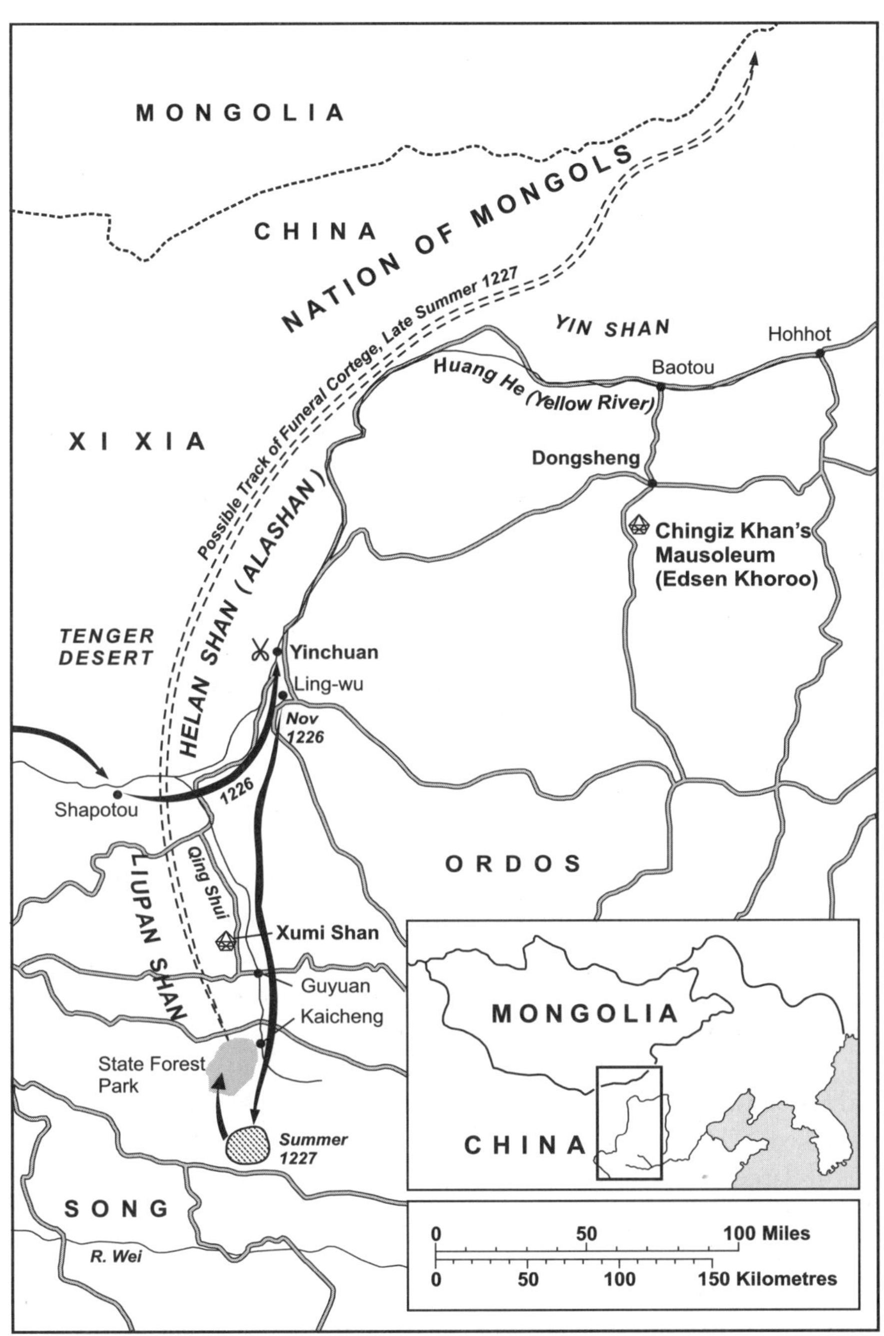

Map 4. The Last Campaign and Death, 1226-7.

Ilu Burqan (Shidarqu) and his attendants having been put to death, the body of the dead Khan was taken up and the mournful procession started homeward and, in due course, they reached the ancestral yurt of the Great Khan, which was within the limits of, but not at, Qaraqorum. On the way, in accordance with their ancient traditions, they killed all whom they met.[50] 'In his time,' relates Marco Polo, 'the Tartars were accustomed, at the funerals of their Khans, to slay all those they met on the way, and they did so, on the way to the place appointed for the sepulchre of Chinghiz Khan.'

It is odd that during the mourning procession they put to death 'all those whom they met on the way', but this was probably the 'nomadic tradition' to ensure that the news of the death of a great leader did not spread until the succession had taken place. It appears that no tombstone was placed to mark the final resting place of the reckless soul, either. Whether it was in accordance with his wish, the decision of his family members and his close companions, or simply the general nomadic practice, is not certain. The choice of the place may be presumed to imply an unexpressed wish/decision for 'anonymity' and/or to remain undisturbed after protracted and tumultuous life. Whatever may have been the reason, it was certainly not a reckless or thoughtless decision. It was in keeping with the character of Chingiz Khan and in consonance with the political culture of the nomads. The denizens of the Gobi were unfamiliar with the adage that all controversy is silenced in the presence of death and the civilian concept of discretion but knew the 'law of revenge' only too well. A tombstone, much less a sepulchre, would have been an easy target for the 'deprived' family members and the disgruntled chieftains to give vent for the 'wrongs', real or imagined, done to them by the Great Khan. If a sepulchre was indeed built to commemorate the legacy of Chingiz Khan, the Persian chroniclers would not have failed to mention it. And the Persian architects and artisans would have provided a memorial worthy of the Great Khan.

The corpse was buried at the foot of a tree, under which, one day, he had rested while following the chase, and which so tickled his fancy that he remarked: 'This place is suitable for my burial.' After the burial, the place was declared an 'exclusive or especially prohibited' area; a guard was posted there to keep people away.

The utmost care taken to conceal the burial place, by his son and successor, Tuli Khan, was, perhaps, the general nomadic practice. Perhaps the practice may have been dictated by the harsh living conditions in Mongolia and the nomads could hardly afford the luxury of (non-productive) graveyards, and the construction and maintenance of tombs to commemorate their heroes and ancestors.

It is related that nature also cooperated to make the area inaccessible; the plain soon became such a dense forest that one could not pass through it. 'There is no trace of the sepulchre,' relates Rashid-ud-din, 'and the forest is not easily accessible.'[51]

Death, according to the oft-repeated maxim, is a great leveller. And what a great leveller it is, ironically enough, attested by the death and burial of the two 'great kings' of their times, namely, Sultan Ala-ud-din Khwarazm Shah and Khan of Khans, Temuchin Chingiz Khan. The sultan was the greatest Muslim ruler of the largest and most powerful Muslim empire of the time while the Khan was the builder of the largest empire of all times; one died a fugitive and was buried in the clothes he was wearing, the other was laid to rest by his family, companions, and commanders.

Fate or death, however, did not cooperate. For Ilugu Burqan arrived before the Khan could die. Chingiz Khan was, however, too determined a man to waver or change his well-considered decision and game of deception. Burqan was allowed to pay homage with presents like golden images of Buddha, golden and silver bowls and vessels, geldings and casuals, and many other objects of different forms and colours but the 'conscientious' Khan did not receive him or the presents himself; they were accepted 'outside the tent'. Ilugu Burqan was made to change his name to Shidarqu and then killed by Tolun Cherbi. Tolun Cherbi reported this to the Khan in person, who rewarded him with the bowls and vessels and the 'movable palace' brought by the ill-fated Tangut ruler.[52]

Notes

1. Browne, *A Literary History of Persia*, vol. I, p. 47.
2. 'He was of a fair colour and medium size. His mother tongue was Turkish but he could also speak Persian. In bravery and valour he was the Rustam of his time. He was of a clement and forgiving nature, fond of doing justice and being kind to others. He loved his soldiers from the core of his heart and made every possible sacrifice to keep them happy. He talked very little and seldom talked ill of anybody. He simply smiled when he heard of anything unusual.' Nassavi, pp. 240-1.
3. Rashid-ud-din, fol. 209.
4. Nassavi, p. 57.
5. According to Nassavi (pp. 59-62) Istawa was near Nasa, the spot where that Jalal-ud-din broke through the Mongol cordon, and that later Aq and Arzlaq defeated the Mongol contingent but were overwhelmed by the sudden arrival of a large army while they were encamping.

6. Rashid-ud-din, fol. 209; *Tabaqat-i-Nasiri*, pp. 347-8; Nassavi, p. 80.

7. According to Nassavi (pp. 62-3) the Sultan relieved Qandhar.

8. He was at the head of 30,000 men to guard the route to Ghaznin, Kabul, Gharjistan and Zabul, and also to act as the vanguard of the Khan. Rashid-ud-din, fol. 215.

9. Rashid-ud-din, fol. 216.

10. According to Ibnul Asir (vol. XII, p. 183) Saif-ud-din's brother was killed in the altercation; the sultan's appeals and tears could not move him. The more the sultan tried to placate him, says Nassavi (p. 81), the more adamant he became.

11. Rashid-ud-din, fols. 215-16.

12. *Tabaqat-i-Nasiri*, p. 349.

13. Juwaini, vol. I, p. 106; Rashid-ud-din, fols. 216-17.

14. Nassavi, p. 84; *Tabaqat-i-Nasiri*, p. 349; Juwaini, vol. I, pp. 106–7; Rashid-ud-din, fols. 217-18.

15. *Rauzat-us-Safa*, vol. IV, p. 146. For details of the battle, also see, Juwaini, vol. II, p. 43. Nasavi, vol. I, p. 306. Howorth, Part I, p. 9, however, says that the sultan's family at their own request were put in a boat and lowered into the fast flowing river to drown. They had wanted to avoid falling into the hands of their enemies. Like the sultan, they preferred death to dishonour. Qazi Minhaj, however, makes no mention of the fate of the sultan's family. See Bartold, *Turkestan,* pp. 445-6; Raverty; notes in *Tabaqat-i-Nasiri*, pp. 292-3, *Notes on Afganistan*, pp. 332-448.

16. Morten, H. Desmond, *The Rise of Chingiz Khan*, Baltimore, 1950, p. 245.

17. Juwaini, vol. I, pp. 106-7.

18. Rashid-ud-din, fols. 217-18.

19. Juwaini, vol. I, pp. 108-9, 112; Rashid-ud-din, fols. 218-19. According to the *Mongolian Chronicle*, Bala Noyan crossed the Indus in pursuit of the sultan but could not track him, though he penetrated deep into the 'country of the Hindus'. He retraced his steps without the fugitive sultan for he had moved towards Lahore and returned laden with immense booty, including many camels and gelded bill-goats.

20. *Tabaqat-i-Nasiri*, pp. 348-9, 355; *Rauzat-us-Safa*, vol. V, p. 38.

21. *Tarikh Nama-i-Herat*, p. 76; *Tabaqat-i-Nasiri*, p. 356.

22. *Tabaqat-i-Nasiri*, p. 356.

23. *Tarikh Nama-i-Herat*, pp. 76-7.

24. Ibid., pp. 77-9; *Tabaqat-i-Nasiri*, pp. 356-7.

25. *Rauzat-us-Safa*, vol. V, p. 39.

26. The remainder of the narrative in this section derives from the *Tabaqat-i-Nasiri*, p. 357-72.

27. Ibid., pp. 358-9.

28. *Tabaqat-i-Nasiri*, pp. 375-6; Rashid-ud-din, fol. 219; Sharfuddin, fols. 128-9, 131.

29. *Rauzat-us-Safa*, vol. V, p. 40.

30. Rashid-ud-din, fol. 219.

31. Ibid., fol. 223; *Rauzat-us-Safa*, vol. V, p. 40.

32. Howorth, Part I, p. 92.

33. Ibid., p. 99.

34. *Secret History*, p. 109; I.R., pp. 196-8 provides a more detailed and interesting account.

35. *Tabaqat-i-Nasiri*, pp. 375-76; Rashid-ud-din, fol. 219.

36. Rashid-ud-din, fol. 223.

37. Ibid., fols. 223-4; *Rauzat-us-Safa*, vol. V, pp. 40-1; *Habib al-siyar*, vol. I, Part III, p. 17.

38. Rashid-ud-din, fol. 224.

39. Ibid., fol. 224; *Rauzat-us-Safa*, vol. V, p. 41; *Habib al-siyar*, vol. I, part III, p. 17.

40. Rashid-ud-din, fol. 224.

41. Juwaini, vol. I, pp. 143, 130.

42. Ibid., pp. 30, 143-4.

43. Rashid-ud-din, fol. 225.

44. *Rauzat-us-Safa*, vol. V, p. 42; *Habib al-siyar*, vol. I, part III, p. 18.

45. Rashid-ud-din, fol. 225.

46. Ibid., fol. 225; *Rauzat-us-Safa*, vol. V, p. 41.

47. Rashid-ud-din, fols. 235, 240; *Rauzat-us-Safa*, vol. V, p. 41. He died, says Rashid-ud-din, 'in the Turkish year of the Hog, which was the year of his birth, of his ascending the throne, and of his death. It was also the year of his father's death.'

48. Rashid-ud-din (fol. 235) says very explicitly that Chingiz reached the good old age of 73 years according to the Turkish calendar, but 75 years according to the lunar calendar. Qazi Minhaj, whose information was quite independent of Turkish or Mongol sources, says that Chingiz was sixty-five years old when he came into Khurasan; this was, of course, an approximate estimate of his age by a 'trustworthy person', and it was at the beginning of 1221 that Chingiz came to Khurasan. (*Tabaqat-i-Nasiri*, p. 373; Tr. p. 1077). And, as such, the estimate of Qazi Minhaj's 'trustworthy' informant was approximately correct.

49. Rashid-ud-din, fol. 225; Rauzat-us-Safa, vol. V, p. 241. According to *Tabaqat-i-Nasiri*, p. 377 and the *Secret History*, p. 118, Shidarqu was put to death by Chingiz himself.

50. Rashid-ud-din, fol. 225; *Rauzat-us-Safa*, vol. V, p. 41.

51. Rashid-ud-din, fols. 225-6; *Shajratul Atrak*, pp. 199-201; *Rauzat-us-Safa*, vol. V, pp. 41-2.

52. *Mongolian Chronicle*, p. 199.

7

Building an Empire

EW FIGURES IN HISTORY have been more misunderstood or misinterpreted than Chingiz Khan. His exploits and astounding achievements dazed his contemporaries and dazzled modern historians, so much so that the man has been lost in his work. Great as were his qualities as a general and his abilities as a statesman, he was equally great and good as a man, who enjoyed his life as he enjoyed his work. But the chroniclers both of the East and the West have painted him in such dark and lurid colours that posterity has taken him for a fiend, a heartless demon devoid of human feelings. The Mongols aroused horror, disgust and fear wherever they went. 'They gloried', says the chronicler Vincent, 'in the slaughter of men; blood to them was spilt as freely as water. They employed lies and deception to delude their victims, and then destroyed them.' 'Since the beginning of time,' mourns the Chinese historian quoted by Curtin,[1] 'no barbarous people have ever been so mighty as the Mongols are at present. They destroy empires as a man plucks out herbs by the roots; such is the power in their possession. Why does Heaven let them have it?'

The man should not, however, be judged against the ideas and institutions of our times but in accordance with those of his own age and modern real politics. He embodied and expressed the fierceness, the pride, the grandeur and the simplicity of the steppes. It was in the fires and chills of the bitter struggle for survival that his life was forged and tempered, and, consequently, he valued men and things only from the standpoint of his own security and success. But of wanton cruelty there was hardly any trace, and, if flourishing cities were reduced to smoke, soil and ashes, and if none was left to groan or cry, none to mourn the fallen, it was all purposive and prompted by military necessity, vengeance, or in order to strike terror.[2] No strategically important city or fortress was allowed to remain so as to become a beacon of hope and a refuge for the enemy.

Machiavelli philosophized that it is better for a prince to be feared than loved by his subjects. 'It is only by a salutary terror,' advised Napoleon to his brother Joseph, King of Naples, 'that you will keep in awe the Italian populace. It is not by being civil to people that you obtain a hold on them. . . . The people of Italy, and in fact of every other country, if they do not feel that they are mastered, are disposed to rebel. . . . You should order two or three of the larger villages that have behaved worst to be pillaged, it will be an example, and will restore gaiety and desire as action of your soldiers.' Napoleon and his Minister of Police, Fouche, established a police regime in France for peace, order and stability, and revived detention without trial which created fear and awe. Czar Nicholas in Russia and Metternich in Austria followed suit, thus 'causing uncertainty, fear and apprehension all around Europe'.

Chingiz was neither the first nor the last to indulge in vandalism and massacres. Alexander devastated Thebia. He massacred the Thebians on a large scale, and sold thousands into slavery. The Romans not only destroyed but ploughed over the proud city of Carthage. The Crusaders massacred thousands indiscriminately when they captured the Holy City of Jerusalem, and the Roman Catholic Church tried to save 'errant souls' through the Inquisition and the stakes. The 'Expansion of Europe' caused as much, if not more, suffering for the 'natives' of Asia and Africa as did the eruption of the nomads had ever done in the past but with one significant difference: the nomadic 'holocaust' was sporadic and the nomads were ultimately absorbed by the vanquished whereas the 'expansionists' steadfastly remained exclusive.

Chingiz Khan's cruelty was calculated, not capricious or purposeless. One of his most striking qualities was that he never relished the needless torture of the captives such as that exhibited by Jalal-ud-din Mangbirni after his victory at the Battle of Parwan or a century later by 'Ala-ud-din Khilji after the defeat of Ali-Beg and Tartaq. Nor did he enjoy, like Tamerlane, the sight of his victims being covered with brick and mortar and their bodies being cemented into a wall. Though generally condemned as a 'barbarian', he was never guilty of the kind of vengeful ferocity such as that displayed by the British after the events of 1857.

He must have possessed great personal charm, which kept people attached to him even in his darkest days. 'This Prince Temuchin,' reported Men Huang, according to Barthold, 'takes off the clothes he was wearing and gives them away; gets off the horse he was riding and makes a present of it.'

He was an ideal leader of men; essentially humane and took a deep interest in the welfare of his people. 'I hate luxury and exercise moderation,' he wrote to the Chinese sage, Ch'ang Ch'un,

I have only one coat and one food. I eat the same food and am dressed in the same tatters as my humble herdsmen. I consider the people my children—I have not many distinguished qualities—But as my calling is high, the obligations incumbent on me are also heavy; and *I fear that in my ruling there may be something wanting.* To cross a river we make boats and rudders. Likewise we invite sages, and choose our assistants to keep the empire in good order. Since the time I came to the throne I have always taken to heart the ruling of my people— (italics added)[3].

During the Mongol invasion of northern China, Chingiz Khan heard of Ch'ang Ch'un's repute for wisdom and sanctity. Anxious to learn the doctrine of the Tao to which Ch'ang Ch'un had devoted his life, and keen to benefit from the monk's wide experience and deep knowledge, Chingiz invited Ch'ang Ch'un to visit his court.[4] 'Since the time I came to the throne', Chingiz wrote, '*I have always taken to heart the ruling of my people; but I could not find worthy men to occupy the places of the three (kung or highest councillors) and the nine (kings or administrators).* With respect to these circumstances I inquired, and heard that you, master, have penetrated the truth, and walk in the path of right. Deeply learned and much experienced, you have explored the laws— we are separated by mountains and plains of great extent, and I cannot meet you—*I implore you to move your sainted steps.* Do not think of the extent of the sandy desert. Commiserate with the people in the present situation of affairs, or have pity upon me, and communicate to me the means of preserving life.' Chingiz was sincere in his protestations; during his expedition against the Khwarazm Shah, he came across a Muslim who raised water for the thirsty people, and 'ordered that he should be exempted from taxes and duties'.[5]

On attaining power, Chingiz never forgot what he owed to others, nor did he shut himself off from his old associates and friends. He remained to the end what he essentially was: an unsophisticated nomad chieftain. Power did not change him. When he became the Khan of Khans, he lavishly rewarded his companions and followers; what is, however, more important is his *telescopic memory for every valuable service* rendered by them, and the supreme confidence in himself, which prompted him to acknowledge openly how much he *owed* his survival and triumph to others. *The order of Tarkhanship, which he instituted, was a unique manifestation of his generous nature.* In his hour of triumph and glory, he did not forget to honour his stepfather, Munlik, even though he had been guilty of deserting him in his earlier days of dire distress and difficulties. He was also generous and hospitable to foreigners.[6] Nothing illustrates better the hospitality, liberality and simplicity of Chingiz Khan than his invitation to, and reception of the Chinese philosopher, Ch'ang Ch'un.[7] 'Your sanctity is become manifest,' wrote the Khan.[8] 'You are endowed with the eminent talents of celebrated men—I can only descend from the throne and stand by this side. *I have fasted and washed.* [Chinese phrases of politeness]. I have ordered my adjutant to prepare an escort and a cart for you—*I shall serve you myself.* The philosopher was reluctant to undertake such a long and exhausting journey. Court life did not appeal to him and he had already refused several invitations from the Kin and the Sung. He begged to be excused on the plea that he was dull and without talent, and that public affairs were beyond him. But the keenness and insistence of the Khan obliged the sage to start on a long, trek to the camp of the Mongol Khan in the west. On the personal instructions of the Khan, the philosopher was accorded the best facilities on his journey across the steppe, and, on reaching the camp of Chingiz Khan, was immediately ushered into the royal presence. The Taoist sage was also exempted from the usual court ceremonial of kowtowing to the Khan, and Chingiz invited him to dine with him daily. The sage declined on the plea that he preferred seclusion. Chingiz appreciated the candour and tastes of the Chinese philosopher and allowed him to live as and where he liked.

Chingiz was frank and straightforward in private life and appreciated the same qualities in others. 'Who was he who in the battle of Koidin broke the neckbone of my horse with an arrow?' asked Chingiz. 'I shot the arrow,' answered Jirguotai,[9] 'If you order me to be executed, my blood will hardly cover more than a palm breadth of the earth; if you spare my life, I will serve you to the best of my ability. I will cross deep torrents for you and crumble rocks to sand.' 'Whenever an enemy has injured us,' remarked Chingiz, 'he has remained silent about it. But you, who have hidden nothing, are worthy of being my companion.'

Frankness along with bravery and loyalty were the qualities Chingiz Khan always valued, even among his enemies. Bravery he appreciated, even admired among his enemies and adversaries. For people who were not true to their salt and betrayed their master or companion, there was only one fate: death. 'How could I accept the services of such a man?' observed Chingiz,[10] when he heard how Kokchu had treated his master. Kokochu was put to death while his wife was rewarded for her loyalty to Sengun. Similar was the treatment he meted out to the attendants of his deadliest enemy, Jamuka, for having turned traitors. 'Those who have dared to seize and betray their own master shall not go unpunished', said Chingiz.[11] 'Execute them together with their sons and grandsons.'

Once Chingiz asked Bogurchi Noyan what was the highest pleasure of man. 'To go out hunting in the spring, riding a good horse and holding a good falcon in one's hand,' was the answer. 'No,' said Chingiz,[12] the greatest joy a man can know is to conquer his enemies and drive them before him; to ride their horses and take away their possessions; to see the faces of those who were dear to them bedewed with tears, and to clasp their wives and daughters in his arms.' This anecdote is important in that it reveals his militaristic outlook as well as the instinct of acquisition. Victory and vengeance were not by and in themselves enough to lure and lull him; the instinct of acquisition was also strong, and he was ever after the fruits of victory: material possession. When the Battle of the Indus was over and Jalal-ud-din had crossed the fast-flowing river, he ordered the divers to fetch the ornaments and valuables which had been thrown by the vanquished into the river.[13] Again, when bestowing his wife Ibaha upon Jurchidai, he asked her to leave behind, *out of her dowry*, a hundred men and Ashik Temur as a keepsake![14]

War and hunting were the favourite activities of the Mongols and, like a true son of the steppes, Chingiz Khan enjoyed the chase and took part in the terrible hunts till shortly before his death.[15] His all-round innovativeness led him to convert the chase from a mere pastime into a well regulated and systematic training for war. The Mongol hunt as governed by the Yassa might very well be compared to modern periodic military manoeuvres.

Sharing the tastes of his people, Chingiz was fond of kumiz or mare's fermented milk, but disapproved of getting drunk. But he was also a practical man, and added, 'If you cannot refrain, get drunk only three times a month', he said.[16] 'It would be better never to get drunk at all but it is difficult to find a man who can abstain altogether.' We never find him overcome or incapable, when his army needed his command or the enemy was at hand. He could never have waged his wars in the west and east after having reached the age of sixty unless he had kept himself in control.

Chingiz's temper was held under the control of a firm will and, even under the greatest provocation, he could display surprising self-command and could listen to his trusted companions and accept their advice or request, or pleas. He wanted to put his uncle, Daritai, to death for having deserted him and for going over to Wang Khan. 'To destroy one's own kin is the same as to quench the fire of one's own hearth,' pleaded Bogurchi; 'you have nothing left to remind you of your father but this uncle of yours. Have you the heart to destroy him?' Chingiz agreed and forgave his uncle. When Oyelun upbraided him for the murder of Bektor and, again, for interrogating Qasar as a criminal, 'Will not a mighty name remain behind me?' Chingiz enquired of Qazi Wahid-ud-din,[17] 'If the Khan will promise me the safety of my life,' said the Qazi, 'I will answer the question.' 'I have promised you its security.' 'A name continues to endure where there are people, but how will a name endure when the Khan's servants massacre each and all; there will be no one to tell the tale (and the glorious name of the Mongol Emperor).' This answer enraged the Khan. Dashing his bows and arrows to the ground, he turned his face away from the qazi. 'When I beheld the effects of rage upon his impious brow,' related the qazi,[18] 'I washed my hand of life and gave up all hope of existence. But a minute later, he turned his face towards me again, and said: 'I used to consider you a prudent and sagacious man, but, from this speech of yours, it has become evident to me that you do not possess complete understanding, and that your comprehension is but small. There are many kings in the world, and, wherever the hoofs of the brigand Muhammad have reached, there I will carry slaughter and cause devastation. The remaining people who are in other parts of the world, and the sovereigns of other kingdoms, will (preserve my name and) relate my history.' The qazi was left unmolested and, then, escaped to narrate his strange experience, and the still stranger facet of the great conqueror's personality. The Khan was right and the qazi went off the track in assessing the devastation and its impact, as described by the Khan, all around. The great medieval historian, Ibn al-Athir comments:

For several years I put off reporting this event, for I found it terrifying and felt revulsion at recounting it and, therefore, hesitated again and again. Who would find it easy to describe the rise of Islam and the Muslims. If anyone were to say that no time since the creation of man by the great God had the world experienced anything like it, he would be telling the truth. In fact nothing comparable is reported in past chronicles. The worst they recall is the treatment and destruction of Jerusalem by Nebuchadhezzar. But what is Jerusalem compared with the areas devastated by those monsters, where every city is twice the size of Jerusalem? What are the atrocities in comparison with (the number of) those they massacred, for a single city whose inhabitants were murdered numbered more than all the Israelites together.

His assessment has been belied by the increasing brutalization of man, and by the unlawful unhealthy nexus between science, war and ethnophobia.

'I know when to exchange the lion skin for that of the fox,' said Napoleon. It was Chingiz Khan rather than Napoleon whose powers were held in check by moderation and common sense. Impetuosity never dictated his actions. When some of his men wanted to jump after Jalal-ud-din into the fast-flowing Indus, he stopped them.[19] Perhaps the best example of his self-control and patience is the incident[20] when Chaghatae challenged the paternity of his elder brother, Juji, in the presence of their parents and the two brothers came to grips. Bogurchi and Muquli separated them and Kokochus managed to pacify the brothers, mad with rage; but Chingiz Khan remained seated and motionless, closing the whole affair with a mild rebuke to Chaghatae.

Chingiz Khan was a most methodical person and established the most rigid discipline in his army and the strictest order in the empire. 'What have ye fixed on today?' enquired Yeke Cheren, a Tartar captive belonging to Belgutai. 'We have resolved,' said the unsuspecting Belgutai, 'to exterminate all male Tartars who are as tall as the axis of the cart.' When the other prisoners learnt this, they fled to the mountain and sought safety in the fortress thereon. 'Go and capture their stronghold,' ordered Chingiz, and it was only after a sanguinary battle and heavy casualties that the Tartars were defeated and all those who were as tall as the axis of the cart, were put to the sword. 'Belgutai', said Chingiz, 'has been guilty of the leakage of an important resolution passed by the conference of our clan and this has led to numerous casualties on our side. Hereafter Belgutai is forbidden to take part in any important conference of our clan. He will be entrusted only with outdoor administration—cases of dispute, riot, robbery, theft, and the like. He and Daritai will be permitted to enter the conference after the discussion of the agenda is over and all its members have drunk their cups.'[21]

He was an ideal leader of men, who took a real interest in his men and even in their mounts, and rewarded every gallant deed or feat of uncomplaining patience. He knew when to be gentle and when to be firm; and never allowed his men to do or suffer what was beyond their strength or endurance. 'You are going to cross high mountains and big rivers,' he advised Subutai[22] on his expedition against the Merkits in 1205. 'You must be thrifty and economical while the horses are still fat and provisions have not run short. Pray do not hunt except from necessity; even if it be for the sake of provisions, you should be reasonable and moderate. Do not let your men use croupiers or breast-straps lest they run their horses to exhaustion. Of all those who violate your orders, you need send me only those whom I know personally; the rest you can execute on the spot. Have caution and fortitude—though you may be far away, you will be near (to my heart). The Sky will give you His aid and protection.'

He took a keen interest in his men and, as his conquering career shows, he was an excellent and unerring judge of men. 'He gave,' says Rashid-ud-din, 'the command of troops to those who had the necessary courage and skills. To those who were active and alert he confided the care of the baggage; to the dullards he confided a pole and made them tend the cattle.' 'It is thus,' Chingiz once commented, 'I have won my victories, and my sons will continue to be victorious if they follow my example.'[23]

Chingiz Khan was, at the same time, leader of his people, who looked to him for safety and security of their persons, their family and their possessions against the covetous and evil eyes of the neighbouring, rarely neighbourly, nomadic tribes, and further, they expected him to look after and satisfy their needs and requirements, pastures for their cattle and women for household functions and assurance of a continuous supply of man power for the safety of the yurt and strength of the tribe. And the loyalty of the tribesmen and the tribes to the leader was dependent upon, and in proportion to his capacity and ability to live up to the expectations of his fellows. It was, therefore, neither necessary nor advisable for Chingiz Khan to indulge in horses and expose his life and limbs like one belonging to the ranks. Petty skirmishes, scouting, and probing operations were neither required from him nor did they suit his position. There were hundreds and thousands of loyal and brave warriors for that. He was to plan, to decide, and to command and it was for others, around and under him to hear and obey, and to carry out the mission.

He was brave but had no passion for romantic bravery. In his youth he was timorous, 'afraid of dogs', but said to have showed on several occasions both his courage and skill in combat.[24] In later life, however, he never engaged in hand-to-hand or close combat; for he was no longer a soldier of fortune but more than a modern commander-in-chief, who led his forces from behind with the responsibility to plan the campaigns and, in pitched battles, to control and conduct the operations, and the employment of the reserve forces, whenever required. Muquli, Subutai and Yamah Noyan, to name only a few, who were capable of independently carrying out arduous operations, invite comparison not with the Marshals of Napoleon, but with Napoleon himself.

Great as he was as a general, statesman and administrator, Chingiz Khan was equally good as a respectable family man. 'I have,' he could have said with Napoleon, 'two men within me, the man of head and the man of heart.' In the treatment of his relatives he reminds one of Napoleon; the Khan shared his greatness and glory with his relations, and gave them people to rule over.[25] His mother, younger brothers and nephews all had *hazaras* or contingents (units of thousand men) assigned to them.[26] Like a true son of the steppe, Chingiz Khan had many sons and daughters from his wives and concubines, whose number is said[27] to have exceeded five hundred.[28] The names of five, who were held in the highest respect and esteem, have been preserved by the chroniclers. These women were faithful to the end except Ibaha who was, rather strangely, given away to one of his companions as a mark of the Khan's appreciation. The first and the senior-most was Bortei.[29] Next came Qulan, daughter of Dair Usun and she was followed by Yesukan and Yessui, both of them Tatar ladies, Konju, daughter of Kin Emperor, and Gur Besu, widow of the Tayang Khan. The chroniclers, however, differ not only in respect of their precedence but even in spelling their names.[30]

Since the status of the sons of a man, according to Mongol custom, depended upon the rank of their mother, the sons of Bortei got preference and precedence. By Bortei, Chingiz had four sons, who, says Juwaini,[31] 'distinguished themselves in great battles and in other important affairs. They were like the four steps of the imperial throne and the four pillars of the palace of Khanship.' Juji, the eldest son, was made Master of the Hunt. The harsh and inexorable Chaghatae was selected for the strict enforcement of the Yassa and the administration of justice. Chingiz assigned to his youngest son Tuli the management, equipment, and despatch of expeditions. And with his unfailing judgment the Khan chose Uktae for administration and government; Uktae was shrewd and insightful. Chingiz assigned to each one of them a yurt; to Juji, he gave all territories from the boundaries of Qiyaligh and Khwarazm down to the extremities of Bulgaria and from there as far into the west as the troops of the Tartar horses had trampled; to Chaghatae, he allotted the territory from the frontiers of the Uighur land down to Samarqand and Bokhara; to Uktae, his successor, Chingiz gave his own capital while the appanage of Tuli was in the neighbourhood of I-mil and Qunaq.[32]

The assignment of appanages did not, however, mean division or partition of the empire as in the case of Mamun and Amin, sons of the Abbasid Caliph Harun-al-Rashid; it was akin to the policy of Napoleon, to found a stable dynasty and, therefore, to throw out 'anchors of safety on all sides to the very bottom of the sea'. Chingiz strove hard to create goodwill and mutual helpfulness between them and, to strengthen the foundations of concord between them, he even resorted to parables. One day he assembled his sons and took out an arrow from his quiver and broke it; then he took out two arrows and broke them also. Then he added arrow to arrow till they were a large number and the strongest men could not break them. 'Look', he said, 'that is what will happen to you. When the weak arrows are joined to their fellows, they all hold together, and the warriors cannot break them. Be sure of it that if you all hold together and support one another, your enemies, however strong and powerful, will not triumph against you.'[33]

With robust, slit and piercing eyes, wide and long forehead, scanty hair on his head but a long beard, Temuchin Chingiz Khan was endowed with a magnetism and charisma such as few great historical figures have possessed. A keen observer, gifted with an unerring judgment of men, their merit and matter, and analysis of situations, he was also a generous leader, magnanimous in acknowledging bravery and rewarding service and loyalty, even of his adversaries and just and impartial in awarding punishment to the guilty, irrespective of rank, race or relationship. None of Chingiz's confidants or companions failed to justify his choice of them except for once and that was the failure of Shigi Qutuqu as a commander. Transferred to the civil side, he turned out to be an excellent chief judge.

In his incomparable, masterly and inimitable pen-picture of Chingiz, Qazi Minhaj has brought out the personality of the Mongol Khan:[34] 'a man of tall stature, of vigorous build, robust in body, the hair on his face scanty and turned white, with cat's eyes, possessed of great energy, discernment, genius, and understanding, awe striking, a butcher, just, resolute, an over thrower of enemies, intrepid, sanguinary, and cruel.' And herein may be found an answer to the query Jawaharlal Nehru[35] posed in one of his letters to Indira. 'But the man fascinates me. Strange, is it not, that this fierce and cruel and feudal chief of a nomadic tribe should fascinate a peaceful and non-violent and mild person like me, who is a dweller of cities and a hater of every thing feudal.'

The People

GENERAL APPEARANCE

With their broad faces, protruding cheekbones, small but flat noses, and tiny eyes, the Mongols looked quite strange and different from the people upon whom they descended as the 'scourge of God'. 'For our sins, unknown tribes came, none knows who they are, nor what their language is, nor what race they are, nor what their faith is—God alone knows who they are and whence they came out,' said the Russian chronicler of Novgorod.

They were of short stature, had small feet, slender waists, shaven crowns and scanty beards.[36] Notwithstanding the unparalleled death and destruction wrought by the Mongols in Muslim lands, and the consequent bitter feelings against them, one hardly comes across any responsible scribe, drawing 'pen-portraits' so horrible, or so terrifying, and narratives so full of venom, as the following repulsive caricature mixed with fear and hatred, from Gregor of Arrano: 'terrible to look at and indescribable, with large heads like a buffalo's, narrow eyes like a fledgling's, a snub nose like a cat's projecting snout and like a dog's, narrow loins like an ant's, short legs like a hog's, and by nature with no beards at all. With a lion's strength, they have voices more shrill than an eagle.'

'That the joys of mortal man be not enduring, not worldly happiness long lasting without lamentations', in this same year, i.e. 1240 'a detestable nation of Satan, to wit the countless army of Tartars, broke loose from its mountain—environed home, and, piercing the solid rocks (of the Caucasus) poured forth like devils from the Tartarus, so that they are rightly called 'Tartars' or Tartarians', wrote Mathew Paris,[37] echoing the same horror, awe and self-guilt as by the learned and pious Muslims of Khurasan and Transoxiana. Mathew Paris went on to add that 'they are inhuman and beastly, rather monsters than men, thirsting for and drinking blood, tearing and devouring the flesh of dogs and men, dressed in ox-hides, armed with plates of iron, short and stout, thickset, strong, invincible, indefatigable, their backs unprotected, their breasts covered with armour; drinking with delight the pure blood of their flocks, with big,[38] strong horses, which eat branches and even trees.'

No wonder then, that Carpini, too, found them as 'differing from the rest of mankind' or that the pious Muslims and Christians looked upon them as of the tribe of Gog and Magog, 'gathering captives as the sand; heaping up earth against every stronghold and taking it.'

CHARACTER

Undaunted courage and reckless daring in battle distinguished a Mongol of the thirteenth century. 'Bravery is the heritage of the Turk,' says Lane-Poole, and the Mongols of Chingiz Khan were no exception; among the nomads the valiant alone claimed the admiration of the tribe, the bards, and the women.[39] According to them, mankind would be divided into two classes, the cowards who fly for their life and the exalted souls who hunger after honour and glory on the battlefield. But the concept of chivalry was unknown to a Mongol. Nursed and nurtured in an atmosphere of danger and distress, always carrying his life in his hand, death held no terrors for him, and a Mongol faced death with courage, hardihood and an indifferent eye. Neither did he ask for quarter nor would he spare a fallen foe. Sex or age meant nothing. The martial and ferocious spirit of the men was also imbibed by their women, for whom the sight of blood and the sound of arms had no particular abhorrence, deterrence, fear or awe. 'The maids and women', reports Carpini, 'ride and race on horseback as skillfully as the men; we saw them also carrying bows and arrows.

The women are able to stay on horseback for a very long time as well as the men; they ride with very short stirrups.'[40] All contemporary accounts are unanimous about the masculine virtues of Mongol women. Fine archers, they used the sword and donned armour, took part in the carnage, were as valiant as their men, and showed no compunction for the victims.

The Mongols led a pure and uncorrupt life. Prostitution was unknown while promiscuity was practically non-existent. Polygamy, early marriages and freedom of the sexes practically insured that no person of marriageable age would remain a bachelor or unmarried. Strict and severe punishment held in check the few unfortunate ones who could not acquire a wife or whose spirits were more daring and wanted some romance.

Nomadic Life

In accordance with the requirements of their primitive economy there was a rough division of labour between the two sexes.[41] The comparatively gentle tasks of driving the carts, milking the cows, making butter, dressing and sewing the skins, etc., were assigned to the women. But the tasks, requiring stronger work were performed by men, e.g., making of bows and arrows, manufacture of stirrups and bits, making saddles, carpentry, care of the horses, etc.

Mongolia was in the thirteenth century inhabited almost entirely by tent-dwellers whose livelihood depended upon hunting, sheep and cattle. 'The nomad's life is, indeed, a triumph of human skill', as observed Toynbee. 'He manages to live off coarse grasses that he cannot eat himself by transferring them into milk and flesh of lame animals, and in order to find subsistence for his cattle, in season and out of season from the natural vegetation of the bare and parsimonious steppe, he has to adapt his life and movements with meticulous accuracy to a seasonal time-table.' Pastoralists depended for their livelihood on their flocks of cattle and sheep, and on such cultivation as could be had by the side of the riverbeds or the hollows of the land, where rain water could be collected; they had to live in tents, and be always on the move and look out for a shady grove and pasturage. It would be, however, a mistake to think that the tribes were at liberty or had a license to roam at large throughout the length and breadth of the steppes. Having their fixed abodes and determinate pastures and streams of water,[42] no tribes could transgress its own camping ground or trespass on that of another without provoking the hostility of the injured and aggrieved tribe. But within the limits of their own grazing lands, they could move freely in search of water and forage. On their seasonal migrations, the whole tribe, or confederation of tribes, held together. The state of inter-tribal warfare and the law of self-preservation taught the unruly nomads the importance of mutual help and of acting together against the outsiders.

Not content with pasturing their flocks, the virile nomads enjoyed and exercised their valour in chase and foray, and often varied the monotony of their life by raiding and plundering defenceless travellers. They often organized marauding expeditions into the fertile lands near and even beyond the Great Wall.

The Mongols were divided and organized into tribes and clans. Originally the descendants of one common ancestor, real or supposed, along with their families, dependants and slaves, formed a clan or tribe. 'A tribe,' as observed by Robertson-Smith, 'was but a large family, the tribal name was the name or nickname of the common ancestor.'[43] But as the power and prestige, or even the very existence, of a tribe depended upon its fighting strength, and as the continual state of tribal warfare was a drain on the manpower of a tribe so much so that despite polygamy, their numbers and strength could not be easily and quickly replenished, they increased their numbers by taking recourse to adoption, 'blood-brothership', and even the incorporation of clans and tribes. Yet, over time such a group again 'broke up into two or more tribes, each embracing the descendants of one of the great ancestor's sons and taking its name from him. These tribes were again divided and sub-divided on the same principle....As time rolls on the sons of a household become heads of separate families, the families grow into septs, and finally the septs become great tribes or even nations embracing several tribes.'[44] Thus by the end of the twelfth century, we find that the tribe was no longer an aggregate of blood relations. Besides the blood kinsmen, the tribes also contained a number of slaves and adopted sons. There was no difference between a real and an adopted son; for all practical purposes the adopted son was counted as of the blood of his new father.

There was also a tendency for the tribes to form groups and confederations. Alliances were usually based on an oath. Allies were held to have formed a life and death union. The form of the oath varied according to the importance and value attached to the alliance or the circumstances during which it was concluded; sometimes they would sacrifice beasts swear by them,[45] while occasionally to emphasize the binding and solemn nature of the alliance, the contracting parties drew blood from their persons and mixed it to become 'andas' or blood brothers.[46]

Having no settled life, the Mongols owed neither obligation nor duty to any entity outside the tribe. They had no body politic to govern and control them, no code of social morality to regulate their actions against strangers.

The innate conservatism of the nomads, however, provided them with a number of settled customs and usages which, in the rough and tumble of their life, served as tribal law.

Independent of kinship, a tribe was usually formed by a voluntary association of groups of men, who rallied round a rising star or a hereditary chief, who assumed prominence on account of his abilities and achievements. Wealth and valour were the indispensable qualifications for a leader, and a cursory glance or review of the tribal leaders during the age of Chingiz shows that always and at the head of each tribe or confederation whether by right of election or inheritance, he alone was leader, who was the bravest and the most generous. The chief common link of union between the leader and the tribesmen was the desire for self-protection and the craving for loot and conquest. The leader who led and fed his people, exercised immense power, including that of life and death in cases of treason and indiscipline, all of which were voluntarily delegated to him. 'We want you to be Khan,' for instance, said the tribal nobles addressing Chingiz before electing him as their leader: 'When you are our Khan, we will be in the front in every battle against your foes; if we capture any beautiful women and good horses, we will first present them to you; at the hunt we will start first to encircle the games for you to shoot. If we disobey your commands in battle or in times of peace we do you any wrong, take from us our wives and our herds, and drive us into the imperiled desert.' In making decisions and deciding disputes, the tribal chief was required by custom to consult the heads of the families or tribes under him. His authority and control understandably lasted only as long as he was able to feed them and protect them and their pastures against hostile encroachments and enemies.

The individual Mongol was, however, personally free: the authority of the leader and the control of the tribe extended only to the waging of war, the seasonal movements and migration of the tribe, and measures relating to the protection of the group as against all other groups.

Dwellings

The influence of geographical factors in Mongolian life was best reflected in their[47] yurts or movable dwellings. Leading a hard and nomadic life, always on the move for fresh pastures, they could ill afford to have fixed dwellings. In winter they had to go down to warmer regions in the south while in summer they moved up towards the cooler regions of the north. Like their predecessors, the Scythians and the Huns, they lived in tents, big and small, carried from one camp to another. 'Some of the huts,' says Carpini,[48] 'are specially taken to pieces and put up again; such are packed on the wagons. Others cannot be taken to pieces, but are carried bodily on the wagons. To carry the smaller tents on a wagon one ox may serve; for the larger ones three oxen or four, or even more according to the size.' 'They set up the dwelling in which they sleep', observed Rubruck,[49] 'on a circular frame of interlaced sticks converging into a little round hoop on the top, from which projects above, a collar like a chimney, and this (framework) they cover over with white felts. Frequently they coat the felt with chalk, or white clay, or powdered bone, to make it appear whiter, and sometimes also (they make the felt) black. The felt around this collar on top they decorate with various pretty designs. Before the entry they also suspend felt ornamented with various embroidered designs in colour. For they embroider the felt, coloured or otherwise, making vines and trees birds and beasts.'

An equally interesting account of a nomad's house was given in the nineteenth century by Sir Charles Eliot[50] in a truly European style. Visiting the house of a Turkish family, he observed that the interior contained only as much furniture 'as could be carried off at a moments' notice on a wagon into Asia'.

The very aspect of a Turkish house seems to indicate that it is not intended for a permanent residence. The ground floor is generally occupied by stables and stores. From this a staircase, often merely a ladder, leads to an upper storey. Usually consisting of a long passage, from which open several rooms, the entrance to which are closed by curtains and not by doors. There are probably holes in the planking of the passages and spiders' webs and swallows' nests in the rafters. The rooms themselves, however, are beautifully clean, but bare and unfurnished. … The general impression left on a European is that a party of travellers have occupied an old barn and said, 'let us make a stay, the place is clean enough to live in; it is no use taking any more trouble about it. We shall probably be off again in a week.'

These movable dwellings were made sufficiently large to serve their needs for summer and winter. Rubruck[51] was astonished by the huge dimensions of their yurts and wagons. He once 'measured the width between the wheel-tracks of a cart 20 feet, and when the house was on the cart it projected beyond the wheels on either side five feet at least.' He saw a cart hitched to 22 oxen carrying a house, 'eleven abreast across the width of the cart and the other eleven before them. The axle of the cart was as large as the mast of a ship, and one man stood in the entry of the house on the cart driving the oxen.'

Bedding and valuables were placed in coffers of black felt coated with grease or tallow (making them waterproof) and then piled upon high carts drawn by camels. These precautions enabled them to negotiate rivers without unloading the carts. The women took pride and delighted in making their luggage carts beautiful. The wealth and status of a Mongol could be judged by the number of such carts with coffers; for while visiting the court of Mangu Khan in the heyday of Mongol prosperity, Rubruck found that it was not unusual for a rich Mongol to have a hundred or two such carts. A solitary female driver could conduct a caravan of twenty to thirty carts; the country being flat,[52] the carts were tied together, one after the other, the girl seated on the front cart, and driving the ox or the camel; 'all the others', observed Rubruck,[53] 'follow after with the same gait. So they go along slowly, as a sheep or an ox might walk.'

When they fixed their camp and pitched the tents, the Mongols took particular care to have the doors of their dwellings facing south. The dwelling of the master of the house was fixed in the centre while that of the first wife was placed on the extreme west and that of the last in the extreme east, the others being sandwiched in between in accordance with their ranks. The distance between the yurt of one wife and that of a stone's throw, perhaps to keep them at a safe distance from. The luggage carts (with the coffers) were placed on either side of the camp at a half-stone's throw so that the ordu stood between two rows of carts as between two walls and, as Rubruck noted[54] 'the ordu of a rich Moal (Mongol) seems like a large town, though there will be very few men in it.' Inside the master's tent, the women always sat on his left while the men were seated on his right. 'Men coming into the house', says Rubruck, 'would never hang up their bows on the side of women.' The master himself sat on a couch in the middle (the northern side) and faced the door.

Food and Drink

The Mongols of the thirteenth century had few inhibitions about food. In the sandy steppes of Mongolia, life was extremely hard. The aridity and severe climate of the Gobi enables only salt plants and hardy grasses to grow. The only places where trees are found in the Gobi are the few river bottoms. Here is the account of Lob Nor by Preschewalski.

It would be difficult to picture to oneself a more desolate landscape, the poplar woods with their bare soil and covered only in autumn with fallen leaves parched and shrivelled with the dry heat, withered branches and prostrate trees encumbering the ground, cane-brakes, crackling under foot and saline dust ready to envelope you from every bough that you brush away in your path. The poplars are so saturated with salt that on breaking a bough a saline incrustation may be seen in the wood. Now again, you come across dead poplars, with broken boughs shorn of their bark, lifeless trunks never decaying, but crumbling away by degrees to be hidden in layers of sand. The neighbouring desert is even more dreary, while not a bird, not an animal, nothing but the occasional tracks of the timid gazelle can be seen, but neither are there any meadows, grass, or flowers.[55]

Under such conditions the nomads ate the flesh of most creatures. They depended mainly on the meat and milk of their animals. 'They eat dead animals without distinction', says Rubruck, 'and with such flocks it cannot but be that many animals die. Nevertheless, in summer, as long as lasts their *cosmos*, that is to say mare's milk, they care not for any other food. So that if it happens that an ox or a horse dies, they dry its flesh by cutting it into narrow strips and hanging it in the sun and the wind, where at once and without salt it becomes dry without any evil smell. With the intestines of horses, they make sausages better than pork ones and they eat them fresh. The rest of the flesh they keep for winter.'[56] Carpini has given a more detailed account of their food and eating habits.

Their food is everything that can be eaten; for they eat dogs, wolves, foxes and horses and, when pushed by necessity, human flesh—I have also seen them eat lice, saying: 'why should I not eat them that eat my son's flesh and drink his blood?' I have seen them also eat rats. They use neither tablecloths nor napkins. They have no bread nor oil nor vegetables, nothing but meat, of which, however, they eat so little that other people could scarcely exist on it. They get their hands covered with the grease of the meat, but when they have finished eating, they wipe them on their boots, on the grass, or something else, though the more refined among them have some little bits of cloth with which they wipe their hands when they have finished eating. One of them takes the food (out of the kettle), and another takes the pieces of meat from him on the point of a knife, and gives to each one: to some more, to other less, as they wish to show them more or less honour.'[57]

Kumiz or fermented mare's milk was a favourite beverage of the Mongols. It was simple and easy to make and could keep long. 'In winter they make a capital drink of rice, of millet, and of honey', says Rubruck; 'it is clear as wine; and wine is carried to them from remote parts. In summer they care only for *cosmos* (*kumiz*).[58] He has also described how the *kumiz* was made.

They fasten a rope to two stakes in the ground, to which about the third hour, they tie the colts; they then proceed to milk the mothers, which in such a case allows themselves to be milked quietly. When they have a great quantity of milk they pour it into a large skin or bottle, and then churn it with a big stick made for the purpose, which is as big as a man's head at its lower extremity and hollowed out. When beaten sharply, the milk begins to ferment or run, and they go on till they have extracted all the butter, and when the liquor is mildly pungent they drink it.

According to Marco Polo, it was usual for the visitors to give a turn or two at the churn stick. The intoxicating power of *kumiz* varied according to the brew. 'The more advanced the vinous fermentation', says Colonel Yule, 'the less acid is the taste and the more it sparkles. The effect, however, is always slight and transitory, and leaves no unpleasant sensation, whilst it produces a strong tendency to refreshing sleep.'[59]

The feasts of the rich Mongols were lively, even boisterous. Rubruck noted that in every big *yurt* there was always *kumiz* before the entry door and, beside the leather vessel, there stood a guitar player with his guitar.[60] 'And', adds Rubruck, 'when the master begins to drink, then one of the attendants cries in a loud voice. "Ha!" and the guitarist strikes his guitar, and when they have a great feast they all clap their hands, and also dance about to the sound of the guitar, the men before the master, the women before the mistress. And when the master is drunk, the attendant cries as before, and the guitarist stops. Then they drink all around, and sometimes they do drink right shamefully and gluttonously.'

DRESS

According to Carpini,[61] there was not much difference in the clothes of men and women; they did not use capes, cloaks, hoods, or skins but wore tunics of buckram, purple or baldachin, which were all of one pattern: open from top to bottom and double over the breast, fastened on the left side with a tape and on the right with hair. These tunics were open to the armpit on the left side. The gown with its fur outside was open behind, with a tail down to the knees. Rubruck[62] remarks:

They always make in winter at least two fur gowns, one with the fur against the body, the other with the fur outside exposed to the wind and snow; these latter are usually of the skins of wolves or foxes or pinions; and while they sit in the dwelling they have another lighter one. The poor make their outside (gowns) of dog and kid skin. They make also breeches with furs. The rich, furthermore, wad their clothing with silk stuffing, which is extraordinarily soft, light and warm. The poor line their clothes with cotton cloth, or with fine wool. And the dress of the girls does not differ from the costume of the men, except that it is somewhat longer. But on the day following her marriage, (a woman) shaves the front half of her head, and puts on a tunic as wide as a nun's gown, but everywhere larger and longer, open before, and tied on the right side. Furthermore, they have a headdress which they call *bocca*,[63] made of bark, or other such light materials as they can find, and it is big and as much as two hands can span around, and is a cubit and more high, and square like the capital of a column. This *bocca* they cover with costly silk stuff, and it is hollow inside and on the top of the capital, they put a tuft of quills or light canes also a cubit or more in length—so it is that when several ladies are riding together, and one sees them from afar, they look like soldiers, helmets on head and lances erect.

With growing prosperity came increased finesse in dress. 'The dress of a Mongol', as described by Babar 'consisted of a cap embroidered with gold thread, or long frock of China satin adorned with flowered needle work, a Chinese belt of the old style, with white stone and purse pocket, to which were hung three or four things like the trinkets women wear at their necks, such as a perfume box and a little bag.'

Beliefs

During the illness of a person it was customary to lay him on his couch; a spear wrapped with black felt was struck outside his tent—to announce the unpleasant news, and to warn the people against inadvertently entering the *yurt*; only persons serving the sick or the shamans could visit him. They went in to chant their incantations and drive away the evil spirits pursuing the sick man. 'For they fear', says Rubruck, 'lest an evil spirit or some wind should come with those who enter. They call their priests, who are these same soothsayers.'[64] Special care was taken to guard the great ordu if anyone belonging to the Khan's family fell ill.

When a sick man showed signs of departing and began to agonize, he was left alone; one and all would leave the tent, for, according to Rubruck, 'if any one is present at the death of an adult, he may not enter the dwelling of any chief or of the emperor, for a year. If it be a child who dies, he may not enter it for a month.'[65]

When the sick person died he was mourned by loud lamentations and wailings, and, curiously enough, his family was exempt from tax for the year.

The Mongols buried their dead. Carpini describes their rituals thus,

When a person is dead if he is of the nobles, he is buried secretly in the steppe wherever it pleaseth them: he is buried, however, with his tent, and a bowl full of meat, and a jar full of mare's milk, and a mare with her foal is buried with him, also a horse with bit and saddle. And another horse they eat, and fill the skin with straw and put it on two or four poles over him, so that he may have a dwelling in the other world, and a mare to give him milk, and that he may increase his horse herd, and have horses on which to ride. And the bones of the horse which they eat they burn for the good of his soul. And often the women come together to burn the bones for the souls of the men, as I have seen with my own eyes, and have been told by others.... Furthermore they bury gold and silver with a person. They break up the cart on which he was carried, destroy his dwelling, and his name may not be pronounced by anyone for three generations.[66]

Qazi Minhaj gives further details:[67]

When one of them dies it is their custom to prepare a place underground about the size of a chamber or hall, in largeness proportionate to the rank and status of the accursed one, who may have departed to hell. They furnish it with a throne and a covering for the ground and place their vessels and numerous effects, together with his arms and weapons and whatever may have been his private property. There they also put some of his wives and slaves, male or female, and the person he loved most above all others. When they have placed that accursed one upon the throne, they bury his most beloved along with him in that place. In the night-time the place is covered up and horses are driven over it in such a manner that not a trace of it remains!

The Mongols 'believed in one god', reported Carpini. He was 'the maker of all things visible and invisible, as well as the author of all blessings in the world and of all punishments.' But they did not worship him.' 'We Moal,' said Mangu, 'believe that there is only one God; by whom we live and by whom we die, and for whom we have an upright heart.' It was a religion without dogma, and without a priesthood.[68] The discussion which Chingiz Khan had with Qazi Ashraf and his companion,[69] gives us insight into the religious outlook of the Mongols. Chingiz expressed his ready concurrence with faith in one God, had no objection against fasting and zakat, and appreciated the principle of prayers but not of the pilgrimage to Mecca. Religion was regarded by the Mongols as the private concern of an individual, who needed no formal or congregational prayers or rites.

The early accounts, however, make it clear that the Mongols revered Nature[70] but had no temples. We have no data on liturgy or ritual, but know that unexplained reverence was shown to the south. They revered the sun, moon, fire, water, and earth. They also appear to have had a belief in the afterlife. Their concept of the hereafter was nothing but a continuation or projection of the life in this world.[71]

Carpini, Rubruck and Marco Polo speak of idols and idol worship among the Mongols of their day. But, by their time, the contact with the civilizations of the East and West had brought a transformation in religion. Juwaini explains that some embraced Islam while some took to Christianity, and many preferred the worship of idols, while some adhered to the old customs and institutions of their forefathers and did not attach themselves to any of the faiths or creeds.[72]

Since the Mongols were free of the trammels of orthodoxy and unburdened by dogma, they were tolerant and showed deference to learned and devout men of all religions. 'As God gives us the different fingers of the hand', said Mangu, 'so he gives to men diverse ways.' Chingiz Khan enjoined his successors to show no preference to the followers of any religion at the expense of the others. He and his descendants (with a few aberrations) were in this respect far ahead of their contemporaries.

Mongol women played a not inconsiderable role in politics. They enjoyed a position of respect and independence nowhere else evident in the thirteenth century. They moved about freely in public, and graced not only the occasions of amusement and diversion but also attended public functions and parades. In court, camp and the tent they had a well defined place. Women of the imperial family intrigued and interfered in matters of state and high policy. They exercised a considerable influence over the iron men of the steppes. Mongol history abounds with the story of notable women who, like Oyelun (when widowed) nurtured the family through the days of destitution. She mothered not only her own sons but also her step sons and the abandoned children of defeated enemies. It is a tribute to her motherhood that these adopted sons, Shigi Qutuqu (Tatar), Gucu (Merves), Kokchu (Besuit), and Boroqul (Jurkin), grew up as brave and exceptionally loyal members of the family. Another fine specimen of Mongol womanhood was Bortei, who retained her hold over the 'man of blood and iron', in spite of her captivity and pregnancy and by her shrewdness and sagacity. It was she who advised him to beware of Jamuka's friendship, and again she warned him against the vaulting ambition of the shaman Teb Tengri, and instigated him to nip the brewing storm in the bud. Further, Yessin, 'though a woman' Chingiz observed, drew his attention to the advisability of designating a successor as he was preparing to go on the long campaign against Khwarazm Shah, and he specifically highlighted her sagacity as against that of his sons' companions and noyans. The chroniclers also mention the masterful widows of Anbagai Khan, Urbe and Sakatai, who took the lead in instigating desertion by Yesukai's cousins and followers soon after his death, Gur Besu, the haughty wife of the

Naiman chief, Tayang Khan, who made any rapprochement impossible, efficient and able administrators, like Soroqo-Tini, or skilled and ambitious intriguers like Turakina, Fatuwa, and Obul Ghamunsh. They also provided that, till the election of a new Khan, the senior widow of the late ruler should act as regent and carry on the administration and government of the *ulus*.

In the political matrix of the twelfth and thirteenth centuries when might was right and the law of the jungle prevailed, marriage (or women) played an important role in the political relations of the Mongols. More often than not, upon marriage depended the mutual attitude of the tribes or their members, friendly or hostile, and it was seldom that a political and diplomatic alliance was not sealed and further cemented by a simultaneous marriage alliance. Chingiz never failed to demand, nor did he hesitate to offer, a daughter in marriage in order to bring and bind his vassals and late adversaries into a closer and more amiable relationship. Not infrequently do we find an explanation about the attitude of the tribes and the policy of their leaders in their marital connections. In times of crisis and extreme danger the armed help and assistance of the marital relations was claimed and was unreservedly forthcoming. Rarely did an individual or hero, like Temuchin, consider it below his dignity to make such an appeal, for 'no one thinks anything of you', he remarked, 'if you come as a beggar'.

Since relatives by marriage also formed a sort of loose military alliance, bound to help each other in times of danger, marriages were sought and arranged with an eye to politics, and not infrequently the grievances and enmity between groups and tribes were settled and solved by marriage. And as such alliances and connections were the need of the day, polygamy became an important feature of their social life—for it rendered easier the alliance and confederation of the tribes.

Women and War

But if women performed the role of being mediators and bringing about peace in the life of the ever-wrangling and warring tribes, they were also often the causes of jealousy, quarrels, feuds, and even wars. Their petty feminine jealousies caused estrangement between their husbands, and sometimes between their respective tribes as happened at the banquet given on the occasion of Chingiz's assumption of the Khanship and the marriage of his mother with Munlik. The feud which arose and existed between Yesukai and the Taichiuts over the forcible seizure and marriage of Oyelun continued to smoulder for more than a generation until they had avenged themselves upon Yesukai's son, Chingiz and made a captive of his young wife, Bortei. And in his turn, later on, Chingiz destroyed the whole tribe. Similarly, it was the failure of marital negotiations which led to the terrible conflict between Chingiz and Wang Khan.

Irrespective of the adversary and the cause of conflict, the object and aim of the tribes was always to get as much booty and captives as possible. In all their raids and plunder expeditions, women formed the chief object of ambition and attraction. How great an incentive and stimulus to fight was the desire to get the women is seen in Chingizd passionate description of his conception of the highest pleasure for a man:[73] 'To see the faces of those who were dear to them his enemies bedewed with tears, and to clasp their wives and daughters in his arms.'

As women formed one of the most coveted prizes in their raids, the tribes took the first and the utmost care to protect their camps and women against a surprise attack. But when, in spite of all these precautions, the women were captured and carried away, they were, just like all other booty, distributed among the members of the tribe; the prettiest and the fairest going to the bravest. The treatment of the female captives usually depended upon their rank, status and personality but were never or seldom killed. Sexually at the disposal of the victors, they were usually reduced to the position of slaves and concubines, and often married and kept as wives. There must have been frequent cases like that of Chingiz wherein the presumptive father could doubt the paternity of his child.

WOMEN AND FAMILY LIFE

The unit of life is the house and the village and then the city. But the unit of Mongol social life was the *akhsu* and the *yurt* (the tent and the encampment), the family and the tribe, and, consequently, the position and status of women depended upon their worth and utility to the tribe. Hearth and home formed the chief sphere of their activities. Within the family circle, they enjoyed a respectable and honourable position. As mistress of the tent the woman had full control and authority over the family possessions; she alone could buy, sell and barter things as she pleased. Just as a man is generally judged by the company he keeps, he could also be adjudged (and so was the case in earlier societies) by the conduct and character of his wife. 'If a woman is stupid and slovenly, without understanding and without order,' observed Chingiz Khan,[74] 'we see in her the bad qualities of her husband. But if she manages her household well, receives guests and messengers suitably and entertains them hospitably, she enhances her husband's prestige, giving him a notable reputation in the assembly. *Good men are recognized by the goodness of their wives.*' (Italics added)

The Mongol women were distinguished for their loyalty and devotion to their husbands. Anecdotes relating to the intimate and amiable relations between men and their wives, such as between Chingiz and Bortei and Qulan, or between Kutimur Noyan and his consort,[75] are amongst the outstanding, though few relieving and almost romantic ideals, in the otherwise generally drab account of the social and family life of the Mongols.

Behind a great man there is a woman: so runs an old adage. It may or may not always be true as notable exemptions can be found in the gallery of the great makers of history. Were there any woman behind the rise and greatness of the Mongol Khan, and if so, then who? For Chingiz had not only one woman, or wife as his life companion to be his friend, philosopher and guide but several wives and a regiment, if not a battalion of concubines. Though, according to Carpini there was no distinction between the son of a wife and that of a concubine, the chroniclers have neither recorded the name of any favourite concubine nor any details about the Khan's sons from them. The names of his wives are duly recorded, and some references are also found about the advice or intervention made by them and appreciated by Khan. Yet, notwithstanding the contributions Bortei, Qulan Qatun, Yessin and Yessulan made in their own way, the adage is true if one looks at Mother Oyelun who had a major influence on the Great Conqueror, and was perhaps foremost among all the 'great women' in category.

It was Mother Oyelun, who dauntlessly tried to persuade and cajole the deserting relations and tribesmen to return to the yurt, and remain steadfast to the banner of Temuchin (Chingiz Khan) after Yesukai's untimely death. It is, however, another story that the wives of kinsmen sabotaged her efforts to preserve the young orphan's patrimony (another instance of women's role in Mongol society). But Oyelun 'intrepidly' faced and overcame the struggle against distress and possible destitution. And it appears that her iron will and determination to struggle and survive against all odds was inherited in full measure by her terrible son. Again, it was she who nursed and brought up not only Temuchin and Belgutai but also the four 'adopted' orphaned sons of vanquished enemies, who turned out to be not only amazingly loyal but also incomparably competent companions and commanders of Chingiz Khan. Their contribution in his struggle for survival, power and supremacy, as well as the unity of the Mongol Empire was both invaluable and enviable until the split in 1260. Unfortunately, the hand that rocked the cradle could not live to see her 'child' fulfill the dreams of Dai Sechen that Yesukai's son will 'rule the world', and the 'babies', nursed by her would turn the 'world' upside down.

Gifted with the powers of quick perception and determination, they could divine the intentions of their menfolk, and several instances occurred wherein women figure as giving their men and the tribe a warning of coming events or by their actions forestall the enemy. Oyelun and Bortei were the first to sense the lofty ambitions of Jamuka and advise Chingiz to be on his guard and break with his blood brother.'[76] 'The eagle nests on a lofty tree; but sometimes, while he trusts in the safety of his tree, the nest is plundered by lesser bird, and eggs and young are devoured,' ran Bortei's message when she warned her husband against the danger threatening Onon from the west during his absence, and he hurriedly reached his *yurt* to find that Sengun and Jamuka had formed a conspiracy and confederacy against him.

The conditions of a hard and warlike life made polygamy for the Mongols almost a law of nature. If that axiom can be applied to the Mongol world and society, when plunder and pillage, rape and rapine, were the order of the day, the only friends one had were his own kinsfolk and blood relations. In such circumstances a large family was necessary for survival in the struggle for existence. 'Man in a barbarous state,' says Westermarck, 'is proud of a large progeny, and he who has most kinsfolk is most honoured and respected.'[77] The high and abnormal death rate, and consequently, the great disproportion between the number of the sexes made polygamy, the only remedy against promiscuity and prostitution. In the intense desire for children to meet the drain on population and keep up the manpower of the family, polygamy furnished them the only effective and speedy means. Furthermore, the hard life of the *yurt* and the frequent exposure of women to harsh weather and the storms of war would have taken their toll on their beauty and youth, and would have been it inevitable for them to lose the respect and devotion of their men; for, lust and not love was 'the paramount factor in the connubial relationship.'[78] And the sexual ardour of the virile nomads hungered for, and fetched others to replace the ugly and the worn out. Moreover, wealth and power, both of the individual and the tribe, depended upon the number of wives and children. In the election of a chief or leader, as with the North American Indians, choice, must have, not infrequently, fallen upon him who had the most numerous offspring and who was, therefore, says Heriot, 'considered as the person most deeply interested in the welfare of the tribe.'

As polygamy prevailed, the position of a wife depended upon the social and political ranks of her husband and upon the fact of her begetting children. In a family, only one woman occupied the pride of place; the first was usually the foremost, the noblest and the full-blooded, who had been 'bestowed' upon the master of the tent by 'his own father' in accordance with Mongol rites and customs. 'My first wife Bortei, to whom I was betrothed in early youth,' as affirmed Chingiz,[79] 'is the wife and house-mother bestowed upon me by my noble father.' And though Chingiz Khan had many wives and concubines, though he loved Qulan most, whom he even took with himself on the Khwarazmian campaign, nevertheless Bortei, notwithstanding her Merkit captivity, enjoyed the pride of place. Her sons, including Juji of doubtful paternities and his descendant(s) alone inherited the empire while the children of Qulan vanished into the limbo of history.

Whatever their position or rank, the women enjoyed in Mongolia, we find that it was not certainly that of mere chattels and slaves, and that they enjoyed a respectable status as far as their own yurt or household was concerned. Nothing illustrates or attests it better than the diffidence of the Great Khan when he sought to find out the response or reaction of his first wife, Bortei, before reaching the ordu along with his newly-acquired second wife. Qulan Qatun; and the beautiful Qulan was assigned a separate yurt for her residence. We also find that the Central Asian Turkish women enjoyed similar status, even the wives of the great and terrible Tamerlane. 'The position of Timur's wives and other women at his court of war as Bebice Forbes Mawa observes,[80] was in keeping with Mongol customs rather than with the requirements of Islam. As can be seen from Clavio's and Ibn Arabshah's accounts of the banquets of 1404, the queens and princesses were present unveiled. The queens and princesses also gave banquets to the invited guests. Timur (Tamerlane) built palaces with gardens in the environs of Samarqand, both for his wives and for other princesses.'

As for the other co-wives, their position varied between the mistress of the tent and the rest of the maidservants, and, like all other property, even they could be transferred by the husband and were inherited by the heirs along with the rest of the deceased man's belongings. 'Ibaha', said Chingiz for instance when he was about to hand her over to one of his trusted lieutenants. 'Ibaha! I do this not because I have ceased to love thee, not because thou hast an evil temper of mind, or art lacking in beauty. I give thee to Jurchidai to reward him in the highest way possible. I give thee to Jurchidai because of his inestimable service, and I desire those of my sons and descendants who shall receive the throne after me to honour the dignity and fame of Ibaha.'

The strange and unprecedented 'award' must have stunned the whole gathering, a wife being awarded to a follower for 'inestimable service', service to which every follower was committed by native and tribal tradition. And the prize, wife of the Khan of Khans, Lord of the Steppes. This was something unheard of and unimaginable, and that is why perhaps, the Great Khan sought to comfort the shattered lady by reaffirming his regard and love for her and also assuring her that her 'dignity and fame' should be honoured by his successors.

The award was as exceptional a case as exceptional was the Great Khan. None of the authentic sources mention such an exceptional gift by any other nomad/Mongol chief. One, however, cannot help but wonder whether it was a well considered decision or was the Khan, for once, carried away by impulse for the 'inestimable' service rendered by Chur Chadai. Whatever may be the 'reason', it is difficult to accept it as 'reasonable', much less estimable, even by the social and moral mores of the thirteenth century Mongols. Moreover, it does not reconcile with his own conduct and behaviour, particularly the 'chastity test' Qulan Qatun had to undergo before her acceptance by Chingiz Khan as his wife, the 'honour war' of extermination that he waged following the Merkit captivity of Bortei and the incomparable calm-headed coolness he displayed over Chaghatae's aspersions against Juji's paternity, whom Chingiz continued, as ever, to call as 'The eldest of my sons'. Finally and most importantly, the 'services' recounted do not seem to be any different, much less higher than those of the Tarkhans or the Great Nayans, such as Subutai, Yaman Noyan and Muquli.

Just emerging from a state of primitive barbarism and moving to Temism, the Mongols still adhered to exogamy, or marriage outside the clan, and though marriage by purchase was the order of the day, no stigma or reproach was attached to marrying the captured. The wedding ceremony of a mock capture was obviously symbolic of the original practice of capturing wives. Since women were looked upon as an entity in the nature of property, ownership or conjugal rights were determined on the basis of possession rather than a mere claim, while titles were based upon ceremonial and marital rites. The case of Chingiz Khan's own mother is an adequate illustration. Though Oyelun's original husband was alive and Yesukai obtained her by sheer force and admitted her into his own *yurt*, nobody ever raised any objections about Temuchin's legitimate paternity. The change that was coming over the Mongols on account of their close and constant intercourse with their civilized neighbours, and with it a gradual modification in their conception of fatherhood, is revealed by the doubts cast on Juji's paternity, even by his own brothers and in the presence of their parents. 'Paternity did not originally mean what it does with us. With us the very foundation of the notion of fatherhood is procreation, and the presumption of law that the husband is the father of all his wife's children rests on a well-established custom of conjugal fidelity, and on the certainty that the husband will object to have spurious children palmed off on him.'[81] But the savage nomads, in utter and desperate need of numerous offspring, could not but look upon woman as a mere child-rearing machine.[82] They did not scruple marrying widows to the younger brothers or the stepsons of the deceased man.

Unaffected by the effeminate culture and luxury of the Chinese and untouched by the vices of the Persians, the Mongols' standard of morality was much higher than among the civilized races of their time, or than their present-day descendants, softened and cultured by the civilizations of the East and the West. 'Whether in Africa or Asia', says Vambery, 'certain vices are introduced only by the so-called bearers of culture.'[83]

As they married early, usually at the age of 14 or 15, and severely punished immorality, illicit intercourse was unknown among them. 'Their women are chaste', observed Carpini', 'and nothing is heard among them of lewdness; but some of the expressions they use in joking are very shameful and coarse.'[84] Notwithstanding his bitterness against the Mongols, Babur has also testified about the fidelity of his Mongol wives. According to Carpini,

Each one hath as many wives, as he can support', 'some have a hundred, some fifty, some more others fewer.... They marry all their relatives except their own mother, their daughters and sisters by the same mother. They may however marry their sisters through their father, and also their father's wives after his death. A younger brother or some other younger member of the family is expected on the death of his elder to take the brother's wife. All other women without any distinction they take as wives and they buy them right dearly from their parents. After the death of their husbands (the women) do not easily make second marriages, except someone wishes to take his stepmother as a wife.[85]

'Among them no widow marriages', adds Rubruck, 'for they believe that all who serve them in this life shall serve them in the next, so as regards a widow, that she will always return to her first husband after death.'[86] Widow remarriage, however, was not uncommon. Hulaku's daughter Tutukai (or Bundugai) successively married Tenker Kurkan, his son Sulamuh and then his son Tijak Kurkan.[87] And Chingiz Khan's mother took Munlik as her second, or rather third husband. The widows of the defeated and slain adversaries were frequently taken as wives by the victor to demonstrate his triumph as well as to effect reconciliation with the vanquished tribe.

Among the Mongols of the twelfth and thirteenth centuries we find no religious ceremonies or rites connected with marriage—no prayers or sacrifices and offerings to the gods nor any consultation of the stars and the shamans to ascertain the right and propitious day for a wedding. According to Rubruck and Carpini, marriage was simply a matter of bargain and purchase—not a sacrament. 'When a person', says Rubruck, 'had made a bargain to marry a girl, her father gave a feast, and the girl flew to her relatives and concealed herself. Thereupon the father said, 'My daughter is yours: take her wheresoever you find her.' Then he searched for her along with his friends until he got hold of her and carried off with a semblance of violence and force.'[88]

It was customary for the bride's father to give is daughter some presents in the nature of a dowry,[89] and which usually consisted of food, clothes, household goods, etc., and sometimes also cattle. She was the sole mistress of her marriage portion and could dispose it off in any manner she liked, though, in practice, this right must have been exercised under the shadow of the all-powerful and towering personality of the master of the tent. But in case of separation or divorce, she was entitled to get back her marriage portion.[90]

'No Mongol', says Vincent of Beauvais, 'deems a woman his real wife till she has conceived or had a child, and if she is barren she can be put away. Nor does a husband get the wife's dower till she has had a child.'[91]

Active and strong, the maids and the women did most of the work. 'It is the duty of the women,' says Rubruck, 'to drive the carts, get the dwellings on and off them, milk the cows, make butter, and to dress and sew skins, which they do with a thread made of tendons. They divide the tendons into fine shreds, and then twist them into one long thread. They also sew the boats, the socks and the clothing. They also make the felt and cover the houses.'[92] They also looked after their herds of sheep and goats, milked them to prepare the *kumiz*, cooked the food and cleansed the bowls. In short, as Carpini observed,[93] their women did all the work while the men led an adventurous outdoor life.

It would be interesting, though provoking, if we ponder the following observations by the writer of the *Habit of Good Society*: manual of etiquette (a nineteenth century publication) concerning women, home and family life: 'It is by woman that nature writes indelible lessons in the hearts of men. Not only when she fills the sphere of a wife, a mother, a teacher, but in every state of life it is woman who has it in her power to influence for good or evil the man with whom she is thrown.' We must not, however,

abuse the poor savage, who lies idle in the sun for days after his return from hunting, while his heavy laden wife toils and moils without complaint or cease; but bearing in view the extreme bursts of exertion which such a life of incessant struggle with nature and his fellows for food involves upon him the consequent necessity of correspondingly utilizing every opportunity of repose to recruit and eke out the short and precarious life so indispensable to wife and weans, we shall see that this crude domestic economy is the best, the most moral, and the most kindly attainable under the circumstances.[94]

The nomad's life was, however, not so dreary and dismal as one might tend to imagine after going through the 'reports' of Carpini and Rubruck. There was also love and laughter; of a life of vigour and zest, be it at the home or the battlefield, the hunt or the marauding raids in search of booty and beauty.

Faith in himself, his prowess and skill, fidelity to the chief, loyalty to the clan, the tribe, and fidelity to the spouse and filial ties characterized the individual's main traits, and which, as Ibn Khaldun later philosophized, contributed to the moral superiority of the nomadic society over sedentary societies, and constituted one of the main reasons for their successes once they left their habitats.

The Conqueror

The Great Khan was the supreme commander of the imperial forces—standing, auxiliary and quasi-feudal. When the Khan himself took part in a campaign, the army gathered round him. Whether on the march or in the camp, the troops had their places only with reference to him.[95] In the field of battle he formed the pivot and the focal point round which the whole army was organized. It was only when the Khan was himself in command of the army that the essential unity of the government and the army, was revealed. Surrounded and protected by his devoted bodyguards—the Personal Ming—he formed the nucleus of the army and guided and controlled its actions on the battlefield.

Army Organization

The chief feature of the Mongol army organization was that the whole population[96] was kept in a state of full military preparedness and was capable of undertaking military operations, whether offensive or defensive, at a moment's notice. The soldiers always had their arms and ammunition ready and at hand; the cavalry was always in fighting form, every soldier had a number of horses ready, trained and tested for battle. The different wings and divisions of the armed population had their permanent positions fixed, in camp as well as at court, and when on the march, always in touch with each other and ready to assist, support and protect one another.

When on the march, there were always advanced guards and flank guards to reconnoitre and observe the enemy's movements and protect the army against being surprised or ambushed. The guards, usually two hundred strong, marched at an arrow's distance or a short gallop, both to remain in touch with the main army as well as to allow it to deploy and manoeuvre without hindrance.

The Mongol army was usually divided into seven divisions—the Booljoonghar, the Boroonghar, the Oonghar, the Joonghar, the Qool or the Ghool, the Ookjoonghar, and the Bustoonghar.[97]

The Booljoonghar was the advanced guard, consisting of about 200 horsemen and marched ahead of the army at a distance of two marches.[98] In Turkish it is called *Qarawal*.

The Boroonghar, which followed the advance guard, occupied the space between it and the main army. It consisted of the bravest and the choicest troops and guarded the route, kept intact the communications between the Booljoonghar and the army. It was also known as '*erawul*' and '*Munqulai*'.[99]

The Oonghar and the Joonghar were the two wings of the main army and marched on either flank at a distance ranging from an arrow shot to two marches. The strength of the wings is given by Marco Polo as two hundred cavalry each.

The Qool or the Ghool was the centre of the army and it moved in between the two wings. The commander of the army occupied the central position and his 'tuq' or standard was planted there.

The Ookjoonghar, also called 'Chikdawul', followed the main army 'at a distance, at which the dust of the ghool might reach it, or that its dust might reach the ghool.'[100]

The Bustoonghar may be said to form the rear guard. It covered and moved behind the Ookjoonghar 'at such a distance that an enemy may not be able to discover the horses or dust of the Ookjoonghar.'[101] By the Persians, it was styled Kumeengah. Hence there was 'a good look-out on all sides against a surprise.'[102]

The 'decimal-cum-appanage system' of a hierarchal organization was somewhat similar, but also different from that of the great Turkish leader, Meghder, who, according to Parker,[103] could very well be regarded as 'one of the great conquerors in World History, and may fairly be called the Hannibal of the Tartary,' and added 'it is not unlikely that the Genghis Khan or Zenglis Khan of the Mongols may be the old word Zenghi in a highly changed form (the Turkish title of 'king' Meghder, that is, Tengrikudu Zenghi meaning 'Heaven's son Immense'.

The 'Meghder system' was similar to the 'Mongol system as it, too had twenty four commanders of deca-chiliar rank, that is, the right to command 10,000 warriors, that each of them had 'his own area within which to wander after pasture' and also had 'the right to appoint his own Chiliarchs, centurions deco-centurions, etc.' The Mongol system was, however, a strait-jacket organization, in which authority flowed downwards from the Great Khan, and each person, whatever his rank, exercised autonomous authority.

In the Mongol system, moreover, appanages were allotted to the Khan's sons but they were all subordinate 'sovereign' authorities, subject and accountable to Chingis Khan and his successor, who was duly elected by a Quriltai or General Assembly of his descendants. Till the time the new Khan was elected, the late Khan's wife could act as Regent. Meghder, on the other hand, appointed two vicegerents, under the title of dogis, next in rank to the Zenghi only, one for the East and one for the West; dogi meant 'worthy' or 'virtuous'; the eastern dogi was regarded as higher in rank and usually heir to the throne. Next to them were, similarly, two ruksee, two marshals, two chamberlains, two marquesses, one each for the East and one for the West, the eastern ranking higher than the other. The system overshadowed the Zenghi as against the Mongol system wherein the Khan was the 'sun of the power system' around which all authorities revolved. Perhaps the merit or strength of the system, coupled with the 'Favours of Eternal Heaven' in the form of numerous gifted descendants enabled them to preserve and further promote the legacy of Chingiz Khan, both in time and space as against any ancient or medieval conqueror.

'Our armies ought to be marshalled after the order of the Tartars, and under the same vigorous laws of war,' advised Carpini. 'Such an organization of the army', observed Juwaini, 'is not found in any history from the time of Adam down to the present day.' And there are no two opinions about the efficiency of the Mongol war machine: its organization was superb but simple. Juwaini remarks:

They have invented a new kind of muster-roll abolishing the old army registers and dismissing the old officials. The whole population is divided into units of ten men, each unit with its amir, who command the other nine; out of such ten amirs one is appointed an Amir-i-sad, who is the commander of the whole hundred. Similarly, there are appointed amirs of the thousand and the ten thousand. The commander of ten thousand is called the amir of Tuman. When any expedition of importance is undertaken or any work is required, it is sent to the amirs of the Tumans and by them to the amirs of the thousands and so on till it reaches the amirs of ten.[104]

The decimal principle had, therefore, the merit of speed and simplicity. As each amir was accountable to the commander immediately over him, the system made for better supervision and closer coordination. Responsibility was both direct and immediate; and all were treated as equals.

The motto of 'one for all and all for one', was inculcated by the merger, even absorption, of the chosen vanquished tribal adversaries into Mongol formations, obliterating age old inter-tribal rivalries and jealousies; all were to be united by invisible links of loyalty and 'bonds of booty' to the Great Khan. 'No man', says Juwaini, 'can desert his comrades—the man of his 'ten' 'hundred', 'thousand', which are all fixed and determined. He cannot go and join another officer, nor is any person permitted to shelter or harbour such a deserter. If any person transgresses this *Yassa* (rule), the deserter is publicly executed, while the person who sheltered him, is put under rack and torture. No one gives asylum to a deserter. Even a *Shahzada* would never give shelter to such a person.'[105] The sense of unity was tested and whetted during the hunt when they had to drive the game forward, hold the circle of the hunt for a month or more and, above all, maintain strict watch so that no beast may escape the circle. If any game escaped, all those adjudged guilty were severely punished.

'They have few arms except arrows and bows and fur gowns,' said Rubruck.[106] Carpini, however, gives a few details:

All of them must have at least the following arms: two or three bows, at least one good one, three big quivers full of arrows, an axe and ropes to pull machine.... Their helmets are of iron or steel on top, but that portion which goes round the neck and throat is of leather ... some of them have spears, and at the lower of the heads is a hook to pull people out of the saddle. Their arrows are two feet one palm and two fingers long ....The heads of their arrows are very sharp, and they always carry files to sharpen them....They have shields made of wickerwork, but I do not think they carry any except in camp, and when on guard over the Emperor and the princes, and then only at night.[107]

But it is remarkable that *the soldiers, not the Khan, had to provide the arms and equipment*. 'Whenever they plan to attack an enemy or a rebel', says Juwaini, 'everything that is necessary for the enterprise is prescribed—all kinds of arms and other equipment from banners to needles and ropes, and horses and beasts of burden from asses to camels. Thus, everyone in the units of ten and hundred provides his requirements. On the day of muster the weapons are inspected and if any are found deficient, they are severely dealt with and punished.'[108]

'In the world there are no troops that can match the Mongols', said Juwaini, 'in the hour of battle and attack they behave like trained lions during a hunt, while during the days of peace and leisure they are as docile and useful as sheep which gives milk, wool and other profitable things.' 'They are a people very obedient to their chiefs,' observed Marco Polo.[109] The contemporaries of Chingiz Khan and Mangu Qaan were struck and bewildered no less by the discipline and devotion of the Mongol soldiers than by their capacity to adapt to circumstances. As soldiers and subjects, they obeyed and loyally carried out orders about the supply of provisions and stores, payment of regular taxes as well as of extraordinary contributions, facilities for couriers and travellers, besides, the maintenance of the *Yam* and the supply of horses and provisions for the same. 'During accidents and vicissitudes, both in adversity and prosperity,' says Juwaini, 'they do not mind separation from their near and dear ones nor do they fear or care about the hostility and opposition of their enemies .... The subjects are also soldiers and in times of war, the young and the old, the nobles and the commons, all of them become swordsmen, bowmen and lancers.'[110]

'His warriors are as brave as lions,' reported the spy of the Khwarazm Shah, 'so that none of the fatigues or hardships of war can injure them. They know neither ease nor rest, neither flight nor withdrawal. Wheresoever they go, they carry everything they need with them ... their horses need neither straw nor wheat, being content to scrape through the snow with their hoofs and eat the underlying grass, or pawing the earth and munching roots and vegetables ... no mountain or river can arrest their progress. They cross every ravine or swim their horses over the rivers, themselves holding on to the mane or the tail.'[111]

The chief characteristic of the Mongol army, which stands out in sharp contrast to the medieval and feudal armies, was the fact that the army was divisible and separable from the person of the monarch, and its capacity to carry on separate campaigns in different directions at one and the same time.

This gave an advantage to the Mongol Khan who could and did easily take advantage of opportunities and conquered territories in the East, South and West with the result that the Mongol banners proudly fluttered from the Caspian Sea to the shores of the Pacific Ocean.

STRATEGY AND TACTICS

'We are not fit to lead an army on the march unless we are familiar with the face of the country ... its mountains and forests, its pitfalls,' observed the veteran Chinese general, Sun Tuzu. 'They ask exhaustive questions,' remarked Rubruck and in fact, the secret service of the Mongols was one of the most efficient known in history. The Mongols by means of their excellent espionage and by questioning their prisoners,[112] always obtained a thorough knowledge of the topography of the country they were invading, and also an insight into the character of the generals opposing them, and above all, the political conditions and factions inside the doomed country, of which they made the fullest use. 'Subutai was better acquainted with the Russian climate and Russian conditions than Napoleon proved to be six hundred years later,' as Michael Prawdin says, 'He had begun his campaign in midwinter, despite the intensity of the cold; he had hounded his men onward across the snow through these vast expanses, but he led men and horses, intact into the steppes, before the melting of the snows should transform the north Russian plains into an impenetrable morass.'[113] For though unconquered and with no enemy worth mentioning to face, he renounced the plundering of the richest Russian towns and turned southward into the steppes. The message which Chingiz Khan sent to Turkan Khatun or the forged treasonable letter which he caused to be intercepted by the Khwarazm Shah shows the complete and accurate knowledge the Mongol Khan possessed concerning the relations between the sultan and his stepmother and the character of the Khwarazmian nobility. Similarly, two decades later, Batu displayed a thorough knowledge of the political factions and divisions inside Hungary and Poland, or again when Mangu surprised Carpini by telling him that the French king, not the Holy Roman Emperor, was the greatest and the most powerful of the European monarchs of his days. It was on account of such thorough and comprehensive information about foreign lands that the Mongols were able to move and manoeuvre in 'unknown' territories as if they were fighting on their own ground. This knowledge, again, enabled them to select points of vantage and fight on the ground of their own choosing, e.g. the battle on the river Kalka.

'An army can march anywhere and at any time of the year, wherever two men can place their feet,' observed Napoleon, and this dictum applied too well to the Mongols of the thirteenth century. 'Neither the Great Wall of China, nor the fortified passes nor the mountains nor the enormous walls of the fortress cities had been able to save the population of a fifty-million empire (of Cathay) from the two hundred thousand Mongolian riders.'[114] No barrier was too strong to withstand their onslaught, no obstacle too great to bar their progress so that the Mongol horsemen traversed, within the short span of six years, one fourth of the globe. Such was the mobility and self-sufficiency of the army that the armies of Chingiz Khan crossed the 400-mile wide sandy desert of Qizil Qum without the loss of a single life where six hundred and fifty years later the Russian cavalry lost its horses while campaigning against Khiva. When Chingiz Khan invaded the Muslim lands, crossing the waterless waste, known as the 'hunger steppe', consisting of wild mountains, sandy and rock-strewn deserts, he performed a feat which rivals, if it does not surpass the crossing of the Alps by Hannibal, and centuries later, by Napoleon with his bare-footed 'warriors of the Revolution'.

'The art of war', said Napoleon, 'may be reduced to a single principle—to unite on a single point a greater mass than the enemy.' Concentration of superior forces at the decisive point is, as a matter of fact, the sole aim and art of strategy. The extreme mobility of Mongol divisions and the speed of their cavalry enabled them to switch over thousands of reinforcements in a single night over a distance of 200 miles. The great twin battles of Sajo and Leignitz were won only by the unexpected and timely junction of their troops. 'The tactics of marching separately and fighting in unison were brought by him (Chingiz) to the highest perfection, with the result that the Mongols were always turning up to surprise the enemy by effecting junctions at the most unlikely places, and yet, when a decisive battle occurred, all their armies were re-united.'[115]

Though holding life of little worth in general, the Khan always strove to spare his Mongol warriors, and praised the commander who did not overwork his men or his horses.[116] The Mongols always distributed their forces on the basis of calculations, and choice troops were always kept in reserve to be thrown in at the decisive time and point. The Battle of the Indus as that against Wang Khan, earlier was won by the free and bold use of the reserve. So sparing and considerate of his men was Chingiz Khan that he allotted Yamah Noyan only 20,000 men to fight the Qara Khitais. It was also the Mongol practice to put the auxiliaries in the forefront so that they constituted the holding force and, functioning as shock-absorbers, enabled the Mongols to participate at the decisive moment or to bring home to the enemy a shattering counter-attack. Napoleon boasted that he always fought on the interior lines but the Mongols won their victories independent of the problem of interior and exterior lines; for the Mongol armies moved independently and without any base of supplies or lines of communication. 'They are excellent soldiers, and passing valiant in battle,' observed Marco Polo. 'They are also more capable of hardships than other nations; for many a time, if need be, they will go for a month without any supply of food, living only on the milk of their mares and on such games as their bows may win them. Their horses also will subsist entirely on the grass of the plains, so that there is no need to carry store of barley or straw or oats.'[117]

Interestingly enough we find a similar contemporary appreciation or account of the Mongol warriors from an adversary, Falak-ud-din Muhammad, who had fought against them at the battle of Nahr Bashir, one of the tributaries of the little Tigris on the western side of Baghdad in 1258, and was fortunate enough to survive the Mongol fury to recount the sorry tale of defeat and disaster that had overwhelmed his 'Garden of Eden'—the 'City of Peace' (Baghdad). The anecdote has been reported by the author of the *Kitabul Fakhri* directly from him, as follows:

I was in the army—to meet the Tatars (Mongols) on the western side of the city of peace (Baghdad) on the occasion of that grievous catastrophe, which befell in the year AH 656 (AD 1258). We met on the Nahr Bashir, one of the tributaries of the little Tigris; and from our side would go forth to challenge an adversary a horseman mounted on an Arab horse and wholly clad in mail, as though he and his horse were a mountain in solidity. Then there would come out to meet him from the Mongols a horseman mounted on a horse like unto an ass, and holding in his hand a spear like unto a spindle, unclad and unarmed, so that all who beheld him laughed at him. Yet ere the day was done, the victory was theirs, and they scattered us in a dire defeat which was the key of disaster, so that then there happened what happened in this matter.[118]

Speaking of their diet during a march or journey, Carpini said, 'when travelling, the Mongols do not eat in the morning: the one meal of the day is taken in the evening.'[119] 'Times out of number,' complained Rubruck 'we were hungered and athirst, cold and wearied. They only gave us food in the evening: in the morning we had something to drink or millet gruel, while in the evening they gave us meat, or shoulder and ribs of mutton, and some pot liquor.'[120] While marching against the Khwarazm Shah, Chingiz Khan ordered his men, one and all, to carry with them three dried sheep, some *Kumiz*, an iron cauldron for cooking purposes and one skin for water.[121] Like an avalanche they moved on, gathering momentum in their march; they were not handicapped by the necessity of establishing a base of supplies and guarding their lines of communication.

'Obey the *Yassa* and carry to an end any action you may begin,' the Great Conqueror advised his descendants.[122] Chingiz Khan laid it down as an unchanging law that a campaign should never be called off until the enemy had been brought to his knees. The commanders of the various tomans were given a fixed objective to achieve and attain, and under no conditions were they to be 'led off at a tangent' to waste their time and strength on alluring and unessential objectives, such as the enemy's capital. He correctly realized that Kushluk and Khwarazm Shah were more important than their capitals and citadels. Once they were put out of the way or capitulated, he could be assured of the surrender of their armies and the obedience of their subjects. 'When you have begun anything, you must, whatever happens, carry it through to a conclusion,' advised Chingiz Khan. 'You must never stop fighting until your enemy has been brought to his knees.' In his Khwarazmian campaign, for example, he left small detachments and garrisons to contain the well-fortified places while the main forces were concentrated on smashing the enemy forces and their spirit of resistance. The moment he came to know that the Khwarazm Shah was not inside, he lost all interest in Samarqand and Bokhara.

'Ability to defeat the enemy,' said Sun Tuzu, 'means taking the offensive'. Throughout the career of Chingiz Khan, we find a predilection for offensive action and it was only during the early stages of his life, when he was fighting just to save his skin and teeth, that he was on the defensive. Since offensive implies and secures initiative and the right to choose the time and place of action, it is no wonder that the Mongols were invariably at an advantage and victorious. Initiative and offensive action secured them strategic security by throwing the enemy on the defensive.

The aim of such a strategy has always been to lessen the possibility of resistance by the enemy and, therefore, the foundation of almost all the tactical and strategical combinations is to 'surprise' the enemy because it means creating a situation for which the enemy is not prepared. 'Mystify, mislead, surprise your enemy' advised the brilliant confederate general Stonewall Jackson. The Mongols were adept in delivering sudden and surprising blows and thereby attained some of their most notable victories. The feint by which he led his main army to cross the Great Wall took the Kins by surprise, and similarly, the Khwarazm Shah was, later, stunned by the sudden appearance of the Mongol in his rear.

'What else is war but a game of deception'. The Mongols believed more in gaining their objectives rather than the means employed. Ambushes, night attacks, stratagems and simulated retreats were usually craftily employed, to mislead, mystify and surprise the enemy. They did not believe in reckless daring and the unnecessary sacrifice of their men.

War means deception and forestalling the enemy and the Mongols employed all sorts of tricks and stratagems. Amongst the favourite tricks of the Mongols was that of sowing discord, dissension and suspicions in the enemy's ranks by sending bribes or by despatching treasonable letters[123] to officers and contriving to have them fall in the hands of their monarch or the commander-in-chief. Another favourite ruse was the trick of leaving a gate unwatched to allow the besieged to leave the town, and then the enemy was pursued and hunted down as at Bokhara. The stratagem by which the fortress of Volhoi was tricked and stormed was a masterpiece of cunning and craftiness. Ilu Burqan was removed by the Mongols in accordance with Chingiz Khan's dying advice in a manner scarcely consistent with the letter, and certainly opposed to the spirit, of the solemn word and promise of the Khan. The pretext on which the war with the Kin was resumed was feeble and unworthy of a hero. The surprise, which secured, later on, the easy conquest of the Sung Empire was designed with craftiness, if not with duplicity. When Subutai was beleaguered by the fighting mountaineers of Caucasus, and was in dire distress, he bought off the Kumans by false and treacherous promises. If the Georgians were defeated by trick, it was by stratagem that Subutai and Yamah Noyan contrived to get out of Derbend.[124]

The most amazing and perhaps the most effective element of their strategy was 'the first blow'—a deliberate and carefully thought out campaign of terror. 'It is by the fear which the reputation of your arms inspires that you maintain the fidelity of your allies and the obedience of conquered nations,' once remarked Napoleon.[125] It was part of their plan of campaign to strike 'awe and fear' into the hearts of their opponents. When they entered the enemy's territory, they rained death and destruction and converted the once-conspicuous scene of bustling, striving activity into a lost, forsaken darkness. 'Flaming houses, depopulated towns and smoking ruins marked their passage.'[126] The terrible news of how they massacred old men and children without compunction, 'violated' the women, burnt cities, razed the fortresses to the ground sent a paralyzing wave of panic and terror. 'So great was the dread that Allah put into all hearts,' says Ibnul Asir, 'things happened that are hard to believe. Someone told me that a Tartar rode alone into a village with many people, and set himself to kill them, one after the other, without a person daring to defend himself. I heard also that one Tatar, wishing to kill a prisoner of his and finding himself without a weapon, ordered his captive to lie down. He went to look for a sword, with which he killed the unfortunate one, who had not moved.'[127]The speed with which they moved and manoeuvred, their superior technique of warfare, their use of incendiaries, and the charge of cannibalism against them, all combined to make the credulous and superstitious people look upon them as of the tribe of Gog and Magog, devils incarnate, the Scourge of God against whom it was fruitless to contend. Slaughter of non-combatants, rape, rapine and even sodomy[128] were used to terrorize the enemy.[129]

There is a similar anecdote about Qazi Minhaj's escape from certain death on his way to India. He was fleeing with sixteen other persons during the war in Afghanistan. His caravan was stopped by a solitary Mongol horseman, who gave them a rope to tie one another's hands with it. The poor dispirited, awe-stricken refugees submissively carried out the command, and the horseman went to fetch a stone as he did not want to waste his valuable arrows. Qazi Minhaj, thereupon, urged them to untie their hands as he had managed to do his own. They refused saying that, if caught, they would be slain. The Qazi tried to argue that they should try to flee with him and, perhaps, they might have a better fate, but in vain! The Qazi, however, ran away and reached Sind to narrate the tale, and write out his invaluable *Tabaqat-i-Nasiri*. The lagers stayed behind and, perhaps, met the inevitable end.

Even before the 'fatal battle of Leighnitz (9 April 1241)' observed Brount, 'the terror inspired even in Western Europe was so great that the contemporary chronicler Mathew Paris, residing at St. Albans, records under the year AD 1238, that for fear of the Mongols, the fishermen of Gothland and Friesland dared not cross the North Sea to take part in the herring-fishing at Yarmouth, and consequently herrings were so cheap and abundant in England that year that forty or fifty were sold for a piece of silver, even at places far from the coasts.'[130]

As the operations of the Mongol armies extended over degrees of longitude and latitude, they always saw to it that the enemy never got an opportunity to thrust himself in between their far-flung columns and encounter them one after the other. The extreme mobility and the surprising speed of their cavalry corps enabled them to muster and join their troops at any threatened point and crush the unsuspecting foe. While, on the other hand, the detached column armies were given independent commands with fixed objectives and with orders to converge at a particular point. The plan was outlined for them but they were independent in their operations and, therefore, like Subutai and Yamah Noyan when they were ordered to hunt down the sultan,[131] they could, as Napoleon would put it, 'march without hesitation, and without new orders.'[132] 'It was wonderful', says Bury,[133] 'how punctually and effectually the arrangements of the commander were carried out in operations extending from the Lower Vistula to Transylvania. Such a campaign was quite beyond the power of any European army of the time; and it was beyond the vision of any European commander.'

On the battlefield[134] the army was usually divided into a fighting line, a supporting line, reserves behind them and detachments on the wings to turn the enemy's flank and also to protect that of their own army. Speaking of their tactics Marco Polo observed:

When they come to an engagement with the enemy, they will gain victory in this fashion. (They never let themselves get into a regular medley, but keep perpetually riding round and shooting into the enemy.) And as they do not count it any shame to run away in battle, they will (sometimes pretend to) do so, and in running away they turn in the saddle and shoot hard and strong at the foe, and in this way cause great havoc. Their horses are trained so perfectly that they will double hither and thither, just like a dog, in a way that is quite astonishing. Thus they fight to as good purpose in running away as if they stood and faced the enemy, because of the vast volleys of arrows that they shoot in this way, turning round upon their pursuers, who are fancying that they have won the battle. But when the Tartars see that they have killed and wounded a good many horses and men, they wheel round bodily, and return to the charge in perfect order and with loud cries; and in a very short time the enemy are routed. In truth they are stout and valiant soldiers, and inured to war. And you perceive that it is just when the enemy sees them run, and imagines that he has gained the battle, that he has in reality lost it; for the Tartars wheel round in a moment when they judge the right time has come.[135]

And very significantly, as Juwaini added,

Quite unlike is the position of the ruler of a Muslim country (of course, the Khwazam Shah), who talks with fear with his own purchased slave, rather possesses ten horse in his stake, lest some soil should result from it. If an army is placed under his command, and he attains to a position of authority, he simply cannot command it. And often it happened that the officer himself, he continues, rises in revolt (against his king or master), and whenever the king wishes to attack an enemy or an enemy wishes to attack, they take months and years to put the army in order and treasuries and territories are required for their salaries and pay.[136]

Herein, most probably, lay the fundamental and fatal weakness and vulnerability of the Khwarazm Shah against better organized and better disciplined 'hordes' of Chingiz Khan. Juwaini, perhaps mockingly, if not mournfully, recounts a parable which holds particularly true of their (Muslim armies) organization. 'At the time of realizing stakes, a revenue officer demanded a number of goats from a farmer. The farmer said "where from?" The officer answered "in the records". The farmer continued "yes, but there is none in the flock." The same is true of Muslim troops. The amir shows that he has such a number of men under him in order to receive more than the legitimate pay, but at the occasion of review, they practise deceit so as to make up the total.'

'Victory in war,' said Vegetius, 'does not depend entirely upon numbers or mere courage; only skill and discipline will ensure it.' And the discipline which Chingiz Khan enforced was that of blood and iron, unsurpassed in, and the wonder of his day. 'Such is their discipline,' says Juwaini, 'that if an amir commanding a hundred thousand men and so remote from the Khan as West is from East, commits a fault, the Khan sends a single horseman, who punishes him according to the Khan's order; if his head is required, it is cut off; if money has been demanded, it is realized.' So strict and severe was the discipline, and equity and justice, said Juwaini, were so enforced without consideration of 'outward status or position' that none, however, highly placed, even a Gurgan like Toghachar, was immune.[137] Capital punishment was laid down for those guilty of deserting their comrades or surrendering to the enemy while serious view was taken of acts of indiscipline such as taking to booty without orders or not keeping one's arms and armour in good condition.[138] Such discipline was necessary if the ambition of world-wide conquests was to be fulfilled. Napoleon observed:

No sovereign, no people, no general, can be secure, if officers are permitted to capitulate on the field and lay down their arms by virtue of an agreement favourable to themselves and to the troops under their command, but opposed to the interests of the remainder of the army. To withdraw from peril themselves; and thus render the position of their comrades more dangerous, is manifestly an act of baseness. Such conduct ought to be proscribed, pronounced infamous, and punishable with death. The generals, officers, and soldiers, who in a battle have saved their lives by capitulating, ought to be decimated. He who commands the arms to be surrendered and those who obey him are like traitors and deserve capital punishment.[139]

Chingiz Khan was equally firm and stringent against deserters. No man, reports Juwaini,[140] could desert his comrades nor could any person harbour such a deserter. The deserter was publicly executed while the person who sheltered him, was put under rack and torture.

The decisive element in their tactics was the *Tulughma* or envelopment. By means of their *Tulughma* movement they did not allow the enemy to recoil before their blows, which made an attack on the enemy more effective and decisive. With unfailing consistency the Mongols strove hard to apply the hammer and anvil principle. The double envelopment was applied with shattering effect on the banks of the Sajo.

Better armed and informed, the Mongol cavalry was always better able to manoeuvre while their attack was delivered with great speed. Napoleon remarked that the power of an attack depended upon its momentum—that is, speed plus mass. Thus, according to this dictum, the Mongol charges and counter-charges must have been very powerful.

'The secret of war', said Napoleon, 'is to march twelve leagues, fight a battle, and march twelve more in pursuit.' Once having gained an upper hand the Mongols never lost time in taking up the pursuit of the vanquished. Eastern Europe was laid low by the twin blows of Sajo and Leignitz only on account of the relentless pursuit. Chingiz Khan was not content with the victory he gained at the Battle of the Indus; he despatched Chaghatae and then Turbei Taqahi to hunt down Sultan Jalal-ud-din. Surprise, espionage, superior cavalry, and speed were always on the side of the Mongol battalions, and, thereby, the Mongols denied their opponents time and space to manoeuvre. Mobility, good communications, bold and resolute commanders enabled them to successfully carry out their operations covering thousands of miles. The rapidity of their movements denied their opponents the chance of striking any one of the converging Mongol armies hard while there was yet time and space to do so. This they achieved by advancing rapidly and by preventing the enemy from moving rapidly—and were able to do so by the disciplined cavalry; while they also achieved the second by blinding the enemy and paralyzing him. The enemy was blinded by the strategy of indirect approach and the movement of independent and parallel columns; he was paralysed by 'the First Blow'. Since the entire army consisted of cavalry, the invading forces were never in danger of outstripping their supporting columns, and thereby rendering their flanks vulnerable. By the rapidity of their movement and the character of their manoeuvres and tactics, the Mongols always concealed, and made up, their inferiority in numbers.

Moreover, the thirteenth century Mongols formed the most brilliant troops of the day. Their superiority arose from natural causes. Trained from infancy to war-like exercises, and following no profession but that of arms; their only pecuniary resources arose from the plunder of their neighbours; their habits of life, the celerity of their movements and the excellence of their armour and discipline, rendered them the choicest troops of their age, perhaps the best cavalry of all times.

Boulger[141] has admirably summed up the causes of the success of the Mongol army against one and all as follows:

The Mongols owed their military success to their admirable discipline and to their close study of the art of war. Their military supremacy arose from their superiority in all essentials as a fighting power to their neighbours (and other opponents, too). Much of their knowledge was borrowed from China, where the art of disciplining a large army and manoeuvering it in the field had been brought to a high state of perfection many centuries before the time of Genghis (Chingiz Khan). But the Mongols carried the teaching of the past to a further point than any of the former or contemporary Chinese commanders induced, than any in the whole world had done; and the revolution which they effected in tactics was not less remarkable in itself, and did not leave a smaller impression upon the age, than the improvements made in military science by Frederick the Great, and Napolean in their day. The Mongol played in a large way in Asia the part which the Normans on a smaller scale played in Europe. Although the landmarks of their triumph have now almost entirely vanished, they were for two centuries the dominant caste in most of the states of Asia.

The following lines from James Elroy Flecker's play *Hassan* partially described the march by the Mongol warriors:

We are they who come faster than fate; we are they who ride early or late;
We storm at your ivory gate; Pale kings of the sunset beware;
Not on silk nor in *samet* we lie, not in curtained solemnity die
Among women who chatter and cry and children who mumble a prayer.
But we sleep by the ropes of the camp, and we rise with a shout and we tramp.
With the sun or the moon for a lamp, and the spray of the wind in our hair.
Our steel we have brought and our star to shine on the ruins of Ghor, Ghaznin and Gharjistan.
We have marched from Volhoi to the Caspian, from the Indus to the Volga, and by Tengri we will go there again;
We have stood on the shore of the plain where the Waters of Destiny boom.
A mart of destruction we made at Nisabur and the Sajo from the inner stock volga, where men were afraid.
For death was a difficult trade, and the sword was a broker of doom,
And the spear was a Desert Physician, who cured not a few of ambition.
And drove not a few to perdition with medicine bitter and strong.
And the shield was a grief to the fool and as bright as a desolate pool.
And as straight as the rock of Stamboul when their cavalry thundered along;
For the coward was drowned with the brave when our battle sheered up like a wave.
And the dead to the desert we gave, and the glory to Tengri in our song.[142]

The Statesman

By his marvellous and impressive conquests, Chingiz and his generals had been able to bring under unified control some of the nations of the East and the West and unite almost the entire civilized world into one empire. In the brief span of two generations, Persia, Iraq, China, Central Asia, a large part of modern Russia and Austria-Hungary were theirs; while they also threatened Central and Western Europe and even Egypt. Thus holding together the ancient Celestial Empire of China and the whole of the Saracen Empire minus Asia Minor, North Africa and Spain, they ruled over a heterogeneous collection of races and religion (Map 5).

By right of conquest and by the old Turkish traditions of the old monarchies it had submerged and subjugated, the Mongol Empire was a despotism based upon and limited by the Great *Yassa* (also written Yasa, Yassak meaning Supreme Law of the Land). The authority of the Great Khan or the Qaan was limited by the *Yassa*, which was above and beyond him. He might contravene or circumvent it by doubtful interpretations but he could not straight away transgress its provisions. The *Yassa* shared with him the respect and devotion of his Mongol subjects. 'Written on leaves and preserved in the treasury of the principal members of the dynasty', says Juwaini,[143] 'it was consulted on the occasion of the election of a new Khan, on the despatch of a large army, and on the convocation of the Qurlitai to deliberate on affairs of state, and the matters were decided according to its contents.' Its observance was obligatory not only on his Mongol subjects but even upon the Khan himself and the members of the imperial family. The Great *Yassa* or the Regulations of Chingiz Khan may be compared to a written and rigid constitution, incapable of amendment. It was designed and supposed to regulate for all times to come the problems and destinies of the Mongol Empire. Only slightly susceptible to change and amendment by means of interpretation, it was as rigid a constitution as can ever be conceived.

Besides the *Yassa*, the prevalence and presence of deep-seated prejudices and deep-rooted ancient customs, together with the conservatism of the illiterate masses further acted as effective brakes and checked the arbitrary exercise of the Khan's despotic power.

The Mongol empire consisted of the homelands of the Mongols, directly and immediately administered by the Great Khan, a number of appanages[144] belonging to the sons and descendants of Chingiz Khan, enjoying almost complete autonomy but owning allegiance to the Khan at Qaraqorum. These were joined together by ties of blood and marriage; and tributary provinces

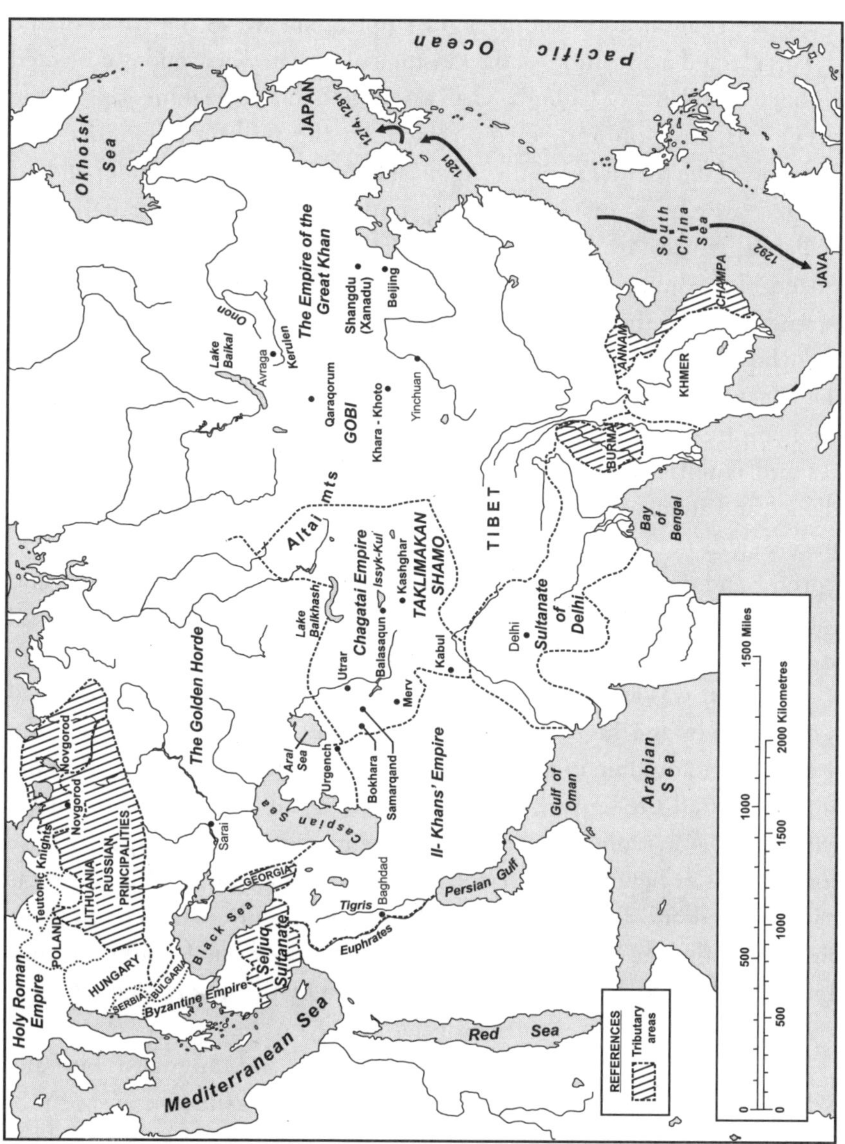

Map 5. The Height of Empire, 1290

and vassal states possessing their own rulers and like the former Indian States, enjoying internal sovereignty. Beyond and outside the frontiers of the empire, were lands and countries which it was the duty and mission of the Mongols to subdue and conquer.

The supreme head of the Mongol empire, known as the Khan or the Qaan, was elected from amongst the kinsmen of the late Khan and was elected by all the descendants of Chingiz Khan assembled in a special meeting of the Qurlitai. His position and power rested on the willing allegiance and cooperation of the members of the imperial family, who ruled as independent sovereigns over their distant appanages and principalities. Actually and immediately, it rested upon his control of the Mongol homelands and the command of the 'pure' Mongol army. His authority was further supported and strengthened by their old traditions of loyalty and obedience to the elected leader, who led them in times of war and fed them during the days of peace. As the successor of Chingiz Khan, he was the symbol of the unity of the Mongol empire and the buckle which united the Mongols spread over many climes and countries; and as such, he claimed and received the absolute obedience and allegiance of all the Mongols.[145] Supreme head of the Mongol commonwealth and empire, the Great Khan was their leader in war and peace, interpreter and executor of the *Yassa* of Chingiz Khan while his Muslim and Christian subjects looked upon him as their lawful ruler, who was imposed upon them by the wrath of God as a punishment for their sins.

The Qaan was an elected but irresponsible head of the State. Limited and supported by the *Yassa*,[146] the powers and the prerogatives of the Qaan were extensive. Fountain of law, justice and honour, he was also the supreme commander of all the empire forces. Fountain of all authority in the state, the ruler of Qaraqorum was not a mere figure-head but a despot, whose authority, (like in Egypt), penetrated the hearths and homes of his subjects and was obeyed and feared throughout the nooks and corners of the vast empire. Even the Yarlighs and the orders of the previous Khans were not binding upon him, and were in practice revoked by the newly elected Khan if they were found in contravention of the *Yassa*.[147]

The powers of the Great Khan, however, were not unlimited. Literally a despot, in practice he was hemmed in by the customs and conservatism of his people, the laws of his subjects, and, above all, by the Great *Yassa*, which did not confer on him the powers of a legislator.

The *Yassa* or the Regulations of Chingiz Khan were like the Twelve Tables, which merely simplified and codified the existing and well-established usages and customs and raised them to the dignity and status of law. More than that, since the *Yassa* was believed to be heavenly inspired and promulgated by Chingiz Khan, it enjoyed the superstitious reverence of the credulous and believing Mongols. The *Yassa* goes beyond present day conceptions and scope of positive law: it was the sacred law of the Mongols and claimed to govern all the various aspects of their life. It sought to regulate their daily life and was believed to provide them precepts and guidance on all the problems of life. Though the whole of the *Yassa* has not come down to us, but from the fragments which have survived one finds that the *Yassa* attempted to provide the Mongols with a complete code of life.[148] From such important matters of state as the election of the Great Khan and the conduct of foreign wars down to the mode of cattle slaughter and the washing of clothes, nothing was too trivial or sacred to be left out. In short, it sought to regulate their social, economic, and even ethical life.

Having only a nomad's conception of property, Chingiz Khan divided his whole realm and bestowed it on his sons and relations—the latter coming under the control of the former,[149] and these appanages of his four sons were so many autonomous principalities and, like the British Dominions, united by ties of blood and professed allegiance to the elected Khan, who was also the head of the ruling family.[150] But in respect of their internal administration and even foreign affairs they were free from central interference or control. They paid no tribute to the Khan at Qaraqorum, and had their own separate and independent standing armies. There was thus no relationship of an overlord and a feudatory. Neither unitary nor feudal, the Mongol empire closely resembled a 'family corporation'[151] and joint ownership system of the Hindus and to a great extent the Shansbaniah kingdom of Ghaznin and Ghor. 'There are two eyes in the head,' remarked Mangu explaining his relationship with Batu; 'but though they be two, they have but one sight; and when one turns its glance there goes the other.'[152] Such was actually the relationship between the Great Khan and the appanaged rulers in the times of Uktae and Mangu. Among them kinship[153] seemed to know no kingship. 'It is indispensable', Chingiz Khan had observed, 'that one of them should be constituted King and all the rest of his sons and relations should be obedient to him, and serve him with one heart and accord so that quarrels might not arise among them and, in consequence of such quarrels, their enemies overcome them. For, although the *title of King would be confined to an individual yet in fact all his sons and relations were partners and participators in the possession of the country and its wealth.*'[154] (Italics added) The appanaged rulers were like so many important members of a great 'family corporation', who were free to do as they liked with their possessions but who were expected and obliged to respect and carry out the wishes and commands of the head of the family, who was in charge of the patrimony—the Ordu Baligh. In spite of their worldwide conquests and imperial ambitions, the Mongols of the early thirteenth century could not emerge from the nomadic conception of law and property.

The vassal princes and chiefs were doubly subordinate to the Great Khan and the appanaged ruler to whom they were responsible for the peaceful administration of their states, the payment of taxes, the tithes of furs, beasts, men, gold and coined money. Like the British sovereign in his relation with Indian States before 1947, the Mongol chief had nothing to do with the internal and routine administration of the vassal states nor was he concerned with the welfare of their peoples. He, however, decided their family disputes and settled the order of succession. The princes had to obtain the approval and charter of government from the Mongol chief. In times of war, they were called upon to furnish contingents for active service. Normally, they acted as they pleased without any let or hindrance by the paramount power, which interfered only in cases of gross oppression and injustice, as in the case of the Idiqut of the Uighurs in the time of Mangu Qaan. A Mongol Shahna or agent lived at their court, who must have, like the British Residents in the former Indian States, exercised a considerable, sometimes overbearing influence on their administration and policy.

The Mongol empire had no hereditary nobility, with the solitary exception of the *Tarkhans*. Every one was 'his own ancestry'. Office and public services alone conferred rights and privileges. The Mongol nobility, such as existed, was only personal and official. Though the descendants of Chingiz Khan constituted the *Altan Uruq* or the Golden Family, from amongst whom alone could be elected the Great Khan of the Mongol commonwealth and empire; they could not as such aspire to and achieve key posts and offices of honour. Whatever privileges they enjoyed on the mere score of their birth and position were like those of the French nobility of the *Ancient Regime*, only social. Even the privileges of the *Tarkhans*, enviable and extensive as they were, could not be inherited beyond nine generations. This lack of hereditary nobility accounts for the durability of the Mongol empire, and the fact that it did not suffer the fate of that of Charlemagne or of the Seljuqs. Since honour and privilege depended upon the individual's service and merit, it furnished the empire with a constantly increasing stream of devoted, ambitious and efficient workers and warriors. Besides, it prevented any group or family from monopolising property and power.

The Law Giver

Chingiz Khan was, however, not merely a conqueror, who had a mania for bloodshed nor was he a chieftain, even a conqueror, who raided and looted for the subsistence and survival of his people. His conquests were also not motivated, like those of Tamerlane, for the love of his homeland and the beautification of his capital/*yurt*; nor were they achieved in a fit of absent-mindedness. It was, perhaps, in the cauldron of captivity that he could have dreamt of not merely a day of deliverance but also a heaven of leisure and pleasure for himself. As victory after victory justified the saying that 'there is a blessing in his arms and a crown over head' and steady accretion of strength, power, and status followed, his mind and vision would have, become wiser and progressively better able to constrictively imagine, think, and plan a better future for himself and a secure inheritance, for his children.

Chingiz Khan would have felt the absence of a law and a law-giver, along with the absence of a law-enforcing authority, and instead sought its remedy or solution in the establishment of a polity based upon law administered by a supreme authority: the *yassa,* and a supreme Ruler: The Khan.

The *yassa* was, in a sense perhaps the most valuable and ineffaceable contribution that Chingiz Khan could make for the well-being of the Mongol people and for the better management of the Mongol polity. Unlike the contemporary monarchs and chiefs he had a firm will, strong sense of duty and justice, and was exceptionally stern in the enforcement of rules and regulations, particularly the administration of justice. And, by all accounts, the mongol domains were different from the kingdoms and dukedoms of the times, as Chingiz Khan showed no favour or partiality towards anyone in matters of justice, even if the culprit concerned could be one of his confidants, relations, or even his highly trustworthy companions. For as he wrote to the Taoist Monk, no work was 'noble and great' as the 'task of well-governed'. He could also add that no task is harder and more exacting or, as Harold Laski was to put it seven centuries later, that the test for the nature and excellence of a state is the quality of justice it administers. And it was, probably, with reference to his quest for good governance and the humility and the spirit of sincerity permeating the great Khan's invitation, that induced the aged and reluctant monk to undertake the arduous journey of thousands of miles from Peking to Samarqand and then to the Hindukush mountains, where the Khan was then camping. That the Khan was serious about his desire for the welfare and good governance of the people is borne out by his requests to the monk to delay his departure on account of his sons' delayed arrival, and to favour them with the benefit of his learning, experience, and saintly advice so that, after he was gone, they could carry on the tradition and policy of 'good governance for the people'.

A kingdom may be conquered but cannot be governed from horseback, and no conqueror was, perhaps, more alive to the wisdom of this adage than Chingiz Khan. Mere conquest was not his aim; he wanted to found a dynasty which should last for a good length of time. For the stability of the 'new order', the first and foremost requisite was sound organization and efficient administration. It was essential that tribal warfare should cease, the brave fighters of the steppes should be moulded and welded into one solid 'nation of archers' on horseback; there should be no more expeditions for loot and captives, and law and order should prevail throughout the dominions of the Khan so that, as the Persian chroniclers would put it, '*a virgin carrying a sack of gold could ride unharmed from one border of the Mongol Empire to the other*'. It was not an easy task; the odds were heavily loaded against Chingiz. Born and bred among the ignorant and illiterate nomads of the Gobi, who had no alphabet of their own, he had, unlike Alexander and Justinian, neither the philosophers of Greece nor the jurist of Rome to aid and advise him in his stupendous venture nor, unlike Alfred and Charlemagne, had he any glorious and hoary past to derive his principles and laws from. He was a simple and terrible nomad, and he remained a nomad chieftain to the last, knowing and learning no language but his mothertongue. Cities and city life did not appeal to him, and, though conqueror of two civilizations, he was not in the least, affected or attracted by them.

He was, however, a hard-headed nomad, resilient and intelligent, a keen observer of men and the rough and tough tumble of life around him and, at the same time endowed with a cool, calm and calculating mind, extraordinary common sense, and sagacity to an uncommon degree. Born with no silver spoon in the mouth but a clot of blood in his clenched fist, Chingiz Khan had to learn the art of politics and the science of government the hardest way possible: initially through the struggle for survival, followed by the struggle for power, and, finally, the struggle for supremacy in his land of birth, and, ultimately, overlordship from the Great Wall of China to the Caspian Sea, and from the Athai Mountains to the Hindukush mountains and the Basin of the Indus. Incredibly tough and incomparable was this achievement, still greater and, perhaps, more important was the problem that confronted the Great Conqueror, namely, holding together and governing the vast empire and its overwhelming huge population as one unit in spite of all kinds of imaginable differences such as languages, cultures, customs, creeds, class structures, history and geography.

Chingiz Khan was, however, no ordinary person, or merely a soldier of fortune in search of 'fresh fields and pastures new' or campaigning only for 'booty and beauty'. He was a man made of a different and finer mettle. Gifted with an extraordinary personality, he had graduated through his struggles into a cool and calculating practitioner of the game of politics, that is, *realpolitic*, and may be said to have been a precursor of some of the great 'makers of modern Europe', namely, Napoleon, Metternich, Bismarck, Cavour and Garibaldi! He used his charisma and magnetism to gather around himself devoted and gifted companions and followers to 'aid and advise' him not only for the intelligent and efficient organization of the Mongols as a 'people in arms' and the skilful use of fear and awe' to win an empire for himself but also to hold it together as an entity through law and justice, that is, the *Yassa* and discipline. This stupendous feat was not achieved for his own greatness or glory but was in pursuance of his dream-wish to assert the stability of his conquered domains and to leave his descendants an extensive, safe and secure empire. For, as he himself declared, that he had won the empire for his mother and family.

It is hardly necessary to emphasize that Chingiz Khan was not the first nor the last conqueror who sought to bequeath his conquered domains to his descendants. Even Napoleon, the 'son' and great hero of the French Revolution desired to found a dynasty and, for the sake of an heir to the throne, married a second time after divorcing, as he confessed, his 'good fortune', namely, his first wife. The 'Divine Right of those in authority' was generally accepted, and, as indicated previously, Chingiz Khan had exploited the Shaman Tengri to strengthen his hold over the credulous Mongols as their leader 'chosen' by Tengri. The old Aristotelian maxim that 'some are born to rule and some to be ruled' was the generally accepted political norm in the Middle Ages, and even survived until quite recent times. It is, therefore, neither strange nor surprising that Chingiz Khan sought to organise the empire and secure legitimacy for his dynasty's continuance and permanence through law and justice.

The prime purpose or object of the *Yassa* was thus, the preservation of the Mongol empire and polity and was, therefore, mainly concerned with such problems as the organization and mobilization of the army, military operations, destruction of towns and cities, and subjugation of empires and kingdoms. It was in this context that capital punishment was enacted for deserters and spies. Death penalty was also enacted for theft and adultery, but not for adultery outside the tribe, probably, for the safety and tranquility in the family and among the tribesmen. The *Yassa* prescribed religious tolerance and exemption of the clergy and saintly persons of all faiths, but it also forbade the slaughter of cattle in the Muslim fashion, bathing and washing of hands and utensils in rivers and streams (as the Mongols believed them to be 'alive' and sacred).

The *Yassa* was, however, neither written down nor dictated on a particular date. Comprising the *Biliks* (sayings), the *Yarliks* (decrees/decisions) and *Yassas* (commands/ordinances) of the Khan; it was recorded on occasions requiring the Khan's intervention. Shigi Qutugu's decisions (civil and criminal) approved by the Khan were also decreed to have the same legal validity as the *Biliks* and *Yassas* of the Khan himself.

The *Yassa*, therefore, could be considered an attempt to immortalize the Khan and his legacy, to provide solid foundations for the empire founded by him, to educate his descendants in the art and science of not merely acquisition and maintenance of power but also of good governance; power to meet challenges, both internal and external to authority and imperial rule, good governance or the welfare of the people through impartial enforcement of law and order, proper maintenance of the trade and travel routes. The *Yassa* was, therefore, much more than a mere code of law. It was applicable and valid in a number of situations or contexts other than judicial. It was a curious mixture of Mongol customs, customary law and even Mongol superstitions and taboos, with some later interpolations such as the Christian beliefs and teachings to love one's neighbour as oneself or to do no evil, tax exemption for the descendants of Ali, the son-in-law of the Prophet Muhammad, lawyers, etc. The *Yassa* does not seem to have mentioned compensation for murder, any new law for the abduction of women or for murder; perhaps, as Juwaini observed, he 'laid down laws which he deemed necessary', and as the complete text has not come down to us.

Quick learner that he was, Chingiz Khan not merely 'wished' but also took precautions and steps necessary for the continuity and perpetuity of his dynastic rule. History shows that the sons/descendants of one and the same parents do not inherit their qualities to the same extent and in measure, as has been prominently exhibited in the lives, careers and achievement of great men, philosophers, scientists, saints, conquerors and rulers. Chingiz Khan was no exception to the general rule, as he discovered that none of his sons was like him though each one was distinguished: Juji (hunt), Chaghatae (discipline), Uktae (conciliation) and Tuli (generalship). Though he consulted them all in regard to his successor, he nominated Uktae as his choice but made it contingent upon his election by the Qurlitai or General Assembly of his family members. Departing from the tribal tradition of heredity and primogeniture, Chingiz Khan further decreed by his *Yassa* that the Great Khan was to be elected by the Qurlitai or the General Assembly comprising all his descendants so as the most suitable and the best from amongst them should hold the reins of the worldwide empire.

The *Yassa*, as it has come down to us, does not measure up to our concepts of a code of law much less a guidebook for good governance or a constitutional document defining the rights and duties of the citizen, and the distribution and exercise of power in a pluralistic empire. While it would not be fair to talk about such loopholes and shortcomings in a document, (which has been lost though said to have been bound in three volumes), the scattered bits that have come down to us can serve as samples of what the '*Yassa* of Chingiz Khan' could have been. The elected Khan was, however, bound by the *Yassa* and had no power to amend or override it. He was more or less an aristocrat similar to many elected prime ministers and presidents of modern times. There were, however, two practical limitations; trials as well as political proceedings were to be held in public, and the Khan had to take notice of the general feeling of his subjects, advisors and ministers.

The *Yassa* (the Law) was, and had to be, therefore framed and designed to organise the empire on a new basis quite different from the earlier and traditional nomadic practice of tribal leagues and to unite and weld the different and differing tribes into one people, or rather into one single tribe, the Mongols, subject to only one chief or Khan, namely, Chingiz Khan (and after him, his descendants). There were to be no divided or diluted loyalties as under European feudalism or later on, the semi-feudal Mansabdari system of the Great Mughals of India. Everyone knew and had to accept the fact that he owed his position and assignment in accordance with the will and command of the sovereign chief. The process began in 1201 when, on accepting the Khanship, Chingiz had exacted an oath of obedience and fealty from the tribal chiefs that they would obey and carry out unquestioningly all his orders and commands even if they were required to behead a son or a father, in Tennyson's words, 'Theirs to do and die, not to question why?' According to the testimony of chroniclers and travellers, the strictest discipline was actually enforced irrespective of the status, high or low, of the errant involved, which ensured peace and order and enormous safety and security on transit and trade routes.

The *Yassa* was a selective amalgam of the old Mongol customs, practices, common law and even taboos and superstitions, and of new norms, rules and regulations to help the Mongols adapt to the needs and requirements of the new political order created by the Great Khan's conquests and the consequent new responsibilities assumed for the governance of the far-flung empire. It was also motivated by the desire of the Great Khan to consolidate the hard-won domains and the empire for his descendants for generations and may be, as reported by Rashid-ud-din, 'for thousands of years'.

The *Yassa* was neither a systematic nor a comprehensive document. It was rather the appellation ascribed by the son and successor of the Great Khan, Qaan Uktae to the compendium comprising the laws, commands, orders and decrees pronounced, rules and regulations prescribed, even sayings and precepts pertaining to a good and healthy life of the individual, family and the polity, which Chingiz Khan had pronounced from time to time as required by the circumstances. They were written down on scrolls in Uighur script, bound in volumes and kept in the State archives. They were known and available to senior members of the ruling family and consulted on important occasions such as war and peace, diplomatic relations, the meetings of the Qurlitai and election of the Qaan. It was Utkae who promulgated the compendium as the *Yassa* of Chingiz. The *Secret History of the Mongols* makes no mention of the *Yassa* though other Chinese sources refer to it as the *Great Yassa*. Juwaini, however, refers it as the *Yassai Naimai Buzurg* or *The Great Book of the Yassa*s (laws, etc.).

Rashid-ud-din, however, devotes one chapter of his history under the heading of *Biliks* (sayings of the Khan) and *Hukumuhai* (orders/decrees of the Khan) with incidental references to *Yassaq* (law). The chapter details innumerable sayings of Chingiz Khan ranging from household management and evil effects of alcoholism to details for the reform, rehabilitation, admonition and, finally, the trial and punishment of the incorrigible errant member of the royal family, and warning against deviation from, and dereliction in the observation, much less transgression against the *Yassa* lest their dominion should go to pieces and their rule come to an inglorious end. From Rashid-ud-din's account it seems reasonable to assume as suggested by Paul Retchnevsky, that there were two separate collections, not one, of the *Yassa*s (laws), *Yarliks* (orders and decrees) and *Biliks* (sayings) including the decrees and judgments pronounced by Shiqi Qutuqu as the chief judge and approved by Chingiz Khan, one exclusively for the members of the ruling family and the other for general use, consisting of sayings and precepts.

However, some of the outstanding Mongolists hold contrary and divergent views about the existence of the *Yassa* of Chingiz Khan as a code of law. In this academic debate David Ayalon, Rachewiltz and Ratchnesty are ranged against David Morgan, Reruin Amitai and Robert Irwin. With no claims to be a Mongolist, one can only observe that, according to Persian sources, there is no mention of a *Yassa* of Chingiz Khan but only *Yassa*s and that Uktae and Kuyuk speak only of *Yassas* and not of a *Yassa* (Code of Law). 'In his wisdom', says Juwaini, 'he made a law for every matter, a regulation for every affair and prescribed a penalty for every offence.'[155]

That the '*Yassas*' were written in Uighur script or that they were not formally published did not matter much as the Mongols were generally illiterate, had no script of their own, and, more importantly, the *Yassa* did not materially affect them; it left untouched their traditions, customs and practices concerning family and inheritance, property and debt. The *Yassa* seems to have been primarily meant for the Mongols and also left untouched the private laws and customs of the subjects as well as their local administration. The *Yassa* was, however, specific and stringent in matters concerning public order and peace, safety of roads, trade and travel traffic, even Mongol taboos and superstitions (detailed later) even overriding the religious sensitivities, and susceptibilities of Muslims regarding slaughter of cattle and washing of clothes and bathing in running water, and of Christians regarding Levitate marriage.

The *Yassa*, however, does not refer to abduction, adultery outside the tribe or compensation for homicide though it provides for dealing with cases concerning stray cattle and lost baggage. For, as Juwaini, remarks, the Khan 'laid down laws which he concluded necessary.'

The *Yassa* of Chingiz Khan exhibits a deep knowledge of political science, military art and penetrating insight into the problems and needs of a nomadic people. The *Yassa* was held in esteem and observed by no less a conqueror than Tamerlane while the precepts and principles of Chingiz Khan were adopted and acknowledged by several mighty monarchs. 'My forefathers and family', said Babur, 'had always sacredly observed the Rules of Chingiz. In their parties, in their courts, their festivals, and their entertainments, in their sitting down, and in their rising up, they never acted contrary to the Institutions of Chingiz.'[156]

As the fundamental law of the Mongols, the *Yassa* required the head of the empire to be elected from amongst the descendants of Chingiz Khan by a specially summoned Assembly or Qurlitai of the princes of the royal blood and the high officers of the State.[157] The *Yassa* required implicit obedience to the orders of the Khan.[158] No empty and ceremonious titles were affixed or suffixed to the name of the Khan. 'Khan' or 'Qaan' was the only word which was added to the ordinary appellation of the newly elected Khan. 'Besides this one word', says Juwaini, 'they had no other title to his name. His sons and brothers continue to be addressed by their ordinary and common names. In their presence and in their absence, in private and in public and in the written Royal orders, they are addressed by the same appellation. They make no distinction (in addressing) sultans and commoners; they write briefly and to the point; and they avoid unnecessary titles and unnecessary writing.' Chingiz Khan, thus, discarded the practices and traditions of the older monarchies, pompous and haughty and completely aloof from their subjects.

On the death of a 'Khan' there was to be necessarily an interregnum before the Qurlitai could meet and elect the new head of the empire. During this period the mother of the late Khan's eldest son ruled as regent. Again, the youngest son by the senior wife was to inherit the Khan's hearth and ancestral property.

Another innovation, introduced by Chingiz, was that he insisted on royal proclamations being concise and clear. 'In the proclamations which he used to send in various territories, calling upon them to tender obedience and homage,' says Juwaini, 'he never used terrifying words or threatened with extreme penalties as had been the practice of the tyrants who (always) referred to the strength of their troops and followers. "If you do not obey and surrender," he simply wrote, "we do not know what will befall you; immortal God alone knows."[159] He was bitter against the use of unnecessary writing and the string of high-sounding words as the Katib of the Khwarazm Shah found to his cost.[160] The Katib had deserted the Shah and Chingiz Khan was pleased to have an experienced and cultured person in his service, especially for handling his correspondence. When Yamah Noyan had conquered Azerbaijan and wished to move on to Syria via Mosul, Chingiz instructed the Katib to draft a letter to Badr-ud-din, Amir of Mosul, to give passage to the Mongol troops. 'The Almighty God has bestowed the government of the earth on us and our clan,' dictated Chingiz. 'Whosoever submits and gives passage to our troops, prospers. His life and property, his country and his family remain with him. But whosoever dares to defy and disobey us, his fate God alone knows: he perishes. If Badr-ud-din yields and submits, he would receive our benefactions. If, however, he acts otherwise, when our formidable forces arrive and appear, Mosul would cease to exist on the face of the earth.' The Katib drafted the letter in accordance with the traditional etiquette and in ornate style. When Danishmand Hajib interpreted the letter to Chingiz Khan in Mongol, his ire was kindled as it did not conform to the brief and brusque message which he had dictated. 'This is not the letter which I dictated,' thundered the Khan. 'But', replied the tactless Katib, 'this is the way such letters are and should be written'. 'Thou art in sympathy with the rebel and has written a letter which would increase his resistance,' shouted the enraged Khan and ordered him to be put to death.

Chingiz was a typical nomad chieftain and fully shared the tastes of his people. He was one with them in his preference for the untrammelled, though hard, life of the steppes as against the easy but effeminate life of the towns. It was, however, not through blind prejudice or passion that he preferred the life of the steppes or prescribed a nomadic life for his people: 'always to wander, never to remain settled'. The wise Tun Yu Ku had said six or seven centuries age:

The Turkish population is small, not one hundredth part of China's, and the only reason we have ever been able to cope with her is that we are all nomads, carrying our supplies with us on our own legs, and all of us versed in the arts of war. When we can, we plunder; when we cannot, we hide away where no Chinese army can get at us. If we begin to build towns and change our old habits of life, we shall some fine day find ourselves annexed altogether. Moreover the very essence of monasteries and temples is the inculcation of mildness of character, but it is only the fierce and the warlike who dominate mankind.[161]

The Mongols loved the life of the steppes and it was probably on this account that Chaghatae, in preference to the historic towns of Samarqand and Bokhara, made Almaligh his capital.[162]

The twin principles of religious toleration and secularism in politics were especially emphasized by the *Yassa*. The Mongols were no less catholic in their outlook than their great leader. Himself attached to no religion, Chingiz Khan showed equal respect and deference to the learned and devout men of all religions. He refrained not only from religious intolerance but, as Juwaini says, 'from inclining towards any creed and from preferring one religion to another.'[163] Not only that, the learned divines of all religions were also exempt from the payment of taxes. 'The Catholic inquisitors of Europe', said Gibbons, 'who defended nonsense by cruelty, might have been confounded by the example of a barbarian, who anticipated the lessons of philosophy and established by his laws a system of pure theism and perfect toleration....In the mosque of Bochara (Bokhara), the insolent victor might trample the Koran under his horse's feet, but the calm legislator respected the prophets and pontiffs of the most hostile sects.'[164] The *Yassa* enjoined, and the descendants of Chingiz Khan did not, but for aberrations by some of his descendants, particularly Kuyuk, Abaqa and Qubilai, deviate from, the principle of religious toleration:[165] to treat their subjects alike and to show no preference for the followers of any religion at the expense of the others. As Vambery observes:

Amidst the terrible ravages committed by the Mongolians, the science of theology and its votaries alone continued to flourish. In the days of the earlier Chaghatay Khans the Mullas of Turkestan had enjoyed a certain amount of protection, thanks partly to the principle of religious toleration, and partly to the superstitious awe in which every class of the priesthood was held; and in almost every town there was some one or other holy man to whom the Moslems had recourse in the day of peril. The spiritual teachers thus became at the same time secular protectors, and from this time forward we find the *Sadr-i-Shariat* (heads of the religious bodies) and chief magistrates, and in general all men of remarkable piety, attaining an influence in the towns of Transoxiana unknown in the rest of Islam, an influence which maintains itself to this day, though the land has been for centuries governed by Musulman princes.[166]

The Mongols were an army before they became an empire and the *Yassa* organized them along military lines. Every man had his place and station fixed—with the men of his 'ten', 'hundred', 'thousand' and the toman. No man could desert his comrades and his station nor could any one, not even a noyan or prince of royal blood, dare, shelter and harbour him. To right and left, as the children of Israel had their appointed places about the Tabernacle, the tribes had their fixed stations in peace and war, in camp and court.[167] The amirs (officers and commanders) of the troops were appointed by the Khan and he had personal contact with and control of officers. The amir was expected to be a god of war and to behave accordingly. He was to be a father to his soldiers, considerate and kind to them, attentive to their needs and economical in the use of manpower.[168]

The *Yassa* laid down as an unchanging law of war that no quarter was to be given to those who offered resistance; the wholesale and horrible devastation, in the words of Juwaini, 'right from the borders of Turkestan down to the remote corners of Syria', was nothing but the ruthless application of the same principle. The *Yassa* exhorted them to be as ruthless with their enemies as it advised them to be peaceful and friendly amongst themselves:[169] to behave like trained lions during a hunt and during the days of peace to be as docile and useful as sheep. The great conqueror further cautioned his descendants against half-hearted measures in dealing with rebels and enemies: 'obey the *Yassa* and carry to an end any action you may begin.'[170] The *Yassa* also regulated the disposal of booty acquired in a battle. None was permitted to plunder the enemy without the express permission of the commander and the booty acquired after victory was distributed equally; an exception, however, was made in the case of Tarkhans who could retain their booty.[171]

The *Yassa* regulated not only the public and martial life of the nomads but also sought to give them a code of morality to govern and guide them in their daily lives. It is pleasing and refreshing to find the *Yassa* embodying and enjoining such homely precepts[172] as that the young should be attentive to what their elders say, or that they should not express their views unless their elders and superiors had spoken, or that the young should not insult the elders. Besides, the *Yassa* acknowledged and emphasized the role women have in the life of their menfolk no less than the life of the nation.[173] 'A man is judged by his wife,' said Chingiz Khan and the *Yassa* required women to be so trained as to assist their husbands in all tasks. As mistress of the house, it was the function and duty of the wife to uphold the name and fame of her husband, to keep the yurt well, and to entertain the couriers and the travelling Noyans, if and when they happened to call for a halt at night. The women were dutiful partners of their menfolk; if a man, for example, required for forced labour was absent, his wife would come forward and perform his task.[174] The importance of the yurt and family life was recognized by the maxim that a man is judged by his household.[175]

The Mongols were fond of the chase and the foray, which were quite in harmony with the needs and mode of their primitive economy. The foray was, however, interdicted by the *Yassa* as it was inconsistent with the new order of things in and beyond the steppes; but the chase was retained as the safety valve for the exuberant energy of the wary sons of the desert. Chingiz had the sagacity to fathom the potentialities of the chase in the military training of the Mongols. The *Yassa*, accordingly, changed the nature of the chase; it was so governed and regulated as to exercise the troops in horsemanship and archery, and teach them to be steady and cautious in the field of battle.

As the territories of Chingiz Khan became very extensive, immediate and constant communication with them became imperative and indispensable. To remain in touch with his far-flung outposts, Chingiz instituted and organized the Yam or the horse-post service. Relays of horses were stationed at different places and the *Yassa* provided for their proper maintenance and regular inspection.

'According to another *Yassa*', says Juwaini, 'the most beautiful girls in the army (i.e. captured girls) are selected. The Amirs of the Ten forward them to the Amirs of the Hundred, everyone handing them over to his superior officers till the Amir of the Tuman, after selection, takes them to the Khan or the *Shahzadas*. Here they are sorted again, those who are considered worthy or please, are detained properly; the others are distributed generously as servants of the Khatuns, so that (the Khan or *Shahzada*) may sleep with them or give them to those he likes.'[176]

The *Yassa* was also a penal code and laid down punishments for various offences. Capital punishment was prescribed for grand larceny, adultery witchcraft and false envoys;[177] it was, however, to be awarded only if the accused was caught red-handed or confessed. Severe punishment was to be meted out to those guilty of minor thefts[178] and insult to the elders.[179]

For the erring members of the 'Golden Family', the *Yassa* detailed a specific and special procedure. In the first instance, it was to be only a verbal admonishment and advice. If this did not prove effective, serious admonishment and warning were to be given. The next step was to exile him from his patrimony. Failing all these, the incorrigible miscreant was to be imprisoned and, as a last resort, to be tried and punished by all the members of the 'Golden Family'. The family council could award him any punishment, even death, if deemed expedient and appropriate.[180]

The *Yassa* ordained that the property of a person, who died intestate, was to be handed over to his chief servant or slave; under no circumstances the property of such a person, whether government officer or subject, was to be confiscated and appropriated in the name of the Khan.[181] The *Yassa* also determined the amount of compensation to be paid for murder:[182] the blood-money for the murder of a Muslim was fixed at forty gold balishs while that for a Chinese it was only equivalent to the price of a donkey. There was also a prohibition against pollution of water: bathing or washing of clothes in reservoirs or in running water were made heinous offences and severely punished, even with death.[183]

'During the seasons of spring and summer,' says Juwaini, 'no one (according to the *Yassa*) should immerse himself in running water, nor wash his hands in streams, nor wash his garments, and afterwards spread them in the open country to dry; and water should not be taken from running streams in vessels of gold or of silver, because, in the belief of these people, such acts are the cause of increase of thunder and lightening, which, in their localities, from the beginning of spring to the end of summer, prevailed to such a degree that the lightening was fearful and the roaring of the thunder tremendous.'[184]

There was also a curious prohibition against slaughtering cattle for sacrificial offerings. It was also an offence to cut the throats of animals slain for food; they were to be killed by cutting their chests open.[185] According to Qazi Minhaj, Chaghatae was vigorous and relentless in the enforcement of this prohibition and, therefore, in his domains, it was not possible 'to slaughter a sheep according to the ordinances of Islam and all sheep used to be thereby rendered unclean.'[186]

Going by Chingiz Khan's nature, his penchant for organization, his desire to safeguard and preserve his hard won achievements against evil eyes, his passion for the permanence and stability of the great empire he was to bequeath to his descendants to be ruled justly with efficiency, tolerance and justice, it may not be unreasonable to expect the *Yassa* to be something more comprehensive and more composite than the remnants of the Mongol Testament that have come down to us—scattered as tit-bits or sayings of Chingiz Khan and his wisemen. It may not be unreasonable to surmise that the *Yassa* could have been something similar in nature to the twelve tables, the *Old Testament, The French Rights of Man* and *The Indian Duties of Citizens*, all rolled into one.

The *Yassa*, we may say, was the 'Fundamental Law' of the Mongols, whose observance was made, for one and all. Chingiz wished the *Yassa* to be the unchanging law of the nomadic people for all times to come. He failed, however, to realize the role of time and distances, economics and environment, the stresses of dynastic jealousies and rivalry in moulding and shaping the course of human development, and that, with the inevitability of fate, the day would come when the Mongols would outgrow the cover provided by his *Yassa*. 'My sons (and descendants) will live a happy and luxurious life', observed Chingiz, 'They will, however, forget their ancestors and the toils and troubles they underwent in founding and organizing the Empire. But if they stick to the *Yassa*, there would be no decline in their power….In vain they would look for another Chingiz to retrieve the situation.'[187]

Notes

1. *The Mongols*, p. 138.
2. It would be worthwhile to remember that the same thing was done in Europe and Asia at this period just as in the best periods of Greek and Roman civilizations.
3. *Med. Res.*, vol. I, pp. 37-8.
4. Ibid., vol. I, pp. 38-9.
5. Ibid., vol. I, p. 76.
6. Juwaini, vol. I, p. 60.
7. *Siyuki*.
8. *Med. Res.*, vol. I, pp. 38-9. Note the change or difference of tone and tenure from the letters addressed to Sultan Ala-ud-din Khwarazm Shah by the Great Khan of the Mongol.

9. *Secret History*, p. 45; *Mongolian Chronicle*, pp. 68-9.

10. Ibid., p. 68; *Mongolian Chronicle*, pp. 109-10.

11. Ibid., p. 79; *Mongolian Chronicle*, p. 11.

12. Rashid-ud-din, fol. 251.

13. Juwaini, vol. I, p. 107.

14. *Secret History*, p. 84; *Mongolian Chronicle*, p. 141.

15. Juwaini, vol. I, p. 111.

16. Rashid-ud-din, fol. 249.

17. *Tabaqat-i-Nasiri*, pp. 352-4.

18. Ibid., p. 354.

19. Juwaini, vol. I, p. 107.

20. *Secret History*, pp. 107-9. The incident, according to the *Mongolian Chronicle*, occurred on the eve of the campaign against the Khwarazm Shah, when, at the instance of his wife, Yissui, who suggested nominating one of his sons as his successor, and he asked as 'the eldest' of his sons, Juji to give him an opinion about the proposal. But before he could say a word, Chaghatae the second son, jumped up to protest against the potential proposal to nominate Juji, with abusive reference to his elder brother's doubtful paternity. And Juji got up and took Chaghatae by the collar of his neck, and spiritedly retorted that their father never said that he was different from his brothers and challenged him to prove his superiority against him in physical strength and archery, and they came to grips. Bogurchi and Muquli, however, intervened and pulled them apart. pp. 182-7.

21. *Secret History*, pp. 49-50.

22. Ibid., p. 78; *Mongolian Chronicle*, p. 127.

23. Rashid-ud-din, fol. 245.

24. *Shajratul Atrak*, pp. 68-9. 'At military exercises I am always in the front, and in time of battle am never behind,' wrote Chingiz to Ch'ang Ch'un in 1219; *Med. Res.*, vol. I, p. 37.

25. Ibid., p. 98; Juwaini, vol. I, p. 30.

26. Rashid-ud-din, fols. 246, 248; *Shajratul Atrak*, p. 77; Sharfuddin, fol. 70; *Rauzat-us-Safa*, vol. V, p. 18.

27. Rashid-ud-din, fol. 259.

28. The earlier authorities are silent; moderation and self-control were the keynotes of his character and life. *Med. Res.*, vol. I, pp. 37-8.

29. Juwaini, vol. I, p. 29; Rashid-ud-din, fol. 95.

30. *Shajratul Atrak*, p. 77; Sharfuddin, fol. 70; *Rauzat-us-Safa*, vol. V, p. 18.

31. Juwaini, vol. I, p. 29.

32. Ibid., pp. 30-2.

33. Ibid., pp. 29–30.

34. *Tabaqat-i-Nasiri*, p. 373; Raverty, p. 1077.

35. *Glimpses of World History* (Allahabad, 1934; reprinted, OUP, 1960).

36. Suyuti (*History of the Caliphs*) and Amir Khusrau (Masnavi, *Qiran u's S'adain*) have given graphic pen-pictures of the terrible nomads. 'A broad flat face, with high cheek bones, wide nostrils, small narrow eyes, large prominent ears, coarse black hair, scanty whiskers and beard, a dark sun-burnt complexion, and lastly, a stout and thickset figure, rather above the average height: such are the distinguishing features of this race.' (Lt. Col. N. Prejevalsky, *Mongolia*, vol. I, p. 48).

37. 'Introductory Note', vol. IV, pp. 76-8, Hakluyt Society Publication, London, 1900.

38. Ibid.

39. *A Thousand Years of the Tartars*, p. 6.

40. Rockhill, p. 75, note 3.

41. Rubruck, pp. 75-6; Rockhill, p. 75.

42. 'Nowhere have they fixed dwellings, nor do they know where their next will be,' says Rubruck. 'They divided among themselves Cithia (Scythia), which extendeth from the Danube to the rising of the sun; and every Captain, according as he hath more or less men under him, knows the limits of his pasture lands and where to graze in winter and summer, spring and autumn. For in winter they go down to warmer regions in the south; in summer they go up to cooler regions towards the north. The pastoral lands without water they graze over in winter where there is snow water, for the snow serveth them as water.' Rockhill, p. 53.

43. *Kinship and Marriage*, p. 4.

44. Ibid., pp. 3-4.

45. *Rauzat-us-Safa*, vol. V, p. 11.

46. *Secret History*, p. 62.

47. Yurt signifies camp or dwelling while Ordu means residence of the Khan. 'Orda', says Carpini 'means the dwellings of the emperor and the princes.' Rockhill, p. 57, note 1. 'A court', observed Rubruck, 'is orda in their language, and it means 'middle', for it is always in the middle of the people with the exception, however, that no one places himself to the south, for in that direction the doors of the court open.' *Travels*, p. 122. Also *Med. Res*, vol. 1, pp. 58, 255; Rockhill, p. 53.

48. Rockhill, p. 53.

49. *Travels*, pp. 53-4.

50. H.A.L. Fisher, *A History of Europe*, Complete Edition in one volume, 1965, p. 409.

51. *Travels*, p. 55. Ibn Batuta had also given a similar account of the Tartar wagon in which he travelled to Sarai. The wagon was mounted on four great wheels and was drawn by two or more horses; 'on the wagon is put a sort of pavilion of wands laced together with narrow thongs. It is very light, and is covered with felt or cloth, and has latticed windows, so that the person inside can look out

without being seen. He can change his position at pleasure, sleeping or eating, reading or writing, during journey.'

52. Russel Smith, p. 323; Carpenter, pp. 159-61.
    Gilmour: 'There are great broad roads running through it (Mongolia) in many directions, roads not made by the hands of man, but may be, by camels' and horses' feet, and they are so well marked that a foreigner and a native, neither of whom had been that way before, followed one of them for two weeks and left it at the very end—it is only in the sandy parts of the country where the winds blow the sands away that the path becomes obscure.'

53. *Travels*, pp. 56-7.

54. Ibid., pp. 57-8.

55. *Travels to Lob Nor*, vol. I, p. 60.

56. *Travels*, pp. 63-5.

57. Rockhill, pp. 63-4, note 3.

58. *Travels*, p. 62.

59. Ibid., pp. 61-2; Yule's Marco Polo, vol. I, pp. 258-60. *Kumiz* is said to be a wonderful tonic and very nutritious. The tribes using it, says Yule, were free from pulmonary disease. Rubruck found *kumiz* to taste like wine and to leave a flavour of milk of almonds. 'With the nomads', said Maqrizi, 'it is the drink of all from the suckling upwards, it is the solace of age and illness, and the greatest of treats to all.'

60. Gilmour (*Among the Mongols*, pp. 265-7) found the Mongol fiddles to be primitive but says the strains of the instrument were soft and low and pleasing in the extreme. According to Pei Shih, the most ancient and commonly used musical instruments of the Turkish tribes were the reed-pipe, drum, and several kinds of guitars with four, five, and nine strings. Rockhill, p. 62, note 2.

61. Rockhill, p. 71, note 2.

62. *Travels*, pp. 70-4.

63. According to Si Yu Ki and Carpini, this headdress was covered, according to the means of the wearer, with woollen cloth, bukram, purple or baldachin. The maidens and young women could not be easily distinguished because they dressed alike and plaited their hair so that it hung down over their ears. *Med. Res.*, vol. I, pp. 52-3; Rockhill, pp. 73-4, note 2.

64. *Travels*, pp. 82-3.

65. Ibid., p. 80.

66. Rockhill, p. 81.

67. *Tabaqat-i-Nasiri*, p. 407. The venerable qazi also gives an astonishing anecdote about the burial and miraculous escape of a Muslim youth who had had the 'misfortune' of being brought up and treated as a son by his Mongol master. (*Tabaqat-i-Nasiri*, pp. 407-9). Vincent of Beauvais and Friar John corroborate the account of Qazi Minhaj (Rockhill, p. 81).

68. There were, no doubt, shamans who can be compared with priests and diviners; but they had no influence or role in the normal life of the Mongols as to merit

comparison with the Jewish rabbis or Catholic clergy. The story of the Teb-Tengri's removal shows that shamanism was not deeply rooted in the consciousness of the nomads; no contemporary Muslim or Christian monarch could have so easily done away with a troublesome divine. Mongols in their primitive and hand-to-mouth economy, could not afford the luxury of priestly castes. *Travels*, p. 60; Rockhill, p. 59.

69. *Rauzat-us-Safa*, vol. V, p. 40.

70. Juwaini, vol. I.

71. *Tabaqat-i-Nasiri*, p. 407; *Rauzat-us-Safa*, vol. V, p. 44.

72. Juwaini, vol I, *passim*.

73. Rashid-ud-din, fol. 251.

74. Ibid., fol. 247.

75. Rashid-ud-din, fol. 18 (Ms no. 186).

76. *Secret History*, pp. 31-2.

77. *History of Marriage*, p. 289.

78. *Marriage: Past, Present and Future*, p. 76.

79. Ssanang Setzen quoted by Howorth (vol. I, pp. 58-9) and Pradwin, p. 61.

80. *The Rise and Rule of Tamerlane*, Cambridge University Press, 1989, Cambridge Edition, 1999.

81. *History of Marriage*, p. 139.

82. According to Carpini, they made no distinction between children from wives and concubines as regards inheritance and other rights. (Rockhill, pp. 77-8). Among the savages, Parker observes, 'the first wife is always the mistress of the household and the most respected in the family. The question upon which the legitimacy of the offspring depends, is not whether the woman is wife or concubine, but whether she has been received into the house of the man or not.'

83. Ibid., p. 69.

84. Rockhill, pp. 79-80, note 2.

85. Ibid., p. 77, note 3; Cf. Marco Polo, vol. I, pp. 222, 245.

86. Howorth, vol. III, p. 213.

87. *Travels*, pp. 77-8. 'Sometimes a son takes to wife all his father's wives, except his own mother; for the ordu of the father and mother always belongs to the youngest son, so it is he who must provide for all his father's wives who come to him with the paternal household, and if he wishes it he uses them as wives, for he esteems not himself injured if they return to his father after death.' The wife of Andrew, Prince of Tebernigov, was forcibly married to his younger brother by Batu.

88. *Travels*, p. 78.

89. Marco Polo, vol. I, pp. 222-45.

90. *Secret History*, p. 84.

91. Rockhill, vol. xxix.

92. *Travels*, pp. 75-6.

93. Rockhill, p. 75, note 3.

94. *Evolution of Sex*, pp. 287-8; Pomerai, p. 61.

95. *Shajratul Atrak*, p. 32.

96. The age of military service may be safely presumed to have been from sixteen to sixty-one years as was the practice of the Hiung-nu and the Turks. Chingiz Khan, however, was in favour of twenty as the minimum age; among the Hiung-nu, says Parker, every male strong enough to draw an ordinary bow was liable for military service. *A Thousand Years of the Tartars*, p. 5.

97. *Shajratul Atrak*, pp. 32-3; Rashid-ud-din, fols. 253, 255, 261-2.

98. Marco Polo, p. 261.

99. Rashid-ud-din, fols. 215-6.

100. *Shajratul Atrak*, p. 33.

101. Ibid., p. 33.

102. Marco Polo, p. 261.

103. E.H. Parker, *A Thousand Years of the Tartars*, p. 19.

104. Juwaini, vol. I, pp. 22-3.

105. Ibid., p. 24.

106. *Travels*, p. 261.

107. Rockhill, pp. 261-2, note 3.

108. Juwaini, vol. I, p. 22.

109. Marco Polo, vol. I, p. 262.

110. Juwaini, vol. I, p. 261.

111. *Rauzat-us-Safa*, vol. V, p. 25.

112. *Secret History*, p. 66.

113. *The Mongol Empire*, p. 252.

114. Ibid., p. 131.

115. Ibid., p. 119.

116. Rashid-ud-din, fol. 248.

117. Marco Polo, vol. I, p. 260.

118. E.G. Browne, *Literary History of Persia*, vol. I, pp. 197-8.

119. Rockhill, p. 132, note 2.

120. *Travels*, p. 132.

121. *Tabaqat-i-Nasiri*, p. 338.

122. *Secret History*, p. 63; Cf. Instructions to Subutai for the pursuit of the Khwarazm Shah. Rashid-ud-din, fols. 205-6.

123. Nassavi, pp. 37-8.

124. Ibnul Asir, vol. XII, pp. 177-9; Rashid-ud-din, fols. 221 and 222; *Rauzat-us-Safa*, vol. V, pp. 30-1.

125. *Roots of Strategy*, p. 236.

126. *The Mongol Empire*, p. 128.

127. Ibnul Asir, vol. XII, p. 174.

128. *Majmaul Ansab*, fol. 191, Raza Library, Rampur.

129. *Roots of Strategy*, p. 223.

130. E.G. Browne, *A Literary History of Persia*, vol. III, pp. 5-6.

131. Rashid-ud-din, fols. 205-6.

132. *Roots of Strategy*, p. 223.

133. *Decline and Fall of the Roman Empire*, vol. VII, p. 344.

134. In his battle against the Naimans the troops were arranged as follows: Tuli was appointed to the Booljoonghar, Koblai and Yamah Noyan to the Boroonghar, and also to act as the advanced guard. Juji was placed near the standard, that is in the division called the ghool or the main body; the command of the Oonghar or right wing was given to Chaghatae and that of the Joonghar or the left wing, was given to Uktae. The rear division or the Boostanghar was commanded by Qarachar while Chingiz with the bravest men in his army took his station with the Ookjoonghar. *Shajratul Atrak*, p. 74.

135. Marco Polo, pp. 262-3.

136. Juwaini, vol. I, pp. 20-1.

137. Ibid. 'No kings have possessed troops equal to those of the Turks; none ever existed so patient in suffering and calamity, so obedient and grateful in prosperity; so attached to their chiefs both in private and public life; so contented with their stations and degrees, whatever they maybe, in life, so brave and expert in the use of their arms.' *Shajratul Atrak*, pp. 94-5.

138. *Roots of Strategy*, p. 234.

139. Ibid.

140. Juwaini, vol. I, p. 24.

141. *A Short History of China,* p. 50.

142. James Elroy Flecker's *Hassan*, pp. 104-5.

143. Juwaini, vol. I, pp. 17-18.

144. Rashid-ud-din, fols. 246, 248.

145. Ibid., fol. 53.

146. According to Ibn Batuta, infringement and violation of the *Yassa* justified and even necessitated the deposition of the Khan. *Cathay and the Way Thither*, vol. IV, pp. 141-2.

147. *Rauzat-us-Safa*, vol. V, pp. 44-5.

148. *Baburnama*, pp. 155, 298.

149. Sharfuddin, fol. 70.

150. For Chaghatae's respect for Uktae as Qaan see Rashid-ud-din, fol. 53.

151. Juwaini, vol. I, pp. 30-1.

152. *Travels*, pp. 237-8.

153. Juwaini, vol. I, pp. 30-1.

154. *Shajratul Atrak*, p. 90.

155. Juwaini, vol. I, p. 17.

156. King, *Memoirs of Babur*, vol. II, p. 7.

157. *Secret History*, p. 109; Juwaini, vol. I, pp. 144, 204.

158. *Shajratul Atrak*, p. 43. According to *Rauzat-us-Safa* (vol. V, p. 62) Qubilai Khan and Irtiq Buqa were both guilty of violating the *Yassa* when they proclaimed themselves Khan. He, perhaps, did not perceive that two crimes always go unpunished: successful revolt or revolution and suicide.

159. Juwaini, vol. I, p. 19.

160. *Rauzat-us-Safa*, vol. V, p. 19.

161. Parker, p. 222.

162. Skrine and Rose, p. 161. 'His Mongol tribesmen and followers—the mainstay of his power—were passionately fond of the life of the steppes,' says Elias; 'the only existence worthy of men and conquerors, was that passed in the felt tents of their ancestors, among the flocks and herds that they tended in time of peace, and led with them on their distant campaigns. The dwellers in houses and towns were, in their eyes, a degenerate and effeminate race;—the tillers of the soil, slaves who toiled like cattle, in order that their betters might pass their time in luxury. They would serve no Khan who did not pass a life worthy of free-born men and 'gentlemen-rovers'; and Chaghatae and his immediate successors probably saw, as his later descendants are described by Mirza Haider to have seen, that the one way of retaining the allegiance of his own people, was to humour their desires in this respect, and live, with them, a nomad's life.' *Tarikh-i-Rashidi*, Intro, p. 32.

163. Juwaini, vol. I, p. 18; *Rauzat-us-Safa*, vol. V, p. 19.

164. *Decline and Fall of the Roman Empire*, vol. VII, p. 4.

165. Juwaini, vol. I, pp. 18-19; *Travels*, p. 182.

166. *Bokhara*, pp. 159-60.

167. *Shajratul Atrak*, p. 32.

168. *Secret History*, p. 78; Rashid-ud-din, fol. 218.

169. Rashid-ud-din, fol. 247.

170. *Secret History*, p. 63.

171. Ibid., p. 48; *Rauzat-us-Safa*, vol. V, p. 12.

172. Rashid-ud-din, fol. 247.

173. Ibid.

174. Juwaini, vol. I, p. 22.

175. Rashid-ud-din, fol. 247.

176. Juwaini, vol. I, p. 24.

177. *Travels*, pp. 79-80; Ibn Batuta, vol. II, p. 364.

178. Ibid., p. 80; Marco Polo, vol. I, p. 259.

179. Rashid-ud-din, fol. 247.

180. Rashid-ud-din, fols. 249-50.

181. Juwaini, vol. I, p. 25.

182. *Rauzat-us-Safa*, vol. V, p. 19; *Shajratul Atrak*, pp. 90-1.

183. *Tabaqat-i-Nasiri*, pp. 381-2; Juwaini, vol. I, pp. 161-3.
184. Juwaini, vol. I, pp. 161-2.
185. Ibid., p. 163.
186. *Tabaqat-i-Nasiri*, p. 397.
187. Rashid-ud-din, fols. 246, 248.

8

Retrospect: The Mongol Phenomenon

THE THIRTEENTH-CENTURY eruption of the Mongols under the leadership of Chingiz Khan was a momentous development in history. Unlike the usual 'raid and run' incursions of the Gobi nomads to which the neighbouring settled societies were accustomed; it was devastative and extensive. Volcanic in its suddenness and ferocity, it created fear and awe far and wide. It was however, not a 'march of barbarians' but a disciplined fighting force controlled by a leader named Temuchin Chingiz Khan, an unfamiliar name and hardly known to its victims. Temuchin came into the world as an orphan child of a petty chieftain of a little known tribe, once quite formidable but at that time (and now) of little consequence, and that in a world where only might and craft counted.

The story of Chingiz Khan is not only gripping, it is an inspiring narrative for young nations and depressed peoples struggling for a life of honour and respect. Temuchin had literally started from scratch, earned a name for himself, attracted a suitable following, and tamed and trained them on a new basis. Neither the milieu nor the available personnel were favourable for such an exercise. Put through the grind in his youth by the sudden death of his father and subsequent misery and two 'captivities', he was then tried and tested in the ensuing inter-tribal wars. Temuchin had mastered the game of power-politics and ultimately was elected successfully, 'Khan of the Mongols' and 'Khaqan' or 'Supreme Leader'. The Mongols had become a dominant power in Eurasia.

In this incredible story of a meteoric rise, the role of the Mongol tribesmen should not be overlooked. There is a saying that saints do not fly, it is their disciples who make them fly. Temuchin was much more than a 'hero':

with a paltry patrimony, disowned by his relatives and deserted by his deceased father's tribal followers, he was in no position to even indulge in daydreams of a respectable life. He seems to have been specially favoured with a strong physique, personal charm, extraordinary self-confidence, and a prodigious memory.

However, as historical irony would have it, the world does not have a complete record of the great man's life and times nor a commendable image of the man and his achievements. This was not for lack of appreciation of his achievements among his descendants or among his people. The European travellers to the court of his descendants and the visitors to the Golden Horde Sarai testify to the veneration in which the deceased Khan was held. Kuyuk's haughty and insulting letter to the Pope also bears testimony to the assumption of a semi-divine status by Chingiz Khan.

That subsequent rulers continued to be awed by the name of Chingiz Khan is further attested by the fact that, notwithstanding his own conquest of lands from Delhi to Angora, the great Tartar (Tattar) Timur (Tamerlane) did not dare to assume the title of Khan; the title was even then deemed by the nomads to rightfully belong to the Great Khan's descendants. Timur contented himself with the substance rather than the pomp of power. He married a Mongol princess, assumed the title of Guregin (royal son-in-law), set up a puppet Chingizide as the Khan, and legitimized his position as the power behind the throne. He could, thus, rule over the nomads in the name of the Khan and as a supporter and well-wisher of the Chingizides, but could not found his own dynasty. So also the founder of a new and great dynasty in India, Zahir-ud-din Babar, was a descendant of Chingiz Khan but the dynasty referred to itself as neither Timurid nor Turkish, but Mughal.

The claim of divinity or semi-divinity has a long and distinguished pedigree. Through the centuries extraordinary men have been seen to partake of some element of the divine which distinguishes them from the general run of human beings. That the halo of divinity hedgeth the king is an old adage, and an instrument of legitimation of the person exercising supreme power. It could have had, and still has, also the social and political function of bonding the people together and making 'will' not 'force' the basis of political coherence.

The adage has been refined since ancient times. Alexander got himself worshipped as 'god' and so did his son. Akbar, the great Mughal emperor of India, attempted to develop an eclectic cult, the *Din-i-Ilahi* (Religion of God), which was in effect but another name for the cult of monarchy; the monarch as a semi-divine personage, obedience to him a religious duty, and disobedience both a sin and a crime. Asoka called himself the beloved of the gods (*Priyadassi*). Even Napoleon who said that 'God is on the side of the biggest battalions' arranged a traditionally religious 'coronation ceremony' for the legitimization of his conversion of the Republic into an Empire, and himself as the Emperor.

Chingiz Khan was, however, a simple man, a 'simple nomad' as he himself explained to the Chinese monk in his letter of invitation. He was unlettered and untutored, keen on good governance but handicapped by a lack of learned advisors; he was afraid that, burdened by the responsibilities of administration he would fail to take good care of his subject peoples. He pleaded like an ordinary mortal for the monk's blessings and was initiated into the art and principles of good government. The correspondence between the two men is charming, and could be described as one between an ardent pupil and his mentor. Such a person could hardly have ever dreamed of claiming the 'halo of divinity'. It is a different matter that the Mongols in course of time, restored to idol worship and that idols of Chingiz Khan were venerated, as reported by Marco Polo and others. Notwithstanding Chingiz Khan's dictum of religious tolerance, Batu, the Khan of the Golden Horde, put to death one of the Grand Dukes of Russia and an attendant knight for their refusal to bow towards the south in front of the idol of the Great Khan.

Like other great men and women, and also his own people, Chingiz Khan too believed in omens, spirits of the air, water, and fire, and some of the provisions of the *Yassa* interdicted some actions that could antagonize them.

Chingiz Khan belonged to the steppe and remained attached to the steppe, even though he was aware of the life and culture in such distant and different societies as China beyond the Great Wall and across the Amu Darya. As a man of action, he could hardly have been impressed by the city-dwellers stereotyped as crafty and cunning, amassing wealth and property, and depending upon the sweat of others. 'I have heard', wrote Batu in his missive to King Bela of Hungary, 'that you have taken the Cumans, our dependants, under your protection. I charge you to cease harbouring them, and to avoid them making an enemy of mine. It will be much easier for them, who have no house and live in tents, to escape, than for you who live in towns. *How can you fly from me?*' (italics added). Western Europe failed to understand the 'Mongol phenomenon', so horrified and terrified was it by what had overtaken eastern Europe. But those who closely observed the Mongols, like the Chinese envoy Meng-Hung, the European missionaries Carpini and Rubruck, the Persian chroniclers, Juwaini and Rashid-ud-din, the Venetian Marco Polo, and the Arab traveller, Ibn Battuta, were all impressed by their simplicity, fidelity, discipline and truthfulness. While Ibn Khaldun, compared nomadism favourable with civilization, and primitiveness with barbarism, the Chinese diplomat Meng-Hung too was impressed by nomadism as a way of life; 'unspoiled customs of antiquity' were being soiled, he noted, by the baneful influence of settled life or the polish of culture upon nomadic simplicity. 'Alas that their preceptors are now Kin officials who have deserted their own country. At present they are beginning to issue from chaos, they are destroying natural heavenly teaching and taking recourse to low cursing. How hateful it is!'

Marco Polo, an ardent administrator of Qubilai Khan, also struck a warning note and observed in his narrative that 'all that has been here related is spoken of the original days of the Tartar Chiefs; but at the present day they are much degenerated.' Strangely, not even the children of the enlightenment could recognize nomadism as a way of life or antiquated fragments of a lost civilization.

Contact with civilization did not affect Chingiz Khan's persona as a nomad, or his attachment to nomadism. Neither the urban culture of the Chinese nor the mercantile culture of the Khurasanis attracted him nor did he adopt their script or their style of correspondence. He advised his descendants, as he himself had done to avoid adopting high-sounding titles and appellations and long-winding and pompous language in their correspondence as was the practice in his days. His letter to Ala-ud-din Khwarazm Shah about friendly and trade relations, and the letter of invitation to the Taoist monk, Chan Chung, are models of prose. He did not erect towers of human skulls nor did he construct victory arches to signal and commemorate his triumphs, as had some conquerors before and after him.

In spite of clear precepts Chingiz's nominee and immediate successor, Uktae founded the great city of Qaraqorum on the banks of the river Orkhan to rival (if not surpass) Baghdad, then reputed to be the best city in the world. In true nomadic tradition, a day's journey away, he also ordered the setting up of a pavilion for which Muslim engineers and master craftsmen were requisitioned. Incidentally or by design, the site chosen was said to be the same where the palace of the mythical King Afrasiyab had stood. It was a huge tent with a capacity of a thousand, supported by innumerable poles of gold. It was named Syr Orda or the Golden Horde, and according to Rashid-ud-din was never dismantled.

Uktae refrained from asserting any special relationship with the divine, but not so his successor, Kuyuk, whose haughty and insulting missive to Pope

Innocent IV is a classic in this regard (1246). 'Through the power of God, all empires from sunrise to sunset have been given to us, and we own them. How could anybody achieve anything except on God's orders? Now you must say from a sincere heart, we shall be obedient. We, too, shall make our strength available to the head of all kings. Come one and all, to pay homage to me. We shall take note of your submission. If you act against it, how can we know what will happen?'

With the immense Mongol power at his disposal and the halo of fear and awe of Chingiz 'hedging' him, Kuyuk was not the last to talk of a divine mandate for his claim to be the supreme ruler of the world. Long before him and even his grandfather, Istemi the Turk had told Zemarchus, the Byzantine envoy, that the Turks had the God-ordained right to govern the world and the great nomad Turkish conqueror, Meghder had styled himself as 'Zenghi, the son of Heaven'. Centuries earlier, Attila the Hun had dreamt of himself as sovereign ruler of the world.

Spuler has reported an interesting episode about the irresistible impact of power and control with contemporary societies on the minds of the members of the Mongol imperial dynasty. Once when a Frenchman came to one of the great Khans and was asked 'what presents he had brought, he replied, 'I have not brought a present since I did not know your power.' 'Did not the birds of the air tell you about it when you entered my country.' 'It may well be that they said something, but I did not understand their language.'

Carpini and Rubruck complained about the rough and rude attitudes of the Mongols towards foreigners although they were cordial and courteous among themselves.

In sharp contrast to the theory pertaining to the 'halo' that hedges and blesses the 'sovereign ruler', Chingiz Khan stands out as 'the exception'. Not only did he avoid fanciful or pompous titles, he did not assert any special claim for himself or for his people as a 'chosen people' / beloved of the Tengri (divine). All peoples, for him, without any distinction and discrimination, were entitled to the protection of his laws. Among the Khan's advisors were, for example, Lu Chutsai (Chinese), Mahmud Yalvaj (Khurasanian Muslim) and Ila Ahai (the Khitan).

The rise and exploits of Chingiz Khan in Mongolia and northern China, and his campaign against the Khwarazm Shah had caused no ripples in Europe except some vicarious satisfaction over the discomfiture of their traditional religious and political rivals and adversaries. But they were unable or unwilling to understand the wide-ranging consequences, and realize the nature and seriousness of the nomadic eruption from the land of Attila and the Huns, this time under the leadership of a greater and a far more powerful chief. Nearer home was the successful passage through Derbend (the Iron Gate) by Subutai, the first person to do so after Alexander, and the worsting of the Qipchaqs and the Bulgars by him. The European monarchs (as unfortunately for the Khwarazm Shah and his courtiers) looked down upon the Mongol phenomenon as a nuisance; whatever happened in the 'remote' steppe was of no concern to them.

Strangely enough, the world around the Mongols and beyond the borders of Mongolia remained calm, and took no measures to insure its own security. China remained unconcerned too. Europe looked the calamity as a well-deserved punishment from God for the heathens and the Muslims for their mutual misdeeds.

In contrast to China and Europe, Chingiz Khan and his descendants were well-informed of conditions in countries around them, even of the value and prices of goods brought in by foreign traders.

For reasons geographic and cultural, the world could not obtain a complete record of the life and times of the Great Khan from his own people, nor a biography or elegy. Ironically, one has to depend upon the records and reports handed down by those whose peoples had the misfortune and agony of being trampled upon by Mongol hooves. We cannot expect an unbiased assessment of the qualities and attainment of their tormentors. Not much attention or value was attached by the people of succeeding ages in the Mongolian steppes. For the Chinese, the world ended with the Great Wall.

Mongol Revolutions

It is said that a great man is the result of a great need. One wonders whether it is one of the iron laws of history, or the three generation formulation of the great Arab historiographer Ibn Khaldun regarding the rise, decline and fall of Asiatic societies/kingdoms or a *post-facto* explanation or attempt at rationalizing of the correlation between the rise of a great talented leader and the then prevalent depressing and socio-political milieu. It is, however, uncertain whether the 'need' is really recognized and there is a longing for a leader to set the house in order or that there is some natural law that governs the emergence of leaders. Another question remains. Should the 'leader' also be in great need and one of them? This adage, however, is literally applicable to Rashid-ud-din, who was in great disarray. The old ties of blood, soft as silk, and strong as links of iron, were no longer holding nor was the traditional system of patriarchal authority governing the daily life of the Mongols. Family life had practically ceased to command respect; the wives did not respect the authority of their husbands nor did they enjoy their confidence and respect. The young did not consider the advice or commands of their elders. There was no law and order (as there was no authority to enforce it). Theft and robbery, particularly those of horses and herds were common occurrences. The horses (so valuable a commodity for the horse-riding nomads) were not properly cared for or looked after.

Temuchin was born at a time when there was no central authority to maintain law order, no known set of laws to govern the activities of the people, and no impartial judge or judicial system to hear disputes according to the law. In other words, the old order was not just in need of reform but had to be abolished and replaced by a new social and political order, based upon a set of totally new principles and inspired by a new vision. This is what he set about to do as soon as he became Khan of the Mongols. His reorganization of his army was in effect, a silent and peaceful revolution'. It introduced new concepts of socio-cum-military organization and good governance.

The social and military organization of the Mongols on a systematic basis as a disciplined social unit (a body-politic) was one of the key factors in the rise of Mongol power in the thirteenth and fourteenth century in Eurasia. It may be said to have been the driving force that carried forward and sustained Mongol imperial power from the Great Wall of China to Caspian Sea and beyond. It was the lynchpin that joined distant and disparate regions together in a strongly welded steel framework.

Unlike the then prevalent practice of each chieftain having a small fighting force of his own, calling in his relations and allies with their soldiers as and when needed (which created potential centres of power and involved depending on the timely assistance of others), Chingiz Khan constituted a special Guard for himself with a supporting regiment, while the whole population owing allegiance to him was organized as a permanent standing army, trained and prepared for civil duties as well as undertaking military operations at short notice. The Khan no longer was the leader of his own tribe but had been transformed into the Supreme Commander of all arrow-shooting horsemen under him. Loyalty was to him alone, assuring unity of command and the status of the Khan as 'the lord of all the peoples living in tents.'

The newly-created aristocracy was based on merit and service to the Khan. Since all loyalties were focused and directed on the Khan, the prince of the appanages (with their own forces) could not claim more authority than that of the followers of the Khan. Discipline was strict, one and all of them, high or low, was accountable and everyone duly punished for violation of his responsibility.

That the Mongol polity was organized along military lines because Mongols were an army first and then became an empire, seems to be as simplistic as the explanation of the astounding revolutionary transformation. With their limited resources in men and war material, the Khan and later on the Mongols required determined and united 'citizen army'. The Mongol social and military reorganization was at least for Chingiz Khan a 'call of the wild' not the product of a 'fevered imperialistic brain', but a desideratum and maybe taken as 'the child of wisdom and milieu'!

The army has always and everywhere been the strong arm of the State. The Mongol polity rested, and could, under the prevailing circumstances, survive only on the strength and support of the army.

The re-organization of the Army was a revolutionary measure. Retaining the Turkish decimal system as the basis of military hierarchy, it was extended to cover the whole Mongol population. As tribes were crushed and absorbed, others who had surrendered and accepted the Khan's overlordship came to be included. Not only tribes but the whole tribal system with its conflicts and clashes over pastures and women and its wars of vendetta, were abolished. A 'new social and political order' had been brought in to being, in which the Khan's word was the law. Discipline was its keynote, discipline in daily life, on the pastures, and on the battlefield. Thus emerged something unknown and unimaginable: the germs of what was in later times to be the concept of a 'citizen army'. It brought about startling transformations in social and military organization as well as in the principles and purposes of governance. Thus, in this respect the Mongolian revolution was silent and bloodless but total.

In Mongolia Chingiz Khan had a free hand and a clean state and an exuberantly loyal people to work this transformation. The Mongolian revolution was like a meteor that lit up the Eurasian horizon for two centuries with justice, the rule of law, tolerance, and discipline. It was through the gains of this revolution that the Golden Family dominated Eurasia for several generations. The conquests may or may not have been initially pre-planned or worked out for stupendous gains. The milieu and the harsh life of nomadic pastoralism would appear to have been hardly conducive to harbouring such vaulting ambitions. But successive and incredible victories against the Tatars (Tartars), Naimans, and Merkits could have whetted the desire and then the ambition for more enduring power to consolidate this hard-won status. Human nature being what it is, it seems both natural and probable that in the course of his struggle for survival, security, and power, Chingiz Khan's vision became wider, his aims and ambitions soared, and his motivation grew stronger. This could have obliged him to plan for the future good of his family and perhaps (though he never talked about it) the good of the homeland of his ancestors. It was only in the twilight of his life that he specifically talked about 'winning the empire' for his family, the choice of a successor, and through the two fables of the 'snakes' and 'sticks' advised his descendants about the wisdom of standing together steadfast. It may not be out of place to say that the specific affirmation by the Khan that the aim of his conquest was to 'win an empire' for his family is not to be taken at face value.

For Chingiz Khan was no ordinary person, no everyday soldier of fortune in search of 'fresh fields and pastures new', or campaigning only for booty. He exploited his charisma to gather round himself devoted and gifted companions and followers to 'aid and advise' him. He too could have acquired as other great conquerors had, the fateful wish to found a dynasty and bequeath his hardworn conquests to his descendants to perpetuate his memory. He held together his territories as an entity through law and justice; the *yassa*, social, justice, and discipline.

The cavalry had traditionally been the main element and strong point of the nomads against the armed forces of the settled societies. Speed and mobility were the chief factors in the successful 'raid, rob and run' tactics of the nomads. Often the cavalry had been only the mobile wing of armies constituted by infantry. Chingiz Khan reversed the role of the cavalry. Since his was essentially an army of horsemen, there was little scope for an infantry in his strategy and tactics. A cavalry ensured surprise and speed (to catch the enemy unawares). The tulughma or wheeling-around movement to charge the enemy flanks, then run away for miles and miles, turn around, and counter-charge the pursuers would cause confusion among the still massed ranks of the enemy. The feigned retreat up to ten or twenty miles would draw the enemy out in hot pursuit and then turn around in a decisive counter-charge and cut down the scattered and disorderly enemy troopers.

The Mongols avoided close combat and street-to-street fighting which was costly in terms of casualties and time and also, tiring. They sought to fight on open ground of their choice: wide and vast open spaces suited them for 'horse-riding, arrow-shooting' warriors and the tactics of the tulughma. Neither the Muslim commanders nor European generals were able to exploit this weakness of the Mongols. The Mongols had learnt from the Chinese experience the effective use of siege-engines, and employed Chinese and Muslim captive engineers and artisans to modify and improve them for heavy duty in the 'Lands of Islam'.

In contrast, the Khwarazm Shah had had all the advantages one could wish for: fighting on home soil, defence in depth, an army of strong 400,000 warriors in no way inferior to the Mongol, well-fortified towns and forts, the Amu Darya as a good natural border, and a great defensive barrier to challenge passage by horsemen.

Whereas Chingiz Khan took time to forestall all contingencies and counter each and every possibility, the Shah wasted valuable time in 'wine, women, and song' and in meaningless discussions with his chicken-hearted courtiers, who could only echo his own nervous and self-defeatist approach. Brave and dashing dissenters like the eldest and ablest son, Jalal-ud-din were sidelined. The Shah did not trouble himself to acquire first-hand intelligence about the Mongol court. He adopted the same fateful policy of locking up the fighting forces within fortified fortresses which the Rajputs had done in India against the forces of Sultan Shihab-ud-din only a few years earlier and once again history repeated itself. Siege after siege ended in disaster in Khurasan as it had earlier done in Rajputana.

Whereas the outside world knew little about the Mongols, Chingiz Khan and his successors were well aware and informed of the conditions in countries where they were to go and operate: their prosperity, topography, the strength and weaknesses of their armies, their internal discontents and dissensions, and even about their saints and learned divines. Chingiz Khan not only knew but utilized and exploited all this to his advantage. The strategy and tactics that he used in his war in the west and those employed by his great general Subutai (comparable to Marshal Ney of Napoleon) against eastern Europeans, exemplify a mastery over detail and thoroughness of knowledge about the enemy, and above all, the confidence in, and the competence of the commanders chosed by the Mongol Khan and the warriors trained by him, to successfully carry out their mission even independently in 'alien lands'.

Moscow provides an excellent case or touchstone for the comparative study of three great war machines in history. Napoleon launched his grand army against Moscow to humble and humiliate the Czar, but was beaten back. His army returned defeated and almost totally destroyed. Hitler and the invincible Weimar made a desperate bid to knock Russia out of war but the debacle marked a turning point in World War II. Subutai in his operation in

Eastern Europe headed straight for his target, reached it, successfully performed his mission and by outsmarting the enemy brought back triumphant his forces intact.

The Mongol horsemen laid waste the towns of Iran and Iraq and their countrysides and drove the proud and powerful Khwarazm Shah to an ignoble death on an island in the Caspian Sea. Similarly Batu and Subutai had King Bela of Hungary on the run across his kingdom to find safe refuge on an island!

Chingiz could not take on China but undertook a probing expedition to the Great Wall and the suburbs across the Wall. He was not a reckless adventurer, nor a mindless expansionist like his contemporary, the Shah of Khwarazm, or even a warlord. He was a good leader and never acted on impulse. His moves were well-calculated and purposive, as demonstrated by the strategy and during his campaign against Ala-ud-din Khwarazm Shah.

The heroic and romantic figure of Napoleon seems to stand in comparison with Chingiz Khan. There is a striking similarity between the two great makers of history. With humble beginnings and grim struggles for survival, both of them, by sheer dint of merit and the heroic mould of their personalities, managed to attain unprecedented power and fame as only a 'chosen few' have done. The similarity lies in their passionate love for their first wives, attachment to family, and a determination to win an empire for their descendants; it also tends to the great qualities of the commanders they trained, and last, in their contributions to the science of war. Among their outstanding feats too there is a similarity. If Chingiz Khan, for instance, transformed the 'rowdy raiders' into one of the finest and most disciplined fighting forces of history, Napoleon tamed the Revolution that was devouring its own children, and successfully led the exuberant volunteers and barefoot soldiers across the Alps into Italy. He made of them the reputed Grand Army. Chingiz Khan fused and welded the ever-wrangling plundering and vendetta-seeking Mongols into a disciplined 'people in arms', or to be exact, 'an arrow-shooting horse-riding people. Russia and eastern Europe were decisively trampled upon and remained under their subordination for about 200 years. The election of a new Khaqan always took considerable time for the members of the Golden Family had to attend the General Assembly or Quzittai meeting to elect him following the death of the ruling Khaqan. Western Europe was saved the ferocity of the Mongol hurricane and the consequent devastation in the lands of Islam caused by the death of Khaqan Uktae and then by that of Khaqan Tuli then by the delayed election of Mangu, and, finally, by the split after his death, as all campaigning was stopped and the Noyan commanders had to head back to attend the Qurlitai meetings.

The Mongol generals, Subutai and Yamah Noyan, can be justifiably ranked with the great Marshals of Napoleon, Ney and Massena. Subutai's storming of Moscow is a classic feat of strategy; notable was his knowledge about the doomed target, its population, city defences and topography, and the weather conditions to be encountered. He outsmarted the Russians by adopting an unexpected and unusual route (from the north), overtaking the Russian defenders by surprise by appearing behind the town; and, after the completion of the operation, departing before the snow melts and turning the land into a vast morass that could have trapped and entangled him and his troops in the same disastrous situation that, centuries later, Napoleon and the Germans and their 'invincible' Webrmacht' were to find to their cost.

Observed Saunders,

The political landscape of Asia and half of Europe, was altered by this tempest of nomadic barbarism, the last and most violent civilization was called to endure; the strength and distribution of the principal religions of the world were permanently changed while peoples were uprooted and dispersed and the ethnic character of many regions were transformed for ever, Asia was opened up to European penetration by land and sea, and these contacts, once made, were later renewed on the initiative of the West, which in its search for a new way to the Far East discovered both America and the sea-route to India round the Cape of Good Hope.

As the ways of the world and the quirks of fortune would have it, the two great conquerors stand poles apart in the last phases of their illustrious careers. Chingiz had a peaceful victor's death, at peace with himself and with the world, having fulfilled his aim to bequeath a safe, secure, and vast empire for his descendants. He had the satisfaction that his sons were well and truly established in their appanages. But Napoleon's sad end took place in a far-off island of the Pacific Ocean as an exiled and humiliated prisoner, betrayed by some of those who were closest to him. To their credit, the grateful people of France brought him back and gave him a resting place worthy of his services to France, the Invalides. Chingiz Khan, on the other hand, in accordance with his own wish and the nomadic tradition, lies in a resting place without even a tombstone; as Rashid-ud-din reported a hundred years after his burial, the grave was untraceable as it was so densely covered by trees that nobody could reach there!

Chingiz Khan devised a new arrangement for the maintenance of the costly and apparently unproductive military apparatus innocuously called 'the army'. He relieved himself (that is his government) of the responsibility and burden of the maintenance of the formidable fighting machine. Chingiz Khan delegated the responsibility and entrusted the burden to the commanders. It was they who were obliged to cater to the needs of the men and horses under them, under strict supervision and accountability. The system had the further advantage of blocking the emergence of rival centres of power and dilution of absolute loyalty to the Khaqan. Marco Polo found that the Mongol warrior often slept mounted and armed while his mount grazed, and could go ten days without cooking food, he would live on his own ration, consisting of ten pounds of dried milk, curd, two litres of *kumiz*, and a certain quantity of cold meat. It speaks of the quality of the warriors 'and their training that they scattered the flower of the formidable Hungarian cavalry 'right and left like the leaves of winter'. And it was the counter-charge at the Battle of the Indus by the Khan's elite guard which turned the table against Sultan Jalal-ud-din as the Guard of Napolean had saved many a day for their leader.

In shining contrast to Napoleon in his private life, Chingiz Khan, exhibited admirable self-control and attachment to his first wife Bortei in going to war against her captors, in glossing over her captivity and concubinage and pregnancy in the enemy camp, and watching in calm and dignified silence the tussle between Chaghatae and Juji over the doubtful paternity of the latter, whom he always referred to as the 'eldest' of his sons, and treated on a par with his other three sons, and like them gave an appanage to him as well.

With no precedent in Mongol history, no distinguished legacy as that of the Greeks and the Romans to guide and warn him, no Kautilya to aid and advise him on governing, Chingiz Khan had to depend on his own wit and wisdom.

The provision of a workable administration system for such a vast plural society in even modern developed and civilized states has proved to be highly taxing. It would have been much more so for Chingiz Khan. For him it was not merely a question of somehow holding together his vast domains but of governing them well and bequeathing an ordered realm to his descendants. The system stood the test of time for the permanent administration of the already conquered territories and was also well-suited, politically and administratively, to the needs and demands for the further, forward and onward, expansion of the empire as there were still lands and peoples beckoning the Mongols!

The peoples to be governed were as different and diverse as can be imagined: city-dwellers and nomads, products and representatives of contrasting cultures, civilizations and clinics, and then they had chiefs of their own, generally crafty and cunning, often without any sense of honour or loyalty, with no character. Loyalty could not be taken for granted. It depended upon and varied with the character of the local chief and the strength and the quality of his power and the extent of social justice within the polity.

For the twin purposes of good governance and stability and security of the empire, Chingiz worked out a new concept and a set of new principles of administration. The concept was decentralization of functions and responsibility. The empire was too vast, the distance involved too long, for quick and satisfactory communication between the central government and the distant local authorities.

The empire was, therefore, notionally divided into two basically disparate units: (a) the steppe, peopled by nomads, and (b) the conquered domains, comprising settled societies with their populous cities, orchards, and fertile agricultural lands. The steppes were divided and subdivided and assigned to the Khan's sons and descendants as appanages. (In medieval India, the Khan's contemporary, Sultan Ghias-ud-din of Delhi, appointed his sons as governors of the two outlying provinces (subas); Bengal in the east and Lahore and Multan in the west). The empire was divided into four large appanages, each allocated to one of the four sons of the Khan, who were to administer them as sub-Khans (II–Khans) and dependencies, under the supervision of the Great Khan or his successor. The novelty lay in the recognition and acceptance of the reality of unity in diversity, that is, the nature of the empire as a 'plural polity', and the appanages were to provide them their due position in the administration and policy-making of the Empire. There was also to be an 'Imperial Council', comprising representatives of the imperial and appanage governments, which, according to Ibn Batuta, met annually and monitored the working of the units and coordinated the policies. The appanage system was probably designed to ensure the security of the empire and assure the continuity of a dynasty. The appanage chiefs and the sub-chiefs of their subdivisions hailing from the Golden Family (the descendants of Chingiz Khan) who, bound by blood ties and self-interest, could be expected to safeguard power bequeathed to them by their illustrious ancestor, Chingiz Bogdo (heaven sent). The system could also be expected to obviate the likely ambitions of the tried and trusted commanders as 'provincial' or 'divisional' administrators to usurp power or indulge in intrigues or attempt to found a dynasty of their own.

The abolition of the principle of heredity was a truly revolutionary action. The succession was sought to be decided by the election of the Qaan or the Great Khan by an electoral college comprising all his descendants and from amongst themselves. Heredity is no guarantee against incompetent succession or maladministration or internal intrigues. Chingiz Khan had innumerable wives and concubines, and children by them. Yet only four sons—Juji, Chaghatae, Uktae, and Tuli—appear to have been singled out by him and specially noticed by the chronicler. Each son was competent and distinguished in his own way but Chingiz Khan felt that none of them was like him. He believed that from among his descendants there would be no 'second Chingiz Khan'. The 'monarch' or Qaan was to be elected by an 'electoral college' but comprising only members of the Golden Family at their assembly (the Qurlitai) and elected for life. During the interregnum, the senior widow of the deceased Qaan was to act in his place but her orders, decrees, and appointments were liable to be cancelled by the Qurlitai, if found to be contrary to the *Yassa*. A radical break and a step in the right direction of the abolition of hereditary monarchy nevertheless served its purpose only for a while—succeeding generations failed to keep up the momentum of change. Although there were no civil wars or revolts against the Khaqan by his relations and children in the lifetime of Chingiz Khan and his immediate elected successors until the time of Mangu Khan (in utter contrast to tragic wars of succession among the Great Mughals of India).

The system was obviously designed to obviate court intrigue, family rivalries and jealousies, and internecine conflicts over questions of succession. Chingiz Khan allocated the four appanages but did not really divide the empire among his sons and relations as had been done by the Turks and the Abbasids earlier. The sons were to be as subsidiary chieftains, and chiefs or unit leaders administering their fiefs according to the provisions of the *Yassa* and policy directions from above. All owed political obedience to those higher in authority, and ultimately to the Khaqan as the Supreme Head of the Empire the arrangement in practice amounted to the federal principle. A remarkable instance of Chingiz Khan's prescience or just coincidence?

Yet the Mongol empire was too vast and heterogeneous to last for long as one unit. The stress and strain of distances were too great; the pressures of rivalry and jealousy among the members of the ever-enlarging 'Golden Family' were too heavy for the ever-weakening ties of blood relationship to keep members knitted together by a remote common ancestry. The inevitable split took place sooner than could be visualized. The split was foretold in the intransigence of Batu in attending the Qurlitai, and the delays in the election of a new Qaan, and the heartbreaks caused by the overruling by the Qurlitai of the decrees and appointments by the Regents during the interregnum as the actions taken were found to be against the *Yassa*. The rumblings of the impending storm were audible even before the meeting of the Qurlitai which elected Mangu, as the intrigues and conspiracy delaying the meeting and election were exposed. The descendants would found empires of their own worthy of their great ancestor. The Mongol empire was thus a unique institution in the medieval world. The Mongol Khaqan was elected by an assembly comprising all the descendants of Chingiz Khan, called Qurlitai. However, Uktae the third son, was nominated the first head by Chingiz Khan himself, and then elected by the Qurlitai after his death. The fourth son, Tuli was to act as Regent until the election. The empire was parcelled (rather than divided and sub-divided) as appanages among his four sons and relations. The sons and the descendants of Chingiz Khan governed for generations the far-flung domains more or less like a 'family corporation'. The arrangement worked well for quite a long time. The secret had lain in the compliance, both by the Khaqan and the Khans, both in letter and spirit, to the will and the last advice of Chingiz Khan warning that united they would flourish, divided they would perish.

The system was however too good to last. The appanage principle did not provide for flexibility. It collapsed under its own weight. Its very qualities proved to be its nemesis. The vast expanse of territory, the heterogeneous nature of the different regions, the wide divergence in the levels of their development, and the wide differences of languages, religions, customs, and usage militated against the durability of the system. Nevertheless, the system sustained, even prolonged, the fear and awe of the Mongols as the dominant and dreaded power in Eurasia for almost a century! Integration and disintegration appear to be the two operative forces in the history of nations, too subtle yet too powerful to be contained for long by the best of monarchs, statesmen or constitutional systems. While the appanages were directly administered by the Mongol prices, the conquered territories were divided and sub-divided and administered by loyal local men (amirs) or Mongol governors, appointed by and responsible to the Great Khan. The steppe appanages were governed by the hierarchically organized Mongol military-cum-civil administration but the conquered territories were to be administered by local authorities by 'indirect rule'. Indirect rule was necessary for effective administration. The Khan did not have the necessary manpower or qualified personnel to govern vast and heavily populated regions, and the Mongols were, by and large, unfamiliar with the cultures and languages of the peoples to be governed. Rule by a tiny minority would have been both unpopular, inefficient, and brittle as it would have had to be essentially a military occupation. Indirect rule, on the other hand, can co-opt local talent and loyalty, at least, that of the aristocracy and the other beneficiaries. This system, with all its limitations, served well the purposes and interests for which it was designed, namely, unity, stability, and security of dynastic rule, up to the death of Mangu and the ensuing war of succession. It also served the subject peoples, firstly by the establishment of a more orderly, efficient, and stable political order.

The descendants of Chaghatae (and there are still a number of Chaghatai families in India and Pakistan, actively participating in the enrichment of the composite Indo-Islamic culture) were fortunate to found an empire in India in 1526, and effectively rule for over two centuries. The gunpowder, sea discoveries, and scientific inventions, fire and economic power, that put an end to the Mongol era, and the emergence of strong and powerful national states pushed the nomads back to whence they had come.

I had referred earlier to the dispute over the election. This was not the cause but only the occasion for the 'split'. The split did not cause irretrievable damage to the Mongols, but it cut the ties linking the appanages, and the 'family corporation' nature of the Mongol empire dissolved. The appanages became separate and independent, sovereign states. Their pride wounded by Ain Jalute, the Mongols had already lost the halo and majesty of a world power. Qaraqorum ceased to be the focus of Eurasian politics. It was deprived not only of its political importance but, perhaps more pinching, also of the much-needed revenues from the seceding appanages. These too, in their turn, were cut off from their patrimonial centre of aspirations, and the invaluable source of constant supply of fresh Mongol blood. Deprived of their base as constituent units of a majestic and powerful 'world Empire', the appanages became independent localized kingdoms, standing on their own.

This break-up howsoever painful and harmful from the imperial point of view, was a blessing for the new states. From being dependencies, they became independent entities. Once alien rulers amongst Muslims in Persia and Turkestan, Buddhists and others in China (while the 'homeland' remained shamanist) they were absorbed into the mainstream of local life and customs. Later, the descendants of Zahir-ud-din Babur, half Turk and half Mongol, the link between Chingiz Khan and Timur, came to be designated as the Mughals in India, not an alien dynasty with a 'home' abroad, but committed to India and a new syncretic Hindu-Muslim, Indo-Islamic culture. Interestingly, the Mongol rulers of Persia (Iran) came to be designated as the Il-Khanid Dynasty of Persia, and those in China as the Yuan dynasty. The task of relief, rehabilitation, and reconstruction, already been taken up in the reigns of Uktae, Tuli, and Mangu, gained fresh momentum, and the two great travellers, Marco Polo and Ibn Batuta, testify to the recovery of regions that had been victims of the proverbial Mongol ferocity.

The political and administrative framework decreed by Chingiz Khan was, however, not without its weak points. The heterogeneous empire was to be governed and guided by what is now termed the principle of 'unity in diversity'. The task of maintaining stability and security, and coordination and satisfaction of the demands and requirements of the different regions, always delicate and difficult, was not stupendous and unprecedented. The appanage system sought to face and solve the problem through decentralization, devolution of authority, all the more so under an unlettered patriarch whose advisors were no better educated or experienced than him. The system was basically unitarian though functionally it partook of the character of a federal polity. Though the Qaan was the supreme head of the empire and the appanage princes were subordinate and responsible to him and were to govern according to the *Yassa*, they were in practice autonomous within their domains with armies of their own. The appanage administration was, however, to be in accordance with the fundamental principles enunciated by Chingiz Khan, including the rule of law, tolerance, and appointments to men of talent. The appanage was, thus, *not* a 'province' but almost a 'kingdom' within the empire. After the disputed election of Mangu's successor, it was therefore a more than Herculean task for any ambitious ruler to wage a protracted war to establish his claim to be the rightful Qaan. With a full-fledged working administrative system under their control, it was but a formality to assume the headship of appanages as independent and sovereign rulers.

I find it difficult to concur with the view of Vladinotsov, however, that the political ambitions and plans of the Great Khan met with failure, that his empire dissolved or that the Mongols 'relapsed into the state out of which they had emerged under his leadership'.

Novel as the system was, it was not too far ahead of the political consciousness of the times. Nevertheless, it preceded by half a millennium, the acceptance of the principle of an elected head of state through an electoral college.

The 'Mongol system' was not the fruitless experiment of a visionary or daydreamer but a serious attempt by a hard-headed practical idealist to tackle a complex problem that still confronts societies namely, how to administer a plural polity. The fundamental principles of the system, an elected chief executive, accountability, and discipline down the line from top to bottom were the keystone of the great arch spanning Eurasia. Missionaries and merchants, Mongols and non-Mongols, one and all, could live and travel under the Pax Mongolica! Instead of a traditional hereditary head of the polity, decentralization of power and functions to the sub-divisions, their responsibility to the central authority, the abolition of a hereditary aristocracy government according to the law, equal protection of law to one and all, and supremacy of the *Yassa* (Constitution) were in place by the thirteenth century. Nobody was too important or too strong to defy or to be beyond the arms of law and justice, be the offender, his stepbrother (Belgauti), uncles (Daritai), son-in-law or the shamans.

The *Yassa* was, however, not a very successful means of providing new norms for the nomadic way of life, or for its administration. The challenges were made more complex by the fact that the empire comprised diverse societies not only different from their new masters, but also higher in the scales of civilization. And it speaks highly of the ambition and versatility of Chingiz Khan that he sought to secure and perpetuate his dynastic rule. He had confidence not only in himself but also in his progeny, as he expressly observed, to hold the empire safe, secure and intact by following in his footsteps and by sticking to the *Yassa*. He warned that deviation from the *Yassa* would ensure the downfall of the Empire. 'My sons (and descendants) will live a happy and luxurious life' observed Chingiz. 'They will, however forget their ancestors and the toils and troubles they underwent in founding and organizing the Empire. But if they stick to the *Yassa*, there would be no decline in their power....In vain they would look for another Chingiz to retrieve the situation.' He failed to realize that the world would change over time.

The *Yassa*, we may say, was the fundamental law of the Mongols and its observance was incumbent on one and all. It was a pioneering effort, pre-dating similar efforts in the West. Perhaps the effort was its own reward.

Chingiz Khan is one of the makers of history. He was not only a conqueror who overturned kingdoms and erased manmade boundaries, he also 'conquered' nature's obstacles, namely distances and dangerous defiles, extremes of climate and inhospitable terrain not with small contingents but with a huge force of six hundred thousand horsemen and their extra mounts.

Terror and Tolerance

All wars cost people lives and property. The conquests of Chingiz Khan and the Mongol military operations were, however, exceptional with regard to the extent of devastation they caused. The campaigns ranged over distances and regions never covered by any conqueror before. The Mongol invasion of Khurasan was ferocious.

The Khurasanians one and all, high and low, rich and poor, men and women had to bear the full brunt of the Mongol ferocity and the arrogance of rampaging Mongol horsemen. The massacre distressing and devastating as it was, served one purpose: the desire of the Khan to overthrow the Shah as quickly as possible, secure the submission of the enemy with the minimum possible loss of his own manpower (by creating 'fear and awe'), to forestall the possibility of any armed uprising thereafter, and to demoralize the garrisons stationed within strong and well-guarded towns and fortresses. Sieges as he had discovered in northern China, proved to be costly, taxing and time-consuming. Fear could have been another factor, as it often makes people and solders go berserk and they tend to kill indiscriminately. There could have been fear of a backlash from the people of the conquered areas, fear of mischief or trouble from the Tangut and / or Chin rulers in his own backyard, and fear of the long delays in getting news or calling assistance from Mongolia on account of the distances and obstacles involved. Both as a strategist and a tactician, Chingiz Khan could have taken all such factors into consideration when he launched his two-pronged operation to demoralize, demolish, and destroy all opposition. Khurasan was laid low in three months while the Shah was relentlessly pursued up to the Caspian Sea. There was sporadic and determined resistance at a number of places, but only two pitched battles were fought, one of which was lost by the Mongols but the second and final was decisively won by Chingiz in person. (However, the mountaineers of Gharjistan gave a tough time to the Mongols.)

Cruelty was a necessity for him. In the grim struggle for survival and then for power, he had undergone all kinds of vicissitudes, suffered humiliation, and pocketed insults. Terror with disinformation is, what is now called psychological war. It aims to influence peoples, mislead the enemy, and demoralize opponents and critics. Unfortunately for Chingiz Khan and his Mongols, the terrifying epithet has been indelibly linked with them as their chief characteristic. The havoc caused on them was the principal reason for the failure to understand them and their achievements accurately and objectively.

One wonders whether the colossal loss of life and property, the misery of survivors, and the manner of causing it by Chingiz Khan and the Mongols can at all be compared with those inflicted by the modern states. Chingiz delivered a clear warning of the impending catastrophe by his simple message: 'Surrender and survive', or 'Defy and perish'. The devastation, death, and suffering caused by Chingiz Khan and his Mongols was obviously far more than what people suffered in World War I.

Chingiz Khan was not a monster who relished bloodshed. He could be touched by the sight of a lonely man at a Persian wheel drawing water for weary travellers and would exempt him from taxation; tears flowed down his cheeks as he discovered that Uktae was being brought home alive from the battlefield; he gave specific instructions to his commanders to take special care of the men and mounts under them and avoid unnecessary loss and casualties; he was pleased and praised Juji with particular reference to fulfilling his mission 'without wounding or causing sufferings to men or gelding'. He could give his own coat or even his own horse to a man in distress. He respected men of piety and learning and exempted the clergy of all religions from taxation. He was also a man of exemplary patience and self-control, who never acted on impulse, who even under the gravest provocation, did not go into paroxisms of rage, and who could, even when he had become Chingiz Khan, calmly bear a fierce tongue-lashing from his mother, and confess that he was frightened! Those who came in contact with him stayed and served him all his life, and he used them to the best of their capabilities. He was also a brave and generous hero, who appreciated bravery among others, even if they belonged to the wrong camp. No service to him went unrewarded, no act of bravery unacknowledged, be it sucking blood out of the neck of Uktae wounded by a poisoned arrow; or the courage of a prisoner to acknowledge that the Khan's horse was brought down by his arrow. (This man was pardoned and he enrolled in the army, coming to be widely known as Yamah Noyan.)

For long Europeans knew about the Mongols but seem to have been unaware of the reports of the two missionaries, Carpini and Rubruck, who had, laboriously and meticulously, pointed out that the nomad Mongols had a definite and distinct way of life of their own. The Mongols were, then, in what Ibn Khaldun could have said, the first stage of human development, though on a higher level, and with education and human settlements coming with economic development. They could also, like so many other societies, cross the threshold of civilization. European prejudice was largely shaped by accounts of the 'Mongol phenomenon' spread by the thirteenth-century European chroniclers and spoken about by wandering minstrels, exaggerated and caricatured in the process of transmission by word of mouth.

Mongol Imperialism

The thirteenth-century Mongol eruption was different in every respect from the intermittent incursions of pastoral nomads into settled areas, to which the concerned societies had become accustomed. Volcanic in its devastative power, the Mongol phenomenon was unstoppable, destroying all opposition and resistance, overcoming every obstacle (Maps 6 and 7). It was not motivated by lust for booty from the marts of towns and celebrated their goods and weapons—nor even their women. The Mongol pastoralists were not driven by the vagaries of their harsh weather or by natural calamities or scarcity of food, nor even by a quest for new pastures and fresh fields. They were fundamentally different in their actions and conduct from the 'rowdy robbers', and were of a different mettle. They were a well-disciplined fighting force, commanded by generals of a very high caliber. And they had been trained and led by a general unlettered and untutored like them, but who was soon to prove himself as the greatest general of all!

Contemporary observers and chroniclers are not to be blamed. In the fourth century, the Huns had driven the Goths out of the Russian steppe towards West Europe and had brought down the celebrated Roman empire (while the Eastern Huns ravaged Northern China). Later the 'White Huns' descended through Afghanistan into northern India and established the celebrated Kushan empire. The Huns were neither the first nor the only peoples to make such incursions. They were followed by the Avors, Bulgars, Magyars, and the Turks, overturning kingdoms, establishing their control over the ruins and ashes of trampled civilizations by their horsemen. All these peoples were pastoral nomads, belonging to northern Mongolia, arrow-shooting archers on horseback and led by a chief who could unite them.

Europeans failed to comprehend neither the nature of the Mongol phenomenon nor that of the upheavals and earth-shaking drama occurring at the time. Ibn Khaldun observed in another context that Asian societies were 'like sick worms which weave a cocoon that they might die in it'. Europeans heard accounts by word of mouth, or from trade caravans passing by the sites of devastation, so that the Mongols appeared to them to be monsters. They heard about the shrieks of waiting women and wounded survivors mourning the loss of their near and dear ones, the great populous and prosperous towns and their splendid buildings in incredible ruins, their streets drenched with the blood of their sons, their celebrated libraries and universities smoking or reduced to ashes. The modern scholars, too seem to have been generally, shocked by the unprecedented deaths and devastation that marked the trail of the Mongols across longitudes and latitudes.

The triumphal march of the Mongol army from the Great Wall of China to the Caspian Sea can certainly be said to match the conquests of Napoleon. It was only in 1269, more than 30 years after the demise of the Great Khan, that it met its first setback. One marvels at its unblemished record over such a long period and in 'alien lands' and all kinds of terrains and climes and

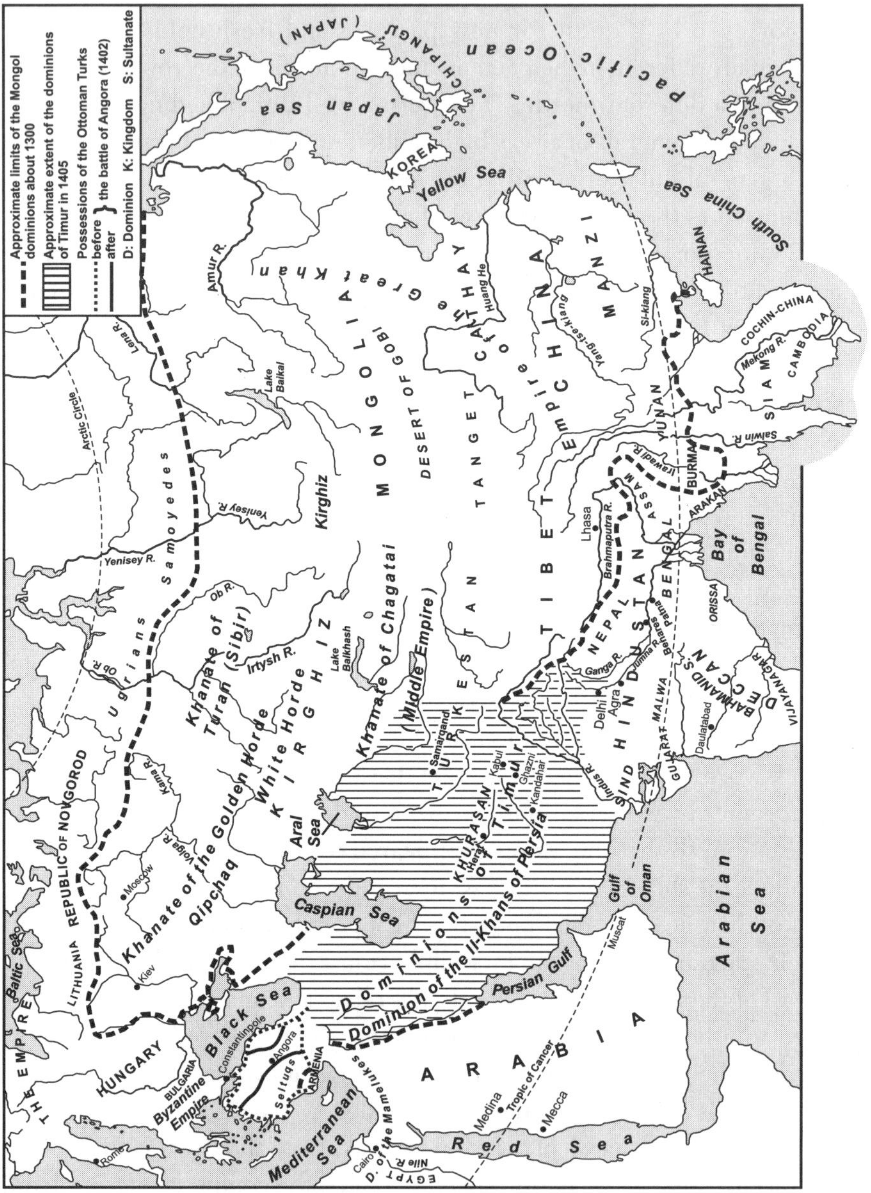

Map 6. The Mongol Dominions, 1304-1405

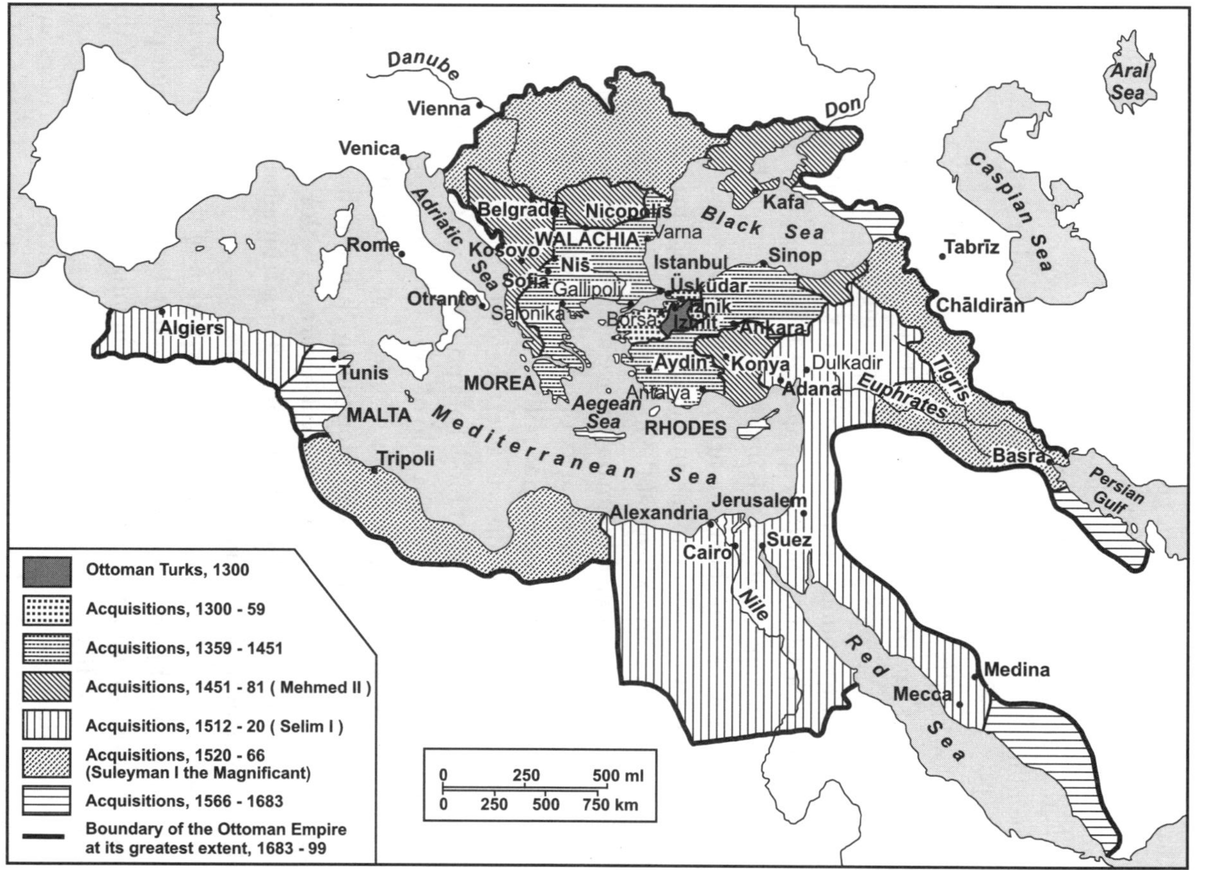

Map 7. The Ottoman Empire

peoples. Always disciplined, with staying power and absence of complaints from the civilians or the country through which they passed except once when inadvertently a town was looted (by a unit which was following the main army) and the town had surrendered and was therefore under the Great Khan's protection. Although the commander was none other than his beloved son-in-law, Toghachur, the Great Khan issued orders for his demotion to the ranks. Toghachur died fighting under the walls of Nishapur as an ordinary soldier. Such an action served as a warning to his own men and an assurance to the others that the Great Khan meant what he said and that he stood by his pledge.

Following the death of Mangu Khan, the disputed election of Qubilai Khan (Kubla Khan of English poet S.T. Coleridge), and the three fruitless attempts to gain Qaraqorum the Mongol empire finally split right downwards, and Qubilai Khan continued to reign as the Great Khan of the Mongols (though actually only as the Khan of his own appanage, China) while the other appanage khans became independent. What is important is not this split but the manner of it, peaceful and acceptable to the army and the Mongol people. Historians wonder at the continued discipline and loyalty of the 'appanaged' units of the army to their respective Khans; at the local army continuing to perform the civilian duties as of yore; at the maintenance and efficiency and punctuality of the horse-post system, the security of travellers, etc. It made no attempt to meddle in imperial or internecine politics and administration nor did the sprit of comraderic incite soldiers to assert themselves to preserve their unity and the imperial unity. A perfect model of a politically neutral army! The year 1277 broke the spell and in 1303 a halo of awe of the dreaded Mongol army near Damascus (Syria) came at the hands of al-Malikun Nasir and al-Malikurzahir Baybar. About 1600 Mongols in chains with a Mongol head round their neck, and a thousand Mamluk spearmen with a Mongol head on his lance in front of the chained prisoners, led a triumphal march of the victorious army back to Cairo.

For an adequate evaluation of the contribution of the Mongols to the art of public administration, one has to bear in mind the medieval principles and practices of administration. If Nessavi highlights the failings of the Khwarazmian officials (corruption and inefficiency), Barthold quotes a scathing criticism of the social and administrative thinking of the rulers and ruling class and that too by none other than the great Seljuq sultan Sanjar who is said to have observed that 'to protect the strong from injury on the part of the weak is more necessary than to protect the weak from the arbitrary actions of the strong, for the insulting of the weak by the strong is only injustice, whereas the insulting of the strong by the weak is both injustice and dishonour. If the masses are to emerge from subjection, the result will be complete disorder, the lesser will perform the duties of the great but the great can not carry out the duties of the lesser.' Barthold also quotes from an official Seljuq document: '... manual workers, artisans and agriculturists/ traders and businessmen do not know the language of kings and any idea of agreeing with theirs or of revolting against them is beyond them, all their efforts are devoted to one aim, to acquire the means of existence and maintain wife and children, obviously they are not to be blamed for this and for enjoying constant peace.' The passive attitude of the Muslim masses could have been due to the reiteration of the implied concept of divinity of the monarch propagated by the Friday sermons. The people by and large could have also regarded the pomp and power of the ruling class as evidence of God's favours to them while they accepted their miserable condition as punishment by God for their sins.

The catalytic role of the conquests of Chingiz Khan and his descendants is amply exemplified among others by the following three developments whose social and political value cannot be minimized. This first is the migration of a small Turkish clan (which grazed its cattle on the pastures around Merv) westwards to Iraq in search of new fields and pastures as well as refuge from the 'ferocious' Mongol horsemen. They then wandered, 'in a fit of absent-mindedness' or under the traditional inputs of wandering further, into Asia Minor and finally settled in Turkey where they were to establish the great Ottoman Turkish Empire, named after its founder Osman (Othman/Ottaman). The Turkish migration turned out to be not only a blessing in disguise for them alone, but also a 'heaven blessed haven of refuge' for the harassed and despised Jews of Europe to live afresh the life of respect they had enjoyed earlier under the Abbasid caliphs and under the Moors in Spain.

The second event is the volcanic rise of Timur and the eruption of the Central Asian (Chaghtai) Turks. It shook Asia from Delhi to Asia Minor. This was by all standards a soulless militarism which ravaged flourishing fields, devastated cities and towns who failed to offer prompt submission or kow-tow to his pride to his pride. His towers of human skulls offer a sharp contrast to the calculated and disciplined devastation wrought by the Mongols. Timur was a great destroyer but also able. He strove hard to revive the lost splendour of Samarqand but failed, and Herat took its place. He was also an unwitting benefactor of Central Europe and Byzantium on one side, and Russia on the other. Not only did he in this triumph at Angora give a blow to the aura of Ottoman invincibility, but he so grievously weakened the Ottoman might that the Ottoman could not penetrate further into Europe for fifty years. Similarly, the Golden Horde was so devastated by Timur's ravaging raids that the attempt to thwart the bid of Dimetri Donskai to throw off the Mongol yoke ended in its own decisive defeat at the Battle of Koulikovo.

Third, there was in 1526 the establishment of the Empire of the Great Mughals in India by the charming Babur, a descendant of Timur. Babur was a half Mongol on the mother's side (!) but proud only of his Turkish lineage. He was orphaned in his teens and had to face many hurdles, but was precocious like Chingiz, his great and distant ancestor. He was fortunate to have in his grandmother Ishan Daulata Begum a woman of great sagacity, courage and prescience as friend and tutor. Far-sighted and gifted with prescience, she forewarned Babur about the intrigues and conspiracies being hatched against his life and power, and thwarted their evil designs. She was also good administrator and is credited with initiating some useful enterprises, rendering Babur valuable advice in matters of state. Babur was however finally forced to forsake his patrimony and leave the Farghana valley. He received a timely invitation from the discontented and disgruntled sections of the Delhi-centred Lodi amirs and notables, to deliver them from the maladministration of Ibrahim Lodi. It was a good opportunity for him to try his luck in India, and he decisively defeated the Sultan of Delhi, Ibrahim Lodi, at the First Battle of Panipat. Babur decided to stay on in India and founded a new dynasty, majestic and illustrious, which effectively ruled (undivided) India for 200 years.

The work of relief and rehabilitation of the devastated land had been initiated by Khaqan Uktae, was continued after him, and was taken up with new vigour and earnestness by the new administration. Persia had been reduced to the position of a mere province both under the Khwarazm Shahs and the Mongol Khaqans. The credit for selling the Persians belongs to the Il-Khanids and to them also belongs the honour of reviving the traditional despotic monarchical system of absolute authority over their subjects dating back to Darius and Xerxes.

The Mongol monarchs were patrons of art and architecture. They instituted observatories equipped with better instruments. Nasirud Din Khusrau as their presiding genius enjoyed the unfettered patronage of Hulaku and could be called his astronomer. Persian astronomical treatises were generally esteemed in Europe and translated into Greek in Byzantium. The *Ziji* or astronomical tables, which he prepared for Hulaku were acclaimed and are still referred to with respect. Alal-ud-din Ata Malik Juwaini and Rashid-ud-din Fazlullah, the two great historians, held important posts under which the Il-Khans and received their unstinted patronage for their histories which are invaluable sources for the life of Chingiz Khan and the Mongols. But along with the great poets and historians and philosophers, the Il-Khanid Persia also produced 'fanatical' theologians. Observes Browne

Even Hulagu (Huluku) Khan, the destroyer of Baghdad and deadly foe of Islam, was the patron of two greatest Persian writers of their period, the astronomer Nasirud Din of Tus and the historian Ala Malik of Juwayn....Two other historians, Abdullah and Fadhlullah of Shiraz, better known as Wassaf-i-Hadrat and Wazir Rashidud Din Fadhkullah, both of whom flourished in the reign of Ghazan Khan (AD 1295–1304), rank amongst the greatest of those who have written in the Persian language on this important branch of knowledge. Persian literature can hardly be said to have suffered from the Mongol invasion, since three of the greatest and most famous poets of Persia, Sa'di of Shiraz, Faridud-Din Attar, and Jalal-ud-Din Rumi were contemporary with it, and many other most famous poets were subsequent to it. ...

With the replacement of Arabic by Persian began a new era in the history of Persia. Persian life and culture began to flourish and flower, Arabic lost its dominant language status in Persia. Even Turkish tribes such as the Ilbaris, the Khiljis and Tughluqs and the Mongols or Chaghatai Turks used Persian as their official language. The influence of Persian is unmistakably clear everywhere in art and architecture, language and culture, life, learning and religion. Persian architecture and miniature painting found patronage in India. The contribution of the Persian language through translations and original treatises, to the preservation and enrichment of the Islamic heritage has been immense. The interaction of the Mongols and Turks from across the Oxus with the Persian language and civilization, imperceptibly influenced their minds and led them to become its unconscious carriers wherever they went, South Asia (where it mothered the genesis and development of the Urdu language which served as lingua franca of the subcontinent till 1947 and thereafter was the official language of Pakistan,) and for a considerable time Asia Minor in the west, where with Arabic it was an important component of the Turkish language, until the Kemalist Revolution. The Persians had been the victims of the ferocious Mongol horsemen, but 'triumphed' over their rulers by the superiority of their civilization. The Persian language became the informal official language of the Mongol court: Kuynk's letter to Innocent IV and Mangu's missive were both composed in it. Persian even became the 'market' language of China as the Muslim merchants used it in their commercial transactions. Persian could justifiably be said to have become the lingua franca of Asia, and the Mongol phenomenon a blessing in disguise for Persia and the Persians! With Persia regaining her past splendour and glory as a great power, and having civilized her conquerors, she was, intellectually and culturally, once again qualified to resume her role of 'conquering' her neighbours.

Turkestan (land of Turks) of the medieval historians was an extensive country bordering Byzantine territory in the west, the mountains of Hindustan in the south, and the Gobi desert and Mongolian steppes in the east. The medieval chroniclers, however, lumped together various Turco-Mongol tribes—Turk, Tattar (Tartar), Turkoman, Mongols and even Tibetan as they were believed to have a common ancestry. Turkestan comprised two distinctively discernible kinds of people—settled town-dwellers civilized and literate and the migratory tribes, of the wilderness, often designated as Tattars (Tartars). According to the *Tarikh-i-Fakhrud Din Mubarak Shah*, 'The Turks living in the forest of Lura (Lawr) had peculiar customs, and whenever a son was born to them, they used to place a dagger by his side so that when he grew he might make it a means of his occupation. Some burnt their dead, and others buried them. The children seem to have justified the expectations of the traditionalists, as on growing up they earned a name for being an exceptionally brave race.'

The land of Babur and Timur was reputed for the bravery of its men and the beauty of its women, for the fertility and greenery of its valleys, the variety and quality of its fruits and natural products, the verdure of its orchards, and gardens, the majesty of its architecture, the delicacy of its arte facts and masterpieces of craft, and the eminence of its scholars. With Khanqahs and seekers of truth, celebrated madrasas and the authentic canonical works, Turkestan seemed to have been an inexhaustible reservoir of human excellence and natural resources. Here were the first nomads to establish a confederacy to govern a vast territory. They were also the first nomads to establish a kingdom so vast that it touched the borders of all the four contemporary civilizations, India, China, Persia, and Byzantium. They were above all, the first to demonstrate that they could rival the settled societies in establishing a large and vast polity with al Farabi, Ibn Sina (Avicena), Burhanud Din, Marghinani Muhammad Ibn Isa Tirmizi, and Muhammad ibn Ali Tirmizi as its distinguished sons. Turkestan could justifiably be said to be the home of Muslim theology, philosophy, natural, history, and astronomy. It was one of the Tirmiz divines Alaul-al Mulk, who was proclaimed caliph by the Khwarazm Shah. The reputed centres of learning, densely populated Samarqand, Bukhara, and Khwarazm, added lustre and splendour to Central Asia. When the Mongols were an obscure tribe hardly known beyond the Gobi, the Turks of Central

Asia were making history as formidable nomad conquerors. It was the same precept that Chingiz Khan followed, advising his descendants to immune themselves against the weakness of sedentary civilization.

Turkestan had been grievously devastated by the fury of Mongol sword and fire. Bukhara, Samarqand, and Khwarazm were the worst affected but they lived up to the reputed bravery of the Turks. The policy of restitution followed by Uktae and his successors paid rich dividends however. Close to Khwarazm rose the equally populous city of Urgunj, which had impressed Ibn Batuta. Marco Polo found Bukhara 'the best city in all Persia'. Samarqand, which had charmed the Taoist monk shortly before its devastation, failed to recover its pre-Mongol primacy in spite of Timur's every effort to restore its glory. He brought artisans and master craftsmen to rebuild and beautify it. He built villages like the earlier suburbs around the main town and named them after the tons of earlier days, for example, Misr, Sultaniah, Damishq Shiraz, and even Baghdad.

Central Asia was allowed to carry on with its old traditional system of local administration which meant the continuation of rule by the old aristocracy which surprisingly, was by and large, theological. Tirmiz, for example, was an important town, and an important spiritual centre. There lived the celebrated Muhammad ibn isa Tirmizi, who collected and compiled a valuable collection of the Hadis of the Prophet, and Muhammad ibn Ali Tirmizi, who founded the Hakimi order of the dervishes. It was to Tirmiz that Ala-ud-din Khwarazm Shah turned to for a suitable but pliant theologian as caliph, undercut the position and influence of the Abbasids. This backfired, as the nominee Ala-ul-mulk Tirmizi did not have, for the people, acceptable credentials. Nevertheless, according to Ibn Batuta, Mawarun Nahar was governed by Ala-ul-mulk Tirmizi for quite some time. Again among the companions there were two prominent Tirmizi brothers, Sayyids with the title of Khudawand-zada, Ali Akbar and Abul Ma'ali. Similarly, there were other dynasties who enjoyed administrative authority in different places. Even in Bukhara and Samarqand there were hereditary office-bearers, all descendants of religious divines: in Bukhara, the privilege of Sadrus Sudur or Shaikhul Islam was enjoyed in different localities by the descendants of the authors of authoritative theological treatises. In Samarqand, the descendants of Burhanaln-ud-din Marghiniri exercised this hereditary privilege. It was these men and their disciples with their Khanqahs in Bukhara, Khwarazm, and on the Syr Darya (Jaxartes) and in the Surkhan Valley (Tirmiz and Chaghaniyan), who carried the message of Islam to the nomads. They led simple and cloistered lives and mixed with the nomads, who were deeply influenced by their simplicity and easy accessibility. Slowly but steadily the message of Islam and with it Muslim culture spread and Turkestan became by the fourteenth century a land of Islam. Similarly, the influence of Persia brought about, over the years, a fundamental change in the culture of Turkestan. The nature and extent of the change is perhaps best illustrated by Ali Sher Nawai. A patron of art and culture, the founder of an academy for the promotion of literary activities and literature, Ali Sher Nawai himself was bilingual in Persian and Turkish, but knew almost nothing about the Turkish poets. Strangely enough, he did not know the names of even the Turkish kings of the pre-Mongol period!

China was late in coming under Mongol control and the least influenced by the split and the internecine conflicts within the Golden Family. However, it fell in the domain of Qubilai who completed the unfinished mission of Chingiz Khan. He defeated the Sung and incorporated south China with the already conquered north, with Beijing as the capital. These are Qubilai's outstanding contributions to the history and culture of China which outlasted the fury of the Ming Revolution, the monarchical whims and changes, and the extremes of the Communist Revolution.

Qubilai was by Mongol standards an educated and amiable person. He was a disciple of Tuta Tatsengo (who was Chief Minister of the Naiman Chieftain Tayang Khan and was brought a prisoner before Chingiz Khan) who recognized his merit, set him free and absorbed his services. Chingiz Khan appointed him Keeper of the Seal and the teacher of his sons. It was through him that the Uighur script was adopted for the Mongol language. Qubilai was a man of taste, a good judge of art and architecture, and receptive to change. As against his grandfather the Great Mongol who preferred a nomadic life, Qubilai was charmed by the Chinese and drew closer to Chinese civilization. He enjoyed, as was pointed by Marco Polo, drinking parties, hunting expeditions, and good company. He identified with China and its people, and after the split, became the founder of the Yuan Dynasty of China. He was a good administrator and, as testified by Marco Polo, the country was prosperous and doing well in every respect.

As the Il-Khanids revived and rejuvenated Persia, Qubilai and his descendants united China, added lustre to its age-old civilization and good governance, and Batu and his Golden Horde indirectly contributed to the unification and emergence of Russia as a strong and powerful country. Pre-Mongol Russia was half-Asiatic and half-European but had remained cut off from both Asia and Europe.

The principal cities were Kiev, Smolensk, Galicia, Suzdal-Valadamir, and Novograd. Moscow was at that time a small village. There was no conception of country, and each city held to fend for itself, on its own and/ or its allies. It was Vladimir (980-1015), notorious for his cruelty and lust who thought of having a religion for his people. He called the divines, the clerics of Islam, Christianity, and Judaism. He rejected Islam on the grounds that it prohibits drink and his people could not live it; Judaism was ruled out as Jerusalem was in alien hands and he was not prepared to accept the designation of a chosen people for his people. As for Christianity, the concept/ doctrines of 'the Holy Bread' and 'The Last Supper' were too abstract. He appointed a 'Commission of Enquiry' to further find out the principles and practices of Christianity. The Commissioners visited Greece and Rome and returned greatly impressed by the mosaics, swinging censors, resplendent vestments, choirs, and rituals and the sensual glory of the Greek Orthodox Church. The Greek/Byzantine Church was also politically more acceptable for an autocrat, who was more concerned with power and politics than questions of ethics. In contrast to the Roman Catholic Church with its principles of Papal infallibility and independence of the Church, the Greek Church was better suited to the unity and stability of his administration. Christianity was made the state religion and Christians were ordered to be duly observed. Vladimir had forcibly married a Byzantine princess, and perhaps, to boost his ties with Byzantium or acquire its cover, he ordained the conversion of his people by force. Kiev, the queen of Russian cities, was made Christian by force.

Russia was not a strong and united country when the Mongols invaded it, first in 1224 and then in 1238. There were three battles, heavy and furious, namely Kalka (1224), Daka and Sit (1238). The Russians fought bravely but were no match for the well-trained and disciplined Mongol warriors. They were out-generaled and defeated by Subutai. It was a long and sustained campaign of six years during which Russia and Eastern Europe were overrun and humbled. Every important city except Novograd was burnt and put to sack. Eastern Europe was paying a heavy price for underestimating the first invasion as a mere raid.

The Russian princes were, however fortunate to escape the fate of the Khwarazm Shah. The Mongols and particularly Chingiz Khan did not seem to have been interested in ruling settled societies. Batu, like his grandfather, remained a nomad and preferred to live with his people at Sarai and live like them. An additional reason could have been that he had more than enough pastures for his cattle in his own appanage.

The terms imposed upon Russia were:

(a) Capitation tax to be paid in money and furs

(b) Succession was to be approved by the Khan and the investiture ceremony was to be held at his court

(c) Infantry regiments were to be provided for service with the army, if and when required

(d) The subsidiary prince was to collaborate in the collection of the taxes, and recruitment for police services

The subsidiary rulers in Mongol Russia were assured internal authority and freedom to carry on their administration on accordance with their customs and traditions. Russia was thus dominated by the Golden Horde for about 200 years. Russia was governed, like other territories, by indirect rule with an iron fist, and Batu was admired by his own people as a good leader but damned as a terrible tyrant by the Russians. The odium was the result of the harshness with which the taxes were collected by the Mongols and the over-zealous Russian officials. To be fair to the Khans of the Golden Horde, Mongol suzerainty had nothing to do with the iron-clad stranglehold of autocracy and despotism which characterized Czarist governance in Russia.

For purposes of the capitation tax and recruitment for military service winter was the best of time of the year for a household census. The harvest had been collected, the people were at home and tax evaders and absconders were put to death. The census was, however, well planned and meticulously carried out; the basis was the household and its composition—sex and age, land and cattle, names of persons, within an age range capable of military service; calculation of tax or tribute was done after taking into consideration the requirements of the district for agriculture and other activities. 'Unfit' persons were taken away for slavery and service. The producers of revenue were grouped/classified into units of men, hundred, thousand, and ten thousand. Mongol officials, called darughchis and bosquaqs supervised and at times also participated in the maintenance of the Yam, and the proper discharge of the above-mentioned functions. Bosquaqs were, in effect, the 'eyes and ears' of the imperial government, and after 1320, the darugchis took over their functions. Tax collectors are never popular and the Mongol officials were no exception.

Indirect rule created two centres of power and loyalty, immediate, and distant. Since the collection of taxes was the function of the local chef, he shared the duty with the Mongol official. Tax collection was onerous but also a profitable business. Ivn Kalita (a Muscovite) was a shrewd politician, a master of flattery, honey-tongued and hungry for power. He succeeded in gaining the confidence of the Khan and successfully manipulated the Sarai court in his attempt to keep others out of contention: 'It shall be for me to know the

Horde and not for them.' In the struggle for power among the Russians, Batu made the strategically important mistake of overlooking the efficacy and dividends of the divide and rule policy.

The Mongols have been, one feels, unjustly condemned for riveting autocracy and despotism in Russia and Persia. They may be faulted for allowing the Sassanian and Byzantine systems of governance to continue.

Mongol Governance

Besides his passionate love for his first wife Bortei as testified by his immediate reaction to her release from Merkit captivity, and unreserved acceptance of Juji of doubtful paternity as 'the eldest of his sons' and restoration to Bortei to her previous status, as the 'first/chief lady of Land', Chingiz seems to have had two more passions, namely, a passion for discipline and the passion for good governance. He took action against his own kinsmen when necessary, for example against Belgauti, his stepbrother for leaking the council decision about the 'fate' of the Tartar (Tattar) prisoners, and against his uncles (for violation of his command against plundering enemy camps) and Toghachar Gurgan, his son-in-law (for the plunder by his troops of a town that was under the Khan's protection). Similarly, he showed exemplary self-discipline when he was greatly angered by the answer of the Persian Qazi Wahid-ud-din to the query about people preserving his name as the mighty monarch. Other incidents have been narrated in previous pages.

The passion for good administration found expression in some unprecedented actions, such as the abolition of hereditary monarchy along with hereditary aristocracy. In the matter of succession, Chingiz indicated his own choice of Uktae, but left the final decision to the Qurlitai. There was besides the provision of a known supreme law of the land. These measures were far ahead of his time. To their credit, the followers of the Great Khan were as quick to learn as he was where efficient administration was concerned. Even after the Great Khan and the pomp and power of the empire became a memory, the *Yassa* of Chingiz Khan remained a treasured legacy, and a code of conduct.

The Yam

The Yam or the horse-post system was a Mongol institution acclaimed for its efficiency and punctuality. There was nothing new about it nor was it a particularly Mongol innovation. It was inherited by them from the Turks and already functioning quite efficiently in China. The capital or the ordu of the Khan was properly connected with the towns and cities through a well-charted network of roads. Horse-post stations were established at reasonable distance of 15 to 20 miles, even greater, but were adequately stocked with provisions, riders, and mounts to speed the post. A number of couriers, Ibn Batuta noted were kept ready day and night, to take the baggage and gallop away without loss of time. The Yam was, however, the only Mongol institution that was not immune against corruption: misappropriation of funds, monetary exactions, and bribes. The official chroniclers, Ata-Malik Juwaini and Rashid-ud-din Fazlullah have specifically mentioned the reforms and disciplinary steps taken by Uktae and Ghazan Khan to root out corrupt practices. Uktae for instance overhauled the whole organization, financing, audit, and disciplinary action by entrusting total responsibility to the chief of the Toman through whose territory the Yam operated. Couriers were banned from passing through the cities. Batu and Chaghatae ordained capital punishment for corruption and misappropriation in their domains. This gives us an idea of the nature and extent of the problem. It also provides a hint that the problem is universal.

The reforms once again put the Yam system on an even keel to perform its catalytic role with efficiency and punctuality. Besides cohesion and communication between the different regions and diverse peoples of the empire, it also brought Asia and Europe closer than they had ever been since the days of Alexander. It facilitated cultural interaction and inter-cultural development. There were excellently maintained roads and crossroads and horse-post stations with 'guest houses' or *sarai*—board and lodging free for official and diplomatic missions. It was not only the 'official' personnel but also their attendants and mounts who were suitably looked after. Merchants were thus encouraged by the enlightened and liberal policies of the Khans by exemptions, lowering of duties, rehabilitation of devastated areas, rebuilding of ruined cities and provision of armed guards for caravans through sparsely populated lands. Missionaries could confidently and conveniently avail the safe and new freedom of travel and, thanks to the unfettered policy of tolerance, could carry on unhampered their missionary activities, perform their religious rites and observe their festivals in the Mongol domains. The Franciscan friars, Andrew of Perngia, Odoric of Pordenone, and John of Marignolli, who travelled long distances through Mongol territories had no mishaps on the roads nor did they complain of any inconvenience.

The Yam was specifically praised for its punctuality. The Yam couriers according to Marco Polo, could cover distances of 200 and 300 miles a day, and added that 'these strong, enduring messengers are highly prized'. The

Yam and safety of road travel established a remarkable cohesion in the vast and empire. To improve the punctuality of the Yam and to avoid inconvenience to the people, Uktae decreed against the Yam couriers passage through towns and cities. Rubruck testified to the afflux of foreigners, Asians as well as Europeans, some of them resident there for ten to thirty years without harassment, living in peace and amity with others and conversant with their customs, habits and language. They were thus good sources of information.

As for China, it was opened to the outside world. It was drawn into closer contact with the outside world than that at any other stage of history.

Marco Polo was the first European who went to China, stayed there about seventeen years and travelled through the length and breadth of the vast country. His report about the Chinese civilization and wealth was disbelieved and he was ridiculed. It was only when Constantinople had been conquered and Venetian merchants were desperate for a cheaper route to India that Marco Polo's report on the sea route to India and China stirred some individuals to follow his path. The exploration of the sea route was undertaken. Italian cities were flooded with Chinese products which then found their way into the markets which of northern Europe, which gave a new impetus to the growth of the towns in social and political life.

The Yam thus, turned out to be a catalyst. The conquests of Chingiz Khan and their innumerable outcomes constitute a dividing line between the Middle Ages and modern times. The Yam may also be said to have demonstrated that peaceful pursuits can have victories more beneficial than triumphs on the battlefields.

The Italian merchant Francis Pegolotti reported that the traders found the road to Cathay (China) perfectly safe irrespective of whether they traveled by day or night except during the period of Regency. The merchants were a useful source for the Mongol intelligence service through their unguarded conversations with their counterparts in the city marts, and way stations. Rubruck and Carpini, themselves on intelligence missions, noted the inquisitiveness of the Mongols and their habit of asking questions. The Khan and his descendants were therefore well-informed about the outside world while their neighbours remained indifferent.

While Europe, looked and worked for the future and surged forward in wealth, in scientific knowledge, in techniques of warfare and in fire power, the East remained mired in the past. While the East was looking backwards and prided itself on its great and glorious contributions to the art and science of good living and good governance Europe was restless, fired with dynamism, discontent, and ambitions to achieve more. Europe could therefore, have been the main beneficiary of the Mongol dominance over Eurasia for more than a century. 'I have no doubt' observed Howorth, 'that the art of printing, the mariner's compass, firearms and a great many details of social life, were not discovered in Europe, but imported by means of Mongol influence from the East'.

Mongol Panchsheel

The Mongols were never hated and despised as 'modern' armies of occupation have been for despoliation and dishonoring women. The Mongol army was allowed no license for such misbehaviour and it was entrusted with civil duties under strict army supervision. For instance, it maintained the roads and safety of travellers and caravans with remarkable efficiency and effectiveness. The army not only earned encomiums for itself for its unparalleled organization, discipline, swift manoeuvres, deceptive strategies and decisive counter-attacks but immortalized the name of the Mongol empire as the largest and best administered till then. The five principles of good rule therefore deserve to be taken at their face value.

Nothing provides better testimony to the genius of Chingiz Khan as the greatest empire builder than the fact that the foundations of the empire were so securely laid that imperial unity outlasted the Khan by more than thirty years. The Mongols remained a dominant power in half of Asia and half of Europe, and European monarchs trembled in their dreams at the clattering of Mongol hooves, for another hundred years. It is to the credit of Chingiz Khan's descendants (as testified by the travellers) that the devastated regions were rehabilitated and renovated, trade, travel and agriculture encouraged, cities and towns rebuilt, and their lost splendour was revived.

The principles of good administration were for Chingiz Khan:

1. Abolition of hereditary system of monarchy and aristocracy and their replacement by an elected executive (by an electoral college); a new aristocracy based on merit with accountability for service to both of them
2. Enforcement of justice through an independent and impartial chief judge (and judiciary)
3. The rule of law (with *Yassa* as the supreme law) ensuring equality before rule of law and equal protection of the laws
4. Religious tolerance. No official religion, no favour to any religion,

no discrimination or favour on grounds of religion, race, creed or class

5. Careers were to be open to all men of ability, punishment for dereliction of duty to be proportionate to the offence as laid down by Law of *Yassa*.

Such was the amazing man and his career, and, similarly the incredible record and catalytic role of the Mongol Khan, his descendants and the Mongols in the evolving history of mankind. It is one of the great ironies of history that such a great man was initially so misunderstood and misrepresented as to be labelled as a barbarian. The forces that the Mongol conquests released and the revolutionary changes they brought about in social and military organization and administration had a catalytic importance for the social and political developments in succeeding centuries. The Mongol invasions may, therefore, be said to mark an indelible dividing line between medieval and modern times.

APPENDICES

A Note on the Authorities

PERSIAN IS one of the most elegant languages of the world, and the Persians are also noted for their contributions to art and culture down the ages. And, perhaps, because of their civilized sedentary life, have repeatedly suffered defeats, devastation, and disaster at the hands of the 'foreigners' or alien invaders as has been the fate of many a civilization in the past, notably, the Greeks. But, fortunately for mankind, history repeated itself as it was to do so often: the vanquished 'conquered' their conquerors by the superiority of their culture and civilization. The Persians, too, conquered the Mongols, and civilization, ultimately, triumphed over 'barbarians'. The Mongols were 'Persianized'. They adopted not only the language of the vanquished, but also their religion. And the Persians provided the administrative bureaucracy, which held together and governed the country for them. The Mongols, had, however, brought a new vigour into Muslim society and culture, and Persian life, learning, and culture rose phoenix-like from the ashes. The Persians in their turn obliged the Mongol Khans in many invisible ways (particularly by preserving the record of their ancestors and their achievements in war and peace) by chronicling them in a systematic way. While the Chinese sources are meagre and perfunctory about the 'war in the west', the Persian chronicles are invaluable and indispensable sources. And, of course, as contemporary records of the Mongol Ilkhanata in Persia, their importance and value is unquestionable.

There is, however, a general impression and criticism that Persian historians are guilty of exaggeration, rhetoric, flowery language, panegyric and euphemism and, therefore, not reliable. This generalization and criticism, though not totally invalid, is not universally applicable, for instance, in such notable cases as Qazi Minhaj-i-Siraj's *Tabaqat-i-Nasiri,* Ata Malik Juwaini's *Tarikh-i-Jahan Gusha*, Rashid-ud-din Fazlullah's *Jamaiut-Twarikh* and many other later chronicles. As Browne has remarked, critics have overlooked the observations of the great French historian of the Mongols, Ohson that 'we should be tempted to charge the Oriental historians with exaggeration, were it not that their statements are entirely confirmed by the independent testimony of Western historians as to the precisely similar proceedings of the Tartars (Mongols) in South Eastern Europe, where they ravaged not only Russia, Poland, and Hungary, but penetrated Silesia, Moravia and Dalmalia, and at the fatal battle of Zicguitz (9 April 1141) defeated an army of 30,000 Germans, Austrians, Hungarians and Poles commanded by Henry the Pious, Duke of Silesia.'

The critics also seem to have overlooked the fact that in the medieval Muslim world, and certainly in the eastern lands of the Caliphate, the 'city' was not merely a walled town but also the suburbs around it. All were populous, as testified by medieval geographers and by Ibn Batuta. The 'cities' were also populated by refugees from surrounding areas, who had fled before the Mongol sword and fire. Balkh, Bokhara, Nusrat-Kuhu, Nasa, Nishapur, Merv, Utrar, Bamian, Khwarazm, and Tirmiz all felt the brunt of Mongol ferocity, one after the other so that, as Juwaini observed, 'not one in a thousand survived'. The contemporary Ibn-ul-asir also wrote in the same vein.

The criticism comes from a lack of appreciation of the milieu in which the Persian chronicles were composed, the requirements of the language, and, above all, the taste and temperament of aristocrats and scholars. The critics, perhaps, also overlooked the fact of the restraints that prevail in an autocratic system: freedom of speech is always the first casualty. Besides, writers of fiction, drama, and history have always to be keenly aware of jealous rivals and detractors eager to pounce upon factual mistakes, insinuation, or unpleasant reflection on the establishment. It is a delicate and exacting task for a conscientious person to be always factually correct and simultaneously avoid the ire of the court. The task becomes all the more difficult when undertaken for suspicious and watchful alien rulers, as under the Il-Khanid in Persia.

'A violent death was, however, commonly the end of those who were rash enough to act as Ministers to Mongols', ruefully observed Browne. 'Thus Jalal-ul-din Simnani, who succeeded the *Sahib-i-Diwan*, was executed in 1289; Sad-ud-daula who succeeded him, was put to death at the end of February 1291; Sadr-ud-din Khalidi, who acted as minister to Gay-Khatu, suffered the same fate in May 1298, and Rashid-ud-din Fazlullah, the most accomplished of all, was executed in July 1318'. Rashid's sixteen-year-old son was put to death along with him. The misfortunes that befell the Juwaini family are detailed later.

It was under such an atmosphere of fear and suspicion, jealousy and intrigue that the Persian writers developed a style of writing florid and ornate, the use of all sorts of figures of speech, exaggerations and eulogy (to the extent of absurdity) allusions and euphemism, which have come to comprise the 'grand style'. It's circumlocutions enabled them to keep their patrons pleased and their own conscience at peace with themselves.

Anyone familiar with the literary and poetic finesse of the Persian language and Muslim culture would be easily able to sift the chaff from the grain and obtain the meaning of the florid verbiage. The *Tarikh-i-Wassaf* is a classic example of 'such pompous, florid and inflated style', but, as Browne observed, 'we could forgive [him] the more easily if his work were less an original authority on the period (1257-1328) of which it treats, but in fact it *is as important as it is unreadable.*' (Emphasis added). Interestingly, he was a protégé of Rashid-ud-din, the master of plain and straightforward style of history writing. But to be fair to him, he was really more concerned with showing off his mastery of language than with history writing as such.

Tabaqat-i-Nasiri

The *Tabaqat-i-Nasiri* of Qazi Abu Omar Minhaj-ud-din Osman bin Siraj-ud-din is one of the earliest works concerning the Mongols, and also covers all the Muslim dynasties of the Indian subcontinent from 864 to the Mongol invasion until 1260. It is only the last chapter (Book XXIII) of the *Tabaqat* that deals with the eruption of the Mongols and their earth-shaking exploits. The chapter contains valuable information pertaining to the war between Sultan Sanjar Seljuq and the tribes of Qara-Khitai, the conquest of Turkestan by Muhammad Khwarazm Shah, and the conquerors of Halaku–Chingiz Khan and his descendants, Juji, Uktae, Chaghatae, Kuzuk, Batu, Mangu, Hulaka, and Barkah. The *Tabaqat* thus provides valuable insight into the political milieu and momentous happenings that turned Central Asia upside down in the thirteenth century.

Qazi Minhaj Siraj was favourably placed for the task of writing an authentic account of the events in Central Asia and northern India. He had a distinguished pedigree. One of his ancestors, Imam Abdul Khalique, was married to one of the forty daughters of Sultan Ibrahim of Ghazni, and all of them were according to the venerable Qazi, 'married to illustrious nobles, or learned men of regime'. The Imam's son was named Ibrahim after the sultan. And Ibrahim was the great-grandfather of our author and an ecclesiastic of repute—another ancestor was the highly respected divine, Siraj-ud-din Muhammad, generally acclaimed as 'the wonder of the age' (*ujubatuz zaman*), and 'the most eloquent man of Persia' (*afsahul mulk*). The Qazi's mother was the foster sister of Mah Malik, which gave him the privilege of spending his early years in the palace of Sultan Shihab-ud-din. Providentially, the ancestors of the author had been high ecclesiastical officers at the courts of Ghazni and the Ghori. Their fame should have preceded the author's and that, perhaps accounts for the ready acceptance, even the welcome he was given in Sind when he emigrated to India (1227) owing to the Mongol conquest of Afghanistan.

On his arrival in Sind, Sultan Qubbach appointed Qazi Minhaj Siraj principal of the Firozia College at Uchchah but soon, thereafter, Qubbch was defeated by the Sultan of Delhi, Iltutmish, and the Qazi was taken to the victorious sultan, who interrogated him about his knowledge of men and affairs. Impressed by his learning the sultan took him to Delhi, and appointed him Khatib and Imam of the Friday Mosque, and Qazi of Gwalior. All these appointments were important and highly respected. The Khatib delivered the Khutba or sermon before the Friday prayers; it was delivered orally, and required high ecclesiastical proficiency and fluency of speech. The Imam led the prayers. Generally the two offices were held by one and the same person, and commanded respect and influence because of the piety, learning, and standard of conduct expected of them. Minhaj Siraj was also, thereafter, shifted to Delhi as Principal of the Nasiriya College, and then, corresponding to the political climate and changes in Delhi, he held intermittently, several important ecclesiastical posts. In between he found time to go to Lakhnauti (1242) and write an account of the place. The authenticity and historical importance of this work is attested by the fact that in writing his *History of Bengal* (six centuries later), Stewart found it 'very valuable'. Interestingly, on his return, the Qazi was reappointed chief qazi (*Qazi ul Quzzat* and *Sadrus-Sudur*) of Delhi. The qazi was the highest judicial officer below the king and exercised both civil and criminal jurisdiction; and according to Ibn Batuta, he also performed the nikah ceremony of the sultan's relatives and the high officials of the government. The *Sadrus-Sudur* was the chief judge in cases involving shariat or the religious law.

The *Tabaqat-i-Nasiri* is, on the whole, a fairly reliable account of the Mongols and no better picture—if not accurate—is to be found of the devastation wrought by Chingiz Khan and his successors. His feelings towards them are extreme but understandably bitter. He claims to have crossed swords with the 'infidels' and would thus have learnt from affected families the accounts of the death and destruction that was brought about by the Mongols in Khwarazm and the mountains of Gharjistan. Writing in the security of Delhi, he had freedom to criticize the Mongols. Sometimes, he mentions the names of his informants and their credentials. He was industrious in the collection of facts, and careful, too, in the choice of informants. Strangely enough as regards facts he is corroborated by Ala-ud-din Ata Malik Juwaini, who was writing the *Tarikh-i-Jahan Gusha* at almost the same time; sometimes, his statements are corroborated by the author/compiler of the *Secret History of the Mongols*, although the three contemporaries lived at distances of thousands of miles.

Besides veracity, the chief merit of the *Tabaqat-i-Nasiri*, lies in its style. Facts are narrated in plain, simple prose, free from flights of fancy and ornate flowery language. The style is direct and unaffected. The *Tabaqat*, however, suffers from two shortcomings. At times, it is too concise to be useful; on occasion, it is irritating as an account of brevity, in regard to the invasion of the 'infidels' of Chingiz Khan into Bengal as far as the walls of Lakhnauti in AH 642 (1245). Yet he is arguably, unsurpassed by any contemporary or Mongol historian in his details about the resistance the all-conquering Mongols received in Ghor and Ghorzistan. Second, his plan is unsatisfactory. Instead of following a linear narrative of events in chronological order, his text is organized by dynasty. This results in overlaps and repetition sometimes with additional information as, for instance, the history of the Khwarazm Shah. And there is some confusion of dates and place-names. Yet, with all its shortcomings and errors of omission and commission, the *Tabaqat-i-Nasiri* remains an invaluable and incomparable source on the invasions of the Mongols and their frequent nightmarish visitations across the Indus, a source of constant concern to the sultans of Delhi.

Tarikh-i-Jahan Gusha

The *Tarikh-i-Jahan Gusha* of Ala-ud-din Ata Malik Juwaini is by far the best book on the subject. The author came from a family that had held the highest offices under the Seljuqs and the Khwarazm Shahs. Musta ad-din, the maternal uncle of his great-grandfather, was secretary and a favourite of the great Seljuq Sultan Sanjar, while his grandfather Shams-ad-din Muhammad, distinguished by the popular titles of 'The Great' and 'long haired', was a member of the entourage of Jalal-ud-din Khwarazm Shah and later Sultan Ala-ud-din Muhammad Khwarazm Shah. He remained faithful to his sovereign and accompanied the sultan in his flight from his Mongol pursuers to Nishapur. The fugitive sultan appointed him *Sahib-i-Diwan*, and Sultan Jalal-ud-din in his turn confirmed the appointment. He served the sultan till his own death in March 1230; he was laid to rest in his native town, Juwain.

Juwaini, too, was a high officer of the Mongol empire. Briefly, his career was as follows: secretary for 13 years to Amir Arghun, the Mongol governor of the lands west of the Oxus (1243–56); secretary of Hulagu Khan on his campaign against the Assassins of Alamut and the caliph of Baghdad, 1256-7; Governor of Baghdad, 1257-81, while the elder brother Shams-ud-din was *Sahib-i-Diwan* and wazir of Halagu's sons Abaqa and Takudar. Ata Malik's son, Baha-ud-din was appointed governor of Persian Iraq and Fars, another son Sharaf-ud-din was a poet of repute and in his turn a patron of poets. The end of the two brothers was rather tragic. Shams-ud-din was put to death while Ala-ud-din died destitute and broken-hearted; he wrote a book on his misfortunes—*Tasli-ul-ikhwan*. It makes painful reading. The charge of corruption had been brought against him but whether guilty or not guilty, the misfortunes of the Juwaini family show how precarious and perilous was the footing of Muslim officers under the Il-Khanids.

About the Juwaini family, Browne wrote: 'Their influence was great and widespread; their connection with literature, both as writers and as patrons of poets and men of learning, extensive; and the jealousy of less fortunate rivals which embittered their lives and finally brought about their destruction [was] commensurate with the power and high positions which they so long enjoyed'.

The *Tarikh-i-Jahan Gusha* is divided into three volumes: the first deals with Chingiz Khan, Kuyuk, and Uktae, the second with the rulers of Khwarazm from A-ti-siz to the death of Jalal-ud-din Mangbirni, the third with Mangu Khan and the Imams of Alamut. Later authors have borrowed heavily from Juwaini. For example, the whole of his third volume is summarized without acknowledgement by Mirkhwand, who among other things repeats our author's errors about the Fatimid caliphs. The *Tarikh-i-Jahan Gusha*, as pointed out by Mirza Abdul Wahab Qazwini, 'by virtue of the importance of its contents, the absence of any other contemporary work dealing with these subjects, and the high position of the author and the unique opportunities which he enjoyed of obtaining the most accurate information about the subjects on which he wrote, attained from the very moment of its publication a great celebrity, won the approbation of all, and was universally regarded by the best judges as authoritative and trustworthy in the highest degree.' A glance through the *Tarikh-i-Wassaf*, the *Jamiut-Tawarikh*, and the *Kitabul-Fakhri*, will indicate the debt which later historians owe to Ala-ud-din Ata Malik Juwaini.

Volumes I and II of the *Tarikh-i-Jahan Gusha* were edited by the great Persian scholar, Abdul Wahab Qazwini, for the Gibb Memorial series. They are the best edited historical texts. Then Qazwini, so Cambridge tradition says, slipped out of the protective guardianship of Browne. A facsimile edition of Volume III (unedited) was then brought out by the Denison Ross. Then Qazwini returned to his work and edited the third volume. All the three volumes have been reprinted in Tehran on the basis of Qazwini's text but without his footnotes.

Juwaini was a highly talented person and enjoyed the confidence of the Mongols at the highest levels, particularly the Mongol governors of Khurasan, Korgruz, and Amir Arghum, and finally, Nulaku; and it was in the company of Korguz and Amir Arghum that he visited the Mongol court several times. There he had the opportunity and privilege of moving in high Mongol circles as well as visiting envoys and traders from far and wide, and thus, acquire first-hand knowledge about those men and events that changed the history and map of not only Central Asia but the world. And it was there that in 1253 he was persuaded to write a history of the conquests of Chingiz Khan and his descendants, which would commemorate their achievements and prompt posterity to emulate them.

Juwaini was eminently qualified for the assignment by his ancestry, by his learning, administrative experience, and acquaintance with Mongol notables. He acquired information about the war, about the West, for which his status, familiarity with the relevant lands and peoples were to his advantage. It was a delicate task and also a tough one. No wonder Juwaini did not take it on his own and had to be persuaded to undertake it.

It was hard for a sensitive son of the soil to relive the agony of the surviving victims of the Khwarazm Shah's greed, foolhardiness, and cowardice, and the consequent wrath of the Mongol Khan. Juwaini journeyed through the scenes of death, destruction and devastation: the desecration of the Bokhara Friday Mosque, the ruins of the majestic architectural monuments of Samarqand, the ploughed-over but one-time great city of Nishapur, the once most-renounced but then the scorched library of Merv, whence on his own admission, the great Arab geographer Yaqut had just managed to run away with four hundred precious books. The sights and signs of devastated heritage must have stirred his heart and soul and, perhaps, that is why he did not cover the destruction of Baghdad, and closed his narrative at 1256.

Juwaini was a conscientious and careful historian, and, he was confronted with the same problems as the court historians of the Mongols. He solved the dilemma in his own way, inventing a style of his own by judiciously and deftly mixing the florid with plain and straightforward narration of events. As an official, he had to be eulogistic with reference to the Great Khan and his descendants, which he did in an admirable manner without minimizing or glossing over the devastation caused by Mongol horsemen. He was, surprisingly, forthright in praise of the daring, who had preferred death over dishonour and waged an unequal fight against the Mongols. His anger against those who betrayed or 'showed their heels without having stretched their hands' is revealed by the invective he carefully used against Ala-ud-din Khwarazm Shah and his mean and cowardly courtiers. He did it all in a careful manner, which testifies his mastery of language. He avoided directly eulogizing Jalal-ud-din Khwarazm Shah but by attributing the tribute and testimony to 'those who saw him', and narrated the compliment paid to the sultan by the Great Khan after the Battle of Indus. He resorted to puns, euphemisms and quotations from the Koran, the Hadith, and sayings of the ancients, legendary figures. He incorporated lines, stanzas from the great poets, and also anecdotes from the classics, to convey his genuine meaning and to reinforce, his arguments. It would, therefore, be unfair to pick out the panegyrics about Chingiz Khan and Mangu Khan or complimentary observations about the Mongol administration and condemn him as a sycophant. Barthold writes, 'It is not to be denied that the author conscientiously endeavoured to give a full and truthful narrative of the events.'

Juwaini has been criticized by scholars for indulging in exaggeration about the massacre in Khurasan and the resistance. But he was a court historian, writing for the satisfaction of his masters; he was going to get nothing from the common people by highlighting any episode which may raise the ire of those who mattered. Besides, it should also be noted that he is very clear about the casualties at Merv, Bokhara, and Nishapur; about Nishapur he mentions that the dead bodies were counted by 40 persons for 40 days. We have also to consider the fact that none of his jealous detractors brought against him a charge of falsifying history. Juwaini used the worst possible epithets against Khwarazm Shah for his folly and cowardice. The testimony of the geographers and travellers about the size and population of the towns and cities concerned is also to be taken into consideration before questioning his authenticity and credibility. Interestingly, the references to and compliments paid to Sultan Jalal-ud-din are unquestionably accepted and endorsed.

Juwaini's ornateness served a purpose; unable to express his ideas in plain speech he hints, according to the accepted tradition of official historians, at his meanings by veiled suggestions in the form of allegories and figures of speech. Juwaini's work will for all times be our main work of reference for the Khwarazm Shahs and Chingiz's campaigns in Muslim Asia.

Jamaiut-Tawarikh

The great historiographer Rashid-ud-din (1245–1318) is an indispensable and invaluable source on the history of the Mongols and the life of Chingiz Khan and his descendants. He is unique among the ancient and medieval chroniclers in that his composition, *Jamaiut-Tawarikh* (Compendium of Chronicles), is not confined to the activities and achievements of one people or one dynasty; it is neither local in its scope nor parochial in its approach but covers the history of almost the then known whole world: from China and Korea to Britain and the Franks (France was not till then a country), and from Russia to Hindustan.

Born in Hamadan (western Iran) to a Jewish family, he converted to Islam along with his parents. His grandfather, Muffaq-ud-Daula Ali, and his father Rais-ud-Daula are said to have been the 'unwilling guests' of the Imam of Alamut and there had the opportunity to associate with the famous intellectual and astrologer, Nasir-ud-Din Tusi in his scientific activities. The family was fortunate to escape after the defeat of the Imam, from the devastation that attended the extermination of his followers, known as the Assassins of Al-Amut, as they managed to leave before Hulaku besieged and then stormed it, and go over to the Il-Khanid court where Rais-ud-Daula and Rashid-ud-din were given both protection and service according to their attainments. Rashid-ud-din so impressed his masters that he was given the prestigious post of *bawarchi* (cook), probably akin to Superintendent of the Royal Kitchen. Pleased by him, the Il-khan Geikhatu (1291–5) recruited him to the civil service, and it was during the reign of Ghazan Khan that he won the respect of the Il-khan and was appointed *Sahib-i-Diwan* (prime minister) in 1296. He retained this important post during the reigns of two successive Ilkhans, Ulzaitu and Abu Said.

It was Ghazan Khan who entrusted to Rashid-ud-din the task of writing a history of the conquests of Chingiz Khan and his descendants lest the succeeding generations forget the deeds of their forefathers. History was to preserve the record and perpetuate their memory. It would also provide them with models and guides to follow in the future. Ghazan Khan was liberal in sanctioning financial and research assistance. The original manuscript was well illuminated and Mirkhwand remarked with envy that Rashid-ud-din was given 60,000 dinars for the preparation and publication of the works, an action unprecedented in the medieval Islamic world. Official patronage enbled him to have access to state archives including the *Altan Depter or the Golden Book*. Rashid-ud-din had the privilege of the assistance of Pulad, Qublai Khan's ambassador at the Ilkhan court, who was considered as the greatest authority on Mongol history and traditions. Writes Rashid-ud-din, 'Ghazan Khan knows the smallest details of the history of the Mongols, the names of their ancestors and of past and present armies, and the genealogy of most of the Mongol tribes. Apart from Pulad no one knows these facts as well as he does. He alone knows Mongol secrets, but he confessed, 'these are not included in this history.' The reasons are obvious. The highly talented physician, great administrator, and public spirited statesman turned part-time historian justified the trust reposed in him by three successive Il-Khans.

Rashid-ud-din supplements Juwaini by giving a more detailed account of the life and conditions in Mongolia before the rise of Chingiz, the early life of the conqueror, his sayings and military organization, but leaves intact Juwaini's account of Mongol campaigns and conquests in Muslim Asia and condenses that of the Khwarazm Shahs. The *Jamaiut-Tawarikh* is, however, invaluable and as Rashid-ud-din was successful in collecting traditions on the early history of Chingiz Khan which seem to have been derived from the *Altan-Depter* or the Golden Book probably through Ghazan Khan and Pulad and his *Yassas*, *Yarliks* and *Biliks*. Our author continues the history of the Mongols as his own work from the death of Uktae to the reign of Ghazan Khan. Rashid-ud-din's style is straightforward and intelligible. Though an official historian, he is not ornate and does not indulge in meaningless figures of speech.

The *Jamaiut-Tawarikh* is unquestionably a landmark in history writing. It is not confined to a chronicle of the life and times of Chingiz Khan and his family, but is a history of then known world and its peoples. The value lies in the fact that he provides us a complete, intelligible, and authentic record not only of the history of the Mongols but also a valuable and detailed account of the nomadic Tatar (Tartar) and Turkish tribes. Moreover, it gives us an exact and interesting account of China (Khita or Cathay).

The Compendium is not unique merely on account of the extensive field it covers, but also for the great variety and number of sources tapped: Chinese, Mongolian, Turkish, Hebrew, Syriac, Tibetan, Uighur, Armenian, and Georgian. It was an unprecedented achievement to muster so such material, to size and analyse it, and then present it in a coherent and readable form as the world's first universal history. This was made possible, as indicated earlier, by the keen and enthusiastic commitment of the Ilkhans, the unstinted cooperation and support of the establishment, and the dedicated service of the support staff, which the great Rashid-ud-din was able to inspire.

'I will dwell no longer on the proofs of the extreme importance of Rashid-ud-din's compilation', said Quateremere. 'The excellent work, undertaken in the most favourable circumstances, and with means of performing it never possessed by any single writer, offered for the first time to the people of Asia—complete course of universal history and geography.'

Tarikh-i-Guzidah

Although not a historian, Hamdullah Mustawfi was an admirer of Rashid-ud-din and often used to spend time with him. He was in a way a follower of the great historian as he decided to follow in his footsteps by utilizing his spare time to compose a 'Select History', *Tarikh-i-Guzidah*. He refers to at least twelve books, which he used as his sources, including the *Tarikh-al-Kamil* of Ibnul Asir, the *Zubaut-Twarikh* of Jamal-ud-Din Abul Qasim Kashani, the *Nizamut-Tawarikh* of Qazi Nassimud-Din al-Bayzawi, the *Kitabul-Mairif* of Ibn Qutajaba, the *Tarikh-i-Jahan Gusha* of Ata Malik Juwaini, and of course, the work of his patron and idol, Rashid-ud-din. The book was dedicated to his patron's son, Ghias-ud-din Muhammad.

Born in 1281-2 and brought up in the shadow of men of learning and substance, who had learnt from victims or seen the smoked ruins of the devastation caused by Ulugh Noyan armies through Khurasan (then, perhaps the most prosperous province of the Khwarazmian empire), Hamdullah got information from many a lucky survivor of those terrible days, among them his own great-grandfather, who may be reckoned as an almost contemporary authority for what he heard, saw and recorded for the benefit of posterity.

Hamdullah was a man of many parts as testified by his versatility, wide-ranging interests and experience. Among his writings *Tarikh-i-Guzidah*, the *Zafar-Nama*, and the *Nuzhatul Qutab*; the first two are historical in nature while the last is a geographical exercise. And all three are monuments to his industry and substantive interests, and contribute to an understanding of the devastation and misery the Khwarasmians had undergone, as well as their capacity to rise from the ashes.

The three books are written in three different styles. The *Tarikh-i-Guzidah* is a brief compendium of history from Adam to the author's own times (1330) and is precise as to facts and chronology but provides us many interesting details or particulars not found elsewhere. Besides, it is a primary source for the contemporary period of Mongol history, that is, Persia under the Il-khans.

The *Nuzhatul Qutab* (1333–4) is, on the other hand, a geographical and cosmological exercise. It is factual and based on his administrative experience and wide reading and travels through Persia. He mentions among his nineteen sources the following: The *Survival Aqalim* of Abu Zazad Ahmad, the *Tibyan* of Ahmad, son of Abi Abdullah, *Masalik Wal-mamalik* of Abul Qasim Abdullah, son of Khurdadbih.

Having been *mustawi mamalik* or auditor general of the kingdom of the Il-khans in the first half of the fourteenth century, Hamdullah shows a wonderful knowledge of geographical details and the revenue system of Persia. From him one can also glean the effects of anarchy, injustice, taxation, and the arrogance and rapaciousness of the tax collectors on the health of the polity. In a word, the *Nuzhatul Qutub* performs for the kingdom of the Il-khan what *Ain-i-Akbari* did for the Mughal Empire in India in the seventeenth century. It is particularly useful with reference to the fiscal administration under the Il-khans and reveals the decline in the income of the peasant and the state after the Mongol massacre.

Hamdullah Mustawfi's *Zafar-Nama* is a historical narrative in verse. It contains 35,000 complete verses and covers the period from the time of the Prophet down to his own age. It is written in a simple and straightforward manner. The *Zafar-Nama* is the opposite of *Tarikh-i-Wassaf*. It took the poet about 15 years to complete its composition. It is lucid and interesting. The author seems to have taken special care about the veracity of the facts and as he belonged to Qazawin, he saw the effects of the Mongol devastation and could gather facts from people with first-hand knowledge of the Mongols, also from his own grandfather, Amin Nasr Mustawfi, who was 93 years of age. Ironically, on both occasions, avoidable and unnecessary 'avalanches' were invited. The following extract (translation by Browne) will, for instance, testify to his poetic genius and the quality of his descriptive power in narrating what happened at Qazawin.

> In terror of the Mongol soldiery.
> Hither and thither did the people fly.
> Some seeking refuge to the mosque did go,
> Hearts filled with anguish, souls surcharge with awe
> From that fierce so for their straits and plight
> The climbing forms the arches hid from sight.

The ruthless Mongols burning brands did ply
Till tongues of flame left upwards the sky.
Roof, vault and arch in burning ruin fell.
A heathen holocaust of Death and Hell.

The *Tarikh-i-Wassaf* of Abdullah Ibn Fazlullah, better known as 'wars of Hazrat' and as 'The Panegyrist' is another valuable source for the financial administration in Persia under the Il-khans. He too was a government official in the revenue department and, therefore, an authority for the fiscal system, collection of revenue, and the economic condition of the peasantry. Though an experienced research assistant of Rashid-ud-din, the *Tarikh-i-Wassaf* as a contribution to the *Jamaiut-Tawarikh*, is as different in style and purpose as imaginable. Though a masterpiece of the grand style characterized by pompous and exuberant rhetoric, it is hardly readable or understandable by the average scholar, but it is an original and important authority for a student of the revenue system of the Il-Khanid Mongols. When Rashid-ud-din presented the book along with its author to Khan Uljaitu, the Mongol Khan could not make head or tail of it. For the author, however, it did not matter for he was not concerned with facts or advancing the frontiers of knowledge but with expounding his knowledge and his command over language, in which he preeminently succeeded.

The rise of Timur and his dynasty gave a fresh impetus and zest to the study of Mongol history, though all histories of the post-Timurid period give to his ancestors an importance which earlier works like the *Secret History* and *Tarikh-i-Jahan Gusha* do not justify. The *Zafar Namah* of Sharfuddin Yazdi is an official biography of Timur, written under the personal direction of Shah Rukh, the younger son of Timur, who was the ruler of Heart. The book is thoroughly official, though the author makes fairly understandable hints at Timur's crimes. An Introduction, known as *Tarikh-i-Jahangir*, was added by Yazdi to his official work; it deals with Chingiz Khan and his descendants down to the time of Timur. The Raza Library, Rampur has a good copy of the manuscript.

Shah Rukh's son, Ulugh-Beg, wrote the 'History of the Four Ulus' (*Tarikh-arba-i-Ulus*) which has reached us in an abridged form. The original 'History' seems to have been lost but the abridgement—the *Shajratul Atrak*—shows that it dealt with the lineage of the Mongols from the Timuriat viewpoint. The original text is preserved in the British Museum. I have used the English translation of Col. Miles.

Tarikh-al-Kamil

Brought up at Mosul, educated in Baghdad and the institutions of higher learning in Baghdad, Jerusalem and Syria, Ibnul Asir returned home after seeing the 'world' and getting exposure to the intellectual atmosphere at the great seats of learning. After returning to Mosul he devoted himself to extensive reading and literary pursuits. Ibnul Asir was conscientious about the collection of facts and judicious in their selection and analysis. He has, therefore, deservedly enjoyed high repute for his veracity.

The *Tarikh-al-Kamil* of Ibnul Asir is recognized as a standard work of Islamic history. In conformity with the then prevalent tradition, he covers the history of the world from the earliest times down to AD 1230. He thus lived in the time of many momentous events that shook the Muslim world in the thirteenth century and which he recorded in the last two volumes of his great work, singularly free from inaccuracies.

Living in Mesopotamia far from some of the terrible scenes of action, and in no position to verify the devastation caused by the triumphal march of the 'infidels' though Transoxiana and northern Persia, he could only depend upon the accounts of fugitives and survivors of the holocaust; it was rarely that he could get eyewitness accounts as, for instance, in the case of Bokhara and Samarqand. Yet he is, on the whole, regarded as a trustworthy and valuable corroborator and supplementary source of information for the history of Chingiz Khan and the Mongols; and the *al-Kamil*, as De Slane observed, 'merits its reputation as one of the best products of its kind'.

Another contemporary work is *Sirat-i-Jalal-ul-din Mangbirni* by Shihab-ud-din Muhammad bin Ahmad Nassavi. This is a monograph on the romantic career of a dashing sultan whose secretary he had become after the sultan's return from India, and as such he is concerned more with the adventures of Sultan Jalal-ud-din than the campaigns of Chingiz Khan. He does not record in detail the atrocities perpetrated on the peoples of Transoxiana, Khwarazm, or Khurasan but tells a lot about the internal conditions, wrangling, and struggles for power. He provides useful insight into the sorry state of affairs that accounted for the pitiable end of the once powerful Khwarazmian empire. Though contemporaries, Ibnul Asir and Nassavi fail to give us a detailed and complete account of the career and campaigns of Chingiz Khan. Of the early life of Chingiz they knew very little and, what is more surprising, they have not a word about Juji's campaign from Utrar down the Syr Darya or Jaxartes. They are, however, invaluable for the history of Central Asia in the thirteenth century.

The *Wazayatul-Ayan* (Obituaries of Eminent Men), by Shams-ud-din Shan Khallishan, is an interesting composition of immense value to students of biography and history. It may justifiably be ranked with Ibn Khaldun's *Muqaddima* as opening new vistas for a meaningful understanding and appreciation of what happened in history and why.

Of distinguished lineage, claiming descent from the great family of the Barmacides, Ibn Khallikan was himself a distinguished scholar, noted for his diligence and erudition and simple but elegant language. His *magnum opus*, the *Wafaya*, is a five-volume monument of an astonishing quantity of accurate information, both historical and literary, enriched with anecdotes. Arranged alphabetically, he starts with jurists, followed by caliphs (but restricted to those whom he knew personally or who were living in his time), religious scholars, kings, Sufis, warriors, ministers, and all well-known individuals. One wonders if the arrangement reflected the priority accorded to them by Ibn Khallikan.

Explaining the nature and scope of his work, Ibn Khallikan said (De Slane's translation):

I have not limited my work to the history of any one particular class of persons, as learned men, princes, amirs, viziers (ministers) or poets; but I have spoken of all those whose names are familiar to the public and about questions are frequently asked. I have, however, related the facts I could *ascertain respecting* them in a concise manner, lest my work became too voluminous…; and I have cited the traits which may best serve to characterize each individual, such as noble actions, singular anecdotes, verses and letters, … (Emphasis added).

Muqaddima Al-Khaldun

Born in Tunis (1332) Ibn Khaldun is one of the eminent figures in the intellectual history of the medieval Muslim world, and certainly the greatest scholar that Andalusia and Africa produced in the fourteenth century. As a scholar-politician, his career was chequered and crowded with great events. It was characterized by ups and downs. He was a man of action and enjoyed politics as he cherished learning, though with varying success. He was greatly respected for his wide learning, originality of thought, and ability to communicate knowledge but as a politician, he excited in equal measure deep jealousy and great opposition and had ultimately to bid adieu to his field of action. He had to migrate to Egypt and die in self-exile (in Cairo, 1406) among people whom he hardly admired. Nevertheless, he got there not only a final resting place but also everlasting fame as a scholar and thinker, and as the father of historiography.

For the history of Chingiz Khan and the Mongols Ibn Khaldun's monumental *Kitab al-Ibar* is not as important as is the *Muqaddima* (Introduction) to his great composition. The *Muqaddima* is in reality more than an introduction, as it, is an entity in itself. For in it he propounded and elucidated at great length, with relevant examples, a new method of studying and writing history and understanding events. History is not, according to him, a mere narration of facts and events, the lives of great men, or the rise and fall of dynasties, it is more than that. For a man does not stand alone in the universe and does not live or operate in a vacuum; he lives in an interdependent universe. History is, therefore, a special or autonomous science to study things, events and men in correlation with the compact habits of food, climate, soil, etc. and their interdependence in the evolutionary process of human development and civilization.

Ibn Khaldun finds that nomadism and civilization are two stages of history, one imperceptibly leading to the other, but not two isolated or conflicting situations. Human history should be understood as a process and nomadism and civilization constitute a syndrome—the nomadism-civilization syndrome—as we now accept and appreciate the rural-urban syndrome. Nomadism is the first stage while civilization is the second. Nomadism, is according to his first-hand knowledge, notable for its simplicity and purity of manner, faithfulness, hard and harsh life, and, in modern terminology, free from the 'diseases' of civilization. Another distinguishing feature of nomadism is what he terms *asabiyzah*, namely, commitment, loyalty, and devotion to the welfare and security of the family and the tribe, or the principle of 'one for all, and all for one'. This accounts for many of the features of tribal nomadic society. However, the situation undergoes a sea change when the nomads pour out of their inhospitable terrain, be it the Aryans, the *Huns*, the Arabs, or the Mongols. They 'raid', plunder and return, and also go on to conquer the richer societies and settle down to consolidate their valuable gains and govern the conquered. They then tend to acquire the habits of their subjects, adopt their religion, and in the process become more civilized (as happened, for instance, with the Il-Khanids in Persia and with Qubilai Khan and his descendants in China). Civilization is characterized by higher standards of living and luxury, intellectual and cultural pursuits, settled and secure life protected and defended by others, namely rulers and their armed forces. These characteristics, cumulatively lead to 'distance' between the rulers and the citizens. Such a development leads to selfishness and the loosening of social ties and a weakening of the sense of belonging, of responsibility and loyalty to the polity (*or asabiyzah*) or, in modern terms, patriotism and nationalism.

Ibn Khaldun enables us to appreciate Qukhan's advice to his people to 'always wander, never settle', and the fascination of Chingiz Khan for the nomadic life and his contempt for the contemporary civilized or sedentary societies. Ibn Khaldun's analysis was based on the corruption and degeneracy he discovered in the Muslim dynasties and in the very texture of his contemporary civil societies. He was, thus, a historian of civilization without compare.

Amir Ali Sher, the first great poet of the Turkish language, whose *Diwan Babar* copied out with his own hands, was also the Wazir of Sultan Husain Mirza, King of Heart. He was himself a man of letters, a patron of art and letters; he used his official position to organize an academy by providing houses, books, and pensions to authors of eminence. The centre of this circle of eminence was Maulana Jami, who wrote his *Nafhatul-Uns* (Encyclopedic Notices of Muslim Mystics) on the basis of material provided by Amir Ali Sher. The duty of writing the history of the world was assigned to Mirkhawand, who planned his work in seven volumes. It is only concerning the history of Ajam beginning with the 'Minor Dynasties of Persia in the ninth century' that the work can be considered authoritative. Volumes V and VI deal with Chingiz Khan and the later period. The author was bedridden while writing the history of Sultan Husain Mirza and his work was completed by his son.

The value of *Rauzat-us-Safa* for historical purposes lies in two facts. First, the author had access to books like *Tarikh-i-Herat*, which gives an account of Mongol slaughter, and has not reached us. He has incorporated almost all that was of worth in those works. Second, in spite of the slaughter by Timur that followed, there was in his time a living tradition of the bitter days of Mongol conquest. The *Rauzat-us-Safa* thus enables us to fill many gaps in the accounts of Juwaini and Rashid-ud-din, who wrote under Mongol patronage.

The *Habib al-Siyar* of Khwandmir is, on the whole, a compendium based of *Rauzat-us-Safa*. But the author discovers new facts in addition to the account given by his grandfather. The two books have also the merit of being illuminated and enlivened by interesting anecdotes.

Sino-Mongolian Sources

The *Secret History of the Mongol Dynasty* is one of the earliest contemporary accounts of the life and career of Temuchin Chingiz Khan. It is the first and only account of the Mongol leader in the Uighur script while others are in Arabic and Persian.

The *Secret History* shows no influence of China, Islam, or Christianity. Its anonymous compilers and editors had apparently an excellent knowledge of Mongolian geography from personal experience. It is equally clear that they knew nothing of Muslim lands; Chingiz's historic campaigns in Central Asia, Persia, and Afghanistan are dismissed in two paragraphs. On the other hand, the early legends as well as the historical traditions of the Mongols and Chingiz's career up to his second accession are described in great detail. There is no other record of the early career of Chingiz Khan except this book; other Chinese histories merely borrow from it.

The early Persian records give us no reliable account of the early career of Chingiz Khan. Qazi Minhaj had the vaguest idea of Mongolia and its people as is proved by his chapters on 'the Mongols' in his *Tabaqat-i-Nasiri*. Ala-ud-din Ata Malik Juwaini, writing in about 1258, gives the vaguest description of the early career of Chingiz and the Mongols in general, though he gives a very detailed and reliable account of the Mongol conquest of Muslim lands. Under the influence of the Timurid rulers, the historians manufactured a legendary history of the Mongols which we find in the *Shajratul Atrak*, based on a work of Timur's grandson, Ulugh-Beg. But this moves in the realm of legend. It is this fact which gives a unique value to the *Secret History*. The first chapter of the book is legendary, but after that it comes to the historical tradition and later to incontrovertible historical facts. The authenticity of the book is proved by its geographical details, which are accurate, and by the fact that Rashid-ud-din, writing independently in the early part of the fourteenth century, with access to state archives and to the *Altan Depter*, and with the benefit of research assistance and traditions possessed by Ghazan Khan and Pulad available to him, is mostly in agreement with the facts and statements as given in the *Secret History*.

The *Secret History* is a novel and unique chronicle in its own way. The title is neither correct nor truly indicative of its nature and scope and a bit confusing. There is nothing 'secret' in it or about it, no startling facts, no incriminating revelations, much less scandals or court intrigues. It was, perhaps, meant to be *secret* in the sense of 'confidential' 'for safe keeping' or 'for private circulation only'.

Another misleading feature of the book is that though it is titled *Secret History of the Mongol Dynasty*, it covers, and covers very well, the life, career, wisdom, foresight and organizational skill of Chingiz Khan excepting the campaign 'war in the west', and provides us a life-size account of his public and private life, but only a perfunctory account of some good deeds and actions of Uktae. The Mongolian version had no sub-divisions or chapters, but the Chinese editors/translators, in keeping with their tradition, arranged it in twelve chapters disregarding their contents, so that topic-wise, there is neither neatness nor continuity. The bulk of the book (10 chapters) deals exclusively with Chingiz Khan, one chapter with both Chingiz and Uktae, and only the last covers Uktae, and his reforms, particularly concerning the post system (the *Yam*) and taxation.

Another distinctive feature of the *Secret History* is that is was written in the Uighur script. Even if it had been made 'public', the Mongols, by and large, would have had no access to it given that they were mostly an unlettered people. This leads to the question as to why it was written and for whom. The author(s) provide no hint.

What may have prompted, if not actually inspired, someone from amongst the entourage of the Great Conqueror to record the amazing life-history and achievements of the illustrious hero, was, perhaps, the impact of the Chinese tradition of preserving records of their past rulers of their long and distinguished past, or else the dismal fate of contemporary empires, three in number, the distant and dimly known Khwarazmian Empire (extending from the Syr Darya to the Caspian Sea) and the nearby Hsia-Hsia, and the Chin. Alternately, the *Secret History* was to be something in the nature of a hand-book, *a la* Machiavelli's *Prince*, for the members of the ruling family and their trusted advisors to inform, encourage, and even guide them to purposeful activity and fruitful for themselves and also for their people.

The authorship and authenticity are a matter of sustained controversy in academia. There are two main divergent but highly esteemed schools. Some scholars like A. Walez regard the *Secret History* almost worthless as chronicle; they point to glaring incongruities and mistakes such as its unreliable chronology, Qgodei (Uktae) being referred to as Qaan in Section 198 though elected later as mentioned in Section 269. There are, however, other scholars like Rene Grousset, who accept its authority as a historical and useful record of the social, political and religious life and activities or history of the 'Golden Clan' of Chingiz Khan and his conquests. They regard the biases and incongruities or unreliability on certain events as aberrations, the result of later additions, deletions, and editorial whims. There are, however, some other Mongolists such as S. Bira and Igor de Rachewiltz, who take a middle position and I have followed them in accepting the *Secret History of the Mongols* as an authentic and important source of the life of Chingiz Khan as far as his early life and their activities east of the Amu Darya are concerned.

Nothing can be said with certainty, about the authorship, but, as demonstrated by de Rachewiltz, the most likely person could be Shigi Qutuqu. He was an adopted brother of Chingiz, nursed and nurtured by Mother Oyelun as her fifth son, brought up as a family member and so an insider. He was brave and intelligent, tested and trusted by Chingiz, and made chief judge and entrusted with the keeping of legal pronouncements. Also appointed military commander, he accompanied the Great Khan on his west Asian campaign. Significantly, he was also the only commander who was crushingly defeated by Sultan Jalal-ud-din *but* neither reproached nor disgraced. And the campaign to western Asia is dismissed in just two paragraphs in the *Secret History* though Shigi Qutuqu was, perhaps, one of the best suited to give us the victors' view of the stupendous feat. Perhaps he did not wish to tell about Parwan and so decided to slant out the whole campaign as a bad dream.

Notwithstanding the problems detailed above, the *Secret History of the Mongol Dynasty* is generally and rightly regarded as an indispensable and invaluable document of the career of Chingiz Khan. Written in the Year of the Rat (1228) by the side of the river Kerulen and under the shadows of the Aral Mountains, admirably suited for poetic fancy and epic fantasy, the *Secret History* partakes the character of both. It is written in plain and simple language but liberally interspersed, at appropriate places, with attractive and poetic passages amounting to about one-third of the entire book that make for interesting (as well as irritating) reading. But they give the narrative an authentic Mongolian flavour. Such is Oyelun's description of the destitution and dire straits to which Yesukai's family was reduced after his death, her harsh words and rebuke to Chingiz on his quarrel with his brothers, or Chingiz Khan's own declamations recounting the valuable services of his boyhood friends and subsequent associates and followers. In epic style, Chingiz Khan's descent is ascribed to 'a blue grey wolf, with his destiny ordained by Heaven above', whose 'wife was a fallow doe', with a son born to them by the source of the Onon River on Mount Burqan.

In similar epic style is described Yesukai's journey to find a suitable girl for Temuchin, their chance meeting with Dai Sechin, and Temuchin's betrothal to Bortei. These are splendid pieces of epic narrative, and so are constant references to 'Mighty Heaven' and 'Mother Earth' aiding Temuchin in his struggles. Nevertheless, the *Secret History* is not an epic, but a down-to-earth chronicle of the vicissitudes, toils, and troubles which Temuchin underwent on his rise to power and grandeur. The unseemly flights to save his own skin by abandoning family to the mercies of his enemies, his unheroic cunning and chicanery to get rid of the Tangut ruler, and even the last journey to his final resting place, all are narrated in a style prosaic and matter of fact, with no alliterative passages for a ballad-singer, no crying and mourning for the 'mighty tree fallen', no 'hard stone broken'. The narrative rather reflects a stoicism, fortitude, and wisdom.

Whatever the controversies, doubts and uncertainties concerning the authorship and authenticity of the *Secret History*, there is hardly any doubt regarding its general acceptance as one of the basic sources for history of the twelfth-thirteenth century Mongols and their great Khan. It is also a repository of information about their customs and beliefs.

The importance of the *Secret History* lies in its being the earliest, almost contemporaneous, extant account of the life and times of Chingiz Khan, the first and the only one outstanding Mongol warlord and a worldwide empire-builder. It remained 'suppressed' or 'a close preserve' for quite some time but ever since its discovery and publication, the *Secret History* has been the subject of intense scholarly interest and as mentioned in earlier debate. The most important of all Chingiz Khan's organizations was the Guard (Kishk), not just an elite corps under the direct command of the *Khaqan*, but also the effective instrument or institution for holding and defending the hard won domains. How it was organized, and its privileges, are described in the text. The writ of the *Khaqan* ran throughout the length and breadth of Chingiz's domains. It assured the fear and majestic awe of the *Khaqan*, the strict enforcement of the *Yassa* and maintenance of the *Yam* or the horse-post system. The *Secret History* also served as a handbook for the self instruction and guidance of the ruling family: a manual for administration and governance.

This history has the added merit of complementing the gaps and omissions in Persian sources, particularly about the early life of Chingiz Khan, his struggle for survival and, ultimately, his attainment of overlordship of the steppes. Besides, its epic style provides both flesh and soul to much that we learn from other sources. We are, thanks to the anonymous author of the *Secret History*, able to see Chingiz Khan not only in his 'robes' and arms, or even in his 'awesome and fearful' glory but also as a human being. The *Secret History* gives some wonderful pictures, as, for instance, the tongue lashing of Temuchin by Mother Oyelun, tears flowing down the cheeks of the 'Man of Blood and Iron' at the sight of the wounded Uktae being brought by Bogurchi with Uktae's feet dangling from the horseback, or seeking through the 'good offices' of his Noyans the reaction and response of his first wife Bortei, to his taking Qulan Qatun as wife and bringing her to the *yurt*!

The *Secret History* covers not only Chingiz Khan's life and work but it also indicates that the great achievements were not just a one-man show. It accords due recognition to his valiant companions of early days such as the 'four hounds' and 'the four steeds'; it even remembers the 'commanders of a thousand'. Thus one wonders to whom should be given the greater credit—the superior commander for his skill, wisdom and leadership qualities, or the valiant warriors for their commitment to the leader and his commands. None ever betrayed his trust, much less turned traitor; and hardly any one (except Shigi Qutuqu and that too, against none else but Sultan Jalal-ud-din) failed to deliver.

The importance attached to the study of the *Secret History* is attested by its seven versions in Chinese, and by its large-scale incorporation in the seventeenth-century *Altan Tobch* (Golden Book). There are translations and transcriptions in Turkish, Mongolian, Chinese, Japanese, Polish, English and most European languages. For it is the only primary and extant source on the role the Mongols played in the great Eurasian epic of the thirteenth century.

A Note on Rashid-ud-Din Fazlullah and The Date of Temuchin's Birth

THE DATE of birth of Chingiz Khan was generally accepted as mentioned by Rashid but has become a subject of controversy. One wonders why, against the general consensus about the authenticity of Rashid-ud-din, doubts were raised as regards the date of Temuchin's birth. They seem to overlook the fact that Rashid was an official historian with unparalleled, access to information, unavailable even to later historians. They also overlook the fact that such a 'great' mistake or blunder would have been immediately pounded upon by his jealous and ambitious rivals to malign and denigrate him and certainly by Ali Shah who had a grudge against Rashid and even had his body exhumed from the grave and transferred to a Jewish cemetery. One of the scholars has, however, delved deep into the dark recesses of the psyche and seems to insinuate that it is an expression of the deep dislike of his co-religionists and, perhaps, of his own, against 'The Great Khan' as they may have had in mind the holocaust in Khurasan and other cities of the Khwarazmian Empire. According to him, the Jews and the Muslims hate the pig, and Rashid was a Jew by origin and a Muslim by choice, and, so logically, the year of the pig (Hogg) could have been ascribed to Chingiz Khan to get vicarious satisfaction or pleasure that the 'infidel' was born in the 'hated' month. This argument is not just far-fetched but also flawed and factually untenable. Far from what I know of Muslims and the teachings of the Koran (the Muslim Holy Book), there is nothing like enjoining 'hatred' against any of God's creatures, even against one's adversaries. The Prophet set admirable examples in this regard. The pig, however, figures in the list of 'prohibited foods' and the list also includes blood and carcass but even the listed items are permitted in emergencies. And what 'vicarious satisfaction' could be had after more than one hundred years particularly when Muslims do not believe in such horoscopes which have been acknowledged, even acclaimed by some of his bitterest critics.

A more plausible argument revolves round the 'age' of Chingiz Khan and the arduous campaign against Khwarazm Shah at such an advanced age of, more or less, sixty. A still more plausible argument could, perhaps, have been on the basis of health. But age has no necessary correlation with health. Moreover, all accounts testify to his robust health till the last campaign and none mentions any incident, infirmity, ailment or even 'exhaustion' and tiredness during the war in the west, such as, for instance, like the fall of the Khan from horseback or 'fever' in the course of the campaign against the Tangut chief.

He was, and remained all through, a man of robust health and virility. He took Qulan Qatun along with him on his campaign against Khwarazm Shah, and Yessui Qatun in the campaign against Tangut chief. Besides, there was, according to Juwaini, the arrangement of systematic supply of concubines for the army, its leaders and the Great Khan, and according to Barthold, a choir of maidens always accompanied him. Even the Taoist Monk noted the presence of concubines in the camp, felt uncomfortable to be so near their tents, and, at his request, was allotted a quieter place.

The 'age' factor can be, and is generally applicable to 'ordinary' and 'average' persons. Born 'with a clot of blood' in his hand, distinguished by fire in his eyes and light in his face in his childhood, strong will and grim determination to have his due and in his own way as against Qasar and the Shaman Teb-tengri and the char-devil for the recovery of the stolen horses from the robbers' camp, endurance and presence of mind during Taichuit captivity in boyhood, strong will and grim determination to succeed against all odds, generous, even lavish in praising and rewarding his companions of boyhood days and his followers for their steadfast loyalty and valuable services, even to the extent of giving away a wife of his own, Ibaha, as a memento of his appreciation and utmost regard for invaluable services, in his days of triumph and power, and so on till his last breath when he awarded the movable palace, and bowls and vessels that the unsuspecting Tangut chief, Ilu Burqan had brought as presents for the Khan to Tolun Cherbi for executing Ilu Burqan with his own hands.

In the absence of more credible evidence to the contrary, it is difficult not to stick to the date of birth given by the great Il-Khanid historian Rashid-ud-din Fazlullah, specially chosen for this task by one of the 'greatest Mongolist', of the day, the Mongolid Khan, Ghazan Khan.

Besides, the Muslims never imposed such prohibitions upon their non-Muslim subjects anywhere throughout their history. They, on the other hand, followed a policy of toleration in matters of religious beliefs and practices in accordance with the Koranic verses that 'there is no compulsion in matters of religion' for them their religion, for us our religion'. And this policy was being followed in Muslim lands when Christendom was going through the throes of the Inquisition and the stakes, when Wycliffe's remains were being dug up and burnt while John Hubs was being consigned alive to the flames. When in Europe the Jews were derided and marginalized, the Ottoman Turks provided them refuge, safety, and livelihood. Ironically, and contrary to the eulogistic appreciation by modern scholars such as Dozy, Scot, and Lane-Poole concerning the Moorish contribution to the development of Spain, street-lighting, public baths, widespread literacy, rich libraries and institutions of higher learning and education, which made Andalusia (or Modern Spain) a beacon of light, learning and enlightenment, the policy of tolerance and enlightenment boomeranged against them. And in the 'Apostasies and Treasons of the Moriscoes (Moors or Muslims)' listed in a Charter drawn up (1602) by the Archbishop of Valencia recommending the expulsion of the Saracens from Spain besides the crimes of washing and bathing, it was specifically recorded: 'They committed nothing so much as that liberty in all matters of religion which the Turks and all other Mohammadans, suffer their subjects to enjoy.' And, according to Dozy, Scott, Lane-Poole, and other scholars, more than 80,000 rare and precious books were put to flames in Granada alone, hundreds and thousands were massacred and hundreds burnt alive. Thousands were baptized compulsorily or forced to declare themselves Christians, and around three million Moors against all solemn pledges and code of 'civilized' conduct were expelled, bag and baggage, out of Spain in the name of none other than Jesus Christ. And with such a legacy and the circumstances and reason detailed above, how and what a vicarious satisfaction an erudite, enlightened and universally respected historian could derive by ascribing a wrong date of birth to the ancestor of his patron, and that too, after no less than 80 years of the death of the Great Conqueror, and when the devastated lands were well on the road to recovery, rehabilitation and rejuvenation.

Rashid-ud-din was conversant with Islamic jurisprudence and theology as well as the shining legacy of compassion and tolerance bequeathed for instance by the Holy Prophet, who issued a general amnesty on the occasion of his triumphal but peaceful march into Mecca for all those who had persecuted, socially boycotted him and his followers and, after their emigration to Madina, waged two wars against them, in one of which his uncle was killed, and by Caliph Abu Bakr, who issued strict instructions to his troops against harming the old and the infirm, women, children and travellers, even against destroying crops or cutting trees. A similar paradigm was set by Caliph Omar, who accepted the proposal of the High Priest and undertook the arduous journey to Jerusalem on camel back and on foot, for the sake of avoiding unnecessary blood, and to personally receive the keys of the Holy City. He even went a step further, and out of respect for Christian sensibilities and to avoid the creation of any precedent, he politely declined the offer of the Patriarch to offer his prayers inside the Church. Centuries later, following their footprints, Saladin the Great proclaimed a general amnesty at the re-conquest of Jerusalem from the Crusaders. We have already noted at another place that, notwithstanding his bitterness against the 'infidel' Chingiz Khan and his horsemen, Qazi Minhaj Siraj, a contemporary eyewitness has given us an honest picture of the Great Conqueror and which the best of the 'histories' of Chingiz Khan seem but to elucidate and elaborate at great length.

Bibliography

Abdullah Ibn Fazlullah, *Tarikh-i-Wassaf*, ed., Muhmmad Mehdi Asfahan, Bombay.

Abul Fazl, *Akbar Nama*, Eng. trans., H. Beveridge.

Adabul Harb Was Shuja'ah, MS, Raza Library, Rampur.

Al-Rawandi, *The Rahat-us-Sudur wa Ayat-us-Surur*, Luzac & Co., 1921.

Ali, S.M., *The Arab Geographers*, Aligarh, 1959.

Allen, W. E.D., *A History of the Georgian People*, 1932.

Amitai, Reuven and Biran, Michal, *Mongols, Turks, and others—Eurasian Nomads and Sedentary World*, Leiden, Brill, Boston, 2005.

Babar: Memoirs of Babar, tr. Erskine.

Babarnama, tr. A.S. Beveridge.

Barthold, W., *Turkestan down to the Mongol Invasion* (Gibb Mem. Series).

Barthold, V.V., *Four Studies in the History of Central Asia*, tr., V. and T. Minorsky, 3 vols., Leiden, 1956.

Beazley, C.R., *The Dawn of Modern Geography*, 3 vols.

———, *The Texts and Versions of John de Plano Carpini and William de Rubruquis*, Hakluyt Society, 1903.

Bertold, Spuler, *History of the Mongols*, London, 1976.

———, *The Mongol Period*, London, 1971.

Boulger, D.C., *A Short History of China*, 1893.

Bretschneider, E., *Medieval Researches from Eastern Asiatic Sources*.

Browne, E.G., *A Literary History of Persia*, CUP, 1978.

Cable and French, *The Gobi Desert*, London, 1942.

Carpenter, F.G., *Asia*.

Carpini, Plano, *Travels*, tr., W.W. Rockhill, Hakluyt Society Extra Series, I, 1903.

Cleaves, Francis Woodman, ed. and tr., *The Secret History of the Mongols*, Cambridge, Massachusetts, Harvard University Press, 1982.

Curtin, Jeremiah, *The Mongols*.

————, *The Mongols in Russia*.

Curzon, G.N., *Persia and the Persian Questions*.

David Morgan, *The Mongols*, New York and Oxford: Basil Blackwell, 1986.

Dawlatshah, *Tazakiratu'sh-Shu'ara*, ed., E.G. Browne.

Douglas, R.R., *The Life of Jenghiz Khan*.

Elliot and Dowson, *History of India*, vol. II, edited by Mohd. Habib, S.A. Rashid and K.A. Nizami.

Haidar, Mohammad, *The Tarikh-i-Rashidi*, English version ed., N. Elias, tr., E.D. Rose.

Howorth, Sir H., *History of the Mongols*.

Ibn Batuta, *Kitabur Rahlah*, also called *Tuhfatun Nuzzar*, Urdu trans., Hyderabad, 1933, abridged Eng. trans., H.A.R. Gibb.

Ibn Khaldun, The Muqqaddima—An Introduction to History in 3 vols., tr., Franz Rosenthal, London, 1958.

Ibnul Asir, *Tarikh al-Kamil*, Cairo.

Jurjani, Minhaj Siraj, *The Tabaqat-i-Nasiri*, ed., W. Nassau Lees, Khadim Husain and Abdul Hai, Bib. Ind., 1864., Eng. tr., H.G. Raverty, Calcutta, 1857.

Juwaini, *Tarikh-i-Jahan Gusha*, ed., Mirza Muhammad Qazwini, Gibb Mem. Series, Eng. tr. J.A. Boyle, Manchester, 1958, 2 vols.

Khwandmir, *Habib al-Siyar*, Tehran, Eng. tr., W.M. Thackston, Harvard University, 1994.

Lamb, Harold, *Genghiz Khan*.

————, *March of the Barbarians*.

————, *Tamerlane*.

Lane-Poole, S., *Babar, Rulers of India Series*.

————, *The Mohammadan Dynasties*.

Le Strange, G., *Baghdad under the Abbasid Caliphate*.

Marco Polo, *Travels*, Marselan edn.

Margoliouth, D., *The Eclipse of the Abbasid Caliphate*.

Mirkhwand, *Rauzat-us-Safa*, Lucknow.

Muhammad bin Ali, *Majmaul Ansab*, Rampur Library.

Muhammad Habib, *Sultan Mahmud of Ghaznin*.

Mui R, Sir William, *The Caliphate: its Rise, Decline and Fall*.

Nassavi Nurad Din Muhammad, *Sirat-i-Jalal-ud-din Mangbirni*, tr., C. Scheffer.

Newton, A.P., *Travel and Travellers in the Middle Ages*.

Nizami-I 'Aruzi-I Samarqandi, *Chahar Maqala*, ed. and trans., E.G. Browne, Gibb Mem. Series, xi, and J.R.A.S., 1899.

Onon, Kugerange, *The Secret History of the Mongols: The Life and Times of Chingiz Khan*, ed. and tr. with an Introduction.

Parker, E.H., *A Thousand Years of the Tartars*.

Pei-Shi-Ki., *Notes upon an Embassy to the North by Wu Ku-Sur*, extracts in English in Bretschneider's *Medieval Researches from Eastern Asiatic Sources*.

Phillips, E.D., *The Mongols*, London, 1969.

Prawdin, Michael, *The Mongol Empire*.

Qazwini, Hamdullah, *Nuzhat-ul Qulub*, Geographical Section, ed. and trans., G. le Strange, Gibb Mem. Series.

—————, *Tarikh-i-Guzidah*, ed. with abridged trans., E.G. Browne, Gibb Mem. Series.

Rachewiltz, Igor de, tr., *The Secret History of the Mongol Dynasty* in *Papers* on *Far Eastern History*, Canberra, Australian National University, 1971-1984.

—————, *The Secret History of the Mongols—A Mongolian Epic Chronicle of the Thirteenth Century* (English translation and commentary), 2 vols., Leiden: E.J. Brill, 2004.

Rashid-ud-din Fazlullah, *Jamiut Tawarikh*, MS no. 87, Raza Library, Rampur, ed. with Introduction, Bahman Karimi, Tehran, AH 1338.

Ratchnesty, Paul, *Genghis Khan: His Life and Legacy*, Eng. tr., Oxford, Basil Blackwell, 1991, rpt, 1994.

Raverty, H.G., *Notes on Afghanistan*.

—————, *The Tabaqat-i-Nasiri*.

Robertson Smith, *Kinship and Marriage in Early Arabia*.

Ross, E.D., (with F.H. Skrine), *The Heart of Asia, a history of Russian Turkestan and the Central Asian Khanates from the earliest times*.

Russel Smith, J., *Human Geography*.

Saif bin Muhammad, *Tarikh-Nama-i-Harat*.

Saunders, J.J., *The History of the Mongol Conquests*, London, 1971.

Secret History of the Mongol Dynasty, tr., Wei-Kwei-Sun.

Siddiqui, A.H., *Caliphate and Kingship in Medieval Persia*.

Yeliu Chu Tsai, *Account of a Journey to the West (Si Yu Lu)*, *1219-1224*, abridged by Sheng Loo-sing of the Yuan dynasty. Extracts in English published in E. Bretschneider's *Medieval Researches from Eastern Asiatic Sources*, Trubnor's Oriental Series, London, 1910.

Si Yu Ki, *An account of Chang Chun Chin Jen's Journey to Chingiz Khan*, written by his Taoist disciple Li Jih-chiang. Palladius' Russian translation. Extracts published in English in Bretschneider's *Medieval Researches*.

Stein, Sir M.A., *Serindia*.

Suyuti, *History of the Caliphs*, tr., H.S. Jarret.

Sykes, Sir Percy, *A History of Persia*, 2 vols.

The Rehla of Ibn Batuta: India, Maldive and Ceylon, tr. Mahdi Hussain, Baroda, 1976.

The Shajratul Atrak, tr. Colonel Miles.

Toynbee, Arnold J., *A Study of History*, abridged by B.C. Somerville, 2 vols., 1974.

Vambery, A., *History of Bokhara*.

Wei-Kwei-Sun, *The Secret History of the Mongol Dynasty*, Yuan-Chao-Pi-Shi, Aligarh.

Westermarck, F., *Origin and Development of the Moral Ideas*, 2 vols.

————, *History of Human Marriage*.

Willoughby, C.A., *Manoeuvre in War*.

Yate, C.E., *Northern Afghanistan*.

Yazdi, Sharfuddin 'Ali, *Zafar Namah*, *Tarikh-i-Jahangir*, Raza library, Rampur.

Yule, Sir Henry, *The Book of Sir Marco Polo*, ed., H. Cordier, with supplementary vol. *Cathay and the Way Thither*, 4 vols.

Index